PRIZEFIGHTER

Democratic Ideals in Global Perspective

Jacqueline Arthur-Montagne and
Emily S. Burrill, Editors

PRIZEFIGHTER

Yankee Sullivan and the Hands That Built the Modern World

Patrick Griffin

University of Virginia Press
Charlottesville and London

Published in association with the University of Virginia's Karsh Institute of Democracy

The University of Virginia Press is situated on the traditional lands of the Monacan Nation, and the Commonwealth of Virginia was and is home to many other Indigenous people. We pay our respect to all of them, past and present. We also honor the enslaved African and African American people who built the University of Virginia, and we recognize their descendants. We commit to fostering voices from these communities through our publications and to deepening our collective understanding of their histories and contributions.

University of Virginia Press

Printed in the United States of America on acid-free paper

First published 2026

1 3 5 7 9 8 6 4 2

LIBRARY OF CONGRESS CATALOGING-IN-PUBLICATION DATA

Names: Griffin, Patrick, author
Title: Prizefighter : Yankee Sullivan and the hands that built the modern world / Patrick Griffin.
Description: Charlottesville : University of Virginia Press, 2026. | Series: Democratic ideals in global perspective | Includes bibliographical references and index.
Identifiers: LCCN 2026013429 (print) | LCCN 2026013430 (ebook) | ISBN 9780813955940 hardback | ISBN 9780813955957 ebook
Subjects: LCSH: Sullivan, James, 1813–1856 | Social history—19th century | Industrial revolution—History—19th century | Free trade—History—19th century | Capital movements—History—19th century | State, The—History—19th century | Democracy—History—19th century | Boxers (Sports) | LCGFT: Biographies
Classification: LCC GV1132.S9 G75 2026 (print) | LCC GV1132.S9 (ebook)
LC record available at https://lccn.loc.gov/2026013429
LC ebook record available at https://lccn.loc.gov/2026013430

Cover art: Yankee Sullivan, ca. 1846. (Library of Congress, Prints and Photographs Division, LC-DIG-pga-04356)
Cover design: Cecilia Sorochin

To Mary Hope and the rest of my family

With deep gratitude to Kenneth J. Lamb
for his research assistance

So I got no illusions about boxing—none. This is a brutal business. It's the hurt business. But I'm a fighter—that's all I can do. It's my destiny.

—Mike Tyson, quoted in Donald McRae, *Dark Trade: Lost in Boxing*

CONTENTS

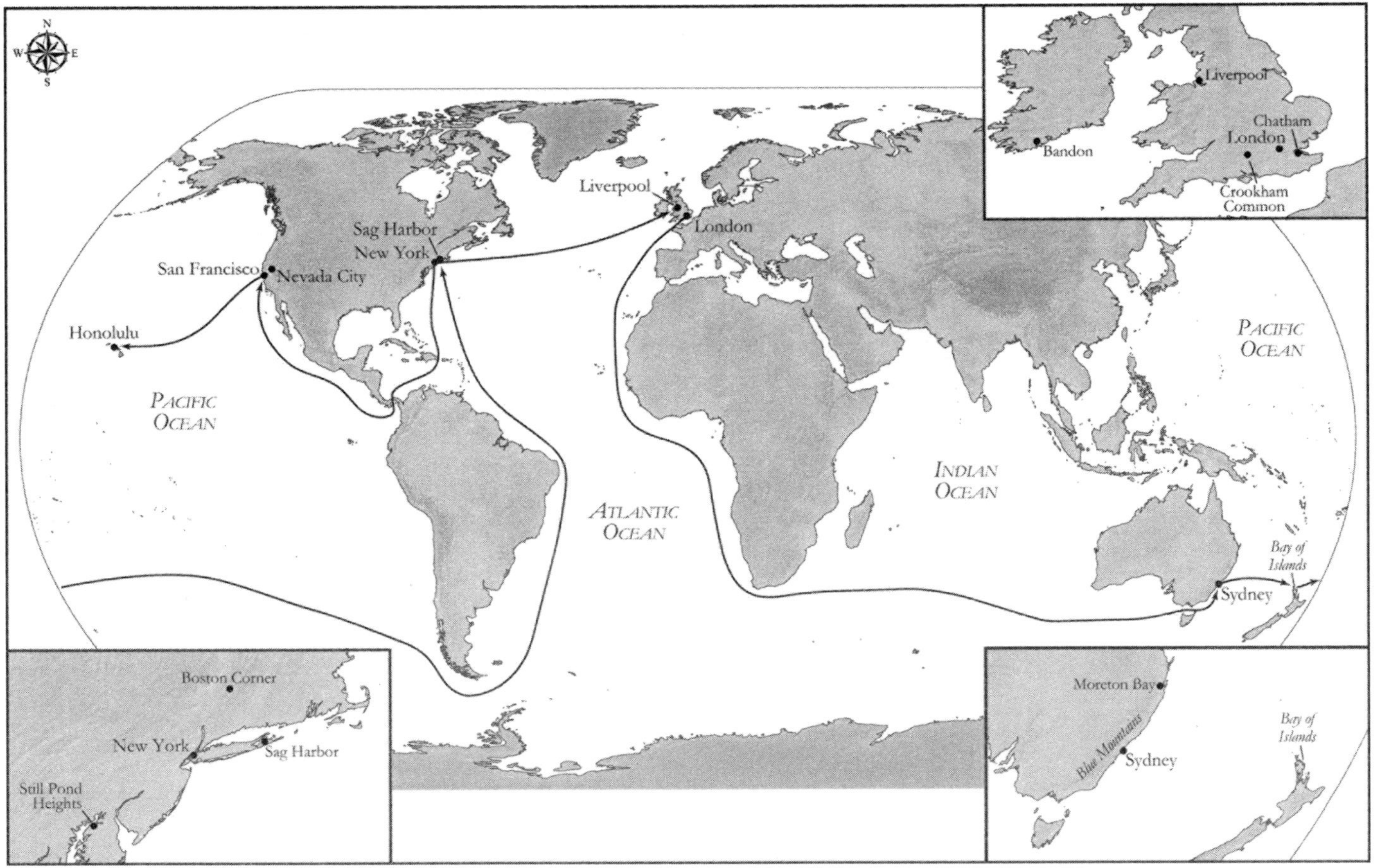

The journeys of Francis Ambrose and Yankee Sullivan, 1813–1856. (Map by Gabriel Moss)

PRIZEFIGHTER

Introduction

BACK IN THE DAY, a now-forgotten prizefighter by the name of Yankee Sullivan was one of the world's most famous, and infamous, characters. By the late-1840s, in fact, he had become nothing short of a cultural phenomenon. Here's just one example. As I was researching his life, I came across, of all things, a piece of scrimshaw with his image on it, housed in Boston's Massachusetts Historical Society. The figure of Sullivan that some sailor had fashioned was carved into a walrus tusk about two feet long, as heavy as a baseball bat. Or better, a heavy belaying pin, the club-like piece of wood that held the rigging down to the deck on sailing vessels and that doubled as a weapon. We have no idea of its provenance. We can only make educated guesses about it.[1] The scrimshander had probably traded for the walrus tusk with an Inuit. That meant he was whaling in the Arctic. As a rule, whalemen did not hunt walrus; rather, they traded for the tusks.

I was amazed that I had discovered Sullivan on a piece of bone. But on more closely inspecting it, I was staggered.

I was not stunned because someone chose to score the image of a fighter. Sailors etched all sorts of things on whalebones and teeth in the mid-nineteenth century, including pugilists.[2] Nor was I surprised by the crude nature of the rendering. On this tusk, the scrimshander had used his jackknife or sailmaker's needle to create a likeness of Yankee Sullivan. Undoubtedly, the sailor did it freehand. Done with an amateur's enthusiasm, and with the name misspelled as "Sulivan," the image portrays him in what was called "fighting attitude." Sullivan stands in an orthodox stance, that is, he is right-handed, with his left foot in front of the right, the left hand prepared to jab, and the right ready to deliver a cross. The whaler, no doubt, rubbed the tusk with soot, tar, ink, or even tobacco spit to fill in the

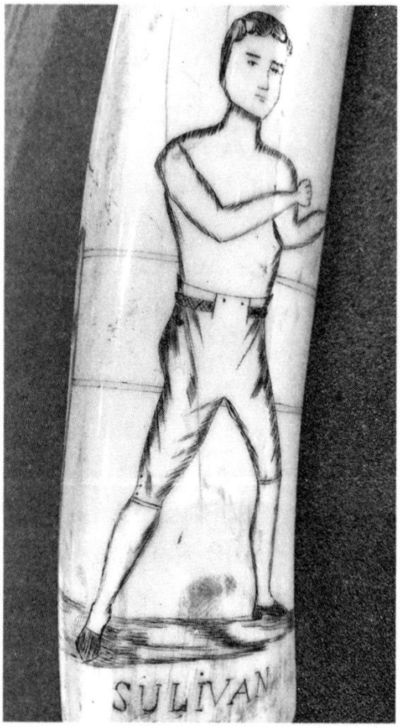

Scrimshaw bearing an image of Yankee Sullivan, 1849. (Collections of the Massachusetts Historical Society; photo by the author)

carved grooves, to make the image come alive. He then wiped and buffed it to a high sheen.[3] Nor was it a shock that he also carved other images into the piece. Above the fighter, for instance, the folk artist—if we can call him that—scratched the likenesses of three women into the tusk. But women appeared on scrimshaw all the time.

No, what gobsmacked me was what I saw at the tip of the tusk as I held it. Standing erect above all of the figures is a monument with an American shield perched atop it. It is inscribed to "the Memory of George Washington." During the long, lonesome voyage with plenty of downtime for carving, the whaleman produced a piece of art featuring a prizefighter and the father of the United States. To this unknown laborer, Yankee Sullivan—an ordinary and uneducated fellow—stood toe-to-toe with America's founding father.

The juxtaposition suggests a bracing and challenging story of how the world in which we live came to be. It is easy to conjure images of the great and the good, like Washington, and to argue that they—enlightened men in an enlightened age—made the globalized modern world. The rise of new class sensibilities, a new industrial economy, new patterns of trade and migration, new sorts of states, and new forms of political participation—all apparent in much of the world and binding it all together—may have dwarfed the ability of anyone to manage, but a few, perhaps, could give a shape to such dynamics. Theirs are the names that appear in history books as world-makers. Individuals such as Washington or Cornelius Vanderbilt seemed to ply the stage as actors with agency as the world transitioned from an older order to a new one. They could, they believed, harness and direct forces that overwhelmed others.[4]

The world of Sullivan appears very different from the one Washington helped fashion. Sullivan lived a life marked by violence, suffering, criminality, incessant movement, and defiance. The adjective "notorious" was consistently attached to his name, no matter the region in which he lived. Throughout his life, he lived with horror and inspired it. He was victimized. He also played the role of victimizer. His enemies saw him as if he were drawn by the pen of Mary Shelley. He seemed the handiwork of some "Modern Prometheus," every bit as frightening as the monster she conjured that the world in which she lived seemed to create. A monster or a menace, however, could not act as a world-maker. A man like Sullivan was more a product of the world around him than a producer. Or so it would appear.

But there is another side to him. In carving Sullivan, the whaler was honoring a kindred spirit. Sullivan, like him more than likely, had sailed the world in search of work, even if often not by choice, including a stint hunting whales. The scrimshaw artist had probably circumnavigated the globe. So had Sullivan. The carving whaleman had, no doubt, traveled far from home and did dangerous work in heaving seas to fuel the industrial economy. He had probably ventured farther than he could have imagined, to lands where people very different from him lived. The same went for Sullivan. Both grew up poor with few options but took what their worlds had to offer. Both toiled with their bodies, yet each would have believed they were entitled to a political voice. Only Sullivan, unlike the sailor, had hit it big and become a champion for the anonymous men who did the hard work that made the world go round.

The whaler was not alone in adulating this figure. When Yankee Sullivan reigned as the world's most dynamic fighter, American newspapers—from California and New Orleans to Boston and New York—regaled readers with his travels and exploits. More than one thousand stories on him circulated around the country from 1840 to the mid-1850s. English,

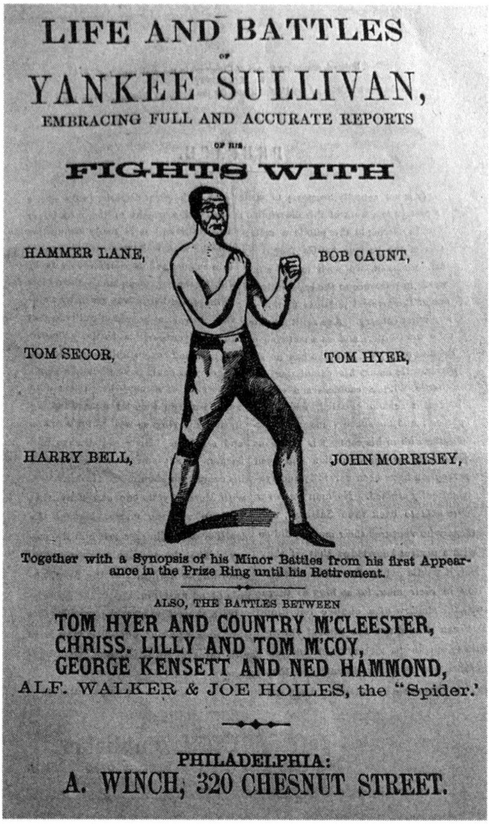

Title page of *Life and Battles of Yankee Sullivan* (Philadelphia: A. Winch, 1854; HathiTrust)

Irish, and Australian readers also could not get enough of the champion. He was an American—and a global—sensation.

Today? Hardly anyone has heard of him. Even among boxing historians, only those who cover the bare-knuckle era know Yankee Sullivan, and then in only the vaguest terms. For those who study New York in the 1840s, he also makes an appearance, looming as an archetype of the violent men who trolled the streets and as the antitype of ordered liberty. For the rest of us, he remains, at best, a ghost. That's the challenge of tracking him. Ever elusive and restless, he appears only in the shadows, and we cast furtive glances at him throughout much of his life. That is, until he emerges on the world stage, but then only as a one-dimensional figure. He is a bit like a white whale. Most certainly dare not, as a rule, mention this shadowy character in the same breath as George Washington.

The scrimshander dared to do so. Yankee Sullivan was celebrated by our unknown whaler for a good reason. As this book will demonstrate, Yankee Sullivan lived a life of extraordinary adventure—one of the most amazing epics we are likely to come across, in fact. Few saw the things he saw and did the things he did. He accomplished much more. He, like the whaler, animated the physical and cultural contours of a new era coming into being, even if Sullivan did it more spectacularly and on a public stage. The sinews of our world, if we take his story seriously, were hammered out not only by figures like Washington but also, in an often-violent crucible, by exploited and exploitative men like Sullivan. He was neither clear-cut hero nor spotless innocent; rather, he was tailor-made for an in-between world. Yankee Sullivan was a complex man for a complex age.

Sullivan's life offers a three-dimensional view of all the tableaux he moved to and through. What the far-flung places he visited shared in common was that they were points of connection in an increasingly interlinked world. After a period of upheaval in the late eighteenth and early nineteenth centuries, when many countries throughout the Atlantic world, and then even farther afield into the Pacific, experienced extraordinary tumult, Sullivan reigned. After an age of revolution, the brave new world that emerged was one of free trade, free movement, industrial development, and popular sovereignty. The period ushered in new empires and nations and new forms of oppression and Native dispossession.[5] It was a bendable, plastic time, when things were not set and people could shape these new realities. All was in flux and in-between. The places that attracted him and people like him were becoming something new and doing so in conjunction with one another, exhilarating some and frightening most. Sullivan lived through it all. More to the point, he helped forge it all.

It is no coincidence that he made a name for himself when he did and where he did. His time as a champion coincided with the rise of a new mass society. This was the moment of new mass politics, mass migration, and mass culture. His rise to prominence also witnessed the creation of a new mass media covering each of these dynamics, all of which were globally enmeshed. Sullivan was in the middle of it all. He also helped define resistance to much of the change that the new mass world betokened. In the contexts through which he moved, he was less a victim than a catalyst, someone as expert as fighting as he was at surviving.

Common people usually feature in these stories just as they do in the historical record: as nameless, faceless, and victim to the forces that buffeted them. Yet every now and then a few emerge from obscurity. Sullivan was one such man. He proved ever-adaptable, mobile, opportunistic, and agile. He was able to sense the limitations and possibilities his world offered and so take advantage of what he could. In the process, for a brief moment, he proved able to rise above his circumstances and against those who would put him under the heel to shape the world around him.

Though "notorious," Sullivan was not exceptional. So many more people lived similar peripatetic hard-to-trace lives in in-between places-in-time. They displayed a sort of toughness that is difficult for us to appreciate. They came from areas where they were oppressed. Many, like Sullivan, had no education and could not read or write. These were the expendables of the societies in which they lived. They had to be mobile. And they could treat others deplorably. With their numbers, with their experiences of discrimination in all sorts of places that were developing, with their history of violence and intimidation on both the giving and receiving ends, with their attraction to the nodes and connecting points of a world growing smaller, they were perfectly suited for such a place as New York. The same goes for Sydney. And San Francisco. And London and Liverpool.

Men like Sullivan did not only navigate a new world. They constructed it. They built the roads, the ports, and the bridges that connected the world. They dug the tunnels and the mines that bound place and industrial process together. They hunted the whales and sailed the ships. They created infrastructure with their hands, enabling key places to become part of a networked global modern economy. And then they loaded and unloaded the goods in ports that were exploding in size and significance. Faceless and nameless, they moved from place to place, searching for opportunity, propelling the growth of global shipping as they did so. Most cruelly, these men cleared out Indigenous peoples to make way for settlers and "polite" society, sometimes in places oceans away from where they had set off. Their work did not end there. Through violence and insistence, they gave form to modern politics and urban democracy. They did not strive for consensus or engage in reasoned debate. They fought to win. They pilloried opponents. They did not shrink from competition but embraced it.

Sullivan excelled at all of this. He also brokered culture in these dynamic places. He epitomized the swagger that defined how workingmen were stepping onto the global stage. Sullivan also exposed the more toxic aspects of the masculinity that went hand in hand with the brutality of the contexts he moved through. And the racial tensions. All of these phenomena were, once again, manifest across the globe.

So, this is the story of the making of a prizefighter but also a tale that reveals a great deal more. Yankee Sullivan bobbed, weaved, and punched in his many rings as the world lurched. Fighters like him did not only witness the birth pangs of an age, however; they also served as midwives to its birth. This should not surprise us. Prizefighters moved better than others. They knew how to evade and when to attack. They were master improvisers. They chose where they went and what they did. They were perfectly suited to their tasks of invention and reinvention. They had to enter the ring as individuals. No one looked out for them. Pugilists were as self-actualized as they came. Sullivan and his ilk realized better than others what animated society at moments of flux. Prizefighters were often the first to arrive in places in transition and proved the most entrepreneurial. They possessed all the virtues and the vices of common people in extremis. They stood at the pinnacle of the competitive cauldrons that bound the modern world together, and because of this, workingmen rallied to them.

Sullivan was the ultimate example of both the prizefighter and the nature of kaleidoscopic changes he helped bring about. He and other prizefighters were among the first moderns. They were not incidental to the creation of a globalized world; they proved instrumental. On the face of it, this seems a strange case to make. Prizefighting would not appear to be associated with progress. Nevertheless, fighting in the ring played a vital role in allowing people and a global system to graduate to a new age. It helped usher people through bewildering changes. Sullivan punched back. He represented defiance. Yet, prizefighting dampened as much violence as it engendered. Prizefighters certainly contested the worst of what globalization had to offer for common people. They also channeled grievances and became rallying points for the disaffected. Bloodshed in the ring, given what prizefighters meant to the exploited, limited bloodshed in the streets.

Thus, for a brief window of time, pugilists proved indispensable to a world that was being connected by the labor of mobile men. This is why this book does not use the words "sport" or "pastime" or "game" to characterize prizefighting. It was far too important for any of these terms. Prizefighting or boxing, the writer Donald McRae argues, "is not really a sport. There is such danger and damage, and even death."[6] In the nineteenth century, when Yankee fought, the stakes were especially high. Fortunes and power and status were determined by prizefighting. Fighters like Sullivan controlled politics and workforces. They shaped the culture of growing cities, brokered power in transition zones, and organized the marginalized. Death, danger, and damage stalked prizefighting then as well. They were more the rule than the exception. Mike Tyson called prizefighting "the hurt business." He is right. But it was more consequential than this. Where world-making was taking place, it featured. The whaleman knew this.

We know one other thing about the piece of scrimshaw. The whaleman rendered it in 1849. This year marked the very height of Yankee Sullivan's popularity and his power. It also featured his nemesis, a fellow named Tom Hyer, on the flip side of the tusk. The first-ever "fight of the century" pitted one against the other. From an obscure background, Sullivan, like other prizefighters, emerged on the global stage at this very moment. To the anonymous scrimshander, at this critical juncture, a menace like Yankee Sullivan was champion, someone who could be mentioned in the same breath as a George Washington and someone who made his competitive and often cruel world sensible.

This book charts the story of one prizefighter, just as it uncovers a story the better sort in the past were reluctant or unable to recognize: that men like Sullivan and the whaleman plied the global stage for a brief and critical moment when the world was being knit together; and that they did much of the knitting. It moves to the many places around the world Sullivan toiled and fought. The book tracks him from Ireland, to England, to Australia, to New Zealand, to the United States, and even Hawaii. His story draws us to the rise of great global cities like London, New York, Sydney, Liverpool, and San Francisco. It also takes us to parts of the world where common men like him did the inglorious work that made the modern world go round. He visited gold-mining regions, built roads, went whaling like the scrimshaw artist, and labored on docks and at navy yards. Throughout his journeys, Sullivan played the part of victim and victimizer, hero and villain. He was a man of violence but also an improviser and shape-shifter, the epitome of the self-made man in Darwinian places-in-time, one well-skilled at adapting and readapting.

I invite the reader to enter the ring with Yankee Sullivan over the sixteen rounds that formed his life, the same number as in the 1849 "fight of the century" that some anonymous whaler thought worthy of memorializing. Some of these chapters in his life, and in this book, were and are long. Some were and are short. Just like a prizefight in the mid-nineteenth century. Rounds could go for many long minutes; they could also last for only a few seconds. Yet each had its own rhythm. His life started with some trying episodes. Those early rounds saw him travel the world, but as a victim, a refugee, and a runaway. He then mastered the possibilities and constraints of the world that was becoming. He re-created himself and chose his path. Those were the proverbial middle rounds. For this short period, he emerged ascendant. The final rounds conclude with his fall from grace, when it became clear that he no longer fit in the world he helped create. The window of time when a prizefighter like him was needed was brief. The ebb and flow of his life was akin to the give-and-take of a prizefight, a fact that made him what was called an "adept" in and out of the ring. At least for a while, before he and others like him would fall out of memory. Then only the Washingtons would remain.

THE EARLY ROUNDS

ROUND 1

Bandon

WHAT MAKES A fighting man? For a start, a fighter has to have the requisite abilities and the right inclination. But there are always other considerations. The place he calls home, the circumstances of birth, and his parents all come to mind. Add to these what is happening when he is young, as well as the fighting culture of the place-in-time he is born and raised. When it comes to fighting, history shows that nurture matters as much as nature. Yankee Sullivan had a great deal of nurture on his side. But discovering all of this took some gumshoe detective work and a great deal of luck.

Yankee Sullivan was an exceptionally elusive character, even for a period of time when most common people led anonymous lives. Even the most basic bit of information about him proved hard to pin down: his name. He was not born "Yankee" Sullivan, of course. Nor was he christened "James Sullivan." Throughout his life, he used a number of aliases, usually with James as the Christian name. He called himself, or others did, Murray and Ambrose. One writer even called him Frank Amor, a name certainly not his.[1]

He was, without a doubt, born Francis Ambrose. The name sounds so serene. Francis Ambrose.[2] It has the ring of a priest or a poet. Only proving, as the philosopher and historian Will Durant put it, that "there is no humorist like history."[3]

Ambrose is a name found in Ireland, where Francis came from; however, it is not common. Mac Ambróis, the Irish version of the name, has been associated with West Munster, Ireland's southwest province, since the fourteenth century. It means simply "son of Ambrose."[4] It is not a typically Irish name. More than likely, the first Ambroses came over to Ireland in the Middle Ages with Norman invaders. Soon they, like so many others in Irish history, would intermarry and go native. In certain parts of Ireland, especially where Irish and English interacted over centuries, mixing and merging were par for the course.

In the early nineteenth century, Ambroses lived in Limerick and especially County Cork. They hailed from places in and around Cork City and to the northwest in the county. A good number came from West Cork, near the towns of Skibbereen and Clonakilty. Some held around one hundred acres or so. Some scratched out existences on only a few acres. Most worked farms of a size somewhere between the two. Most Ambroses were on the poorer side, but, then again, so were most Irish people. Ambroses certainly did not come from the ruling class in Ireland, from those of the Protestant establishment, who through a history of conquest and appropriation owned much of the land. As such, Ambroses tended to be fairly typical.[5]

They appear to have been fairly typical when it came to religion as well. The records of the local Church of Ireland, the official Protestant church in the kingdom, contain no traces of Ambroses in the years around the time Francis Ambrose was born, 1813.[6] The same pertains for Catholic records, though for different reasons. The Catholic baptismal records for the year 1813 in the place where he was born have not survived. Yet, other clues make it clear that he was baptized Catholic.

A number of Ambroses, Murrays, and Sullivans of about the right age and the right place to have been his parents married in the Catholic Church. Since he used these names throughout his life, it's a good bet that these were names found in his family. The same goes for burials. Ambroses and Murrays appear from time to time in the same records, suggesting that they were close and moved in the same circles. Sometimes they formed unions. On January 29, 1814, for instance, a John Ambrose and a Neal Murray witnessed the marriage of Timothy Leary and Margaret Murray.[7] To witness marriages and to stand in as godparents represent intimate forms of association. They imply networks. Usually, those who married into a family would serve such roles. So, we are on solid ground assuming that this John Ambrose had wed a Murray as well. It is not surprising, therefore, that Francis would use the name Murray later in life.

Murray, therefore, was almost certainly his mother's maiden name. In one instance, a Catherine Murray married an Ambrose. The time and place would be about right. There is no way to know much about her, but the name Murray was more common in the area of Francis's birth than Ambrose. Catherine was a Catholic, as evidenced by the records she appears in. A few Catherines of about the right age can be found in the area of Cork that Francis reportedly came from. One of them was baptized in Saints Peter and Paul Church in Cork City in 1791. Of the Catherines in these records, one seems to have been his mother, putting the age at which she gave birth to Francis sometime in her early twenties.[8]

His father was much more complicated to find. Taking the Ambrose-Murray unions as a guide, it made sense his name was John Ambrose. But no John Ambroses in the area where Catherine Murray was from can be found. The name does not make an appearance in recordings in land records, for instance, which would tell where he came from. Nothing except some marriage or funeral records, but none of these put him at an address. Only one John Ambrose, a soldier, fit the place and time.[9] Moreover, if genetics mean anything, he seemed cut from the same swashbuckling, globe-trotting cloth as his son.

That John soldiered for Britain is not all that surprising. Ireland was an ideal reservoir for British manpower. Ireland had an excess of aggrieved men, perfectly suited for military service, so long as the British could get past their religion. Irish Catholics were second-class citizens in the British state, even though they made up three-quarters of the population of the kingdom. The English tended to look down their noses at the Irish, but they also feared them because of a history of rebelling. For centuries, England, and then the new superstate of Britain—one that combined England with Scotland—had tried to bring the Irish to heel. Officials planted Protestants in some regions to undercut Ireland's stubborn Catholicism after the Reformation. And all the Irish did was rise and rise again. In the eighteenth century, the British passed laws, though not much enforced, to punish Irish Catholics who were holding out. They were institutionally and legally discriminated against. They only rose again.

After a failed rising in 1798, the British tried to end the Irish menace once and for all. It mattered all the more because revolutionary France had tried to exploit Irish anger in its fight against Britain. In the competitive world of European power politics, Ireland had to be bound to Britain. In 1800, the Parliament in London passed an Act of Union. At the same time, the Irish Parliament, which was wholly Protestant, voted itself out of existence to join the British. These churchmen, too, feared Catholic wrath. Ireland became part of a union that included the kingdoms of Scotland and England. That "union," however, tended to serve the purposes of the English.

Most Irish were doubly discriminated against because Catholics enjoyed few of the rights other British subjects did under the Union. Presbyterians in the North also suffered discrimination because they dissented from the established church. Catholics, though, had it worse. Because of their associations with rebellion and sedition, and English prejudice, Catholics could not own property or serve in many professions. Hamstrung economically from getting ahead and from owning land, most Irish Catholics languished in obscure poverty. John Ambrose was one such man. The British listed him as a "laborer." This meant he owned no land.

For him, and for so many other Irish, the British army proved their way out. It also became a safety valve to any sort of intrigues in the kingdom. Young men were encouraged to join the British cause, which meant that fewer angry people would be at home to contest their second-class status. After the American Revolution, given the increased demands of global empire, manpower proved a pressing issue, and the British military lifted any formal prohibition on enlisting Irish Catholics. Recruiting parties fanned out across Ireland. They found an eager—or rather, desperate—audience. For a laborer like John Ambrose, the possibility of steady pay overcame any objections. As it did for many Irishmen. As a laborer, John would have been looking at a future in which he farmed a small plot that he rented. Instead, at age seventeen, around 1808, John joined a unit comprised of Englishmen and other Irishmen, the Fifty-Ninth Foot. Elements of the Fifty-Ninth Foot did garrison duty in Cork and recruited in Kildare. He would spend most of his time with the First Battalion of the Fifty-Ninth. The Second Battalion was destined to serve under Lieutenant-General Sir Arthur Wellesley, the future Duke of Wellington, in the Peninsular Campaign against Napoleon.

In 1811, John Ambrose, more than likely, was involved in a forgotten, but telling chapter of British global history: the conquest of Java. The British sought to invade this island on the other side of the globe, now a part of Indonesia, for the oldest set of reasons: to snooker a foe—and to grow an empire. The foe was revolutionary France. The empire was centered on India. In 1811, the two aims of thwarting and extending converged and made an invasion and then conquest of Java almost overdetermined. In that year, the Fifty-Ninth, along with Bengal Sepoys and men from Madras, set off from India for Java. In one memorable episode, John Ambrose's unit took a fort at a place called Cornelis. He and his comrades faced grapeshot, engaged in hand-to-hand combat, and suffered appalling casualties. "The number of dead and the shocking variety of deaths had better not be imagined," one remembered. The commander of the Fifty-Ninth hailed his troops' "reputation and gallantry," but he acknowledged the human toll.[10] They then did garrison duty in the aftermath of massacres. It seems the people who lived there "had undergone a period of extreme terror," as one eyewitness put it.[11] The Fifty-Ninth fought under the motto "victory or death," a phrase that would be uttered by John's son years later in a much different fight.[12]

John Ambrose was wounded in Java. He was sent to Chelsea and laid up in the royal military hospital just on the edge of London. He then was probably back in Ireland for a bit in 1812, when he fathered Francis. The Second Battalion was stationed in Ireland and England at this time, and he could have been attached to the unit doing garrison duty in Cork. Or perhaps his wife joined him in Chelsea.[13]

Wherever he was in 1812, John Ambrose, all in all, served nine years with the Fifty-Ninth. He was mustered out in 1817, and military records detail how he was given a travel allowance to travel from Cork to the place Catherine lived. He was still a young man, but he had seen a world of action and travel, all in the service of the Crown, the East India Company, and empire. Though he spent only four of his nine years in India, he was listed as part of an "East India Party." With the Fifty-Ninth, he had seen service in the Cape Colony—now South Africa—and in Mauritius, in addition to Java and India. For all his sacrifices, he was regarded as an "Invalid soldier." He was hobbled with "Rheumatism, of long standing and general debility." Others at Chelsea in the Fifty-Ninth Foot were "worn out" and suffering from "general debility." One comrade lost an eye in Java in 1812. Given the horrors he witnessed and survived, John likely struggled with PTSD.[14] Yet he had to feel lucky when he made it home to his wife and four-year-old son.

Overall, John's experiences were not exceptional at all. He remains nearly as faceless as his wife, Catherine. Maybe they met in Cork City, where he might have been doing some garrison duty. Maybe they met in

Catherine's hometown. But he, like so many other Irishmen at this time, was involved in the grand stories of the day: the age of revolution and the expansion of empire. And, though Irish, he and others fought and suffered in the service of Britain. Ireland, after all, was part of the United Kingdom, however fractured the union.

In 1813, Francis was born poor, and he was born of hard people, two critical ingredients for becoming a prizefighter. Francis Ambrose also had something else in his corner. Where and when he came into the world contributed a lot to creating a man apt to fight. His birthdate was April 12, 1813—a momentous time in Ireland. Place only adds to the momentousness. Francis's birthplace of Bandon—the town in Cork to which John returned after his service—was defined by a tangled mix of flux, promise, violence, and hardship. And fighting culture. John Ambrose was given a few shillings after he was demobilized, enough to get him back to Bandon. More than likely, he was returning home. Few Ambroses lived in Bandon, but there is a record of a Thomas baptized there in 1798. He was the son of Francis and of Catherine Ambrose, and John was quite possibly Thomas's older brother. That would make this Francis the grandfather of our Francis. If this is the case, the grandfather probably moved into the area from regions farther afield.[15]

Bandon sits in a tranquil valley, with a river from which the town takes its name running through it—though it was not and is not navigable. In 1835, a chronicler described the areas surrounding Bandon as "agreeably wooded and . . . ornamented with several mansions, villas, and cottages, that give the environs a pleasing and picturesque appearance."[16] But looks can be deceiving. Being a Catholic in Bandon was daunting. There, as an old saying goes, "even the pigs are Protestant." It was, to borrow a phrase from twentieth-century Northern Ireland, "a Protestant place for a Protestant people." Although located on the southern end of Ireland, Bandon experienced the same pressures and tensions that animated the vexed relations in places like Belfast or Derry/Londonderry.[17]

This was a town built on exclusion, and John and Catherine stood on the wrong side of the line. Early settlers, Protestant all, established enclaves on each side of the river in the years of the Munster Plantation in Ireland. This was part of that grand plan to civilize Ireland and to make it English. It did not work. After settlement, the new landlord in the area,

Richard Boyle, Earl of Cork, decided to enclose the small settlements. He constructed mighty walls, all finished by 1627, and, per one admirer, turned "a mere waste of bog and wood," no irony intended, into "a spacious, handsome, and well fortified place, continuing to flourish and to increase in extent and importance." Boyle designed Bandon to serve as "an asylum for the English."[18] The walls around the asylum wove right around all the structures that Protestants needed to survive and to thrive.

Still vulnerable to their Catholic neighbors, however, the inhabitants suffered in 1641 when Catholics rose up against the policy of Plantation throughout Ireland. Bandon became an impoverished refugee center in these years, as violence swirled around it. But it did not fall. Those in Bandon saw the world outside the walls as a forbidding place teeming with unsympathetic Natives. Inside, they created an administrative center for the region, with bustling markets. Soon, they specialized in textiles, though the town had plenty of other artisans. All served the intramural community.

Perhaps apocryphally, but tellingly, a sign used to hang on a gate into the city saying, "Enter here Turk Jew or Atheist, Every man except a Papist." And it was meant to stay that way. In 1688, some of the walls were knocked down as armies under the Catholic British King James II laid waste to part of the area and occupied the town for a bit, but soon it reverted to its fortified tranquility. With the rebellion of 1798, violence gripped much of Ireland, but it did not really touch Bandon. Militias peopled exclusively by Protestants ensured the town remained inviolable. At the very end of the eighteenth century, Bandon boasted as many Orange Lodges as most places in the North. Orangemen banded together to intimidate Catholics and officials. They sent an insistent message to all who doubted that Protestants would hold onto what they had. These associations tended to attract the "lower order of Protestants," those most apt to feel anxious about their privileges.[19] Catholics were only permitted within the walls on market days.

There was much to protect. Bandon served as a connection point between the fertile hinterland of West Cork and the cities of Kinsale and Cork just to the east with their established ties to Britain and the Atlantic. Functioning as an entrepôt, the town thrived during peaceful moments. In 1787, Bandon had two architects, four chandlers, one doctor, five linen drapers, two saddlers, one cabinet maker, eight clothiers, seven grocers, six merchants, four shoemakers, one carpenter, one comb maker, two innkeepers, two pressers and dyers, seven linen and cotton manufacturers, one calico manufacturer, one cooper, one land surveyor, and two publicans. These were all Protestants who lived within the walls, occupying a self-sufficient Protestant island amid a sea of Catholics.[20] Yet Bandon was poised for transformation.

Walls stem change. But sometimes change has a way of overwhelming even the staunchest defenses. By the early nineteenth century, just when Francis, the grandfather, was likely arriving, Bandon's walls were becoming permeable. Like many places in Ireland, the town was transitioning to a market economy, especially in the wake of the explosion of trade in the late eighteenth century and during the Napoleonic Wars. Tanneries, distilleries, breweries, mills for weaving fabric, including a cotton mill, tied Bandon to Atlantic trade networks to meet the increased demand of a wartime economy. Bandon boasted nine tanning yards. More than one thousand people worked in the spinning mills. One distillery would eventually produce three hundred thousand gallons of whiskey a year. Five ales and porters were brewed here.[21] It was an "industrious" place.

But these tasks required more labor than Protestants could provide. So, Catholics from its hinterland streamed into the area. They needed to find new places to live, as rents were rising due to the rising population. Given the difficulty of fixing the name Ambrose to this town, it's a good bet any Ambroses were part of that incoming migration surge at the end of the eighteenth century, even if they lived just outside the walls, where most Catholics settled. Moreover, at this time, and for the first time, a few Catholics were admitted to live in the town. The walls had been breached.[22] The population in Bandon and the surrounding region jumped, doubling between 1798 and 1821, as more Catholics came into the town and its immediate suburbs to serve as farm and industrial laborers.

New people meant new places of worship. Although a small Catholic chapel stood well to the north of the town, the new arrivals required a newer one closer to town. It went up right outside the walls on the southwestern side of Bandon. By definition it sat outside, but only just. The new chapel was built on Gallows Hill in 1796 on lands donated by the Earl of Bandon and paid for by subscription, and it became the chief Catholic site of worship. In 1798, amid fears of civil war, Protestants burned the older one to the ground, and this newer one became the lone place for Catholics to gather. In 1855, one resident would remember that the "Roman Catholic chapel was a rather mean-looking edifice, situated in a back street and not erected like the fine buildings of a similar kind that I have seen in the south, in the most prominent places, so that they generally attract the attention of all who pass by."[23]

The vast majority of Catholics lived in what was called Irishtown. Neighborhoods throughout Ireland bear that name. These products of settler colonialism sprung up next to Protestant enclaves and represented sites where Catholics were permitted to live.[24] Today it remains visible just to the east side of Bandon, across the bridge called "Irishtown Bridge." While practically all of the town inside the walls lay on lands owned by the Duke of Devonshire, Irishtown, ironically, sat on lands owned by the Earl of Shannon, the famous Boyle family that built the walls in the first place.[25] By the early nineteenth century, Irishtown was spreading to other areas just outside the walls.

The Ambroses settled on the western side of the town, on Chapel Lane right next to the relatively new Catholic chapel on Gallows Hill. They therefore lived on lands of the Earls of Cork and Bandon. These would have been bilingual areas. Around the town, 25 to 50 percent of the people spoke Irish as their predominant language. In the immediate vicinity of the town, in its Irishtown suburbs, however, everyone spoke some English.[26] So, the Natives learned to live dual lives, especially those who were entering Bandon looking for opportunity—as most probably the Ambroses did.

Thirty lots, dotted with cabins, lined Chapel Lane outside the wall and the adjoining Church Street. Nearby stood a mill, which employed hundreds, as well as a distillery and a brewery. One of the barracks kept watch close by. Beyond this small area lay a river called the Bridewell and then field after field. Francis's early life, in this suburb, would have been intensely urban and rural at the same time.[27] And intimate. Murrays lived side-by-side with Donovans, Regans, Learys, Mahoneys, and Sullivans—all common names in West Cork. John Ambrose, in fact, served as godfather to a James Sullivan, so Sullivans were likely related to Ambroses and Murrays.[28] Many would have been newcomers from surrounding areas, with the surge of development. All this suggests that the Ambroses migrated in from places to the west of Bandon, like Clonakilty or Skibbereen, where some Ambroses lived. Typically, these families worked their land collectively, binding them to each other.

So, the Ambroses lived amid a colony of Catholic newcomers—men and women who relied on each other and created an extended family to weather the challenges of the day and to help each other scout out opportunities. They were separated from their Protestant neighbors by walls of about ten feet in height. But now they could enter the town as laborers. They had no schooling. Few could read or write. The number who could not presumably included young Francis. Nonetheless, their presence suggested that what had been a Protestant stronghold, with Orange Lodges when young Francis was coming of age, was becoming more and more Catholic, with all the tensions inherent in such a shift, turning a "Protestant showplace" into a more typical Irish provincial town.[29]

The Ambroses were landless, or more properly subtenants, that is, tenants-at-will who enjoyed no security. They lived in one of the simple cabins that lined Chapel Lane. A cabin did not carry status like a "house." Houses housed Protestants inside the walls. On this side of extramural Bandon, cabins tended to have a ramshackle appearance, despite their thatched roofs. Chapel Lane resembled an overcrowded slum of "wretched cabins composed of wattles, plastered over with cow-dung and mud," as someone from inside the walls evocatively put it. Francis was, no doubt, born in one of these.[30] On one of the lanes by Gallows Hill, one tenant was responsible for twenty-five subtenants. The Ambroses probably lived within this sort of arrangement.[31] Nonetheless, the spread of cabin-suburbs betokened an expanding, open environment.

Much more was changing in Bandon. In the town today, an old quay serves as a focal point. It was brand-spanking new in the early nineteenth century. By it stands a bridge across the Bandon River. This had also gone up just around the time Francis, the grandfather, arrived. The quays and the bridge comprised part of a design to open Bandon to a wider world. The town's fathers had heady hopes. They constructed new roads into the city and out of it, thinking that Bandon would soon have a direct route to the Atlantic, via a hoped-for canal to Kinsale. The two sets of quays that were constructed in the early nineteenth century would prepare the way for canals. This dream drove the development of Bandon at just the time young Francis was born.

In fact, improvement mania swept Ireland in the opening decades of the nineteenth century. Throughout the kingdom, men and women worked to tie remote parts of Ireland into the broader Atlantic. The quays in Bandon were meant to bind Bandon and what was made and raised in and around the town to Kinsale, and from it to places farther removed, in much the same way the Erie Canal would yoke the American Midwest to New York City or canals tied places in the industrial North of England to London. The quays along the Rivers Bandon and Bridewell were constructed between 1804 and 1820, when all was hope and promise. Commercialization, no doubt, displaced people, just as it tied more and more people into a sometimes bewildering broader world of flux.[32] Ambrose and his family were just a few more souls whose lives were transformed by the commercial change of the age and all it wrought. With Francis's birth, all seemed in transition.

Or perhaps not everything. Time, in fact, had and had not passed Bandon by. Though the town was developing, it was almost as if the age of revolution had not happened. Certainly, democracy and autonomy were nowhere in evidence. Many buffers of authority existed between the Ambroses and those who ruled Bandon, such as the mighty Duke of Devonshire—who visited only twice—and his chief subtenant, the Earl of Bandon, on whose lands their cabin sat. With him, they never interacted. All was done through layers of subtenants and local officials. Between the mighty and the meek lay level upon level of hierarchical authority. The Ambroses enjoyed few rights to speak of and no status. They could not vote. Then again, who could? Few would be able to until the reforms of the 1830s. To be Catholic and landless meant no access to power in Bandon at the time of Francis's birth.[33] Bandon may have been modernizing, but that process of change was distorted by Ireland's colonial status.[34] Yet, with examples of politicization and change throughout the Atlantic at this time, even the seemingly powerless realized they possessed some power, if only the power of threat. The rebellion of 1798, though a failure, proved that. Maybe such a time would come again, even in a Protestant bastion.

To keep this volatile mix of settler and Native from exploding due to a surging population and to ensure that politicization of the lower orders would be kept at bay, the British government rotated units in and out of the two barracks in the town. Highland regiments and soldiers from Argyle came and went from Scotland, as did units from all over England—like the Thirty-Sixth Foot from Hertfordshire, the Thirty-Fourth Foot, which would leave Bandon to travel to India, and the Wiltshire Militia.

The South Cork Militia, a Protestant unit, garrisoned the town from time to time, and men from Fermanagh, Kilkenny, Waterford, Sligo, and King's County, too. All of these visited in the years Francis was growing up, with an eye toward keeping the peace while Bandon joined the modern, connected world.[35]

Things did not work out as planned or hoped for. The problem was simple: The economy was staggering under successive blows as soon as planners began working on quays and bridges and just as Francis entered the world. For a start, the economic dislocations stymieing much of the Western world after the Napoleonic Wars wrecked Bandon. Wars bring economic prosperity, as supply surges to meet demand; the end of them occasions recessions, as demand collapses. Another hit: Ireland was outpaced by industrial changes in Britain. Bandon, for instance, had a flourishing weaving culture before. Weavers specialized in lighter wools and in linen. They were a sophisticated lot. By the time quays were going in, and locals were clamoring for canals, roads, and bridges to be built tying Bandon into the exploding world of commerce, the town was sideswiped by the newly competitive world of free trade with Britain. New steamships connecting Britain to Ireland in the early 1800s accelerated the penetration of the Irish market by British goods. After the Battle of Waterloo ended the Napoleonic Wars, the woolen trade languished. "Trade at present is in the very worst state," a person involved lamented, "very few of the looms in this whole town are going." Provisions cost more; the wages for labor remained low. Weavers in Bandon were resorting to "beggary." In 1815, Bandon had more than two thousand weavers; within twenty-five years that number would fall to 150.[36] To make matters worse, rents were going up, as the population was rising and as landlords wanted to turn more land to pasturage. Rents went unpaid, especially as landlords were not adjusting them to reflect the difficulties peasants and the poorer sort were facing. Moreover, churchmen, as a rule, did not relent on tithes.[37]

Economic downturns radicalized politics in Bandon, which remained stubbornly a town separated by walls. And soon all those Catholics who had streamed in bore the brunt of the blame. Authorities pleaded with Orangemen not to march, as was their custom, within the town and, more problematically, outside of it. With so many angry and anxious people, fears emerged of a return to the awful days of 1798. The bad turn transformed what had been a town opening up into the "Derry of the South," a place marked by aggressive political cultures.[38]

Just after Francis was born, Bandon was mobilizing, and it was politicizing.[39] Unsurprisingly, politicization took on a ritualized cast. Ireland had an old, old tradition of rural violence. Decades earlier, what were called "Whiteboys," armed vigilantes who wore white costumes, had tried to right historic wrongs and stand up for the Catholic peasantry. Whiteboys defended the poorer sort against the wealthy and officials who had forgotten their obligations, terrorized those who enforced tithing too rigorously, and threatened anyone who hindered laboring men and women from earning a living. To officials, Whiteboys were terrorists. There was nothing new about such groups. Anytime tenants felt their traditional rights were being violated, they formed into secret societies to contest their subordination and to remind their overlords that even peasants had a right to subsistence. With failed harvests and excessive rents due amid a contraction of trade, and the war years coming to a close, secret societies sprung up.

In this area, a figure calling himself "Captain Rock" arose as a champion of the downtrodden. Throughout much of Munster, men who called themselves followers of this mythic being sent chilling messages to the wealthy in their midst, warning them that they might meet their deaths unless they relented and remembered their responsibilities to the poor. They donned masks to hide their identities, an old Irish tradition, and a few went further by wearing white linen frocks. This, too, was an Irish rural custom, with insurgents trying to invert conventional roles and power relations. (Incidentally, Ned Kelly's gang in Australia, emulating these Irish secret societies, would do exactly the same thing.)[40] Inside Irishtown, men were swearing oaths, joining secret societies, and planning to subvert the status quo. Soldiers garrisoned the town to impose order and, in the minds of Catholics, to keep them in their place.

After one such movement arose nearby in Limerick, Cork seethed with intrigue, including Bandon. Insurgents known as "Rockites" in Bandon and throughout Munster believed that the world could be redeemed through bloodshed. They indulged in apocalyptic thinking, seeing in economic catastrophe a sign of the end times, when Protestants would be disinherited and vanquished. All around Bandon, Rockites raided the houses of the wealthy for arms and torched the homes of those they deemed

Captain Rock, Commander of the Insurgents in Ireland, 1822. (Chronicle/Alamy)

most vile. If anyone "canted," or turned out the poor, he was intimidated or killed. Rockites refused to pay rents or tithes, and they threatened those who did. They crippled cattle and men. All of Munster was more or less in a state of emergency. West Cork especially so.[41]

Working-class Protestants in Bandon did not take things lying down. Sectarianism is complex. It relies on history but also on socioeconomic issues, changing religious sensibilities, and ignorance and paranoia. Bandon's crash seemed to have hit all of these notes.[42] Protestants transformed their Orange Lodges into militia companies and did their best to intimidate their Catholic neighbors, fueled as they were by renewed evangelical piety, older hatreds, and fears of a collapsing economy. An old anti-Catholic ballad from 1798 that is still heard in Northern Ireland, "Croppies Lie Down," perfectly captured the mood. In fact, this period could bear the name "the Troubles" for Bandon. This term was pulled out of the proverbial closet whenever Irish men and women of different persuasions killed each other. It sanitized the grim reality that pointed to how, given the nature of power relations, Ireland remained a divided society. The Orange Order tried to reassert control and revert to the old apartheid-like ways. For them, Bandon remained a walled place, and one now on the edge.

Francis was born in the right town to become a fighter. In the Bandon of his youth, violence was not the exception but the rule. Here, a practice known as "faction fighting" thrived. The faction fight was an old Irish tradition, and it occurred most frequently in the South and West of Ireland, in the province of Munster. In a place like Bandon it had special appeal. The Irish feuded with one another to defend family, clan, townland, and honor. Factions fought to control people and territory. They regulated behavior and policed the bounds of their communities through organized violence. It was not unusual for fair days to be fight days. Or for a hurling match to turn into massed warfare. Gangs of men insulted one another, edging for a fight, and they usually did not leave disappointed. Hundreds could savage one another with fists and sticks, as well as firearms from time to time. Drink was generally taken. Deaths could occur.[43]

This form of ritualized combat baffled authorities. But the meanings were pretty clear. Factions fought over access to scarce resources and opportunities to work. Fights also represented a form of resistance against those who held the resources. As such, a faction fight always had purpose. In an Irish society that was modernizing and more competitive, and during which normal people were getting increasingly squeezed, it took on even greater significance. In Bandon faction fighting flourished. Concerns which could not be quite uttered or fully appreciated were enacted through violence.[44] And in Bandon, factions operated in sectarian ways.

A faction served as Ireland's version of the mafia. Neighborhoods, counties, parishes—all could serve as salient dividing lines and rallying points for faction fighters. But family came first. As some family names popped up time and time again, gangs became associated with their leaders, some of whom preferred single-combat to a massed clash. The Ambroses would be one of these families. The name Ambrose appeared regularly in faction fighting in Limerick.[45]

Bandon, then, was a fighting town. People, like the Ambroses and Murrays and the Sullivans, clung together and competed and fought together. Catholics fought Protestants, but they also fought each other, and some fought for the British, having joined the military. Bandon created hard people inured to violence and who engaged in all sorts of combat. The nature of the competitive world they were helping create dictated as much. Moreover, it seems all fighting, even sectarian clashes, was ritualized. All this meant that young Francis Ambrose was well-designed for the prize-fighting world he would eventually move through.[46]

Bandon was as broken as Ireland. As George Bennett, an early historian writing a generation after Francis was born, put it, "The history of a town, or of a locality, is often but the history of a nation in miniature." Bandon represented Ireland in extremis. All the ghosts that haunted Ireland had amplified voices in Bandon. Here "two communities [were] peopled by different races." Protestants, or "Saxons," as Bennett called them, did all the hard work to reorder a wilderness, and then the "barbarous Irish" wanted it back. The place was defined by a struggle "between those who lived in cheerful homes, and who supplied their tables with beef and mutton," and the cabin-dwellers "who lived on roots and whey." Bandon was a fighting town because, like Ireland, it was a zero-sum place.[47]

These many tangled tensions coalesced and came to a head over two trying years when Francis was a young boy. In 1821, the population of the town and its surroundings reached a high-water mark of just over ten thousand, making Bandon the eighth-largest city in Ireland. Then it all fell apart. Banks failed, leading to the "consequent distress of Tradesmen." Similarly, farmers saw the value of their crops drop. There was a "total suspension of Trade in this country."[48] Smuggling was increasing, and taxes could not be collected in "disturbed districts."[49] Weavers, the very symbols of Bandon's prosperity, could not put food on the table.

Those like the Ambroses, landless laborers, fared even worse. Many were put on relief works, doing improvements, including building roads or leveling out ones that had been constructed already to make them more useable for traffic. Anxious officials tried to devise such schemes to tie the evident distress of the community into hoped-for improvements, such as a new wider road between Bandon and Kinsale. Maybe, they reckoned, they could kill two birds with one stone: address the potential discontent by offering employment "to a numerous and starving population" and pave the way for a future of possibilities.[50] But they were grasping at straws. In the face of a decline in Bandon as rapid as its rise had been, there were "spirited attempts" to introduce the cotton trade. Factories went up. But because of the distance to raw materials and markets, these attempts also failed. A cotton factory was turned into an "auxiliary workhouse." Corduroy manufacture and linen weaving also were tried. These did not succeed either.[51]

Cue the sectarian tensions. The local powers that had worked to keep the town "tranquil" wrote officials in Dublin promising to "excite and perpetuate a feeling of concord and good will between all His Majesty's Subjects in this part of the United Kingdom."[52] They had no chance. In 1821, Bandon experienced a huge "riot" in the town. On July 2, three Orange Lodges marched to commemorate the Battle of Boyne, when in 1691 the Protestant William had defeated the Catholic James and asserted Protestant hegemony in the kingdom, and to announce their status as the natural rulers of a town in decline. On this day, the Orangemen wore sashes and carried orange lilies, and they entered a church to hear the Rev. William Sullivan preach. "Fear God, honour the king," he implored. Their "custom" was to march, to the beat of drums, past all of the churches in the town and its suburbs, and finish up at the gates of the Earl of Bandon's house by firing a cannon out of respect. This announced, in very Northern Ireland fashion, their supremacy over Catholics. Marching was designed to "perpetuate the remembrance of their degradation."

On this day in 1821, they left the Church of Ireland church "without the slightest unpleasant occurrence taking place." Then the provocation began. After they had nearly wrapped up near the earl's gates, they reached Gallows Hill, near where the Ambroses lived and where the Catholic chapel stood. Here, the road formed a cross. At the cross, "the state of things became sadly changed." Standing athwart the road was "a mob" of a few hundred people, led by men armed with guns. The assembled heaved stones at the Orangemen and fired shots at them at the same time. The Catholics told them that "if they attempted to approach the cross the people of that neighbourhood were prepared for them, and were determined to prevent their passing."

The Orangemen had guns and pistols at the ready as well, and they did not back down. They opened fire with a cannon loaded with gravel and marbles, buttons and penknives. The two sides fought for an hour. Men on both sides were wounded. Margaret Crowley, pregnant, lay dead. John Shee would die of his wounds a few days later. The crowd then dispersed. An inquest was held, and a jury, composed of equal numbers of Protestants and Catholics, convened. Among those arrested were two Sullivans,

Timothy and William. William Motherway, from a family also closely associated with the Ambroses, was hauled before a court as well. Ten of the Orangemen were tried in the matter of the death of Crowley, but most were exonerated. Two were found guilty of manslaughter. This incident would bear the title the "Battle of the Cross." Catholics then retaliated and killed an Orangeman at Timoleague.[53] More trouble followed the next year.

A few months after the battle, 2,134 persons were "in receipt of charitable assistance," and a committee formed to provide employment for the poor. There was "Great distress in Bandon this year."[54] On top of all this, prices fluctuated, crops failed, and farmers slaughtered calves as they had no market. Then, the final blow: Famine struck. Potato crops failed in the late 1810s and early 1820s, just as all of these other afflictions hit Bandon. At the end of the terrible decade of the 1820s, a new Church of Ireland curate detailed his feelings on entering the town for the first time: "I shall not forget the state of depression I was in when I arrived there." All hope had faded. "Bandon was a noisy, dirty town, uncouth and squalid in outward condition." He feared "the place where I had come to live was savage and uncivilized."[55]

Jails in West Cork were bursting at the seams. In 1821, more than 150 men and women were committed and tried for a number of crimes, including rioting and killings associated with sectarian hostility. In addition, dozens upon dozens of people were charged with theft of all sorts. Some for clothes or cloth, some for potatoes, others for sheep, pigs, or cows, as was the case for a James Sullivan. Others were convicted of smuggling, fencing stolen goods, or passing "forged notes." Murders of passion and assaults also seemed to have been on the rise. The system was overwhelmed, so much so that about thirty-five men and women were sentenced "under the rule of transportation" and dispatched to Australia. Most of these were accused of common theft. The number of these crimes spoke to the distinctive difficulties of the times.[56]

Insurgency was tipping into insurrection. The Rockite disturbances reached a new peak in 1821 and 1822 as well. Faction fights were taking on a troubling, insurrectionist edge. During a fair in 1821, an "affray" led to the destruction not of rivals but of the homes of a number of "reputable persons." Witnesses refused to give any information.[57] In late 1821, just after a series of not-so-silent nights around Christmas, local authorities noted "multiple acts of outrage" breaking out in Bandon. The town was caught in the grips of "agitation and wicked incendiaries." Men were openly marching about armed with blunderbusses and guns. If any persons paid taxes, it was reported, they were warned they "shall have their cattle houghed and their heads cut off." Most chillingly, "a violent, threatening, and inflammatory notice" was "signed Captain Rock" and posted on a chapel door.[58] Local gentry figures asked for more troops and even for the establishment of a yeomanry cavalry corps to start patrolling the area.[59] They had good reason to worry. A "spirit of discontent and disobedience to the Laws" was spreading.[60] Rumors flew. The French were preparing to invade. Priests were writing secret notes in Latin. Rockites were flashing secret signs. A cache of arms lay between Bandon and Kinsale. Rebels were making gunpowder. The end was coming.[61]

At this febrile time, insurgents broke into thirty-five houses looking for arms, and frightened gentry reported that five to seven hundred people were out searching for weapons. Most troublingly, these secret-society types were operating out in the open, leading to clashes. "The whole country," a West Cork Protestant declared, "was thrown into a state of confusion. Men ascended the hills, sounded horns, and raised the peasantry." Around Bandon, men left their homes to join the Rockites en masse.[62] Alarmed, Bandon police paraded with Orangemen, who amped up their sectarian cant.[63] A number of the Rockites captured were also dispatched to Australia, later inspiring Ned Kelly. Between 1822 and 1825, 330 insurrectionists from Munster were tried in special court sessions and sent on prison ships to Sydney.[64]

At least one member of the extended Ambrose family, but probably more, was directly involved. A John Ambrose was threatened in 1821, but he was living near Newcastle in Limerick, well north of Bandon—so likely not the father of young Francis. This John had attempted to take over the lease of someone evicted, taboo in a period of rural insurgency. In fact, this Ambrose incident represented the first time someone used the name "Captain Rock" to intimidate a neighbor.[65] Whatever side men and women ended up supporting, there was little doubt that common people like the Ambroses found themselves in awful and constrained circumstances. Few had free choices. These years, as a contemporary witness put it, were marked by "the wretched and desponding state" to which all "had been reduced by the effects of the Whiteboy warfare of the winter of 1821 (in which they were all engaged) and the dreadful famine of the spring and summer of 1822."[66]

People began to note deserted houses. The population of Bandon had increased ever since Francis's grandfather had arrived, peaking in 1821. Then it fell.[67] In a story that would be repeated generation after generation, from the eighteenth through the twentieth century, someone lamented how "great numbers are leaving this poor Kingdom for the United States and British Settlements."[68] The 1820s fueled movement. "The condition of the town of Bandon," a writer recalled in 1830, was "peculiar—no other district probably in the United Kingdom, either Manufacturing or Agricultural, suffering so much distress in proportion to its population."[69]

A chronicler writing a generation after remembered these dark days. "Then commenced an exodus, the like of which, considering the extent of our population, we have scarcely seen paralleled even in history," he wrote, "and which has left us, after an interval of fifty years, with not ½ the number of inhabitants the town contained in this year. Family circles—indeed, we are told, entire communities—fled to Manchester, Leeds, London, and even to Paris." Many, he continued, "have not left even a trace of their whereabouts." In these years, "Lodgings were unlet; houses were unoccupied; whole streets were deserted."[70] People spoke of abandoned cabins in and around where the Ambroses lived. Like many other towns and villages throughout Ireland, those that were tied to a wider world, Bandon spewed out men and women.

Bandon had long ties through Kinsale and Cork to London. Here, many would flee. We don't know the exact year, but it's a good bet the Ambroses left for London during the awful years of 1821 or 1822, just as the town was collapsing economically, seething with sectarian hatred, and hemorrhaging people. That would have made Francis eight or nine years old. He, more than likely, would have retained his Cork accent. He would have certainly remembered the trying times and the Troubles in Bandon. Maybe his father left because he was involved in insurrection. Maybe he just wanted out because of declining opportunities. Maybe, having seen the world, he knew that boundless possibilities awaited elsewhere.

Whatever the specific reasons, Catherine, John, and Francis, their oldest child, likely headed to Cork, boarded a new steamer like the *George IV* or the *St. Patrick*—the chief vessels of two vying steamship lines that had been set up to tie Cork to England—and made for Bristol. Both began plying the route weekly in 1822. Or they could have shipped on the *Ivanhoe* or *Talbot*. These were ferrying people and goods in 1821. Maybe they sailed. In any event, Bristol had been tied to Cork for a long, long time, as evidenced by the Earl of Cork courting Protestants from there to settle in Bandon at the time the walls went up, but the steamers represented a leap in scale and reliability. They came and went on scheduled days, a necessary innovation because of increased trade.[71]

He was entering a new world. In Bristol, Francis beheld a wealthy city of canals, traffic, and modern docks that had made its money from the transatlantic slave trade and more modest endeavors like the import of goods and people from Irish ports. He landed not far from where a statue to the Irish-born statesman Edmund Burke still stands and where a statue of the slave trader Edward Colston would be toppled.

From here, along with a train of others, the Ambrose family made its way to the teeming capital, a city John knew from his days convalescing in Chelsea.[72] Young Francis was about to experience the immigrant's dilemma, the same mix of attraction and repulsion that more than likely had defined his grandfather's existence when he had made his way to that strange town of promise and perdition that was Bandon. Only this time, a Francis Ambrose made his way to a place a bit more alien than the Bandon of his grandfather.

ROUND 2

Whitechapel

THE FIRST THINGS we hear out of the mouth of Francis Ambrose are a threat, a bribe, and a lie. After leading an anonymous existence, he burst onto the scene, and into the historical record, on December 6, 1827. Here is how that happened. On an evening just a week before, between six and seven o'clock, a fellow named John Beckett squeezed himself between two other passengers in the back of a coach and took a seat. He was heading from a neighborhood on the East End called Whitechapel to a dockland area even farther east. Right by the white church that gave the parish its name, on a lane that intersected with Whitechapel Road, Francis, now fourteen years of age, clambered on the back of the coach to skitch a ride. He hauled himself up and held on for about one hundred yards, then he jumped down to make a run for it. Someone ran up to the coach to tell the men aboard they had been robbed.[1]

Beckett felt around his person and realized his handkerchief had gone missing. He probably knew his coach was traveling right between two infamous rag markets, one on Petticoat Lane to the north and the other on Rosemary Lane to the south. He was riding through London's silk-stealing ground zero. Unhappily for Francis, an officer, or a "beak," as the boy would have called him, was watching all of this unfold before his eyes. As soon as Francis jumped off of the coach, Francis Keys ran after him and caught him. Keys looked around the corner of Whitechapel Road and Church Lane and saw some other boys hanging about. They could have been accomplices. But he could have nothing on them. They "were not in company with the prisoner," he concluded. Joseph Fryer, another beak on the beat, confirmed what Keys saw. He then ran to catch the coach and to tell Beckett that Ambrose had indeed robbed him.

Keys dragged Ambrose to Whitechapel's watchhouse, the equivalent of the local precinct. Watchmen and the famous Bow Street Runners, of which Keys counted himself a member, were the precursors to the police force which was just about to be created for London. The growing metropolis desperately needed officers and watchhouses. Francis was booked. And not just any booking. The beaks could have beaten Francis or held him at the watchhouse for a few days to put the fear of God in him before releasing him. The judge, however, decided the circumstances called for something sterner. Newspapers covered the arrest, something quite unusual for the theft of only one handkerchief. Francis was labeled "a notorious young thief."[2]

We know what the Notorious Francis looked like. He stood five feet tall and was regarded as "slender" and fair-skinned. He had sandy hair and gray eyes.[3]

He was sent to the infamous Newgate Prison, just in the shadow of St. Paul's Cathedral, the London Stock Exchange, and the Bank of England. "At the very core of London, at the heart of its business and animation, in the midst of a whirl of noise and motion . . . stands Newgate," Charles Dickens wrote. "And what a frowsy, ugly, disorderly, depressing scene it was," he added.[4] Francis was admitted to Newgate and ushered through the grim alleys that led to the gallery of cells. He was consigned to a jail with "the most atrocious felons," those under sentence of death, and some, like him, who had only pilfered a handkerchief. "Those dreadful walls of Newgate, which have hidden so much misery and such unspeakable anguish," a character from one of Dickens's novels intones, brought about tortured bouts of introspection and anxiety. Prisoners lay on stone beds and, in the darkest and most gloomy of settings through many a "dark, dismal, and silent night," were left ruminating on their past misdeeds and their dreadful futures. They "beat their hands against heavy doors and walls" until they bled. The only things they heard were jangled keys, cries in the night, the jeering from other prisoners, the hammering as scaffolds were built, and the incessant tolling of bells from the Church of the Holy Sepulchre, aptly named, across the road. Ambrose spent three days there awaiting trial—pretty frightening and disorienting stuff for a fourteen-year-old, sandy-haired boy.[5]

On December 6, Francis Ambrose had his day in court. He appeared that day not just in any old courthouse but in the famous Old Bailey,

London's chief felony court across the way from Newgate, where some of the most sensational trials in history occurred. Another Irishman, Oscar Wilde, would be tried here, as would two other notorious criminals from the East End, Reggie and Ronnie Kray. The Old Bailey symbolized the terrible power of the state and, situated in the global financial center of the City of London, the sacrosanct status of property. Even a handkerchief mattered. But the poor did not. Nineteen-year-old William Saunders had just been found guilty for stealing two frocks and sentenced to prison for six months. Maybe Francis, a first-time offender, could expect an even lighter sentence. It seemed, though, that with a number of witnesses to his crime, he had little chance of getting off clean.

Then, standing before the judge, Francis Ambrose opened his mouth. "Did you not offer a boy 5 s. [shillings] to say that I was in it?" Francis put it to Keys, charging the constable with framing him for the amount a workingman could expect to make in a day. "I did not," Keys shot back, insulted by the tone and the accusation. Keys then recalled that on the night in question it was Francis who did something that only compounded his crime. Keys had rifled through Francis's pockets and found six shillings and three pence, quite a tidy sum for a fourteen-year-old street urchin to have. "You may take that, and let me go," Francis had offered to Keys. The upright officer, at least on this day, had answered, "that was not the way I did my duty."

Strategies one and two had failed. Francis tried a number three. "I ran to get a ride," Francis now claimed in the court, pleading that he "saw the handkerchief lay where the gentleman put their feet." The judge was having none of it. And with good reason. These cases came up time after time in the Old Bailey these days. Francis Ambrose seemed just one more street-smart kid that the East End of London produced. Judges and officers had heard it all. This was pretty cut-and-dried.

But give Francis Ambrose his due. He was not taking his fate lying down. Threatening, bribing, and lying—in the face of authority and all of its symbols and institutional power—were not for the faint of heart. Most common people in Bandon and in London never appear in records, or just once or twice at most, usually when they are baptized and when they die. Perhaps when they marry. Beyond that, they lived invisible and mute existences. But Francis had done something that allowed him to punch through anonymity, and his first words would be a figurative shaking of the fist at the world and the powers that be. Defiance was his vengeance. And, as we shall see, it would cost him.

He would find his voice in one of the most dynamic places in the world, a city apt to make a young man defiant. London was the center of the world. All roads in England led to it. All oceans of the world poured into it. It was growing by leaps and bounds when the Ambrose family, along with thousands of others, left Bandon and set off for it. It was the world's maw, a gaping mouth that claimed all. London, moreover, was the center of boxing and prizefighting, something the Irish and other minorities featured in, but also of modern urban life—with all the good and the bad that this phrase conjured. London served as the hub of an empire the likes of which the world had not seen. And Whitechapel, where the Ambroses settled, became what it did because of that empire. In Whitechapel, the forces that made young Francis Ambrose insolent also made prizefighting, pluralism, and poverty, in the midst of great wealth and power, defining characteristics.

This chapter of Francis Ambrose's life was a story only a person born one year before him, like Charles Dickens, could bring to life. And perhaps he did.

The Irish had a long history of going to London, but Whitechapel had not, up to this point, featured as the most likely destination in the metropolis. Most from Cork had headed to a neighborhood called St. Giles-in-the-Fields, right by the Seven Dials.[6] Here they built a tight-knit and embattled but assertive community.[7] By the time Francis was born, the area had a reputation among the middle class for grinding poverty, crime, filth, inadequate housing, prostitution, gambling, gin, and Irishness. All of that ran afoul of the precepts of militant evangelical Protestantism and laissez-faire economics, both of which were becoming staples of middle-class English life and of modernity. Those living in St. Giles were London's outcasts because of their ethnicity, their religion, and their reputation for pugnacity.[8]

When the Ambroses arrived from Bristol in 1821 or 1822, they did not head to an established Irish enclave like St. Giles. Instead, they alighted in an area that was up-and-coming: Whitechapel. Whitechapel had existed as a village just outside the gates of the City of London, the historic heart and financial center of the expanding metropolis that, in our time, bears

High Street, Whitechapel, T. Cox, nineteenth century. (The Print Collector/Alamy)

the name "Greater London." With the explosive growth of the metropolis in the seventeenth century, as the population was rising throughout England and mobile people made their way to the capital, Whitechapel turned from village into suburb. Immigrants had long settled in the area. By the time of the Ambroses' arrival, Whitechapel was becoming an integral part of the urban fabric, swallowed up and considered just a poorer section of the old City that lay just to the immediate west. When Ambrose was arrested, the number of Londoners had ballooned to a staggering one and a half million, and London was spreading out accordingly.[9]

Whitechapel took off because London did. In the years before the Ambroses set off from Bandon, London was growing not just in population but also in wealth. The postwar years would occasion a boom in the greater city. The revolutionary era the world had just passed through left Britain standing as the winner. The upheavals of the period had seen its institutions strengthened, whereas in other places regimes had fallen to pieces. The political economy that animated the world trended now toward free trade, which gave Britain a comparative advantage when it came to global competition. It had the world's finest navy, the best merchant marine, and financial systems that had grown through war-making.

Britain had lost its North American colonies, but the new United States needed Britain, and more particularly London capital, to expand and to enjoy security. The same went for much of Latin America. Argentina, the United States, and Brazil formed part of what could be called an "informal empire." Though not ruled by Britain, they had to play by its free-market rules and depended on money from London banks for their development. When it came to formal empire, Britain still held profitable islands in the Caribbean, which, though they were transitioning from slave labor, still provided riches to the center. Most significantly, it still controlled the Indian subcontinent and, if anything, had deepened its penetration there. It was extending its reach to Australia and what would be the colony of New Zealand.

All of these changes could be seen on the Thames. The City of London was still the beating financial and trading heart of the empire, but now its tendrils stretched over more of the river. With the idea of free trade ascendant, greater London was poised to become the world's greatest port. The metropolis, after all, combined all the aspects of a financial, political, and mercantile capital, and a river ran through it all.[10] Farther east on the Thames from the City, docks were going up. And these just weren't wharves where boats tied up to load and unload. Engineers were creating docking systems that operated like locks on a canal, ensuring that ships did not rise and fall with the tides but remained at a fixed height. Liverpool would take these sorts of "wet docks" to new heights, but in London these "artificial lakes" first began to proliferate along the Thames to the east, creating as they did a system poised to become the greatest port in the world.[11] Right by the Tower of London, the St. Katharine Docks were being constructed in the 1820s, where goods like sugar and rubber arrived from more temperate zones, as well as shipments from the new settlements in Australia. London Docks for American-produced goods like tobacco, in addition to coffee, had been constructed close by just a few decades earlier. Farther east, by the Isle of Dogs, the great docks for the India trade were being constructed.[12] In fact, a canal that functioned like a holding pen for ships cut across the Isle. Scores of ships could tie up here. Between the Isle and St. Katharine's lay the old settlement of Wapping. Coal boats bobbed beneath pubs like the Prospect of Whitby, itself named after a ship. Massive warehouses went up in Wapping. Right by it, huge walled enclosures were arising to protect the goods loaded and unloaded on ships in wet docks.

The Shadwell Basin served as one of these. Meanwhile, new roads cut though old neighborhoods to get so many of these goods to warehouses in the City.[13] All told, when the Ambroses left Ireland, the docks of London were handling 4,500 foreign ships a year carrying about three million tons. All of that tonnage required the grafting of a modern dock system onto a more rudimentary set-up along the river.[14]

And this brings us back to Whitechapel. This section of the capital sat between Wapping and the Tower, just to the north of St. Katharine Docks. It would be remade to accommodate London's spectacular growth through trade. A narrow lane called Dock Street ran from the rag fair on Rosemary Lane to the Thames. Once the walled docks went up, the street had to be widened. Modern trade called for modern roads. So navvies tore down the houses and tenements along the street and then created a channel from the rag fair to the dock so that the increased traffic could be run up to the City in more economical fashion. Much of this building and widening was occurring precisely when Ambrose was there.[15] Whitechapel, then, lay right between two axes of wealth: the docks that tied London to the world and its riches; and the City that financed much of that world. Both axes grew together, with Whitechapel in the middle of it all.[16]

Building roads, docks, and walls demanded labor, and lots of it. Similarly, ships did not load and unload themselves. Dock Street was widened by the Irish, who tended to live in this section of Whitechapel most proximate to the river. They also tended to work the docks that their fellow countrymen constructed. Most Irish, after all, were fated to be "laborers." The system in which Ireland found itself—again, think of second-class subjects in a second-class and populous kingdom—guaranteed that Ireland's surplus population could provide the manpower to people armies and build infrastructure. If London's comparative advantage allowed it to rule the world, Ireland's was to provide the menial and unskilled labor needed to make that happen. For these reasons, Whitechapel had its own boom time. Only it boomed with the poor who began to stream into it, pushed out of places like Bandon and attracted to London and its ceaseless demand for cheap labor. Where development in Bandon had stalled because of Ireland's peculiar place in the British system, Whitechapel grew. In fact, it exploded. In 1801, 23,666 people lived in Whitechapel. By the 1830s, 64,141 did. The Ambroses, therefore, were part of a mighty movement of people to the East End.[17]

It made sense to head here from Bandon. Like Bandon, Whitechapel and the neighborhood it merged with just to the north, Spitalfields, had a long tradition of weaving. Before docks and building became its calling cards, making the fabrics that were traded around the world distinguished it. For generations, skilled artisans, many Huguenots, or Protestants from France, had established themselves on lanes like Fournier Street to work their looms and sell at markets that had popped up nearby. Perhaps John Ambrose came here to weave. But this is unlikely for a number of reasons. For a start, the weaving industry in this part of London was in steep decline, for many of the same reasons it was hamstrung in Bandon. More to the point, if John fought with the Fifty-Ninth, then he spent his time perfecting a craft other than weaving. Killing and marching represented his skills. He had no time to master weaving. Being a Catholic also did not betoken life as a weaver, as most tended to be Protestant. There is one other consideration when we try to fix why the Ambroses were attracted to Whitechapel. Immigrants, as a rule, far from backward, tend to be the most forward-looking people in the world. They scout out opportunities far more effectively than other folks. They adapt, and they improvise. They know where to go and why. Therefore, it's a good bet that John Ambrose had his back and his wits to rely on. Most Irish worked with both, and he would have known the lay of the land and he would have recognized that his fate was to do what nearly all other Irish Catholics did in the booming capital, and that was to provide brute labor.

From what we know, they would settle right off of one of London's most famous—or infamous—streets, Petticoat Lane. Petticoat Lane sat in the southwest extreme of the parish of Spitalfields, right where it merged into Whitechapel, an arching and bending street that ran from the main thoroughfare of Whitechapel Road—right, in fact, where Francis would have his skitching adventure in a few years' time—to the place where the City and Spitalfields run into each other and where Liverpool Street Station now stands. Off it sprang irregular alleys and haphazard lanes.[18] Petticoat Lane was really more of a rabbit warren of courts and closes. On these side streets, weavers futilely worked looms as they grew more and more desperate. A foundry made bells. Factories refined sugar. Nearby, the East India Company had a gun manufacturing center and a proving ground. This was a zone of industry and workshops, as well as a dockland.[19]

They came here for three reasons. It was close to work that John could do. It was where other immigrants congregated, and the Irish tended to settle in "colonies." And it was cheap.[20] The last consideration mattered. Petticoat Lane had a reputation as a place where sellers plied secondhand, and even thirdhand and fourth-hand, goods. Merchants set up stalls all along the lane. Hawkers ranged selling goods of dubious quality. And thieves roamed, particularly gangs of pickpockets. At rag fairs, Dickens recalled, one could find for sale "huge bunches of second-hand silk handkerchiefs of all sizes and patterns, for here reside the traders who purchase them from the pickpockets."[21] It was said that "if you missed your purse or handkerchief at one end of the Lane, you would find it for sale at the other." It earned the name "Petticoat Lane" not for this reason but because it was long associated with the sex trade.[22]

With good reason, Dickens set *Oliver Twist* in the area. All of this, in terms of the scale of poverty and the ubiquity of crime and tension, was new—both for London and for global cities like it that would arise. The place made for good drama. This area, and this street in particular, seemed to epitomize the darkness of the modern world, from its very beginnings with the Ambroses' arrival. Certainly that is how the middle-class and reformers characterized things. Though the area was one in which people pieced together meaningful lives, their betters saw a place like Petticoat Lane as a slum, with all that word connotes.

Francis and his family likely lived in a court that spilled into the lane. We have addresses for them on Mill's Lane and Tuson or Tyson Court, once part of the Halifax estate but now subdivided into tenements.[23] These streets were tributaries of Petticoat, right next to Frying Pan Alley and Sandy's Row, where we know one of Francis's brothers would eventually work. The narrowness—and very name—of Frying Pan Alley gives a sense of what the whole neighborhood once felt like. Right on this spot sat the Freehold Porter Ale and Table Beer Brewery, as well as a storehouse for Constitution Brewery and a Jewish Free School for training boys in the Torah. These went up just as the Ambroses arrived.[24]

In 1821 and 1822, when the Ambroses likely settled, Petticoat Lane served as a teeming migration depot. In fact, all of London was dominated by immigrants. They came from all sorts of places, and shoals of Irish came in.[25] The Spitalfields Ambrose knew was an assemblage of microhabitats, or, as a commentator put it, "pauper colon[ies]" or "rookeries." These were derisive terms for tenements in which people, usually newcomers, flocked together like birds perilously perched on a cliffside. In such places one found "human masses pent up, crowded, crammed in courts and alleys."[26]

Petticoat Lane and its alleys were a strange and lively admixture of people. Stretches of the lane and the alleys that fed into it, especially toward the Spitalfields end, were peopled by Jewish immigrants from the Continent and their children. Most of the hawkers and sellers young Francis would have dodged as he made his way to and from Petticoat Lane would have been Jewish. The Jewish population there would explode in the later nineteenth century. In the 1820s, it was about 10 percent Jewish. The lane was akin to the Lower East Side in New York, a place that had stalls and shops and that buzzed on the day after the Sabbath. Still, large numbers of Irish lived here as well—about 10 percent, too—and like their Jewish neighbors, they congregated together in their own rookeries. The Irish tended toward the dock side of the area.[27] We know the Ambroses consorted in London with Crowleys, another West Cork name, as well as Dempseys—also a name that crops up in records.[28] Here, as well, were Chinese, though they were far outnumbered by others. Arabs and Indians, too, up from the docks took rooms here.[29] With time, Whitechapel would be a palimpsest, as Jew overtook Irish, for instance. When Ambrose arrived, it was something beyond a melting pot, to use Nathan Glazer and Daniel Moynihan's evocative phrase for New York a century later.

Petticoat Lane was home to one of the most "notorious" characters of Victorian London. Ikey Solomons lived on one of the alleys feeding into the lane and had a lair and pawn shop on Bell Lane.[30] Solomons was a reformer's nightmare, and such types made him out to be all that was wrong, in their eyes, with their city as it was developing. He thieved, and he led a small army of urchins who picked pockets and pilfered along the lane. Solomons, a report of the day ran, "initiated himself into the society of gamesters, prostitutes, prigs, and such like characters, [and] began to look round for a wider field for the exertion of his wonderful abilities." He had ambitions, and "he found that the sharing of minor robberies were inadequate to his increasing wants, and having once left the paths of honesty and virtue, he determined to drink deeper into the cup of lasciviousness and vice." Solomons kept lairs around a number of rag fairs in the East End, but his activities were bounded by Petticoat Lane and Rose Mary Lane. And what a thief he was. When he was caught, authorities "discovered a most valuable, extensive, and general assortment of almost every article of British commerce, as well as sundry China, Brocade, and other silks, to the value of many thousands of pounds, including watches, jewellery, diamonds, and pearls, which must from their value have been the property of persons moving in the highest rank of life."[31]

Solomons captured the imagination of Londoners at the time, representing all that they thought evil about the city arising in their midst. So celebrated had he become at the time that Solomons served as the model for Dickens's Fagin, a character at home in narrow lanes and who could wend though "a maze of mean and dirty streets which abound in that close and densely-populated quarter."[32] The name Fagin sounds Irish, but the character was not. In fact, Dickens derisively called him "the Jew." For Dickens and for polite London, Solomons seemed to epitomize all that Whitechapel and Spitalfields meant to the English imagination.[33]

This was Francis Ambrose's world. Penury and, as a later reformer noted, "the poor living off the poor" defined the lot of all.[34] As Dickens would say, "there are many woeful sights in that part of London."[35] Here, he would write in another essay, "there are certain squalid streets, lying like black narrow trenches, far below the steeples" filled with those who "prowl languidly about."[36] Infant mortality, as one would expect, was rampant. Children, often underfed, lived their lives on the street. They had a motley appearance, sometimes turning rags into clothes. Many ran around barefoot. Some had no shelter and slept "rough," such as in haylofts on Petticoat Lane. Whitechapel and the courts around Petticoat Lane in particular represented, along with St. Giles, "the worst places, both as regards filth and immorality."[37] Polite society, embracing laissez-faire ways of seeing the world, mandated that people should be able to look after themselves. In Whitechapel this was a fantasy.[38]

Petticoat Lane turned alienated and uprooted people into enterprising urban creatures. Unsurprisingly, pickpocketing represented both a mark of desperation and a smart strategy. Gangs of pickpockets roamed the area, often sporting flash clothes. This form of theft could be likened to a craft. Some cut their nails at an angle to make them tools for snagging. An expert pickpocket needed "a light tread, a delicate sense of touch, combined with firm nerves." One had to be savvy enough to scope out a mark. A pickpocket may have resorted to the practice because of poverty, but only the wiliest and most street-smart survived. It was not for everyone.[39]

Despite all these challenges, the Ambrose family grew. In 1823, John was born. Three years later Edward came along.[40] The lag between Francis and John and the gap between John and Edward may suggest either deaths or miscarriages. All on Petticoat Lane knew such tragedies. On the East End, such was life. It was an unforgiving place, where ideas about how to address pluralism and poverty had not yet caught up with social reality. With good reason, in 1845 Friedrich Engels set his book *The Condition of the Working Class in England* right here.

It was one thing being poor; it was quite another being poor and Irish. Lanes that the Irish settled in represented "the lowest conditions under which human life is possible," wrote a visitor to the rookeries. The worst sections of the city were filled "with hordes of Irish." Though they made up only 4 percent of the city's population, they gave a place a reputation.[41] Reformers, evangelicals, and do-gooders descended on areas the Irish settled to try to remake the people by handing out Bibles and preaching self-help. They were like an army come to view a subject colony, fulminating against such corrupting pursuits as drinking, rat-killing, and brawling, all the things the Irish indulged in.[42] These people of the reformed faith wanted the Irish to work for their Bibles and their salvation. Then they would drop their superstitious ways and join the modern world. Of course, it did not work out that way.[43] Charles Dickens provided a garden-variety description of the Irish in the Victorian city. One night he took a tour with a local policeman. What he saw repelled him. One Irish ghetto he visited amounted to a "compound of sickening smells, these heaps of filth, these tumbling houses, with all their vile contents, animate and inanimate." He reported he saw "lowering foreheads, the sallow cheeks, the brutal eyes, the matted hair, the infected vermin-haunted heaps of rags."[44] Whether responsible for their behavior or not, "the Irish in this country," a reformer wrote, "have to contend with a prejudice universal against them," a prejudice "of race, not of religion." To their English neighbors the Irish were "nothing better than rogues, vagabonds, and liars."[45]

The Irish like the Ambroses served as bogeymen in London at this time. Minorities even in the sections of the city they inhabited, never mind the broader metropolis, they tended to hope they would be tolerated. They did not approach the city with confidence. They did so with anxiety. They lived and operated like exiles, "comfortless in their arrangements" and "unheralded and often abandoned." Their lot was to survive, to strive at best for acceptance, never mind integration. Their condition was made all the more galling because they lived so close to prosperity. Indeed, the rookeries stood as "symptom" of the imperial grandeur that was transforming London. "These were," one scholar concludes, "the deracinated victims of change." In an undemocratic society, the Irish stood on a bottom rung.[46]

That said, Bandon also prepared Ambrose well for places in transition. He and so many others from Bandon were readied for hard physical labor and for the cultural negotiation of living in a dynamically changing place with a global footprint. These were a modern people, even if their betters did not see or construe them that way. The other thing these people were was adaptable. They could accommodate themselves to urban life because of their experiences of resisting and accommodating in Ireland. They could and did slot themselves into new categories of difference, such as ethnicity, and they appreciated how power could work in new contexts with different social configurations. They were not aliens in this world.[47]

They also had a buttress of faith. Though the Irish did not prove fastidious Catholics, they had the Church. Catholics had erected chapels in the area, particularly as the Irish began streaming in.[48] We know the Ambroses attended a chapel closer to where Liverpool Street Station now sits. The family traveled to a church at Finsbury Square on the eastern edge of the City called St. Mary Moorfields. Brand-new in 1820, it was a large, classical church modeled on St. Sulpice in Paris. It had a number of well-to-do parishioners, but soon it was overtaken by thousands of poor Irish, like the Ambroses. Francis's two younger brothers born in London would be baptized here.[49] Whether the Ambroses attended mass or not is a different story. Most Irish claimed to be Catholic, and that meant a great deal culturally to them. Observance for "Irish Cockneys" was a different matter altogether. The Ambroses, nevertheless, more than likely relied on the Church for a sense of identity. It marked them as Irish, as opposed to English, and this mattered in an anonymous and often-hostile city. It also ritualized the key moments in life: birth, marriage, and death. Sunday church attendance did not rank high on their list of nonnegotiables.[50]

The stakes were high. Catholic clerics were particularly alarmed by the growing numbers of Irish children left to their own devices. They knew what the future would hold: crime and prostitution. They hoped to build a school for these children. Alas, these attempts came too late for Francis. When he lived in Whitechapel, youngsters more or less ran free. Here is a story repeated time and time again in the East End. Seven Irish boys, most with names we would associate with Cork, accosted a beak in Whitechapel weeks before Francis was arrested. For this they were sent away for a year of hard labor. Frankly, this sentence, considering what crimes against property would merit, seems pretty light. In any event, six of the young men, more than likely casual laborers hanging around the rag fairs, petitioned the state for clemency. They sent a letter to Robert Peel—he whose very name is associated with the need for police in the modern city—claiming their innocence. They could not support their families, who depended on them, if they were in prison, and on top of this they did not assault the beak. It was a case of mistaken identity; and it was dark; and they claimed they had not run afoul of the law before. They should, by all that justice demanded, go free to help their families. One of them refused to sign. James Sullivan did not deny he had beaten the beak.[51] This was a hard man. Were the others guilty and just trying to worm out of a conviction? Who knows. But given the time and place they lived, the reality of poverty and overcrowding with the temptations of the goods of the world lying close by, crime and punishment were constants. Youngsters were encountering real urban problems for the first time, and with no educational system for them in place.

What did Francis Ambrose do? We know he did not spend his time in school. He once claimed to work as a trunk maker. That assertion may not be as far-fetched as it might seem. Dozens of firms made trunks, portmanteaus, and the like, and no doubt they hired apprentices to learn the trade. There were legitimate craftsmen, some royal trunk makers, like one on Fernchurch Street, nearby in the City of London, and finer ones on Bond Street, the Strand, Cockspur Street, and Charing Cross in the West End. These catered to the wealthy sort.[52] In Whitechapel, a different kind of trunk was constructed that required a different set of skills.

Ambrose more than likely worked, if he did, as a secondhand repurposer, a fancy term for a scavenger. In poverty-stricken places, nothing was left to waste. Everything could be reused. Scraps of tin and copper, old cooking pots and pans, once they had served their purposes, were sold for pennies to buyers who then cut the metal into strips or "clamps" or "clips" to bind the corners and edges of the repurposed wood that had been painted black. From this, clever street-buyers made trunks. These craftsmen were London's bottom-feeders, struggling on the very margins of the imperial economy. They would have been plying their trade right by what is still called Frying Pan Alley, next to where we know the Ambroses lived.[53]

Or perhaps he lied. More than likely, like his father, Francis worked as a laborer. Whitechapel was filled with "laborers," only now they did what they could in an urban setting. Another time, Francis called himself an "errand boy." Laborer and errand boy essentially suggest the same thing. In London, the terms referred to those doing casual work of any and all sorts. As a contemporary put it, "Many of these men seem to form a body of street-jobbers or operative labourers, ready to work at the docks, to be navvies (when strong enough), bricklayers' labourers, street-sweepers, carriers of trunks or parcels, window-cleaners, errand-goers, porters, and (occasionally) nightmen." This was Francis's likely lot. Critics saw them as shiftless. "Few of the class seem to apply themselves to trading, as in the costermonger line. They are the loungers about the boundaries of trading, but seldom take any onward steps," or so said a contemporary.[54]

We have some evidence that John Ambrose toiled as a coal whipper "in that part of the Thames known as the Pool," a section of the river along Wapping, right by the pub called the Prospect of Whitby. The source of this information claimed to have it on "reliable authority."[55] Whether this is the case, we do not know, but it would fit. As a historian would write, the Irish at this time had a "near monopoly position" on the docks in this area. Whipping, or "getting coals out of ships," was the province of "Irish Cockneys."[56] Coal whippers unloaded ships that arrived from the north of England, like Newcastle. Coal drove the industrial growth of London. Whippers had to be physical specimens. They shoveled and shoveled all day. Coal whippers worked in teams of nine men. Four shoveled in the hold and loaded huge baskets, four raised the baskets to the deck of the ship, and one steered them into place. The tasks required great stamina and strength and terrific coordination. They were renowned as heavy drinkers, sooty in appearance. Coal-whipping was only for the toughest and the roughest. Irish coal heavers had fearsome reputations. Anyone horning in on their trade, like sailors looking for work, encountered a people who knew how to inflict damage.[57]

Wapping was a grim place. Warehouses made the appearance of the river black. It was, as Dickens put it, a place of "dark locks" and "dirty water," where fallen women worked the streets and, therefore, was "a common place for suicide."[58] Sailors strolled the streets, looking for prostitutes. Those loitering to look for work here or to drink were "mostly Irish."[59] For a sense of what Wapping was like, visit the Prospect of Whitby. In it, on the second floor, punters cleared away tables and chairs for bare-knuckle boxing matches. By a bar overlooking the river and the coal boats, as a sign announces, some of the earliest bouts between seamen of different countries took place. Perhaps apocryphally, one of the founding fathers of the English fight game, Jack Broughton, fought here.[60] Cockfights were staged as well. Here was the more Irish side of the Spitalfields-Whitechapel corridor, and anyone working the boats could have bet on, witnessed, or participated in such events.

Perhaps Francis did this work. It would certainly explain his later physique. If he did, it would not have immunized him against uncertainty. Such work was "of such a precarious nature." It depended on the winds. "The sustenance of thousands of families," an observer wrote about dock working, was "as fickle as the very breeze itself." This sort of labor was as "casual" as it came.[61]

The nature of "casual" work in Whitechapel, either coal-whipping or running errands, bred hard men. It also rewarded the clever, those who could think on their feet. The place was defined by the capital development that had become London's pulse, to be sure. In Spitalfields and Whitechapel, that pulse intensified competition among a growing body of poor men and women to keep a hand on the very lowest rung, while older ways of getting ahead, like weaving, were collapsing and newer ones were arising. The effect of clinging to that ladder had to be traumatic and dizzying, especially for the many people from these neighborhoods arriving from places farther afield, whether these be English villages, Irish slums, or European shtetls. Along with hacking out a living, newcomers had to determine the lay of the land and the customs of the country quickly. They had no safety nets beyond kin and neighbors who had made the trek with them. Yes, the local Church of England parish could dole out some assistance. That was the old system that saw after those who fell by the wayside of life. But the ills of a modernizing interconnected world overwhelmed any of the accommodations, and the state had not caught up. In fact, no one really knew what sort of role the state could have or should have played. Who and what were responsible for poverty? Dickens certainly asked this question. So did so many others. But none had real answers to novel problems. The prison and the workhouse were always there for those who could not hold on. The virtues of agility, adaptability, uncomplaining toughness, and moxie proved indispensable for the casual laborer and gave those who lived in this place their fighting sensibilities.

The area, unsurprisingly, bred good fighters. When Francis lived here, the neighborhood was becoming a center for prizefighting. In fact, when Francis Ambrose was born, prizefighting was experiencing something of a golden age in London. Wealthy patrons supported the pastime. They bet on it, drank in pubs that prizefighters owned, happily traveled far afield to watch a match, and packed into exhibition halls close to St. Giles, on the West End, to watch men demonstrate the craft. Some even, as was the case with Lord Byron, wrote odes to it. The man who famously was "mad, bad, and dangerous to know" fetishized boxing, and he even trained under the boxer John Jackson, whom he called "my corporeal pastor and master." Charles Dickens, a connoisseur of London culture in these days, knew of the great fighters and the rituals and slang that surrounded the fight game. Though prizefighting was proscribed, boxing, or sparring with mufflers on, was legal. Fighters could put on exhibitions to showcase the "manly art," as an Irish Londoner from St. Giles and leading promoter of the sport named Pierce Egan put it. [62]

When Francis arrived in London, fisticuffs was king, and London's rise to global status made it the center of the fighting world. Prizefighting and boxing captured the culture of Regency-era London like it would during no other period. Fighting and boxing were the darlings of what was called "the Fancy." We use the words "fans" to describe followers of a sport, as in "fight fans." "The Fancy" is a much more evocative phrase. It meant that human menagerie that lived and died with what happened in the ring. The Fancy included the very wealthiest of England, the landed and the titled and the monied, and the very poorest, those who did the fighting. Lords and carmen, those muscle-bound men who carried people around London, hung out together in taverns and at exhibitions. The Fancy mixed excitement with a bit of skullduggery, some vaunted prose, and lots of drinking to create a culture that animated the fight game in London and made it a magnet that attracted talent, so much so that the capital of the nation became the capital of global pugilism.[63] Though prizefighting ran afoul of the law, the wealthy did not care; in fact, they relished the good fun of flouting the law and slumming it. A trip to a prizefight that was taking place somewhere out in the countryside so as to evade the law could be great sport. To find men in the ring, they scoured neighborhoods like St. Giles and then Whitechapel, looking for physical specimens who seemed to have the right stuff.

The Fancy had its headquarters in the Castle Tavern on High Holborn Road. Men crowded in to hear gossip and to assemble before making their way to a site beyond the reach of the law.[64] Matches were held, stakes were set, and the Fancy met to discuss fighters and drink and to gamble. The Castle was, as promoters put it, "a select sparring club" where "members bring gentlemen selected by ballot and paying a subscription."[65] It was, as Pierce Egan rightly called it, "the Temple of the Fancy."

Prizefighting defined Englishness at the time. It demonstrated how the British stood up to what they regarded as French effeminacy throughout the revolutionary era, and why the English prevailed. Boxing and prizefighting served as both an example of this fact and as a crucible where true Englishness was tested and formed. To be properly English was to be white and Christian, but of the Protestant variety. Fighters like the great Tom Cribb, who opened up a drinking parlor near where Trafalgar Square was being constructed, epitomized the manly virtues that Britons prided themselves on and that they believed had allowed them to defeat the French.

The Irish could only serve as foils in an English stage drama.[66] Nor could Black and Jewish fighters be considered the equals of the English. These were the other two groups that tested the manliness of Englishness in the ring. But sometimes minorities broke through the fistic glass ceiling. Perhaps the most able and famous fighter to take on the great avatar of Englishness, Tom Cribb, was the former enslaved person from the United States, Tom Molineaux, himself trained by another African American in London named Bill Richmond. Egan pointed out how boxing was "unknown" in America, but Molineaux fought Cribb twice to suggest otherwise.[67]

The Irish had their moments, too. Just as the Ambroses were dealing with the era of uncertainty in Bandon, an Irishman named Dan Donnelly was earning a fearsome reputation for a powerful right in Dublin, his hometown, by defeating a top-flight English fighter. Cries of "ould Ireland forever" filled the air as he entered the ring. Donnelly, as far as his supporters were concerned, was fighting for "the honour of Old Ireland."[68] Then he came and took London by storm. But he proved a flop, undone by the drink, and skulked back to Dublin penniless.[69] Nonetheless, in the late 1810s, Donnelly, an Irish fighter, had been the talk of the town in a town that happened to be the center of boxing culture.

A later chronicler of the Yankee Sullivan story would write that young Francis Ambrose had been able to catch a glimpse, or a "peep," of the great Dan Donnelly.[70] Such was almost certainly not the case. But that the two would be mentioned in the same breath speaks to the growing role the Irish would play in London's prizefighting universe.

In the years before the Ambroses arrived, that story was veering toward the East End. With its rapid development and growing immigrant and Irish character, places like Whitechapel were becoming the new center of the prizefighting trade. Where else could you find a critical mass of edgy, hardy, cocky, quick-witted young men who hungered for opportunities in an unforgiving world? Everything the ring valued could be found in Whitechapel and Spitalfields. Whitechapel had a few "sporting houses" where sparring and gambling took place. On Brick Lane, a street that ran parallel to Petticoat Lane, a fellow named Anderson ran such a public house called the Ship. And right between Petticoat and Rose Mary Lanes, close to where Francis would be pinched, Jem Pudney owned another such place called the Coach and Horses.[71] These are only the officially noted premises. Things tended to happen beyond the law and official recognition in the neighborhood. The sporting houses acted almost as satellites of the Temple of the Fancy in Holborn. Prizefighting, to thrive, needed urban and pugilistic infrastructure. The East End provided it.

That's all well and good, but fighting required bodies. And Whitechapel became the new supply center. In fact, in the golden years before young Francis had been born, an East Ender not only dominated the prizefighting circuit but remade it. His name was Daniel Mendoza. The son of Jewish immigrants, Mendoza had all of the fighting virtues that the East End could supply. But he had something else. Mendoza soon became an innovator. He realized that, given prevailing trends in fighting, his size could be a disadvantage. He stood at only five feet seven inches. He turned his small stature into a virtue. He also used the stereotypes of the day and turned them to his advantage. This meant he fought "like a Jew." If fighters clumsily hammered each other, he would be all movement and deception. He understood that the key to fighting is not to get hit. A good fight for him was to avoid "any blow of material consequence." So, he perfected defensive technique. He came to scratch and toed the line, as all fighters had to when a new round began, but soon he used the whole ring and made his opponent chase him, all to tire his adversary out. He parried punches and countered, using agility as a weapon. He slipped punches, what he called "side-stepping," that is, moving his head a few inches to avoid a blow, all the while setting his body up for a counterattack. He punched quickly, using speed as his weapon. Those he fought pilloried him as a "cowardly" fighter, someone who would not stand in the center and take his punishment and mete it out. Mendoza knew better. His job, he believed, was to win, in whatever way he could and with the least damage to him. A match, to him, had to be a "contest of skill." He became known as "a scientific fighter," that is, he prized boxing as a craft to be mastered and not just an opportunity to bludgeon.[72]

Mendoza remade a sport that little resembled the boxing matches we see today.[73] Under the conventions of the day, rounds lasted as long as a man could stand. If he went down, a round ended, and the two combatants went back to their respective corners for thirty seconds. They had then to come up to scratch—a line marked in the middle of the turf ring—for the fight to continue. If one of the combatants did not come up to scratch, it was over. A prizefight only ended if a fighter could not leave his corner, if he lay unconscious in the ring, or if one of his cornermen threw in the sponge. Most proved reluctant to take this course of action, and cornermen did all they could to get their man to scratch. A great deal of money was riding on a fighter continuing. Mendoza worked within these rules, but pushed their bounds. He, for example, chose when to hit the deck, pushing right up against the bounds of acceptable behavior as he did so.

This East End immigrant's son revolutionized the fight game and with good reason would bill himself, as he did in 1820, the "Father of the Science."[74] He even wrote a book, or had it ghostwritten, on how to fight the way he did. Soon the Fancy realized that all would have to adopt Mendoza's more crafty, defensive style if they wanted to win. For boxing is a ruthless profession. A prizefighter either stays up with trends or is gone. Adapt or die could be the watchwords of the craft. Whitechapel kids were made for this way of approaching life and approaching the ring. Mendoza himself recognized this, and upon his final retirement, he ran a pub called the Lord Nelson on Whitechapel Road, just a few hundred yards from where Francis would have his skitching adventure, and opened a boxing academy for young Jewish boys in the area. Francis, of course, did not attend. His education undoubtedly would have come in the streets, though the scientific style that Mendoza championed began to remake pugilism, even for young boys.[75]

Mendoza would settle just to the east of his pub in Bethnal Green. But eventually, he would end up on skid row and have to set up house on Petticoat Lane, at a squalid address on Horse-shoe Alley on the Whitechapel side of the parish.[76] He was Francis Ambrose's neighbor. Did Francis catch a glimpse of Daniel Mendoza? Of course, he would have known of him. By the time Francis was traipsing down Petticoat Lane, Mendoza had turned into a washed-up ex-fighter and pub owner who had fallen on hard times. But he was a cultural icon. He was the living avatar of the defining characteristic of London culture that had Petticoat Lane as its epicenter.

Especially tough fighters came from Petticoat Lane. Another great innovator, Samuel Elias, known as Dutch Sam or the "Terrible Jew," also was born on the lane Francis called home. Elias invented—or better, popularized—the uppercut.[77] His approach, unlike Mendoza's, was to get in close and create great upward force with a quick punch. All that force came from the legs, just as Mendoza's ability to move laterally came from the legs as well.

Finally, Francis lived in the neighborhood of the great Jem Ward, a man who would go on to play an important role in Ambrose's life after a number of twists and turns. Ward oozed moxie. He threw a bout, or "crossed" a prizefight as the saying went, only to make a comeback that allowed him to lay claim to the unofficial British title. He also was raised in the East End of London by Irish-born parents and had honed his physical abilities by working as a coal whipper. Pierce Egan called him the "Black Diamond," hard and soot-covered. He was also known to sport a "green fogle," when he entered the ring. These would be regarded as his "colors," or a symbol of what he represented. A disciple of Mendoza's style, he was regarded by Egan as "a *good* milling cove" and by a later boxing commentator as "a very scientific boxer from East London." He also was what we could call a sharpshooter. As opposed to blows to the body, which bare-knuckle fighters tended to employ to keep fragile hands unharmed, he favored quick shots to the head, the kind that demoralized opponents. Ward gained renown as a fighter who pushed the rules and conventions of the craft to their very limits, and sometimes beyond them, and he did so at exactly the time Francis was living in the East End. He was, as Egan reported, quite adept at "the street business," a style he mastered in the East End.[78] We do not know if Ambrose knew him personally before his arrest; he would certainly sometime after.

So, not only did Petticoat Lane inculcate the necessary mental abilities to thrive in the ring, it also was a competitive crucible that valued innovation. Sites of imperial globalization, like London, tended to be centers of pugilism. There is no doubt that it thrived in just the sorts of areas that were becoming connection points in a modernizing world. Boxing, therefore, was perfect for seething places like Whitechapel.

Did Francis fight? Of course he did. In a neighborhood where prizefighting was king, all boys knew its rules and rituals, and contemporaries reported on how adept youngsters were. They had to be. As a reformer named Charles Booth put it, in the city at this time "violence was common." It was not unusual to meet an Irishman who "had formerly been a pugilist, a hard hitter and hard drinker, as his battered face testified."[79] Another chronicler found that "a fondness for 'sparring' and 'boxing' lingers among the rude members of some classes of the working men." These sorts often became the boxers who were "the pets of princes and nobles." In this neighborhood, "it is called 'plucky' to bear pain without complaining."[80] Kids fought each other in the streets and alleys. People competed for scarce and physically challenging work. Alcohol eased anxiety but fueled violence. And as contemporaries testified, the people of streets like Petticoat Lane could prove fierce when provoked.[81] The residents of Whitechapel prided themselves on becoming what the writer Carlo Rotella argues makes all good boxers: they were good with their hands. They knew how to employ them, in fighting and in laboring.[82] This was the London that Ambrose knew. And even if he did not yet fight in formal bouts—he was, after all, too young—he and other young boys tried to best each other in the street, following the rituals prescribed by those who tried to earn some type of living from the pursuit.

To Londoners at the time, the Irish, like Jews and Blacks, seemed tailor-made for the fight game, perhaps even more so. They seemed prepared for violence, but of a sort that jibed with prizefighting. The faction fight and the actions of the sectarian secret societies functioned in the same way boxing did. Like faction fighting, pugilism, with its rituals, domesticated and channeled tensions. It also bounded violence. It focused group grievances. It made for acceptable outlets of violence in combustible contexts. In Ireland, in urban spaces, the Irish also had embraced pugilism. There is no doubt that it thrived in just the sorts of places, like the East End of London, that were becoming transformed by modern globalization. And the Irish proved enthusiastic participants in the prizefighting world after they adapted Irish ways in a new dynamic context. Young Francis would have been a young disciple.

So, picture Jack Dawkins, the Artful Dodger in Dickens's *Oliver Twist*, a defiant boy becoming a man in an unforgiving crucible, a character very much like Francis Ambrose. Dickens thought these sorts of people defined modernity. In much of his work, Dickens hoped to reveal the human costs of unregulated development; he also wanted to point out the human capacity for self-invention even in the grimmest of circumstances. The Dodger and all that happened to him and around him evinced the good and the bad aspects of this most globalized place. Moreover, Dickens knew the Irish and their relationship to this place. They were the world's flotsam and jetsam, washing up where work was needed and living, and in some cases thriving, along the edges. The Dodger fit this sort of description as well.

Let's get back to Francis's arrest. He was probably on a route he knew like the back of his hand, from one rag fair to another, the way Fagin and his gang of urchins operated in Dickens's novel. That would place him at the spot of the crime, right next to the church at Whitechapel that gives the parish its name. He would have been planning to nick the handkerchief and sprint to Rose Mary Lane. There, right by the church, was where the coaches ran and where he could spy wealthy and easy marks. He could then melt into the sea of humanity and find the Fagin he fenced goods to. If he was indeed heading to Rose Mary Lane, he would have run down a twisting dogleg of a lane filled with tenements and industry, including the East India Company weapons proving ground.[83]

He would have darted around punters sitting outside a pub that remains to this day. The Crown and Seven Stars could be found smack in the middle of Rose Mary Lane, a brand-new establishment that had just gone up in 1826 and, given its location, could have been a "flash house."[84] Today, not so fittingly, the pub bears the name the Artful Dodger.[85] Even more ironically, the pub is known as a place to watch boxing, with images of long-dead fighters on one wall and, on another wall, a kitschy painting of the Artful Dodger—Jack Wild from the film version of *Oliver!*

Back when Ambrose was thieving, Rose Mary Lane was the sanctuary of "Dredgers, ballast-heavers, coal-whippers, watermen, lumpen, and others whose trade is connected with the river." This was "a large district interlaced with narrow lanes, courts, and alleys ramifying into each other in the most intricate and disorderly manner." As around Petticoat Lane, "the houses are of the poorest description, and [it] seems they have tumbled into their places at random. Foul channels, huge dust-heaps, and a variety of other unsightly objects, occupy every space, and dabbling among these are crowds of ragged dirty children who grab and wallow, as if in their native element." Ambrose found kindred spirits here: "None reside in these places but the poorest and most wretched of the population and, as might be expected, this, the cheapest and filthiest locality of London, is the head-quarters of the bone-grubbers and other street finders."[86]

In *Oliver Twist,* the Artful Dodger has his Francis Ambrose moment when he picks a pocket, stealing a silver snuff case. He, too, proves ever-defiant in the face of authority, refusing to bend his neck. The two were not alone in shaking their metaphorical fists at the system. Defiance defined the stance of a good number. For his crime and for his audacity in the face of unsympathetic justice, a magistrate sentences him to transportation to Australia. The Dodger, unbowed, would be heading to the prison colony.[87]

The same fate befell Francis Ambrose. At the Old Bailey, he was herded into a holding pen with fifty or sixty other people accused of other crimes, nearly all against property. The judge confronted miscreant after miscreant; indeed, a quick judge could hear seventy cases a day. The average trial lasted a mere 510 seconds.[88] Francis's did not even go that length. A few sentences exchanged, and the boom was lowered. Though in his case, the judge determined that a sentence of seven years as a convict in Australia, the more or less standard time for a crime against property, was not long enough. Because Francis threatened, challenged, and lied, his sentence was doubled. Because he was a "notorious young thief," he was not given a run-of-the-mill sentence. For one stolen handkerchief he received a fourteen-year sentence to the prison colony at the other end of the world. Fourteen years for a fourteen-year-old.[89] In fact, the judge was taking into account a few considerations when determining if transportation would be a young offender's fate. Was he "hardened"? It seems Francis ticked this box. Did he have any "criminal connections"? More than likely he did. Crimes associated with what was regarded as "the criminal class" also earned transportation. Pickpocketing was associated in the popular mind with the ills of Whitechapel and therefore with the frightening visage of urban crime, which itself seemed to be increasing. Francis was not heading to Australia because of his defiance, but he probably garnered fourteen years, and not seven, because of it.[90]

Although his defiance, his unwillingness to bow his head to what his world considered fitting and proper, guaranteed his fate, it also underscored his character. Francis Ambrose, like the Dodger, was of a place-in-time and made of different stuff. Londoners would not have it. They expected boys-becoming-men like him to know their place. He refused. What he did not know was that his experiences with the darker aspects of modern globalization were shaping him. And they were just beginning. Alas for him, Whitechapel would seem a paradise compared to what awaited.

ROUND 3

Chatham

On October 21, 1805, a ship called the *Euryalus* took its place in the line of battle near HMS *Victory* for what would be known as the Battle of Trafalgar. The day before, it had been patrolling the seas around Cadiz off the coast of Spain, trying to find out for Lord Horatio Nelson, the head of the British fleet, what plans the allied navies of France and Spain had in mind. The ship was also to lure the enemy out to fight, acting almost like a hare to a pack of greyhounds, and start a "Chase." When *Euryalus* and the other frigates of the small reconnaissance fleet spotted the enemy, word was relayed to Nelson, who knew the daring way he would attack the enemy. He would divide the fleet into two columns to break the enemy's line, and *Victory*, a mighty battleship, would serve as the tip on the left, the "weather column." He sent that famous message, recounted on board the *Euryalus*, "that England expects every Man to do his Duty this Day." The action then commenced at 12:15 p.m.[1]

From this point, *Euryalus* played a supporting role. It boasted only thirty-six guns, a small number by comparison. Launched only five years earlier, its game was speed. *Euryalus* was an Apollo-class frigate, a fifth-rate ship of the line. It held a crew of between 220 and 300 on two decks. It could sting, but ships like *Victory* were the ones designed to do the heavy brawling. *Euryalus* was named after a character in Homer's *Iliad*, a fighter of great renown who became one of Jason's famous Argonauts. Homer called him "a god-like warrior" who had the courage to take on the finest fighters in single combat. Think of him as the Mendoza of the *Iliad* and of the ship that bore his name as the Mendoza of the fleet.

On that day in 1805, the British had the weather gauge, the perfect windward position for optimal maneuverability, establishing the terms of battle, and bringing maximum firepower to bear when attacking. The British, and *Victory* in particular, would be well positioned to fire into any hull they came across. To the leeward side sailed *Euryalus*. It would be tasked with improvising, hitting and running as needed, and sending signals to the fleet. *Euryalus* was a "watch-dog." Once Nelson committed, it sped into position, just off of *Victory*'s port beam, running parallel to the main line on the left, right next to the *Temeraire*, which followed close on the heels of *Victory*. When the fighting commenced, *Euryalus* stopped her running and "returned the enemy's fire in a brave and steady manner."[2]

The "glorious victory," of course, belonged to *Victory*, though it was severely damaged. "Valour and skill" had won the day. Nelson was killed in the battle, and for this he would be revered as a martyr for Britain, destined to stand in stone on pillars around the British imperial world. An officer on the *Euryalus* wrote that "that Brave and Excellent Officer Lord Nelson whose Name will never be forgotten" had become "one of the Brightest Ornaments in the British Navy." His flag was taken down and, as a great honor and in recognition of the vital albeit smaller part it played in an epic battle, the commander who took over for Nelson "hoisted his flag on Board of us," the *Euryalus*. For a few days, it would serve as the British flagship.[3]

From this epic moment *Euryalus* would meet an inglorious end. After Trafalgar, it had tours throughout the world during the rest of the war. But then, like all of the wooden ships in a world of steam and iron, it became obsolete. It was decommissioned and demasted. Its fate was immortalized in one of the great paintings of the period. The artist J. M. W. Turner's most recognizable painting is entitled *The Fighting Temeraire*. As the sun sets over an estuary in England, the once-great ship—now stripped of its sails and with a ghostlike pallor, is towed up from Sheerness by a paddle-steamer tug belching fire and smoke. O, brave new world, as the future supplants the past. The *Temeraire* had sailed next to *Euryalus* in the great battle, and it was a ship that could in size stand almost toe-to-toe with *Victory*. Now it was ending its days, to be turned into scrap and, more to the point, a "sacred relic," as the writer William Makepeace Thackeray would utter when he first beheld Turner's masterpiece.[4]

Between victory and scrap-heap or relic, both *Temeraire* and *Euryalus* still had roles to play in the story of British empire. They would do so as floating prisons. Both would serve out their days as what were called prison hulks. Prisons were overflowing during the age of revolution. Since the American Revolution, when rising numbers of convicts could no longer be shipped off to the American colonies, prison authorities used ships to house prisoners. When a new penal settlement was established on the other side of the world in Australia, they served as holding pens for prisoners awaiting shipment. They eased the strain on an overwhelmed system, now teetering because of increased crime in neighborhoods such as Whitechapel. The hulk, then, was an inexpensive way of dealing with one of the seminal problems of the modern world: crime and punishment.

Hulks also could provide cheap labor in naval installations. Dredging rivers, building embankments, enlarging dock capacity to build and service more ships, moving timber and iron, all required labor. Prisoners on hulks, floating next to docks, could do all of this work. They could act as the invisible hands of Britain's military-industrial complex, so critical as Britain's imperial obligations around the world grew and grew. Hulks offered a captive labor force to enable the navy, now with all of its imperial demands, to grow. Most of the hulks sat farther down by the estuary at Sheerness and, most notably, on the Thames farther east of Whitechapel at Woolwich, close by Greenwich. Just below the church of St. Mary Magdalene, where the great Tom Cribb eventually would be buried with a proud lion for a monument, prisoners did menial work at the naval base and arsenal and worked to keep the channel in the river navigable. These men comprised part of what could be called a penal-imperial complex.[5]

Francis Ambrose played his part in this epic drama, not in Woolwich but at an even larger facility near the Thames estuary, a place called Chatham, where the *Euryalus* floated. He would have been destined for Woolwich if he had been arrested just a few years earlier. But in 1825, a reforming Protestant minister by the name of Thomas Price argued that boys would have to be separated from men. "Many of these poor children," he thundered, "might be reclaimed."[6] *Euryalus*, therefore, was established as a juvenile detention center.

The hulk was meant to offer an enlightened approach to imprisonment for boys. Reformers knew what was happening to young offenders on prison hulks, though they dared not speak its name. They used euphemisms instead, focusing on how mixing boys with men could lead to their corruption. They hoped boys would remake themselves in the right circumstances and with the proper education and encouragement. This could not happen around hardened adult criminals. The same sorts of do-gooders who visited the rookeries in Whitechapel and handed out Bibles argued that boys could be redeemed if they were put on hulks of their own. The *Euryalus* would be part of that reform. Price, a Protestant Father Flanagan, made it his mission to see to a new way of transforming the most incorrigible boys. In his floating "boys' town," if we could call it that, those with no "moral and social restraint" would be saved. Here, he would inculcate "honesty, industry, and sobriety."[7]

Francis and other boys also found guilty in the Old Bailey journeyed to the hulks in wagons. One reckons his parents and brothers were at Newgate to see him off. His companions included a boy called James Sullivan. On January 5, 1828, the motley crew arrived to a site of great activity once they passed by the village of Rochester.[8] They were now as far away from Whitechapel and the Old Bailey as one could imagine. The River Medway was chosen for just this reason. It is a lazy river, perfect for building and repairing naval ships. The Medway, where the dockyard sat, lay close to the Thames estuary but not in it. It was a place unbothered by so much of the growing traffic sailing and steaming into London's docks. Here, sailors could enjoy proximity to the capital and to the Channel and North Sea without the fuss and bother.

Charles Dickens said the first thing any visitor to Chatham noticed was the noise: "Ding, Clash, Dong, Bong, Rattle, Clash, Clonk, Bang, Clatter, Bang Bang BANG." On one ship, he heard "Twelve hundred hammers, measurers, caulkers, armourers, forgers, smiths, shipwrights; twelve hundred dingers, clashers, dingers, rattlers, clinkers, bangers bangers bangers."[9] He surveyed the scene in 1869, when an ironclad was being fit out. But the same went for the late 1820s, when Francis was there and they were working with wood. The noise would have been constant. Dickens would know. He moved there at the age of five, when his father was working as a clerk at the Naval Dock Yards.

Chatham Docks Yards were a world unto themselves. Thousands of men, most highly skilled, worked day and night to fit out, repair, and build ships. Lord Nelson's flagship, HMS *Victory*, was built here, as was *Temeraire*. Joiners, shipwrights, ropemakers, smiths, sailmakers, even ministers in the church on the grounds, all plied their trades and crafts in Chatham. These men, and later a few women, took pride in outfitting the world's greatest ships. They played their part in an imperial and military drama that spanned the globe. Tradesmen at Chatham worked so efficiently that a large number of ships could be mobilized quickly. In fact, Chatham had to have one of the highest concentrations of skilled artisans of any place in the world. It also boasted Europe's longest brick building—more than a quarter mile in length—where craftsmen made the rope that ships needed. The place was and is massive.

When Dickens's father worked here, and just around the time Francis arrived, the place needed convicts. In fact, in the years when Dickens was young, when he lived in Chatham, the dockyard was going through a period of explosive growth. The government purchased more land to create more slips to service all the ships needed for Britain to maintain global dominance in the wake of wars with France and the expansion of empire in the Pacific. The facility was creeping farther and farther out toward the Channel, as the demand grew for naval vessels to defend Britain from any threat and to safeguard empire. Chatham, then, was an extension of John Ambrose's labors for empire. And all of this necessitated cheap labor. Enter convicts. So much menial work had to be done in dredging the Medway to prepare for dock extension and to move all the timber around the yard to new areas. One horse could do the work of forty men in hauling beams and masts, but the use of the forty could prove more cost-effective. Convicts loaded and unloaded mud barges. They carted lumber. They swept and cleaned the yard. They even picked nails from rubbish. They did all aspects of unskilled grunt work at a yard that valued skill. They worked from sunup to sundown, with one hour back at the hulk for lunch.[10] The dockyard's expansion onto nearby St. Mary's Island required one thousand men. Their drudge labor increased the size of the dockyard from 97 to 380 acres. They added four new dry docks that could manage the most massive ships of the day.[11] Why have men and boys languish in prisons when they could be put to work?

The *Euryalus* sat in the middle of the Medway, adjacent to the ropery. The ship was a forlorn sight. An artist named John Sell Cotman sketched it in 1828, when Francis first beheld it. It sat solemnly but ingloriously. Only one mast remained. It was sawed-off. On it, a flag fluttered. The prow of the ship was covered with ropes tying down the canvas running past the gunports. At the stern, a flagpole still stood but was flagless. It looked as ghostly as Turner's *Temeraire*.[12]

In fact, *Euryalus* was a floating purgatory, or as prisoners were wont to say, "hell upon earth."[13] In 1825, the boys aboard a hulk called the *Bellerophon* were transferred to the *Euryalus*, so the new regime could get under way in creating what was billed as a floating reformatory. They would be under Thomas Price's spiritual care. The chaplain's plan mandated that young offenders be segregated into classes to ensure the most hardened did not corrupt those young souls that could be saved. They would have religious lessons, as some of them had no idea of religion and God. They would be put to work, and perhaps they would leave with some sort of trade. But they had to be looked after. Price wanted a library in the hulk. He demanded that those overseeing the boys devote themselves to reforming the boys. They were still malleable and could be remade and, God willing, rehabilitated.[14]

If only. This was hardly a system designed for rehabilitation, and before too long, Price ran into conflict with the overseer, John Steadman, who believed more in routine than reform. "It is true," Steadman averred, "that the exercise of power may restrain unruly dispositions, and the operation of sinister motives may produce a degree of obedience." No rods would be spared. Price was sent packing.[15] Although 250 boys were supposed to be crammed into the hulk, because of the growing problem of youth crime in London and other cities, nearly 400 boys could be squashed into the ship at one time. When Francis arrived, 300 were on board.[16] The reformers had not met these sorts of boys before. They could sit still and listen to dry sermons, but they did not seem to take to the lessons. A draconian regime, designed to instill discipline, was their fate. Order would be the order of the day.

Unlike the men, many of the boys were kept on the hulk all day and every day. At least the men left to do physical labor in the dockyards. The boys did tailoring work, making outfits for the convicts laboring there. The men may have expanded the dockyard, itself a symbol of British might. The boys did their bit as well. Making clothes represented their modest participation in the military-industrial complex, but a contribution nonetheless. Life here was drudgery. Their days began at 5:00 a.m. They lowered their hammocks and made their way to chapel for hymns and prayers. After a breakfast at 6:00 a.m., they cleaned the ship. Those in charge also heard complaints about what had happened the night before. Work began, in silence, at 8:00 a.m. Punishments were doled out at 9:00 a.m. This could range from the cat-and-nine tails and caning to being deprived of food and sent to solitary with a bread and water diet. After lunch at noon, they went up on deck, where they walked in circles, again in silence, like old men in a prison yard. "After mid-day dinner," a contemporary remembered, "they were allowed an hour in the open air . . . the slightest noise bringing a severe reprimand." Then back to work below on the clothes. Some boys had the reprieve of chapel for lessons. The rest stayed at their tasks. By 5:00 p.m. their workday was over. They had supper and went back on deck for more walking in circles. They had another session in chapel before turning in at 8:00 p.m. An hour later, the guards mandated absolute silence.[17] Silence, monotonous work, no exercise. It was a recipe for disaster. Some resorted to self-mutilation to escape the hell. Others resisted this regime. The boys proved an endless headache. "Open mutinies took place on at least two occasions," an official reported. "We would call them riots!"[18]

But in truth, the boys faced their sternest tests from each other. Lights-out came at 9:00 p.m. on the hulk. Then the true awfulness began. The young convicts were largely left to their own devices. One can imagine the bullying and the rape. The boys divided themselves into two groups: Nobs and Noseys. Nobs ran the show. They were the biggest and toughest kids who took out their anxieties and their anger to prey on the weakest. They ganged together to bully. They stole the meager rations the young and weak should have eaten. These children were all at the age where they needed nutrition to grow, but, as one argued, "you are half starved to death there." A little bit of protein, like an ox cheek, for the strong; potato peelings and porridge for the weak.[19] In this battle for survival, the strong overwhelmed the weak. Noseys fought back by currying favor with authorities. They told tales. They ratted. Those who were bullied decided they had to find some protection in this world of all against all. Beatings, reprisals, fear, domination . . . all the worst of humanity came out in the *Euryalus*, despite the pious hopes of those who devised the plan for the hulk.

On top of this, the adults could not agree on how to handle the problem. The debates over what to do went over the well-trodden ground of nature and nurture. One group argued draconian measures were needed. Was there any such thing as a bad boy? They answered yes, and if such was the case, why bother with rehabilitation? Punishment was the answer, and in this instance, it would mean allowing nature to take its course on the hulk. The overseer on the ship seemed to subscribe to this approach, and he turned a blind eye to the evils taking place on the *Euryalus*. Others argued that with more religious instruction they could be reformed. Price, the minster, hoped boys could be redeemed, that they could change given the right instruction and the right environment. He was hardly alone. Officials rationalized the awful choices they made—and the fate to which they condemned the victims of the modern world's ills—with the notion that removal from bad influences and proper controls could allow boys to remake themselves.[20]

These would be the same sorts of arguments that would be trotted out to try to address the problems of a modernizing world. The debate raged especially while Francis was confined. He found himself in the gray zone, a pawn in the pressing intellectual issues of the day, listening to interminably long sermons geared to rehabilitation, at one extreme, and dealing with neglect and "the lord of the flies," at the other. He was caught between the Nobs and the Noseys. The grim reality, given how and why the boys were sentenced to be shipped off to Australia, was that most of the miscreants by definition were "hardened" or in the spot they were because of "bad associations." Yet, they were still impressionable. The end result for most would be, as an official writing about the *Euryalus* would put it, "however criminal they might have been before their Commitments . . . previous to their Imprisonment in that accursed Hulk . . . they were comparatively innocent." Though the *Euryalus*, in theory, was "specially fitted for them," the reality was bleak: "If there be any regular and established schools for teaching crime, the ship Euryalus is the place."[21] An ex-convict testifying sometime later before a government committee looking into the juvenile penal system had this to say about his stint on the *Euryalus:* "Frequently when I have seen it in a newspaper that a Judge has sentenced a boy out of mercy to him to the hulks, I have made the observation that was it a child of mine I would rather see him dead at my feet than see him sent to that place."[22]

Francis's only solace was the one hour a day he had on deck, on that space beneath the sawed-off mast. On clear days, at least, he had a view of the lovely cathedral and castle in Rochester, which had to seem the only reprieve from the bustle and noise of Chatham dockyards. Or he could look at the ropeworks, and take in its extraordinary length. Maybe what drew his attention were the warships being built and all the hustle and bustle. That is, if he cared.

Perhaps he was thinking of how to survive. Or, more likely, how to dominate. No doubt, at five feet, he was not one of the bigger boys. But it would be hard to imagine that any were tougher. Whether he had worked as a coal whipper or an errand boy used to hard labor, Francis had become by this tender age a hardened street-smart kid who—given the neighborhood of Irish rookeries he lived in—had to be physically able to defend himself and clever. He, more than likely, honed the fighting skills, or at least the temperament, he had begun to acquire on the East End. It stands to reason. He came from a subculture that vilified informers. And one that favored and rewarded ritualized violence. It's easy to reckon he was a Nob, or at least not a victim. Perhaps a victim of the state and of the troubling world he inhabited. But not a victim at the hands of other boys.

He was to stay here a total of just over two months, until he almost turned fifteen. Then he readied to sail to Australia. Francis now inhabited the impersonal, indifferent world of the state's penal system. In fact, after his time in the hulk, he was inured to it. Herded, trotted off to a new place, he just followed the directions. Resistance was futile, and the whole regime was designed to inculcate this fact. Even if some hoped he could be refashioned into a productive subject through incarceration, the state did not care about such considerations. It, too, had plans for him. Maybe the victims and maladies of a globalizing city could be used to strengthen empire. Officials and authorities thought in this way.

Amid all of these criminals, the Notorious Francis behaved well, or at least his overlords noted as much. What he had endured had served this purpose. "Conduct orderly," the report read.[23] This would be about his last good report card.

In early 1828, his ship to Port Jackson in New South Wales pulled out of the canal that ran across the Isle of Dogs and that contained many ships coming from and going to India. Here the ship moored to allow workmen aboard to repair what had been damaged on the recent voyage and where it was made ready to sail. It then stopped at Deptford at its massive Royal Navy dock, right by the facility and hulks at Woolwich.[24] On March 4, 1828, men from the Thirty-Ninth Regiment of Foot, originally an Irish-raised unit that had seen glory defending empire in India, came on board. The Thirty-Ninth, which now also included men from England and Wales, was tasked with guarding convicts in Australia, mundane work for a regiment whose motto was "primus in Indis," or "first in India."[25] Nonetheless, its new charge also mattered, perhaps just as much as its vaunted role in securing empire in India. Here, convict settlement promised a new grand experiment in empire building. After the loss of the American colonies, perhaps these places on the other side of the earth could bind a new empire together, one designed for the world of free movement and of free trade that had emerged.

Just over a week later, on March 13, the ship was piloted down the Thames. Between March 17 and 22, it would take on convicts at docks with hulks farther down the river and on the Medway. On March 19, Francis, along with nine other boys, was plucked off the *Euryalus* and put on an "open boat" for the ten-mile trip to Sheerness on a freezing night. Here, where the Medway ran into the Thames and in sight of yet another dock facility with hulks bobbing, he would meet the loaded transport. As soon as he clambered aboard, he was fastened in fetters belowdecks. His ship was part of a small fleet of four going to New South Wales and Van Diemen's Land that included 720 male convicts. Two more ships, with an additional 500, were fitting out to depart at any moment.[26]

Alas, for those on board, a Black seaman, "a Man of Colour," showed signs of coming down with smallpox.[27] This was a scourge all feared, that is, those who had not been inoculated and those who had not contracted the illness before and lived to tell the tale. Most of the convicts, one reckons, had not been privy to either. So, the captain had little choice but to get the sailor off the ship. If smallpox broke out on board, well, at least they had a ships' surgeon on hand to address the crisis, and hopefully, if this were the case, the contagion would have run its course by the time the ship reached Australia.

So, to Francis's undoubted consternation, the ship stayed anchored as the men aboard readied to send the smallpox patient to Chatham. They washed, fumigated, and whitewashed the man's berth. Stuck once more in Chatham, he had not yet escaped the dreaded *Euryalus*. He had, he thought, moved on from the experience of being confined and disciplined. In fact, he had not. He had just graduated to another, more mobile, form.

Finally, at 10:30 a.m. on March 27, 1828, the ship hoisted anchor at Sheerness and set out to sea.[28] The odds were not good that Francis would ever see England, his mother, father, and brothers again. But, then again, they are called odds, not certainties.

ROUND 4

The Rocks

THE SHIP'S NAME was the *Bussorah Merchant,* and James Baigrie served as master. It was named after the city of Basra, in present-day Iraq, then a trading center in the Ottoman Empire, as well as a historic crossroads. The ship's name gestured to how the East India Company, which had a long presence there and for which the *Merchant* sailed, was now playing such a role in worldwide trade and in securing Britain's preeminence over its rival France.[1] The *Bussorah Merchant* carried a heady legacy and represented a confident bet on the future.

The ship was made for journeys that tied the world of trade together. It was square-rigged, and a British merchantman, like virtually all the ships used. Narrow, deep, and flat-bottomed, it was designed for cargo, not passengers. Nonetheless, the East India Company liked tendering ships out, as it would make the return voyage profitable. A ship of this sort needed a great deal of ballast, usually in the form of goods filling the hold. Convicts, who numbered 140 on the trip, could also do the trick.

Nevertheless, they would not be treated like cattle. Convict passages, as a rule, proved safer than regular emigrant voyages, whether across the Atlantic or the Pacific. The crew of thirty-one would have been experienced and disciplined. Moreover, if constructed elsewhere, a ship had to rise to Thames-built standards. The *Bussorah Merchant* did. The ship was built in Calcutta in 1818 and crafted from teak. This hardwood put her in league with the stoutest ships in the merchant marine.[2] Because of the pressing need to bring settlers and soldiers to Australia, and to keep the trade to India afloat, the ship had a dual role to play. The *Bussorah Merchant* accordingly had to answer to a number of purposes and officials, including the "military department" and "public department," and "commercial department." It was versatile.[3]

The ship had to be. That empire was stretching out beyond the Levant and India to the Pacific. This is the time when the phrase "the sun never sets on the British empire" came to light. This was an empire designed for growth and wealth and to enrich the center and the elites that helped manage it in far-flung peripheries. And it needed all forty-four of the troops who were sailing on that voyage.

This empire now depended on Francis Ambrose. Well, not just him, but on the thousands of others who were bound to the other side of the world in ships that sailed to and from the Indian Ocean, including the other convicts who were journeying on the *Merchant*. The *Merchant* brought the goods of India and Asia to Britain, to the East India Docks just to the east of Whitechapel, and returned with holds filled with Ambrose and people like him. Settlers, and even the off-scourings in London whom Britain needed but could not support, would serve a role that complemented trade to the East. In this way, the world that the *Euryalus* made possible, with the victory over the French, produced the world of the *Merchant*, one of empire premised on free trade and on convict labor. The function of the ship, therefore, centered on the person of Francis Ambrose. The questions all confronted were simple: Could those transported to the other side of the world, Britain's criminal class and disaffected Irish peasants—and Francis Ambrose checked both of these boxes—make a far-off place a profitable and integrated part of a global empire? Could "punitive mobility," as one historian puts it, serve such a purpose?[4]

Of course, Francis Ambrose had no idea about any of this. As one of two fourteen-year-olds on board, he was simply trying to survive. And he had good reason to worry about what lay in store. One convict transported a few years earlier told a tale of woe about the journey to Down Under. His passage was "truly uncomfortable not to say miserable."[5] Things, however, were not all doom and gloom on the *Merchant*. Indeed, the movement of convicts had morphed into a predictable and consistent system. By 1828, the kinks had been well worked out.[6] Baigrie hinted that he would treat all on the ship with a modicum of respect when he ordered that convicts could be free of their chains when the ship hit blue water, about a week out. The start of the trip to Australia augured well and made the time on *Euryalus* seem awful by comparison.

One of his shipmates, William Maybury, had embezzled funds in London and, like Francis, received a fourteen-year sentence for his crimes. Maybury kept a diary throughout the voyage. Those on the ship suffered through rough seas and seasickness, he reported. Once out of the Bay of Biscay, once they passed through big seas, the ship made good headway, going at a clip of eight to nine knots an hour. "Fresh breezes" moved her along. They traveled south around the West of Africa. Convict ships were noted for their poor ventilation. At night, convicts were confined to a locked hold. Tedium and boredom made the weeks drag on. If the weather was bad, the hatches and air scuttles were closed, making part of the journey always damp and dark. They were bound to run into weather, intense heat, and then freezing cold. The food, though usually serviceable, was often scanty on such trips. As a rule, convicts could expect two-thirds of a Royal Navy ration. Their diet typically consisted of peas, bread, salt beef and salt pork, butter, and rice. Raisins, suet, oatmeal, also. In ports, fresh meat and vegetables were taken aboard to ward off scurvy. Prisoners elected their own mess captain, who saw to the rations.[7]

On this trip they ate well, at least as Maybury recounted. And there seemed to be little fuss along the way. Francis's fifteenth birthday, April 12, for instance, was "a very warm day." They had "fair" winds, and that evening "the setting sun was extremely beautiful." They saw another ship that evening, and as they did "all hands dined upon the Deck." The next day the convicts could make out Tenerife as they enjoyed "a fine pudding with Boiled Beef for dinner" washed down with port wine. The crew fished most days, and what was caught was cooked for all. Other days it was salt beef or pickled pork and biscuits, and cakes for tea. Pudding also. They almost daily had sweetened lime juice with water, or "cordial," to fend off scurvy. They, of course, encountered "trouble and pity," thunder and squalls, which made all miserable. They prayed on Sundays belowdecks. They got caught in the doldrums, and as they neared the Cape of Good Hope after sixty days aboard, it grew cold, and the seas became as high as "mountains." But all in all, they enjoyed a good, swift passage.

And they remained relatively healthy. The ship's doctor, or what was called the "surgeon-superintendent," Robert Dunn, recorded in his log four people who contracted smallpox along the way. He kept each of them isolated, had the hold fumigated, and because he did not have a major outbreak, the ship could continue on its journey without making landfall. Most ailments were run-of-the-mill. He dealt with accidents that happened aboard and basic sickness. In fact, the most challenging cases he faced were those who, like Francis, had arrived by boat from Chatham to Sheerness early on to join the *Merchant.* A few came down with pneumonia, and he bled and purged them. They had one slight case of scurvy, but the lime juice seemed to have taken care of it. Nearly all of them survived. Four died along the way, who were "launched into the deep" after a quick service. The rest thrived on the journey.[8]

The ship of course also held over forty soldiers. They did exercises with weapons during the day, including drills with bayonets. On past journeys on the *Bussorah Merchant,* such as an awful trip just a few years earlier, soldiers had almost staged a mutiny. Their commander had butted heads with the captain of the ship, and they struggled to determine who exactly was in charge.[9] But on this trip, relations remained sound throughout. The commanding officer of the Thirty-Ninth lauded Baigrie for "your unwearied kindness and attention, and your very liberal and handsome Conduct." Dunn also received praise for his humanity.[10]

Francis had probably not been a model convict, though. He remained healthy throughout the journey, and no one wrote him up. This does not mean he steered clear of trouble. Next to his name on the paperwork recording his arrival in Australia, an "I.G." was printed. This probably meant Iron Gang. From time to time the ship's crew clapped convicts in irons for minor offenses, and Francis, for some unspecified reason, was confined.[11] This should not be surprising. After all, the ship's company from convicts, to seamen, to soldiers, were hard men, all crowded together in holds at night. One can figure what happened there and how one of the youngest would have had to ward off advances.

They continued along the way, without bothering or needing to stop in any port, and made landfall in 121 days, below average time for a convict ship, but just. The fastest that year made the journey in 100 days; the slowest 181 days.[12] On July 26, at 2:00 p.m., they could see Sydney lighthouse. Two hours later, they cleared the headlands that served as a gate to Port Jackson and Sydney Harbor, which appeared "narrow but beautiful in the extreme," and took a pilot aboard. By 7:00 p.m., they had anchored.

What they beheld appeared to those on board not a "barren and uncultivated country" but "a Paradise of the Garden of the World."

Because the ship had had a smallpox breakout, however small it was, Dunn alerted the governor. He knew eleven weeks had elapsed since the last case, so he had no worries. But caution was the order of the day. At Port Jackson, all aboard the ship were placed in quarantine, and a small vessel was turned into a hospital ship. Officials ordered the *Bussorah Merchant* to an anchorage just across the bay from the settlement, a place called "Spring Cove," nestled right by where Manly now sits. A guard was posted to see to it that no one came close and none of the passengers left the cordon. The *Merchant* would be the first ship quarantined in Australia. The convicts and troops were permitted to go ashore, but they could not leave the quarantine bay. They pitched twenty tents and waited, lolling around until enough time passed to ensure that those who had made the trip were disease-free.[13] No one reported being ill. By August 21 Dunn sent a favorable medical report to the port authorities, but the convicts were not released from quarantine until September.

From the quarantine station, Francis could see Sydney. One who came on the ship with him could not believe how extraordinarily situated the town was. "No picture could excel for the beauty, the Rocks, the Water and the situation of the Town in general is really Grand," he exclaimed. Granted, he had not seen the settlement up close, but from afar, from the other side of the harbor, it was striking.[14] The earliest convicts from the British Isles, and the so-called First Fleet, had sailed to Botany Bay, just to the south. But by this time, Sydney became the gateway to Australia. Sydney represented a toehold onto the island-continent as a whole and a place for the refuse of England, as America had been in the seventeenth century. In the early nineteenth century, the need to get rid of undesirables was more pressing, as evidenced by the state of places like Whitechapel.

For all of this, Francis was probably in better shape than he had been since his days in Bandon. When he was arrested in London, he stood at five feet tall. Now he was listed by authorities at just over five feet eight inches, about the size of a good middleweight. A spurt of eight inches seems improbable, and either the recorder on the sending or the receiving side must have gotten it wrong. Nonetheless, he had grown while at sea. He was also listed as a redhead now.

His journey also revealed other features. Francis had almost certainly fought on board. He had somehow gotten a "cracked" and "flat" nose and a scar on the center of his forehead. He also sported a scar on his left thumb, as well as a burn mark on an arm. To complete the ensemble, he also had a tattoo. On his left arm he acquired an "F.A.," his initials.[15] Convicts did tattoo themselves, but not a majority. The men who did often displayed their initials or names. In the impersonal world of the penal-imperial system, a tattoo served as a marker of individual identity. Shipmates used needles and gunpowder, guaranteeing the tattoos would fade with time, to create all sorts of images on the bodies of convicts, including, at times, etchings of men prizefighting. The fifteen-year-old Francis went for something simple and, in fact, the most common.[16]

He picked up a few other things as well. When he landed, officials had to record all they knew of him. From this point forward, whenever he ran across authority, he would be known as "Francis Ambrose, Bussorah Merchant." The ship would mark him. So would his religion. Officials wanted to know how to parse or classify convicts in Australia. It made keeping control easier. Francis listed himself as "Protestant." What did this mean? Perhaps it was a clerical error. Or maybe he had seen the light on the *Euryalus*. Maybe the evangelicals who preached about damnation had gotten to him. Given how tedious the sermons were, this is pretty doubtful. More than likely, calling himself Protestant says something about him doing what he needed to do to manage and perhaps survive. On the ship, few Irish accompanied him. Many of the troops were Irish, certainly if we go by the names of the men that Dr. Dunn treated on board. But among the convicts, Francis was an outlier. Most came from England, from all over, in fact, and a few were transported from Edinburgh jails. Few had identifiably Irish names.[17] It may have been helpful to be Catholic when around the Irish but a Protestant on an English-dominated ship. Such a move could ensure protection. Francis Ambrose had the advantage of having lived among both the Irish and English. One reckons he suppressed the brogue and played up the Cockney accent. And who could blame him? He was fifteen years old, after all, on a ship filled with hard men. But his claiming to be Protestant reveals something more. This more than anything demonstrates his ability to shape-shift. It suggests that he knew how power worked and that he could work within systems as he encountered them, playing up different aspects of his identity as needed. He was already adept at fighting and at improvising.

For the record, he would never claim to be Protestant again.

Finally freed from quarantine, Francis made his way to Sydney in mid-September. The settlement had been founded only forty years earlier, but in the time since, it had become a hive of activity at the very verge of empire. "Since I last wrote you," an official in Sydney observed, "three Convict ships have arrived and all the people disposed of immediately, and even sought for." Wheat was growing well, and crime was down, giving everything a more settled feel. "People," he gushed, "may now travel all over the country unarmed as peacefully secure as you do in England and I ascribe it entirely to the system of dispersing them," by whom, of course, he meant the convicts.[18]

It all formed part of what he rightly called "the system." Sydney was bound to the rest of the world by ships. Whalers from Britain and even the United State came and went to and from the Pacific hunting grounds. Ships from Europe and all over the Pacific visited, making this place, like old Basra, a crossroads of culture and commerce. But one on the very edge of the world. Sydney did not have the same dry docks and wet docks that London had, nor the same sort of vast military facilities as in Woolwich or Chatham. It was all more rudimentary and improvised. The Irish novelist Maria Edgeworth, after reading a treatise on the colony, likened New South Wales to a place in the throes of transition from a state of nature to a state of society. She considered it "composed of . . . vagabonds worthy of Romulus and Remus but with the incalculably great advantage of the printing press and the cannon."[19] Sydney presented a striking picture of development. It was a boomtown on the move. And it needed labor. Perhaps, Edgeworth hoped, Sydney could see to "the reformation of these convicts and the transmutation of rogues into honest men."[20] The settlement, though admittedly rough around the edges, could remake the likes of Francis Ambrose. In the process, Sydney was developing. In March 1827, Christina Eliza Brooks, the wife of a captain of a ship that sailed to and fro for the East India Company, described the town she had settled in and how it had changed. "This place which 10 or 12 years ago was a quiet country [and] . . . thoroughly English Town," she found, "is now a crowded and bustling business-like City."[21]

Sydney Cove from Dawes Point, Frederick Garling, 1839. (Dixson Galleries, State Library of New South Wales)

Francis arrived at Sydney Cove, what is now Circular Quay, where the ferries come and go today near the Sydney Opera House. Back then it was the busy maritime center of Sydney. Today, the John Cadman House stands near where convicts alighted, right next to a statue of one of colonial New South Wales's governors, William Bligh of *Mutiny on the Bounty* infamy. Cadman served as the superintendent of government boats, suggesting the official presence there was significant. The same went for the navy, as the Naval Yard sat right next to the Cadman House. The dock was not too far from Clarence Street, where the Oriental Hotel was going up.

Ambrose went right to a neighborhood called the Rocks. The Rocks lay just on the west side of the cove where he landed. It was called by this name because the neighborhood sat on a bluff made of sandstone that juts out into the harbor and comprises the western end of Sydney Cove. The rocks tumble down into Walsh Bay on its northwestern side. The area had once been the home of the Cadigal people. In a story tragically repeated elsewhere, smallpox killed most of the Indigenous people who lived in the Rocks area, though as a people the Cadigal would live on. In the years since, it had been built up in higgledy-piggledy fashion. It was, by the time

Francis arrived, a neighborhood dominated by convicts. The Rocks was "their town," an area they had built. By 1822, more than 1,200 convicts and ex-convicts lived there.[22]

Houses clung together like birds in a rookery. Lanes then ran down into bays. Often these were extraordinarily narrow. The foundations of the buildings were made of stone quarried from the rock below. Behind the facades, there were terraces and alleys, the sort that conjured up memories of the East End in London. The place could be dizzying, and one could easily see how drunken visitors could fall prey to the locals. Things could be rather lawless. Rum was the drink of choice, but grog shops also sold homemade gin. One English official claimed that "you see drunken people in all directions, men and women fighting in the street, and the most disgusting scenes of all descriptions, particularly in that part of Sydney denominated the Rocks." To his prejudiced English eyes, convicts ruled the neighborhood. He concluded, "I should call St. Giles's a paradise as compared with the Rocks in Sydney."[23]

No doubt he exaggerated, but there seems to be some truth to what he said. Convict culture shaped the Rocks. From the get-go, convicts refused to do what they were told. They demanded autonomy, and they got it. Don't think of men limping along and dragging ball and chain. Because officials needed labor to make the colony part of a British imperial system, those coming on ships like the *Merchant* could come and go as they pleased, within limits, so long as they worked. Because of this autonomy, they had a great hand in adapting the culture they had brought with them and thus reshaping what they encountered. The layout of houses, rituals, drinking culture, the rhythms of work all owed a great deal to the tastes and instincts of convicts. Even when more and more convicts glutted the labor and housing markets, beginning in the early 1820s, and more became what were known as "Barracks men," they still enjoyed a great deal of freedom. The "absence of walls and warders" marked the early years.[24]

Thus the Rocks appeared as yet one more notorious area. The "by-streets" of Sydney were home to "persons of the most abandoned character." So said James Scott, a Scottish physician who would go on to serve on the *Bussorah Merchant* on its subsequent voyages. He saw the Rocks as a neighborhood of devolved English culture.[25] Early on, gangs abounded. These people created a sense of menace in the narrow alleys, many of their social betters alleged. Irish and English larrikins, as the rowdy and defiant hooligans were called, mixed together easily and also fought.

The Irish were disproportionally represented as convicts in the Rocks. In fact, so pronounced was Irish rebel culture in the neighborhood that people had the distinct impression that this was the Irish section of Sydney.[26] They would be right. In fact, before too long, a Catholic church dedicated to St. Patrick would be established here to cater to Irish immigrants who kept arriving. The Irish who lived here faced the same sorts of discrimination they did in London, but they had two great advantages. First, they comprised a sizeable minority here. Second, and more importantly, they had a reputation. Whether an Irishmen had been arrested for petty theft or not, he was considered a "rebel," a person who fought the powers that be. In Australia, among so many convicts, that carried some weight. It did not make being Irish fashionable, but it made them estimable. Being from Bandon, and used to Irish culture, would have helped Francis in the Rocks.

Other peoples called the Rocks home. As this was a waterside neighborhood with shipping coming from far and wide, it had a cosmopolitan feel. Here would arise Sydney's first Chinatown. Also Māori from New Zealand who were working on ships found a home, drinking at inns and public houses after stints whaling. The Indigenous people, though many had been wiped away from the area as early as 1816, still made their presence felt on the whalers that came and went from Walsh Bay and Campbell Cove.[27]

The Rocks appeared a distillation of places that had shaped Francis's early life. It was densely urban, with houses made of brick, much like parts of London, with the same kind of rowdy culture. But it had a frontier feel to it, an openness mixed with ethnic enmities, that bore a resemblance to Bandon. It certainly mixed Irish and English. The place bustled. Drinking accompanied work, play, deal-making, celebrating, lamenting. The neighborhood's culture was marked by what one scholar calls "opportunism and risk-taking." But at the same time, residents embraced a "fatalism" and even a "resignation" to the way power in the world worked. The Rocks, like other in-between transition zones Francis knew, housed only the clever and the realistic.[28] It defied easy characterization. Yes, the Rocks witnessed plenty of violence. Archaeological remains suggest, however, that people strived to acquire the nicer things in life. Even convicts, amid the liveliness and poverty of the Rocks, could enjoy some creature comforts and create community.[29]

By the time Francis arrived, the culture was shifting in subtle ways. Convicts could still enjoy a modicum of autonomy, but the frontier phase was coming to an end. As the Rocks became more settled in the late 1820s, and as its distinct culture congealed, convicts were beginning to be treated, well, like convicts. They had fewer opportunities to buy homes. They were increasingly relegated to tenant status. Authorities watched them more closely, and policing took on a more vigilant caste. All in all, those who made it there earlier and had established stable lives wanted to forget their convict origins and planned to make sure they did not revert to what was imagined as a blighted past.[30]

All convicts were there to try to help Australia develop, and they represented just over half of the town's population of ten thousand.[31] As such, they were not placed in prisons but put to work. Many participated in what is referred to as the "assignment system." Private men and women could make use of convict labor on their farms to improve land and in businesses to help them get under way. Or they could be farmed out to government labor gangs to do public works. Assignment worked for the government, and it certainly worked for those who stood to take advantage of the cheap labor. In fact, most convicts worked for free settlers, who made the most out of the assignment system.

At fifteen, Francis was not old enough to be sent to the frontier, so he was assigned to a woman in Sydney. The fifty-year-old Mary Atcheson claimed him as an indentured servant at Sydney Cove. Mary had come over in 1822, on a ship called *The Prince of Orange*. So, she was a relative newcomer as well, but one who came of age in the United Kingdom. One supposes she was a widow, given the fact that she had two teenage boys and was listed as the head of household in the 1828 census. She owned an inn called the St. Patrick on Clarence Street. A woman leading such an establishment would not have raised eyebrows. In the Rocks, women ran everything from respectable inns to public houses and even brothels. She would need what Francis still called himself: an "errand boy." She knew where he was born. He seemed a good fit.[32]

Clarence Street led from the quays to the Barracks, where undoubtedly some of Francis's fellow passengers on the *Merchant* were headed. On Church Hill a few hundred yards away, English settlers had built the first Anglican church in the colony, St. Philip's. It was a simple affair, white with an outsized medieval-looking round tower at the front.[33] Established churchmen were not the only ones who lived by the St. Patrick. A family of Muslims lived on Clarence Street.[34] There were other similar places nearby in the Rocks. A stone's throw from the Clarence Street St. Patrick, the "Sign of St. Patrick" on Gloucester Street was going up, one that at the time was "much frequented and well-known." It came by its name honestly. This was a street of Irish and English settlers, including the owner of lots there who bore the name Cribb. We assume it's no relation to the great prizefighter.[35] The Sign of St. Patrick was, as an ad put it in 1824 when it was rented out, a "desirable house" on Gloucester Street with everything needed to run a public house. We could reckon Mary's place was much the same.[36]

Clarence Street was the Rocks, and even Sydney, writ small. It was configured to face the harbor in two directions, the center of Sydney's life and what oriented all activity in the Rocks. From the houses on the street, men and women could watch executions in the gaolyard below. All around Clarence Street were reminders of the power and reach of the state. The Barracks was really a complex of military buildings that dominated the streetscape. British troops garrisoned the convict town, and it was no mistake that they were billeted right next to the Rocks. Navy, army, police, gaolers—these maintained order and served as vivid reminders that though life could be a bit freer in the Rocks, those who lived there toiled as convicts or had just escaped that condition. All of this lay just outside the house Francis lodged in.

The Rocks also resembled and would bear a striking resemblance to the places he had left and the places he was destined to travel to in the future. It was the hub of seaborne and port life with an eclectic mix of people. An arrival in 1829 observed that "from the variety of strange sounds and divers tongues that met the ear, Sydney at the time might be not untruly described as a City of Babel on a small scale."[37] It was an impoverished area. It had a heavy Irish Catholic inflection, though English Protestants dominated the town. The place had a ramshackle feel to it. The residents seemed to specialize in heavy drinking. To sum it up, it was very much like the Five Points in New York, and Whitechapel, and what would become San Francisco. And it would be cleared away for slum clearance like Whitechapel had been and like the Five Points would be.[38]

Things in the Rocks got off to a rocky start for Francis. In truth, Ambrose had a challenging stay at the St. Patrick on Clarence Street. In less than two months, Mary complained that Francis was "perfectly useless to me." She did not elaborate or mention any problems he might have been causing, and she was wise not to. She wanted him off her hands. She was able to fob him off on a fellow named Thomas Ashton, who ran the canteen at the military barracks on Clarence Street, just a short walk from the St. Patrick. Ashton "had occasion for a lad as a servant."[39] Francis was indeed back to being an "errand boy." He did odd jobs and ran food to the barracks. And Ashton needed the help.

Where there were Irish and English workingmen in plural and bustling port-town settings, fighting thrived. Sydney and then areas farther afield became colonies of British fistic culture. Fittingly, one of the chief pastimes here was prizefighting. Fittingly as well, combatants would abide by the rituals, rules, and customs of the fight game as practiced by the great Cribb, Mendoza, and Ward. In fact, prizefighting in Australia had its origins in the Rocks. An early panoramic view of the Rocks includes a prizefight taking place right next to a windmill. This site, now Observatory Hill, was a hard-to-reach place for officials, but easy enough to get to for convicts. Before Ambrose came, convicts made prizefighting theirs, as a diversion but also as a means of claiming their manhood. Polite society took little notice of it. By the time Francis arrived, those days had passed. Polite society now frowned on the spectacle and argued it epitomized the rudeness of convict culture. In Francis's time there, fighting took place in areas far removed like the road out west toward the settlement at Parramatta. Here pubs sponsored all sorts of bouts. In fact, publicans became early Australia's Fancy. Another spot was the new Sydney Races, which had moved from Hyde Park, right next to a barracks bearing the name. Prizefighting, as ever, settled in the niches of society, and these were filled with the lower sort. Unlicensed fights also were sponsored at public houses in the Rocks. One wonders if men squared off in Mary Atcheson's Inn or at the St. Patrick on Gloucester Street.[40]

We have no idea if Francis Ambrose participated in Sydney's fistic scene. One chronicler later hypothesized that he may have started fighting in Australia at this time, taking on a Scottish convict two years his senior called Stewart in 1828 or 1829. If this was the case, then he already had some skills or at least the moxie, and given the likelihood he had engaged in fisticuffs on the ship, this bout could have taken place. The only source to make this claim would be a popular account from the United States published years later. According to another that recounts the fight, Stewart, "who was somewhat skilled in the use of his 'bunch of five,'" or his fist, accepted Ambrose's challenge, though Ambrose had never had a prizefight before. They fought for twelve pounds a side. Ambrose relied on backers for his stake. He proved too quick and too scientific, or so the account claimed, for Stewart. Ambrose won in two hours and twenty minutes. We should take the details with a grain of salt. This account that explores the bout does not mention Australia at all. As for Stewart's first name, we haven't a clue. But Ambrose certainly could have confronted a Stewart in the ring in Sydney.[41] Given the iron gang, the tattoo, the cracked nose, and the problems with Mary Atcheson, we can only surmise he was doing some sort of fighting.

But whether he did or not, Francis once again lived right by an early center of fighting. A few years later an evangelical visitor, and an appalled one at that, would say, "The 'Rocks' in Sydney are, in roguery and raffery, as vile as Whitechapel." He wasn't wrong, not when it came to skullduggery or fisticuffs.[42]

Though Francis Ambrose by law was regarded as a servant and bonded to his master, if he kept his nose clean, steering clear of rebels and fighters, and just kept doing his job for Thomas Ashton, then he could expect a good life in Sydney. With good behavior he would have been granted a "ticket to leave." This was not a pardon that would have allowed him to leave the colony. Think of it as a parole. He would be free to chart his own course in the settlement, understanding that he was still a convict, but one who now would have enjoyed an in-between status between prisoner and free man. The colony needed free settlers, and its officials wanted to reduce costs. A ticket to leave incentivized good behavior and kept policing costs lower. If he served six years with a master, he could earn a ticket, regain his freedom, and expect the same wages as a free migrant.[43]

Francis would never earn his ticket. On July 4, 1829, he was found guilty of stealing and sentenced to three years "at the penal settlement." He had lived in Sydney less than a year. We don't know what he stole, but what does it matter? Sydney had not reformed him. And maybe, given the nature of the Rocks, it only corrupted him further. He certainly styled himself a larrikin. This arrest, after all, was only the beginning of a rap sheet as long as your proverbial arm. He was cut from the cloth of a Ned Kelly, or rather, Ned Kelly was cut from his cloth. Kelly was seemingly always having run-ins with the law, in jail as often as out of it, and when on the outside, always expecting another arrest. The same held for Ambrose. He would remain the Notorious Francis, particularly as the early years of convict autonomy were giving way to a more vigilant policing regime. For his latest sins, he was sent back to the hulks, in this case, one called the *Phoenix*.[44]

The *Phoenix* was the first prison hulk in Australia, serving as the initial sign of an overburdened system of penology in the prison colony. By 1825, as Christina Eliza Brooks argued, the conditions in Sydney Gaol were appalling because of overcrowding. Officials then decided to resort to the English strategy of employing hulks, "or floating prison[s]."[45] The *Phoenix* seemed perfect for the job. It had been built in England and plied the Atlantic between London and Jamaica, delivering exotic goods to docks Francis was all too familiar with in the East End. Then it transitioned to a convict ship. After a trip with convicts from England, the *Phoenix* struck a group of rocks called the Sow and Pigs, right near the harbor entrance. It was lightened and refloated, but the damage was too much to allow it to go to sea again after it was hove down. The ship was bought for one thousand pounds by colonial authorities and turned into a prison hulk, largely for convicts awaiting transport elsewhere. The *Phoenix* sat in Lavender Bay, which was first called Hulk Bay or Phoenix Bay.[46]

Ambrose was right back at Chatham, though this time as an adult. Prisoners left the hulk each day to labor in chain gangs, performing such menial work as fixing the streets in Sydney. Six men bunked in each cell. The inmates almost immediately complained of scanty rations. Food was not enough to get them through the hard labor. To make matters worse, they had few blankets and their clothes were worn. Floggings were meted out on a regular basis. The *Phoenix*, believe it or not, had a schoolroom in it by the time Ambrose was there. The schoolmaster, though, had been locked in his cell "for attempting a heinous crime." He was sentenced to fifty lashes. The inmates saw it as a place of "cruelty and starvation." It was, in that touchstone phrase of the day, a "Human Hell."[47]

But Ambrose's stay here would be short. The *Phoenix* was little more than a holding pen, a stopping-off point on the way to other, darker holes. His next destination was designed for secondary punishment, the sort of place that was the stuff of folktales and that all convicts dreaded, with good reason. There were worse places in Australia than a hulk.

ROUND 5

Moreton Bay

MAYBE HE HAD finally found hell. Colonial officials had established three colonies for what were known as "secondary" offenses, that is, crimes that those who had been convicted in the United Kingdom and transported committed in Australia. Authorities dispatched criminals to either Moreton Bay, Norfolk Island, or Port Macquarie. Norfolk Island was where the worst of the lot went. A man escaped a hanging offense by being sent to this place where any hope went to die. Port Macquarie was the in-between place, where convicts went for crimes but not necessarily the sort that would have them face the noose. Moreton Bay specialized in those who had committed crimes against property.

Ambrose traveled to Moreton Bay. When he did his time there, it was akin to an Australian Devil's Island, a place known for torture and suffering.[1] When it comes to reckoning with Australia's history, it is easy to overestimate the extent that convicts were exploited and abused. More often than not, they enjoyed autonomy and some ability to assert agency. It's especially tempting to assume that sites of secondary punishment, like Moreton Bay, were the exception. Yet, even on this front, we would be wise to use a bit of caution when it comes to accepting at face value lurid tales of torture. Still, when examining Ambrose's experiences there, the Devil's Island motif would seem to have some purchase.

At least for the years Francis Ambrose was condemned to be there. Moreton Bay epitomized the frightening apogee of that subtle shift that was taking place as soon as Ambrose arrived in Sydney Cove. The fear of growing crime in Sydney drove the creation of these places. Greater policing and vigilance and cracking down on what was regarded as larrikin-convict culture necessitated a more thoroughgoing regime of discipline.

The regime could be seen in barracks and hulks that held convict-prisoners, but it reached its height in those three dreaded places.[2] Moreton Bay, in fact, may have been the most gruesome of all the sites for secondary punishment when young Francis set off from Sydney to the place.

He arrived by ship. The *Waterloo* was tasked with taking a group of convicts five hundred miles to the north. Shipwrights in England had built it for trade to the West and East Indies, launching it in 1815—the fateful year when Waterloo became a place on everyone's lips with a victory as epic as Nelson's at Trafalgar. Now the *Waterloo* was doing runs up and down the Tasman as a supplement to its principal commercial sailing. In mid-August, the ship left the quay where Ambrose had landed just some months earlier and sailed out of the same gateway to the Pacific he had entered. The ship then veered to port, away from European settlements. Francis Ambrose, for all of his adventures, had never seen anything like this. He had moved from growing center to growing center of a globalizing world. Now he appeared to be leaving that world. He was replaying his father's Java tale of a journey into his own Hobbesian world.

On board with him were nearly 250 others who had committed crimes, making this the largest shipment of convicts to the settlement.[3] From a bustling, complicated place, he and the others on board entered a zone of isolation and grim simplicity. The Moreton Bay penal settlement did not sit on Moreton Bay at all, but inland on the north bank of the Brisbane River. The river at this point twists like a snake. Originally a penal station had been established closer to the coast, on Moreton Bay itself, but the ground proved too swampy. Men contracted malaria. It was also too exposed to attacks from the Indigenous people. So, officials in 1825 shifted the site up the river to what they hoped would be a more defensible position on better land. The peninsula between twists in the river that they chose seemed ideal and to the uninitiated almost garden-like. It would retain the name of the abandoned site. Today, it is the center of the city of Brisbane.

Ambrose was only sixteen years of age, among the youngest there. And what he beheld had to make his heart drop. The prison camp seemed close to the ocean, but the effect of zigzagging up an isolated river must have been disorienting. Though he could see no walls, it was clear there could be no easy escape. Around the area local Indigenous bands lived, and from what even an unstudied eye could tell, they found no favor with the new inhabitants. By a river, the new arrivals saw a rude and sparse settlement. On the wharf, where the *Waterloo* tied up, convicts already there ran supplies from the ship into a commissariat. This fortified edifice, simple and Georgian in its proportion, was built with defense in mind—both to protect the colony in the event of attack and to keep the convicts from the stores. Its stone pediment simply read "G.R., 1829": Georgius Rex, a crown, and the year it was finished. The men on the wharf then loaded the *Waterloo*'s hull with what the prison settlement had produced, such as the wheat grown on the very eastern edge of the settlement, where Brisbane's botanic gardens now sit. For these convicts were working in fields in what was supposed to be an almost self-sufficient operation. Behind the commissariat, Ambrose could see the quarters where he and his shipmates would sleep, another Georgian-looking building. Its sublime symmetry contrasted with its purpose. Fittingly, it was surrounded by overseers' huts and a building housing tiny cells for solitary confinement. Nearby stood the barracks for the soldiers who would keep a watch over them and defend the colony from any attacks, a jail, of course, and other structures. On a hill, about a quarter of a mile away, Ambrose would have spied a windmill with a structure standing next to it. He no doubt had heard of outer settlements across the river, on a point, where men labored in fields. Beyond that, nothing.[4]

All around he could hear the racket of building. A hospital was arising. They would need it. For the reigning commandant was busy preparing the settlement for greater numbers, of which the passengers on the *Waterloo* represented a good portion. Undoubtedly, there would be casualties. Whole crews were working in a large lumberyard. Behind them smiths were busy. Convicts forged nails. Stone was coming and going for housing more convicts to endure punishment and for more soldiers to protect them. All lived in barracks.[5]

When Ambrose landed, the guards there affixed to his ankles a set of shackles with chains. These weighed about seven or eight pounds and had a leather cuff on the inside to reduce cutting and chafing. But some unlucky souls also wore double irons, as they were called, usually for some infraction.[6] These chains would be his constant companions for nine months. They could only come off after that time if he behaved himself. If he did not, the heavier set could be fixed to his ankles. That is how things worked here. There were few incentives, only more punishments.

Francis recognized some of his fellow prisoners when he arrived. Their number included fourteen prisoners from the *Bussorah Merchant*. That had to help build up some sense of camaraderie in an alien environment.[7] The convicts sent here would clear land, hoe fields, and move boulders. Once he got off the *Waterloo*, he learned to which work gang he was assigned. He could expect, as the regulations put it, "Hard Labour from Sunrise till Sun Set."[8]

Moreton Bay was designed to punish. But it also represented a new experiment in the development of Australia. Could the continent beyond New South Wales be coaxed into producing anything profitable? Could anything here flourish and so tie this massive continent to the sinews of empire? Instead of languishing in jails or in hulks, prisoners would offer the needed muscle and manpower to see if areas far removed from Sydney, after an investment of cheap labor, could be turned over to productive free settlers. Even these could serve empire.[9]

When Ambrose arrived, the settlement designed for punishment and profit had reached its very height, both in terms of prisoner population and in horror. About one thousand men, as well as a handful of women in a separate settlement, toiled. The numbers would never go higher. It was also filled with soldiers, all there to keep an eye on the convicts. Surveillance and suffering were the operative words.

A Scot by the name of Patrick Logan ran the place. A military man to his core, he participated in many of the big imperial doings of the day. He had fought against the French in the Peninsular War and then took on the Americans in what they called the War of 1812. He was then dispatched to this new experiment in Australia and tasked with paving the way for a new settlement of free settlers in the area around Moreton Bay. He would have as much disposable labor as he needed to turn this place into something profitable.

Logan has gone down in Australian lore as a sadist. In fact, he is the subject of one of Australia's most famous folk songs, an Irish-sounding dirge called "Moreton Bay." The song recounts the suffering of an Irish convict condemned to the place under Logan's watch. "For three long years I was beastly treated, heavy irons on my legs I wore," it recalls. The character in the song recounts how flogging "lacerated" his back. Many starved. He remembers with dread the sites for punishment "where Captain Logan he had us mangled." In point of fact, the folk song is not completely wrong. Logan commanded the settlement like a concentration camp. So cruel was his stint that a former convict launched a publicity campaign to let the world know what was happening in the name of the king on the edge of the known world. The man was named William Ross, a convict in Moreton Bay from 1826 to 1832—a long, long stint, and one overlapping with the sentence of Francis Ambrose. When he gained his freedom from the settlement, he wrote a long, impassioned plea called *The Fell Tyrant* to let the candid world, especially London, where it was published, know what a dystopian new world Logan had created.

Granted, the author took many liberties to drive home his point about the martinet Logan. Those who have interrogated the broadside have argued that he was "prone to exaggeration and misinformation."[10] But there is no denying that the word he uses again and again—"dreadful"—has power and persuades. Ross uses some evocative images, some that he could not have made up out of whole cloth. According to him, for instance, the guards followed convicts to the privy to count the corn kernels in their shit, all to figure out if men were stealing food. Though hard to believe, such a tale had to have some basis in reality, if even it happened only once. That it would at all is telling.

Ross composed a compelling tale of woe. The sun scorched. The men starved. The work broke backs. He was told he had to break up a certain amount of hard ground each day, and he was watched by an overseer. The quota had to be met, or else more punishment awaited. Convict-overseers comprised a core part of the system of surveillance, one of whom "seems to delight in human blood." Ross claimed if they ran away and survived "the cannibals" in the forest, "their doom would be to wear irons of not less than 18 or 20 pounds on their legs" and to "receive from 100 to 300 lashes." Men in his narrative could and did die from excessive flogging.[11]

Ross was not alone in his critique. Others also condemned Logan and wrote searing condemnations of his tyrannical ways. One published in a newspaper in Sydney when Francis was transported on the *Waterloo* affirmed the *Fell Tyrant*'s characterization of events. The word used over and over again was the same one Ross employed: "dreadful." As a former convict argued, "the overseers of the gangs at Moreton Bay are some of the most ferocious of the human race." Days set for punishment were referred to as "Logan's field days." The place of punishment was called "the convincing

Frontispiece from *The Fell Tyrant, or The Suffering Convict,* William Ross (London: J. Ward, 1836; Mitchell Library Collection, State Library of New South Wales)

ground." He made the wild claim that on one such day, three or four floggers administered 3,300 lashes in total, their orders "to strike firmly but slowly." They took turns. Twenty-five a go, and then the next started. The "skulkers" and runaways received such treatment on these days.[12]

The men who ran the colony employed what was called the "triangle" to administer floggings. Australia's version of the "adjutant's daughter," the simple term bespoke its shape and symbolism. Three poles were lashed together at the top to form a structure. The man in question was then tied to it, and the flogger—a convict himself—went to work. The triangle could be erected anywhere and put up quickly. But it was the number of lashes that made flogging so diabolical at Moreton Bay. Usually, convicts who ran afoul of the rules received 50. Sometimes, they had to suffer through more. From February 1828 to February 1829, as recorded by a superintendent named Peter Spicer, one convict endured 300 stripes, and nine suffered through 200. Nearly one hundred men received 50. Twenty-five lashes were handed out regularly, often for malingering or working too slowly. On March 27, 1828, to cite just one day, twenty men received 25 lashes, and another man, 50. On May 20, three prisoners were given 150, one man, 100, three men, 50, and four more men received 25. Eight hundred lashes in one day. On an even more grisly date, August 16, the floggers administered over 1,200 lashes to twenty-six men.[13] For good measure and to have the desired effect, whippings were doled out in front of the prisoner barracks.[14] At the end of a session, salt water was thrown on the ribboned back, even after a "feeler" of 200 lashes, heightening the pain. Convicts dreaded "getting salty back."[15]

The routine proved the cruelest. The men served as beasts of burden. Conventions and rules dictated that the men would do everything; animals to pull plows or horses to drag carts were seen as a luxury. They used hand tools to break the hard ground and to make furrows for the maize they raised. Regulations in the penal settlements mandated that "the use of the Hoe and Spade shall be as much as possible adopted . . . the Plough given up, and no Working Cattle are to be employed in operations which can be effected by Men and Hand Cart."[16] Logan and his henchmen orchestrated everything perfectly at all times to let the convicts know that the regime was totalizing and that punishment was the purpose.

Toward the end of his career, Patrick Logan established what was called a "new farm" on another spit of land jutting into the river east of Kangaroo Point. To reach the new farm and to clear it entailed sailing around three bends, passing the Kangaroo Point Cliffs where much of the rock for the settlement was quarried, and another palisade, which resembled the one Ambrose would see later in his life along the Hudson River. The work started with clearing. The projected new farm was filled with paperbark trees and aquatic ferns and shallow lagoons. The farm itself was a floodplain bottom, much like the point adjacent to the settlement. Crops would be harvested and sent right to boats to make their way to the King's Wharf, then up the hill to the mill, where the grain was ground.

Logan brutalized the men who would not get into line and submit. The treadmill was the chief means to do so. A building housing the treadmill sat next to the windmill that would be repurposed, just like Sydney's, into an observatory. The windmill sat on a highpoint, with the hope that breezes would move the sails. They usually did not. That's where the treadmill came into play. Here those punished toiled for hours in "their irons." Convicts called it "the everlasting staircase" and, more evocatively, the "cockchafer."[17] Treadmills had been introduced into English prisons. Soon, they appeared in Jamaica, where they were used to punish newly freed enslaved men.[18] They then were adopted in Australia. Punishment, too, had a global component in these days. Those who endured the treadmill remembered the sound. The steady clack, clack, clack of the irons against the ever-moving stairs, as they walked up and up without ever ascending, holding onto a rail in front. One leg after another, up to twenty-five men in a row. Those singled out for special punishment would be joined by fifteen others and work the mill for up to fourteen hours. This regimen "robbed even death of its terrors." If Moreton Bay was a place for secondary crimes, or those committed by convicts in Australia, the treadmill in Moreton Bay was for third-time offenders. As witnesses recounted, few punishments led men to want death more, especially in the tropical heat. Men died, such as the unfortunate Michael Collins, who got tangled in the treads and was crushed in September 1829. But the corn had to be ground down. The men, too, apparently.[19]

Once again, as in the hulks, sometimes the worst suffering came at the hands of fellow prisoners. The settlement was filled with abused youngish men doing strenuous labor all day. Bullying abounded. So, too, did rape. Francis, at sixteen, and about the youngest there, probably had the greatest reason to fear. No doubt some consensual unions were formed among men. As one eyewitness at another penal settlement would find, it was not unusual for two convicts to become "man and wife." And jealousies could often lead to violence and even murder.[20] But at night, in the prisoners' quarters, it could become something else still.

Needless to say, many tried to run away. Convicts would often bolt together, hoping somehow to make it to a better life. But to where? No settlement, except another penal colony south toward Sydney, was anywhere near Moreton Bay. Again, it was like Devil's Island, where the sea and the jungle served as walls. But they bolted nonetheless. All told, one-quarter of all the men condemned to Moreton Bay tried to run away. They did so despite what a governor conceded was "the almost impossibility of escape." Many starved. Some even came back. A few made it to another penal station, like Port Macquarie. Authorities there just sent them back to Moreton Bay for punishment.[21]

Francis Ambrose would try to escape. He and three others, Timothy Shea, William Chaffey, and William Puckeridge, absconded on February 18, 1831. This was in midsummer, when temperatures and humidity reached their high points. Ambrose and two of the three made it about two weeks. No doubt they used all of their acquired skills to scavenge in a savage environment, but in this unforgiving place, they would find their abilities wanting. Francis may have been a London boy who knew how to survive in the city, but this was wholly different. Street smarts meant little in a jungle. Shea would not have known much more. He probably came from Cork. Like Puckeridge, he was found guilty of murder and sent to Moreton Bay for seven years. He had run away once before, so he knew the ropes. Timothy Shea lasted a week longer in the bush. He was returned on March 9.[22]

In most cases, Aboriginal trackers returned prisoners. As Captain Logan said just before Ambrose absconded, "the natives" made themselves "useful in apprehending and bringing in runaways." For each captive they returned, trackers received metal goods and food. They especially prized "tomahawks."[23] They knew the area. They also knew in what direction Francis and his fellow bolters were likely to have taken off. Convicts attempting escape had only bits and pieces of information to go on—the word of a returned escapee, rumors, and even myth. The trackers knew this. Since the guards paid the Aboriginal people to find the runaways for them, in the eyes of convicts they, too, were complicit in the regime.

Not surprisingly, race relations in the colony were abysmal. The men who searched for escapees, for their part, despised convicts, who they felt were beneath them. To the Aborigines, the servile runaways were all "croppies," the derogatory term for Irish Catholic rebels and convicts from the era of the 1798 rebellion. One can imagine how the Irishman Ambrose was treated when he was captured. And one can figure what he thought of his captors. That Aborigines attacked men working in the fields from time to time only magnified hatreds. That runaways raped Aboriginal women, as they did while Ambrose was there, made the hatreds mutual.[24]

Running away, then, smacked of true desperation. Convicts knew they would die in the bush, be killed by Aborigines, or be tracked down by them, beaten, and returned to the living hell they had tried to escape. No one, after all, succeeded. But such a fate beat remaining in Moreton Bay. As far as convicts were concerned, the overseers tried to work them to death, and the Blacks in their midst were eager to kill them.

Death in the bush would have been preferable to being caught and returned. When Ambrose and his companions were dragged back to the colony, they had to endure further punishment. That meant a flogging. The returned escapee could expect what the law called for: one hundred lashes. Often they then made their way to the treadmill for more torture.

More than likely, after the initial punishments, they were forced to "be constantly overlooked and worked in heavy irons." Logan started this policy, considering it more efficacious than a mere flogging. The policy seemed to address the problem of mass runaways that were occurring in the hottest summer months when things were at their most miserable.[25] What this more than likely meant for Ambrose was that he would have irons attached to his legs weighing eighteen to twenty pounds. He would drag these around as he worked with an iron gang, closely supervised, doing hard labor.[26]

We don't know how many stripes in total he received in Moreton Bay or how many hours he logged on the treadmill or for how long he wore heavy irons. Given Francis's track record and his penchant for rule-breaking, we have to assume he had a number of visits to the triangle and the mill. We know he was flogged just a few weeks before he absconded. A day after his return, he was in the hospital, presumably being treated for his flogging.[27] Now consider that he was enduring all of this suffering while malnourished and where disease was rampant.

Convicts, of course, rose up. And this was the difficult balancing act the sadist Logan had to negotiate. Could he get the requisite labor out of a bunch of resentful and violent men to make this settlement profitable and fruitful for the broader imperial project? Moreton Bay was the dark underside of empire and existed in the first place to turn the feared men that the system had produced and pulled from its slums to the purposes of imperial expansion. Logan and others like him had to wonder if it was possible to both punish and build. Sometimes the calculation failed. In one frightening and electrifying incident, just before Ambrose reached Moreton Bay, convicts reacted to punishments and food shortages by attacking their overseers. In many circumstances, assaulting an overseer in the fields smacked of payback. Sometimes these men had risen from the convict ranks. They acquired their positions by ratting on others, by striving for preferment, and doing what they had to do to stay alive. In a series of incidents in late 1828 and early 1829, a few groups of men took up their implements and killed a number of these convict-overseers in what authorities characterized as a troubling spate of incidents. At issue, according to one account, was the fact that convict-overseers had turned "informer," and one in particular "was always lodging some complaint against the men, to curry favour with the authorities there."[28]

One of the men was a convict from West Cork named Sullivan. In some renderings, he goes by Patrick. The *Sydney Gazette* called him James Sullivan.[29] In his case, while working out on the farm, he took his brush hook, a deadly implement akin to a bolo knife, and drove it into the head of a fellow Irishman.[30] Maybe Sullivan was planning to escape, and he thought the overseers would turn him in. Some said men like Sullivan killed because they preferred death to another day at Moreton Bay. Perhaps he simply wanted to see Sydney again, where he knew he would be tried. Or maybe Sullivan saw the man he killed as an informer. Whatever the motive, after the killing, Sullivan and his accomplices traveled to Sydney in chains to be tried for the killing. When the court found them guilty, an Irish Catholic priest heard their last confessions and accompanied them onto the scaffold. Though he had been sentenced to transportation for stealing, in his case sheep, it was clear he styled himself an Irish rebel in the penal colony. When Sullivan clambered up to the place of execution, he gave a few last words. He did not utter a word of regret for what he had done. He cried out, "Goodbye, Lads. Pray for me." He was hanged, then his body was sent for dissection, an ignominious end to the life of a rebel.[31] We can only imagine what the story of the rebel Sullivan, a fellow West Corkman, meant to a young Ambrose when he arrived at Moreton Bay.

Did Ambrose fight there? It's a good bet. Some later reports would suggest that he had fought and defeated a man in Australia named Dick Trainor. One such man was dispatched to Van Diemen's Land in 1830. However, no Trainor ventured to Moreton Bay. But someone named Richard Drawnea or Drawnen from Ireland was sentenced to serve there. He also went by Traynor, and he and Francis toiled there at the same time. Perhaps this Irish convict fought Ambrose.[32] According to a later account of the fight, when Ambrose went by the name Yankee Sullivan, Trainor was "a hard knot." They decided to fight for fifty pounds a side, paying the sum out in five deposits. All of this was encouraged by the "fistic community." Where said community existed went unmentioned. In any event, Ambrose, as per this report, took Trainor out in over an hour and a half.[33]

We have to assume the report sanitized the event, if it even happened. Even if the men of Moreton Bay would have enjoyed a modicum of autonomy from time to time, enough to afford the opportunity to stage a fight, they would not have comprised what we could call a "fistic community."

Things at Moreton Bay were more elemental. Moreton Bay certainly did not keep prizefighting records. It had no Fancy. But if not in "official" bouts, or one that could be recognized by commentators as a "prizefight," one can be fairly certain he performed in the ring at some time. His subsequent experience would bear this out. Fighting, no matter how exhausted convicts were, was the only diversion they had. One assumes that the guards and the soldiers also relished having something to bet on, and convicts savaging each other fit the bill. Fighting also offered an outlet to prove their toughness and their skills. It did something more. In this bleak context, being good with one's hands conferred dignity. The prizefight was probably the only thing that would have reminded them they were men, that they came from a culture that valued such abilities. We have to assume Francis honed his fighting skills warding off those who tried to take advantage of him, still just a boy. Again, we just don't know for sure. But it's a good bet his time at Moreton Bay was the rough apprenticeship that began to turn his sensibilities and his defiance into a craft. Moreton Bay was, no doubt, Australia's version of "Fight Club."

When Australians think of the "convict stain," it is places like Moreton Bay which come to mind. All was shame. Fallen men were broken further by British officials like Logan, and human nature revealed its most tarnished aspects. When Francis arrived, Logan was still there but on his way out. His wife was ailing and wanted a change of scenery.[34] A new warden was taking over. A Scot named James Clunie would serve as commandant for the last two-thirds of Ambrose's stay. He would be a bit better than Logan, but not by much. Some claimed he was worse. The regime Logan had put in place still persisted. Nothing essential had changed.

What happened to Logan after his rule had to give Ambrose some hope or at least satisfaction. Logan left the colony and began exploring the area around it, hoping to scout out new opportunities. As he was out in the bush, he ran into a group of Aborigines. They speared his horse and killed him. They buried him face down in a shallow grave. When officials from Moreton Bay went out looking for him, they found the grave and saw that wild dogs had been at it. Word soon spread to convicts, who gleefully noted he was facing down, headed straight to the hell he deserved.

A fellow Scot and a colonial official in Sydney praised Logan. Alexander McLeay wrote of the "Melancholy fate of Captain Logan, 57th Regiment."

He could not even bring himself to recount what had happened, but it grieved him. "It has been painful to dwell," he said, "on the particulars of this distressing event." To him, Logan represented all that would make Australia prosper. Logan was a man of "zeal" and "chivalrous and undaunted spirit." He had undertaken a thankless task that was "arduous" and "troublesome," but a critical one for the colony. If more places could be enmeshed in the imperial system and if more of the continent could be made profitable, all would prosper. "His life was devoted to the public service," even if he had been killed by "an act of savage barbarity."[35]

Men like Ambrose did not see things that way. As the folk song puts it, "Like the Egyptians and ancient Hebrews, we were oppressed by Logan's yoke, till a native black who lay in ambush did give our tyrant his mortal stroke." The Irishman ends his lament exclaiming, "Fellow prisoners, be exhilarated. That all such monsters such a death may find!" Only then, he concludes, and once "liberated," can one's "former suffering . . . fade from mind."

In February 1833, Francis Ambrose finally left Moreton Bay. He had served nearly three and a half years, his sentence lengthened because of his attempt to run away. He was nineteen, having survived some of the most impressionable years of his life in this hellhole. One imagines that Francis Ambrose would not, could not, and did not let Moreton Bay "fade from mind." It just added one more layer to a life that had been nothing short of a trial up to this point. And, cruelly, he was now off to finishing school.

ROUND 6

The Blue Mountains

FRANCIS AMBROSE ARRIVED back in Sydney from Moreton Bay in February 1833. More punishment awaited. The most notable involved a journey he would make a number of times to the west. His path led him through Parramatta, now a suburb of Sydney, and the beginning of a critical road for Australia's development. With time, it became known as the Great Western Road, the path through the Blue Mountains. These formed a formidable barrier between New South Wales and the interior of the continent. Over these mountains lay Australia's manifest destiny. The "conquest of the Blue Mountains," as the mythic ideal would have it, would save Australia from possible "stagnation" and perhaps "failure." The road west could open Australia's port towns to the "wide and fertile Plains" that lay just beyond.[1] The project of building a road formed an integral part of the frontier ethos of the nation, much as breaching the Appalachians, with Daniel Boone leading the way, serves as a central motif of American exceptionalism. The Blue Mountains stood in the way of progress, until some intrepid individuals were sent west to explore and to find a path through the continent. Or so the story went.

The road envisioned by governors and great men was built with convict labor. It followed the tracks and trails laid out by Indigenous people, and its building depended on the hope and expectation of their being pushed away. Ambrose's story, the final chapter of his Australian sojourn, follows this road through the mountains. His experiences there would be the final ingredients shaping him into a fighter and also, as we shall see, putting an indelible stamp on Australian prizefighting. In the process something in Ambrose beyond the victim was emerging. The fighter was coming into focus.

How could one person be victimized so much? His upbringing in Bandon, subject to economic dislocation and sectarian animus; the Dickensian experience in London; hulks and prison ships; being transported to Australia; and off to Moreton Bay. How could the litany keep going? But it did.[2] Ambrose was committed for short stints to Sydney Gaol, an awful place, in 1833, 1836, and in 1837.[3] But, on one of these occasions, he ran away. In 1837, he was doing a year of hard labor on a chain gang in Woolloomooloo. But he ran away. He was placed in Carter's Barracks to work the treadmill, in this case a monster that could accommodate sixty prisoners at a go.[4] But he ran away. He worked on the dockyards, right next to the Rocks. On this occasion, in 1836, Ambrose was still listed as an "errand boy." But he ran away. A runaway ad stated that Ambrose was one of a number of men with "stolen Certificates and tickets of Leave."[5] The following year, after he had tired out authorities with all of his absconding, he secured a pretty nice position working at another tavern on Castlereagh Street just up from the Rocks. But he ran away.[6]

Each time he absconded, authorities agonized over what to do. Should he be sent to Port Macquarie? Or to a new place farther afield called Port Phillip? They considered the former and opted for the latter. But, before he could be shipped off there, he ran away.

He would continue in this vein from the moment he left Moreton Bay in 1833 until 1840. Work gang after work gang, jail after jail. His life was defined by chains and bars. In addition to those listed above, he also toiled on Goat Island, now a feature of the harbor just west of the Harbour Bridge and which goes by an Indigenous name, Me-Mal. Convicts in the 1830s built much of what was on it. It also served as a prison hulk of sorts for a while, a holding pen for the overflow of convicts. Nothing worked. If it wasn't absconding or assaulting a constable, it was "drunkenness on works." For nearly each of these infractions, he earned fifty lashes. Again and again. Here is a typical incident. On August 10, 1837, after he had been in-country for more than seven years, the *Sydney Gazette and New South Wales Advertiser* reported that "Francis Ambrose, arrayed in a blue frock velvetcollar, but a confounded dirty shirt," and who "was charged with having been attempting to do a bit of genteel about Sydney for the last fortnight, instead of hoeing up some corn land," had been "ordered a cheque for 50 for the same, and the Charley who captured him introduced into the pockets of his small's 10s, as a bonne bouche for his activity." This meant, apparently, that instead of working, he was partying and was informed on and caught. The informer received ten shillings; Ambrose received fifty lashes.[7]

Throughout all this time, Ambrose was placed in that holding pen for the penal system, the *Phoenix*, what a fellow prisoner at the time referred to as a "floating Den of Sin and Infamy."[8] No longer would his behavior be deemed "good." In 1833, for instance, his conduct was listed simply as "bad."[9] He also had the misfortune to endure the apotheosis of the surveillance system, a place that still stands today called Hyde Park Barracks. He was a regular at the Barracks, moving between it and all sorts of punishment sites. Here he slept, and here he was tried, and here he was punished. It was from here he ran away in 1833. In 1836, too.[10]

Contemporaries raved about the proportions and simplicity of Hyde Park Barracks. "Although none of these edifices have much architectural pretension," a critic would write in 1848, "yet, the proportions being good, the masses broad, and the lines bold and unbroken, they form an imposing and dignified whole." It had served an important purpose since it was erected in 1819. The building held new convicts coming into Sydney before they were assigned to private individuals. It, therefore, operated as a "depot." More critically, it housed the labor necessary to construct public buildings, functioning as a dormitory for exploitable and cheap labor. The first governor of New South Wales complained about the poverty of the town early on and "the decayed and dilapidated state of all the public buildings," as well as of roads and bridges. Convicts could perform the requisite labor. The Barracks could sleep hundreds of men, who could be farmed out in the day to do the important work of building Sydney under government auspices. They could then return at night. It worked for everyone, especially for the government, which only had to pay for food and clothes.[11]

Soon it performed a new and vital function. By the time Francis Ambrose arrived, the system was overwhelmed with the rising number of "incorrigible" prisoners. Soon, the rationale for the Barracks was changing. Authorities repurposed it into a depot for those shuffling between punishment sites. For this reason, Ambrose became a regular. In 1834, for instance, he spent time here between stints on work gangs and the *Phoenix*.[12] It was also transformed into a court for convict crimes and a processing center, the very heart of the penal-imperial complex in Sydney that was emerging when Ambrose had arrived and that had become full-blown by the time he was back from Moreton Bay. For his part, Francis was held there and tried there "in a summary way before the Bench of Magistrates" on a number of occasions, three times in 1836 alone.[13] While held, he did all sorts of hard labor, but under strict supervision.

Ambrose entered and reentered it during the darkest days of convict discipline when the Barracks was run by a man cut from the same cloth as Patrick Logan. Ernest Augustus Slade came to Sydney about the same time as Ambrose. He was a military man, and afterward became the superintendent of Hyde Park Barracks when Ambrose returned from Moreton Bay. He ran a tight ship. He complained that before, under the laxer regime of old, convicts could bribe floggers to use flimsy whips. Under his watch, floggings became routine. He also ordered new "cats" made, with more knots and sturdier and longer handles. He said his "scourgers" could inflict fifty lashes that would equal another's one thousand. His scourgers could draw blood on the fourth or fifth lash, he boasted. In some cases, it took only one. In 1833, James Burnett had tried to rob the till at Francis's old haunt, the Sign of the St. Patrick on Clarence Street, and was set to receive twenty-five lashes before heading off to a road gang. He had never been flogged before. He cried out on the first lash. The skin flayed on number thirteen. "He seemed to feel much pain," the overseer observed. Slade set up the triangle in the courtyard, so all could witness the punishment. Slade made sure the convicts were under stricter surveillance, and he focused on getting rid of what he regarded as "corrupt" overseers, those who looked the other way as convicts did what they wanted. No more. This "bloodhound," as the convicts called him, was the perfect man for the new regime. But again, convicts often had most to fear from other convicts. The men slept in a single room with hammocks, all cheek to jowl. Slade testified before an investigating committee that "sodomy" was common. "The boys" often complained, he said, that "they could not remain in the rooms along with the men." At times, boys even took on girls' names. Before, convicts in the Barracks had a bit of autonomy, and they could even bribe guards to get out at night. Not now.[14] The time Ambrose was incarcerated there corresponded with this regime.

His crimes also merited multiple sentences of six months to a year in "iron gangs" in yet more sites of punishment.[15] His most significant iron-gang time was spent in the mountains, building roads. He was first sent to the mountains in 1833, and then again soon after that. The government had built a number of facilities along mountain roads as holding sites for convicts and as construction depots. Troops garrisoned these stations, always on the lookout for runaways who could become the worst of all Australian nightmares: bushrangers. These Ned Kelly–like outlaws lived in maroon-like colonies always a step or two ahead of the law and living outside the bounds of civilization. For this reason, they kept a close eye on the convicts within. Iron gangs differed from mere road gangs, whose men labored without shackles on. Iron gangs were a different matter altogether. Those so sentenced did everything in chains, from sleeping to working to eating. In the Blue Mountains, the "incorrigibles" gathered to be worked in gangs of up to sixty men under the strictest supervision.[16]

Ambrose was also invested, whether he knew it or not, in trying to tie Sydney and by extension all of Australia into an imperial network that spanned oceans and aspired to tap into the riches of a continent. Sydney would be the entrepôt yoking the interior to the Tasman. Roads represented the chief means of doing so. Conquering the Blue Mountains promised to ensure Australia's status as a key contributor to the British imperial project of settler colonies and free trade. The conquest of the continent could also aid in bringing "civilization" to a place in need of development. It was understood, following reigning Scottish Enlightenment ideas, that societies could evolve through different discrete stages of development. Australia had its example of the hunter-gathering stage in Aborigines. Then followed a stage for pastoralists and farmers. All would be followed by commercial politeness. Convicts, ever liable to cause a society to backslide, could labor to bring about the commercial stage and so redeem themselves. The road promised a great deal to a great many, just as it was part of the epic story of British imperial civilization.[17]

In 1815, an engineer named William Cox had been tasked with creating the road over the mountains. He relied on convict labor to do so. The first road went straight down the escarpment on the west, following earlier paths laid out by Natives. Cox made a quick job of it, and did so by design. The key was to get it going. For Australia's future depended on broaching the interior. All those fertile plains could produce the crops and the cattle and the sheep and the wool that made it to market in Sydney and thence to the rest of the empire. Here lay Australia's "promised land." But the road proved virtually unusable, traveled mainly by herds of cattle and sheep, dray carts, and soldiers moving in and out from frontier garrisons.[18] The inclines proved too steep, and the road had been made too narrow with too many switchbacks. Another engineer named Thomas Mitchell, and a veteran of the Peninsular Campaign during the war, was brought in to improve the road and make it usable.[19]

Mitchell started in 1828, just as Ambrose landed. The redoing of the road coincided with the transformation of the convict regime that was typified by both Moreton Bay and Hyde Park Barracks. Mitchell was the right man for the job, a leader who would be remembered even a century later as a "stern soldier and disciplinarian."[20] These convicts would be watched and monitored.

Ambrose toiled here for more than two years, starting in 1833. He and other convict-laborers did different work, widening and straightening what was there and forging a new path that could handle traffic. Convicts hewed roads out of solid rock. They built impressive bridges made of massive stones.[21] They also constructed the walls along it. It is still in use. A great deal of inhumanity accounted for Australia's civility. The typical day for Ambrose revolved around waking up and marching miles in chains to worksites. Convicts moved on as they completed segments, almost like railroad workers were doing in America at this time. The work entailed breaking rocks, removing trees and stumps, clearing brush, quarrying, always hauling and hammering. All the while, convicts toiled in chains.

Ambrose worked out of a staging area for much of the western slope road-reconstruction. He was housed in what was referred to as a "stockade." Stockades were temporary structures designed as bases for convict labor. When he was at one near Emu Plains, he worked on the road up the Lapstone Hill. This is the eastern edge of the mountains, and it was part of Mitchell's redevelopment work. Ambrose missed experiencing the more free and open times there, when it was set up as "a convict agricultural farm" and a government experiment. In 1826, convicts did not have it so

Road Builders Memorial, Terrance Plowright, Katoomba, 2005. (Photo by the author)

bad. Prostitutes came and went from Parramatta without "fear or shame," as an inquiry discovered. On St. Patrick's Day, the convicts on the road crews there witnessed a number of the women dance lewdly "in full view of the men's camp." It was as if they'd never left the Rocks. When Ambrose arrived, the men in the stockade were tasked with cutting out a road and doing the quarry work to complete a bridge.[22] But during his stint there, troops supervised and policed, ensuring that convicts did not rise up, as they had earlier on some occasions, and to guarantee they did not run away. Road gangs did what they did and slept where they did, always with someone's eyes upon them. The new regime at Emu Plains scandalized some Australians because of the abysmal conditions. Reformers came through the area and tried to alert the public in Sydney and in London to the dreadfulness they witnessed in much the same way reformers in England had warned people about the abuses at Chatham and the wretchedness of Whitechapel. Here the men would do the work of "bullocks." But to what end? the visitors asked. Would such a regimen reform men?[23]

Near Katoomba, Ambrose worked out of a stockade on Cox's River. It, too, had a Moreton Bay feel to it. Even more remote than the station at Emu Plains, Cox's River Station was designed for control. Here, the stockade was a complex of buildings surrounded by twelve-foot-tall wooden fence, all meant for intensive supervision and work discipline, a new feature of "the deterrence and punishment network for second offenders."[24] Or in Ambrose's case, fourth or fifth offenders. The convicts' huts were made of wood with bark roofs that were always in need of repair. At its height, the stockade housed between five and eight hundred men. Overseers had their own huts. Outside the fence line, a guard house and a hospital also arose. Regiments cycled through, including the Eighteenth Royal Irish, the Seventeenth Foot from Leicestershire, and the Fourth Own King's Regiment of Foot. The troops were garrisoned just outside of the stockade to watch over the iron gangs.[25] They needed to watch. Before Ambrose's time there, the place was renowned for all sorts of crimes. After the troops came, there was "unquestionably a great improvement."[26]

Each day the routine at the dreaded "Stockade No. 2" proved an ordeal. All suffered from the elements. "The winter nights are too cold, and the summer days too hot," a traveler through the Blue Mountains discovered.[27] Nothing brought relief. When the convicts awoke, they grabbed their tools and then marched in groups of twenty-five. Troops escorted them. They could not even sing. On one occasion, when a convict broke into what was regarded as a "defiant" air, he was flogged on the spot. They could travel as far as four miles. At noon, the convicts walked back for dinner. As an official observed, "they often grumble at mess." At the end of the day, back they went into their "wooden prisons." They "have no time for recreation or opportunity for mischief," a contemporary gushed.[28] A Quaker visitor lamented, "We can scarcely conceive a situation more miserable." The men were locked up between sunset and sunrise in "caravans or boxes" that held twenty to twenty-eight men. The men could "neither stand upright, nor sit down at the same time." They slept on bare boards. All day they were "kept to a monotonous employment, under a strict military guard." They were flogged for "obstinacy" or for not working hard enough.[29]

One convict there recorded the wretchedness of convict life. Thomas Cook worked the road gangs when Ambrose did. They must have been bunkmates at Cox's River. Most famously—or infamously—he related a tale of how soldiers fixed bayonets and forced the convicts to run in chains to their worksites for fourteen or fifteen days. The "scourgers with their cats" wore themselves out lashing convicts. In Cook's estimation, overseers were always cruel, dishing out favors to those they liked and punishing people who refused to bend their necks to them. Commandants and military men were invariably martinets. And the men became beasts. Throughout his narrative, he fixates on what he calls "execrable practices," "monstrosities," "horrible propensities," and "Sinful abominations" the men participated in and which the overseers encouraged. Whistleblowers were bullied. Men maimed themselves. The noose seemed better than Stockade No. 2.[30] No doubt prone to exaggeration, Cook nevertheless illustrated that Francis Ambrose's time on the iron gang was marked by a strict regime of discipline.[31] Though an exceptional convict laboring at an exceptional moment, Ambrose experienced what epitomized the worst Australia could offer.

The road across the mountains became the stuff of Australian frontier lore, every bit as much as Ned Kelly. It represented the apogee of the convict's role in "taming a continent," as nineteenth-century Australians would have said. Of course, people lived here. And Europeans had a difficult time fitting these Indigenous into their reigning understandings of humanity. Were Aborgines "innocents," like Adam and Eve before the Fall? Were they devils that attacked without evident reason? Did they represent peoples at an earlier stage of development? The paradigms for making sense of human diversity posited these were "noble savage" types, destined to be expunged by European progress; or Aborigines were inherently violent people who did all they could to stymie progress. For one traveler over the Blue Mountains, the Indigenous people he encountered "appear to be a harmless race, with nothing ferocious in their manners or countenance." Demonstrating that racist assumptions also were globally connected, he compared them favorably to "the American negro," a group whom he alleged also possessed a fixed and unchangeable nature. The convicts corrupted Aborigines. They "sow[ed] the seeds of drunkenness in the prolific soil of savage indolence."[32] Others, just as condescending, argued that Aborigines sponsored "well-planned forays." Settlers should beware. "The ruin and death of many Europeans will be the first result." And after? "Then will follow, a fearful retribution on the natives."[33]

Historians often use the term "settler colonialism" to define the experience of Indigenous peoples when facing European invasion. The idea is that the new arrivals did the dirty work of the state by pushing people off the land to prepare the way for "progress." At about the time Ambrose was toiling away in frontier contexts, the term fits. A Scot who settled in one of these areas to which roads were being built wrote his brother to boast about his farm of five hundred acres on the bank of the Hunter's River. He hoped for even more land. Convicts had helped him clear it. "Nothing wanting to complete the happiness of the inhabitants but morals and good laws," he prophesied. Here was the heartland of Australian development, and if Sydney could tap into it, all would enjoy the bounty of progress. But then again there were what he called "the Native Blacks." He lost a friend, as well as his "convict servant," to an attack on his farm. He conceded that the attack was a payback for the fact that his friend "beat" a "Native Black." Six other settlers met similar ends. But, he concluded, "a great number of Natives have been shot by the Military." On early frontiers, this is how settler colonialism worked, whether in seventeenth-century Virginia, eighteenth-century Ohio, or nineteenth-century Australia.[34]

Did Ambrose participate in such bloodshed? We will never know, but it featured all around him, and given his life in Australia, it's a good bet he hated the Aboriginal people he encountered. And he now had a great deal of experience living in those flash-point frontier regions where violence occurred, where common people were trapped between those who exploited them for their labor and the Natives whose land they were settling, and where tensions, necessarily, were at their highest.

All around where he labored, tit-for-tat murders and even massacres were becoming all too regular. The killings coincided with the more intensive penal regime and with the spread of assigned convicts and work gangs out farther and farther to clear lands and make roads for development. Ambrose was working on spreading "civilization," albeit sometimes at the point of a bayonet, when settler violence and Native resistance were at a fevered pitch. The Hunter Valley and regions to the west of Sydney were areas where convicts and emancipists—that is, those who had served out their terms—clashed with both free settlers and increasingly with Native groups that contested the movement. Ambrose and others like him found themselves in an in-between space with in-between status.[35]

In 1838, just after Ambrose had been working on chain gangs, the most gruesome massacre in Australian history occurred. To the north in a frontier region, what came to be known as the Myall Creek Massacre took place. Twenty-eight Aborigines were bound and marched off to a place of execution, after which their bodies were mutilated. They had not killed any whites or livestock. They stood in the way of maddened and mobilized men, ex-convicts, who wanted what they felt they were entitled to. They became victim of those who had themselves been victimized.[36] It was almost an exact replay of Bacon's Rebellion in Virginia in the seventeenth century or the killings perpetrated by the Paxton Boys in Pennsylvania in the eighteenth century.

Ambrose was not there, of course. But he could have been and perhaps should have been. For he was a fitting representative of convict culture and what it meant to Australia's development. He had also inhabited frontier regions in gangs and where he performed hard labor. Men like him were exploited to do the brutalizing work necessary to make Australia part of a global system. They were certainly victims. But in their efforts to survive a regime that was becoming all-encompassing and coercive they savaged those who contested the spread of empire. Convicts could and did try to reclaim their manhood and their civilized status by targeting Native peoples. In the process, an unbridgeable gulf was emerging between two subject groups as roads drove deeper and deeper into the continent.

In 1841, a writer back in Ireland made the claim that in Australia it was a "universal fact that white mens dogs hate the blacks, and black mens dogs hate the whites."[37] This may seem a trivial point, but it gestured to a firm fact that was emerging. With convict roads being built and a frontier narrative beginning to take shape suggesting the growing chasm between settlers and the Indigenous people, there was no discernible way to reconcile the two. The road through the Blue Mountains wrought this as well. For better and for worse, Ambrose and men like him built Australia. They built it with their muscle but also with their ingenuity. They built it with skill and sophistication, while suffering for being born poor on the other side of the world. And they killed.[38]

Francis Ambrose was clearly a hardened criminal. It would be hard to believe that anyone could scare or intimidate him. He could take anything the state threw at him. He was a cock of the walk, even in a place of hard men. In 1836, at some point during his misadventures, he was arrested once more and sent to Sydney Gaol. The clerk recorded him as transported on the *Bussorah Merchant* and standing 5 feet, 8¾ inches tall. He appeared "stout" and ruddy with sandy hair. He now sported another tattoo, one of

"(Lovers) man and woman on [his] right arm."[39] Who could the "lover" on his arm have been? We have no idea. He was not married, but in Sydney, particularly in the Rocks when he was back in Sydney, that did not matter. The dreaded superintendent in Hyde Park Barracks considered what he called "concubinage" to be de rigueur among the convicts.[40]

It is hard to imagine a tougher or harder man, or a person in better physical condition. Ambrose had been forced to run to and from work-sites in the Blue Mountains in shackles. He had endured stints on the treadmill. He had consistently performed heavy labor. Officials considered him "slender" the first few times he had run-ins with the law. No longer.[41] His harsh regime of roadwork and daily exercise would have prepared him for any ring. The steady train of abuse he had been served also contributed to making him a fearsome fighting machine.

In Australia, during this time of serial absconding and trips to and from road gangs and Hyde Park Barracks, he was fighting. Ambrose did all of this while he was on the lam, assigned to barracks, and while he was living in ganging stations. It is certain that he had picked up a reputation because the press picked up on him. He also had acquired a nickname: "Ginger."[42] This is exactly how the great Mexican boxer Canelo Alvarez acquired his alias. He was known as "Cinnamon"—in Spanish, "Canelo"—because of the ginger color of his hair. He claimed to be Irish, the descendant of the San Patricios, another bunch of Irish rebels. The nickname and all that went along with it set him apart and gave him an identity. So it was for Ambrose.

In these days, fighting in Australia was moving out of the Rocks to the margins, close to where the toughest were either clearing lands, dispossessing Aborigines, or toiling on road gangs. As the fistic scene in London testified, prizefighting was a practice that took off where world-making was taking place. It flourished in in-between places, those zones where things were becoming or transitioning. In Australia, it would thrive in frontier pockets, right where the brute work of globalization occurred and where men apt to enter a ring toiled.[43] Prizefighting, therefore, more or less followed the course of Ambrose's pilgrimage through Australia.

Ginger began to appear in the record. One thing is for certain: His opponents were tough men. We know most about one named George Sharpless, a fellow convict he fought in 1833. George Sharpless came over from London in 1824. One newspaper, *The Australian*, described him as "the Bumble Footed Shoe-Maker." Nonetheless, the *Sydney Monitor* reported on November 12, 1834, how Sharpless, a lifer, ran away from the farm he worked on that was owned by a fellow named Nichols. When Nichols confronted Sharpless, the shoemaker said he would rather die than go back. He "put himself in an attitude to fight," and Nichols had to take up a stick to defend himself.[44] Bumbles suffered from a deformity. But he could fight.

Not as well as Ginger, as it transpired.[45] On Friday, August 10, 1833, they met on the Parramatta Road.[46] They each put up two and a half guineas, "all they could muster," as a newspaper reporting on the spectacle put it. In truth, they probably had backers, suggesting some sort of Fancy. Ginger and Bumbles followed the rules of the game. They stripped ritualistically. Bumbles "squared away as if he had seen science." He looked the part to a discerning eye. Throughout the first round, he "administered pepper to the calf's head of the Ginger." He welted him up, or "jellied" Ambrose a bit. But then the tide turned. By the end of "the mill" Bumbles was forced to acknowledge, the report breathlessly put it, that Ambrose had bested him in twenty-seven rounds.[47]

The correspondent covering "the ring" on this day wanted to make the case that Australia, too, had a Fancy. "The philosophic observer of human nature," he began, "may think that Records of Pugilism ought not to find a place in the Journals of this Colony." The "ethical set," as he argued, thought as much. But these events were becoming more regular and they demanded that someone report on them. Australia, too, comprised part of the fistic empire.[48]

Another opponent was named Thomas Brady. According to one biographical account, Brady was "a pugilist of the first class." He had insulted Ambrose, leading to fisticuffs. Ambrose's friends then set a fight date.[49] *The Australian*, a Sydney paper, confirmed that the fight took place. It published the following piece on June 23, 1837:

> Thomas Brady, free, the antagonist of Francis Ambrose, alias Ginger, in a pugilistic encounter on the Parramatta Road a few days since, was on Tuesday held to Bail by the Police bench, for his peaceable behaviour during Twelve calendar months, himself in £20, and two sureties in £10 each. Having entered into the required securities, he was discharged. Ambrose alias Ginger, being a prisoner of the crown, was a few days since rewarded

> with 50 lashes, for his share in the transaction. Mr. Inspector Jackson, who came in almost at the expiration of the brutal exhibition, was rather roughly handled because he endeavoured to put a stop to it. A summons had been granted at his suit against one individual for assaulting him, and the party summoned failing to obey the mandate on Tuesday last; the time appointed, the Bench issued a warrant for his apprehension.

The report says it all. The convict Ambrose beat Brady in seventeen rounds, but Ambrose paid for it. The fight attracted an audience out on a road leading to the frontier. Ginger had worked on this very road, which had become by this time a regular venue for fights, close enough to Sydney but also proximate to the frontier. The upshot was that Francis Ambrose was becoming more notorious than ever. And his persona, Ginger, was well known to the Fancy Down Under.[50]

He fought a number of other fights, including one against a fellow named Johnny White. He won them all.[51]

Ambrose had not benefited from proper training, so his fighting style was likely akin to brawling. The farther one moved from the center of global fighting in London, the more things deteriorated and devolved. But these were "official" bouts. Even if they were fought with the desperation of abused convicts, they followed the same rules as in Britain. The formalities had to be followed. The onlookers formed a ring for the fighters who entered with seconds and with a referee before stripping down. They fought rounds that were based not on time but on when a man fell. The winner could claim the bout if his opponent could not make it back to scratch in thirty seconds after the end of a round or if the corner threw in the sponge.

These rituals, which followed the aristocratic code duello, did something notable for convicted brawlers like Ambrose. Prizefighting ennobled common men who had suffered and imbued their violence with honor. Through it, Ambrose could claim himself a man and secure an identity in a dehumanizing world. He was a prizefighter, not just a convict. He had started out as "Francis Ambrose, Bussorah Merchant." Australia's Fancy knew him as "Ambrose alias Ginger." He had become, for all practical purposes, a professional.

ROUND 7

The Bay of Islands

IN 1840, THREE GLOBAL STORIES converged. Here is the first. On June 17, 1839, David Hand, the master of an American ship, was setting off from Sag Harbor, Long Island. He skippered the *Hamilton,* named, of course, after the "founding father" Alexander Hamilton, who had been slain in a duel but who also had a great hand in devising what sort of nation the United States would be. The *Hamilton* was a whaling ship. New York craftsmen had constructed it in 1826. Before being refitted as a whaler, the ship had plied the seas between New York and Liverpool as a packet. On the increasingly busy route, it was now outclassed. Just as ships of the line were repurposed into hulks, packets became whalers.[1]

Hand had a lot to live up to. A generation earlier his father, also a David, had played a great role in America's securing its independence from Britain. The elder Hand had been imprisoned by the British numerous times, only to escape time and time again.[2] So dashing had he been that the novelist James Fenimore Cooper based his character Natty Bumppo on him, better known as Hawkeye in *The Last of the Mohicans,* a role Daniel Day-Lewis would immortalize in a film adaptation. Bumppo, like David Hand's father, served as a ranger on the frontier. For generations, this sort of character would come to define what it meant to be American. D. H. Lawrence loved the character. With Bumppo, he wrote, "you have there the myth of the essential white America. All the other stuff, the love, the democracy, the floundering into lust, is a sort of by-play. The essential American is hard, isolate, stoic and a killer. It has never yet melted."[3] After all of this, he would serve as the first master of the *Hamilton.* He was one of the whaling pioneers of Sag Harbor. Though Hand Junior had served as master of a ship called the *Columbia,* this was his maiden voyage on the *Hamilton.*[4]

David Hand, the younger, was engaged on a great adventure as well. He would risk all and endure storms at sea to help the new republic grow. The oil he would bring back by killing right and sperm whales in seas far away from Sag Harbor would help fuel America's industrial development. Maybe not playing as grand a role as his father, he was nonetheless invested in an undertaking that Alexander Hamilton would have seen as critical to America's rise in a global economy. Whale oil made the world go round. It had lit the street lamps in the East End of London, and it was doing the same for New York. Industry depended on it.[5] In his father's day, Americans had been catching up to the British when it came to whaling. By the time the *Hamilton* was readying to depart in 1840, Americans had entered a golden age. No one outranked the Yankees.[6]

In his early days at sea, Hand dashed off a letter to his father. "I have a fine ship," he boasted. He was blessed with "good Officers and I believe a good crew, and a good wind now gowing at the rate of nine knots per hour." Sailing had been pleasant. Yes, they had rough seas the second night out, but the weather "moderated." He had "not sene the spout of a whale or a Blackfish since we left," but it was early days. In a postscript, one he added just before he sent off the letter, he gushed they "saw sperm whales." And they took one that yielded fifty barrels.[7] He had a right to be hopeful. The *Hamilton* was 454 tons, on the larger side and certain to be bigger than many of the competitors he would see on the other side of the world. It was made for a long, tough voyage.[8] With a little luck, he would return with his hold filled with barrels of whale oil. The plan was simple. He would head for the seas off of New Holland for "rite whales" and then sail toward New Zealand, where he was more likely to spot sperm whales.[9]

In no time, his ship ran into difficulties. It started with the weather. The cold as he went south off toward the Pacific was fearsome. Then, when he arrived at the whale fishery—or the grounds where the leviathans usually made their yearly journeys—he was not having much of that luck he had hoped for. On September 29, after another day of failing to spy any whales, he wrote in his log "This is what I call D____ hard times." He meant "Damned," no doubt.[10] He could not find sperm whales. Sperm whale trumped all for its purity and for the price it could fetch. In addition, the heads of sperm whales contained the even more precious spermaceti, a fine oil that could turn waxy and that had myriad uses, ranging from candles to ointments.[11] Herman Melville memorably—and homoerotically—described the process of processing the organ after a kill. "Squeeze! squeeze! squeeze! all the morning long; I squeezed that sperm till I almost melted into it; I squeezed that sperm till a strange sort of insanity came over me; and I found myself unwittingly squeezing my co-laborer's hands in it, mistaking their hands for the gentle globules."[12]

Hand instead only found right whales, worth something to be sure but smaller than the typical sperm whale and with oil not quite as refined and, therefore, not as profitable. But still, these counted as part of the Pacific's "living sea of oil." Throughout his time near the Tasman Sea, his crew spotted right whales on many days, dispatched the smaller boats to chase the leviathans, plunged harpoons into them, tied the lines fast to the boats, and tore through the sea until the whales tired or died. Then the work began on these "floating furnace-factories," hauling, cutting, and then rendering the fat into oil in tryworks—huge vats with fires beneath them on the deck—pouring the hot oil on a rolling ship into barrels, and stowing these below. The tasks required guile, stamina, and skill. One greenhorn who tried his hand at it said, it was "a difficult and dangerous business, and ought never to be attempted by any, except those that have been bred up to and perfectly skilled in the art."[13]

Hand had journeyed a long way from Sag Harbor to slaughter only a small number of sperm whales. On their first foray into the hunting grounds, they killed four when they spotted a pod.[14] But he saw few sperm whales beyond this by New Holland. In his father's time, those leaving the United States for whaling did not have to rove beyond the Atlantic to find their prey. Now? Some had to venture as far as the Arctic Ocean, like the sailor who carved the scrimshaw. Others, like those on the *Hamilton,* were obliged to travel into the Pacific. With the surging and unquenchable demand for oil, skippers like Hand were overhunting. Industrial development demanded that he and his crew sail far from home.

The *Hamilton*'s bad luck continued. On November 11, a boat was stove to pieces as it was trying to take a whale. Two days later, a man was lost overboard, and one of the barrels with the precious oil was smashed in. After sailing off of New Holland, they headed for New Zealand. On February 26, they turned over the boats for sperm whales. No luck. A month later, Hand declared, "Looking for sperm whales is like looking for Angels visits."[15]

Then another crewman died. A newspaper back home got word of the following: "Died at sea, on board the Hamilton, March 21st. David Burnham, seaman. Working his passage from New Zealand to his native place, Portland."[16] With a leaking ship, with his supplies running low, with too few sperm whales killed, with increasingly surly men anxious to see land and its comforts, he looked for a port to pull into, to reassess, and—as he knew—to procure more men. For some were bound to run off. Such was reality in the whaling business. On May 5, after almost eleven months at sea, they reached a port. Hand sent a report back home via another ship headed that way. They had collected 2,600 hundred barrels of whale oil, and 300 from sperm whales. It was not enough.[17]

Now the second story. While Hand was braving the oceans, Francis Ambrose was having an adventure that would have challenged even a Hawkeye in the Australian bush. He had one more assignment in Australia after all the stockades, chain gangs, and escape attempts. After, no doubt, another stay in Sydney Gaol or Hyde Park Barracks, authorities dispatched him well to the south of Sydney. In 1839, he was working as an assigned convict doing public works once more. Near Wollongong in New South Wales, about fifty miles from Sydney, he was most likely doing hard labor to build a breakwater and then a road. He ran away again, this time from the stockade there on March 1, 1840, but not before stealing rations off of some of his fellow convicts.[18] He set off for Sydney. Today you could walk it in a few days. In 1840, when he absconded, he would have had to trek weeks through the bush, steering clear of Aborigines. Then again, he did have some experience. He had been in the bush before. He had run away numerous times.

He journeyed this time to the area by the Rocks, not to avail himself of its many pleasures but to get out of Australia. He knew his best chance: whalers. All kinds of ships were increasingly stopping in Sydney. Those packing away sandalwood and those on sealing expeditions pulled into the port. But whalers were a tried-and-true method of getting out.[19] They came and went from Sydney, particularly to refit, with greater regularity than even a generation before. British whalers, of course, touched down in Sydney on a regular basis. Increasingly, so too did American whalers. Americans, as David Hand could testify, were now becoming major players in whaling, even surpassing the British in their ambitions and in the number of ships they sent out in search of whales.[20]

Ambrose would not have had much luck with British whalers. Officials knew that convicts tried to stow away and get out of Australia, and British masters cooperated with them to ferret out such men. But Americans? Men coming from New York or Massachusetts tended to hate the British. American-ness was premised on anti-Britishness, especially for the sort of working-class men who toiled on whalers. Americans lived in a republic that had broken away from the Crown, something that they thought distinguished them from all others. They felt no compulsion to help the British discover the convicts, who also tended to hate the Crown. With the increased traffic in Sydney Harbor, and with the increased number of whalers plying the seas around it and stopping in port, officials could not police all ships. These difficulties provided the opportunity Francis Ambrose needed.

The third story involves a man named John Howell, the master of a ship called the *France*. The *France* also called the whaling center of Sag Harbor home. On July 16, 1838, John Egbert Howell ordered the anchor hauled for a whaling voyage that would last for a couple of years. The *France* would leave the Atlantic and head to the promising grounds off of Australia in search of whales, where it had had some good fortune. Alas, on the morning of December 23, 1839, now almost a year and a half out, a crewmember found the ship had six feet of water sitting in the hold. All hands were awakened to find the leak. They discovered "a running stream of water" they could not stem. The men began sweating at the pumps. They were making "1,200 strokes an hour" just to keep up with the flow. What became clear was that the ship could not go on. "We have now come to the conclusion," Howell wrote on Christmas Eve, "to go to Sidney for repairs and refit the ship for another cruise."[21] The *France* limped into Sydney, reaching Mosmon's Bay just across from Sydney Cove on January 31, New Year's Eve. Here the men unloaded the oil they had collected, 560 barrels of right whale oil, and 24 barrels of sperm. Alas, the men ran amok in the Rocks. Howell lamented that the "Men are disorderly as ever caused by strong drink." The carpenter and his men, when they were supposed to be fixing the ship, tended to be "dead Drunk."[22]

It was to be a long, tortuous stay. By the time the *France* was pronounced fit for sea, on February 24, twelve men had absconded. To make matters worse, Howell had to discharge the first and third officers. They would, no doubt, find the Rocks more convivial. On March 16, Howell took the ship down to Sydney Cove, or rather more than likely just to the north of it, to take on stores and prepare to continue the cruise. Meanwhile, he had to search for ships' hands, who proved "scarce" in Sydney. He had to offer five pounds in advance to get anyone to ship with him. Howell fumed. "The Ship ready for sea but waiting for the men," he noted day after day.[23]

At this point, two of the three tales intersected. Ambrose skulked right past Sydney Cove, where he had arrived more than a decade earlier. Whalers did not alight here. The stink was too great, and the docks and piers in the Cove were too busy with government vessels. Campbell Cove was more likely. Though close by, it was not policed as vigorously as Sydney Cove. Authorities did indeed board ships and tried to smoke out convicts. From time to time, they would clamber onto a ship, order tarpaulins thrown over the ship to cover it, and light small smoldering fires to fill holds below with smoke. This trick worked to get rats off board. It did the same with men.[24] On March 26, Howell reported that "the Police men took out 4 Prisoners that were secreted in the Hold." The word choice is interesting. It suggests that members of the crew were helping absconders. Or that Howell had a hand in it, for that matter. But apparently, the police missed at least one man.[25]

Ambrose had escaped the police dragnet. The next day, on Friday, March 27, 1840, Ambrose and the *France* weighed anchor and set sail from Sydney.[26] Had he had the temerity to stand on deck, the last buildings he would have seen were the stone warehouses that were just built and that still stand at the Cove. The last island in his view would have been Goat's Island, where he had done chain gang work. The last bays he would have looked out on as he boarded were where he had spent time in quarantine and in the *Phoenix,* which sat just across from Campbell's.

The city had changed so much since he arrived. It no longer suited the improvisers and shape-shifting convicts like Ambrose. Sydney had arrived. Mary Phoebe Broughton noted as much just at the time Ambrose bolted. Sydney now had a "society," she wrote, and clearly had become more refined. She spoke excitedly of ships coming and going between England and Sydney with news and papers and fashion. Broughton led a life akin to something out of *Jane Eyre.* She did not make a single mention of convicts. So great a change in so little a time. This was like an English society now. The convicts and their culture no longer held sway.[27] Ambrose certainly no longer fit.

When Ambrose boarded the *France*, he had no name and no identity. He was not Ambrose or even Ginger. No name appears on the log of the *France*. He would not have demanded what whalers called a "lay," that is, a percentage of profits. Desperate men earned passage and little else in exchange for their labor. Nonetheless, even the likes of Ambrose had some leverage. Sailors were always absconding. They were more or less free agents who could join the ship that offered the best prospects. Ambrose did not have this luxury. He needed the *France* more than it needed him. But it needed men nonetheless.[28]

Herman Melville had a term for such peripatetic men who moved through the whaling world: "Omoo." According to him, this word meant a rover and a rambler. But in a competitive market, and because of the global demand for whale oil, a rambler's labor mattered. Though "Omoo" was a term favored in the Marquesas Islands for "wanderer," as Melville tells us, in the global capitalist enterprise that was whaling, wandering entailed a power and autonomy that common men rarely enjoyed. On board, they could be treated as poorly as sailors in a navy, but in port they gained strength. Even convicts.[29]

Ambrose now would experience a voyage "before the mast," that is, belowdecks, where the rest of the common seamen bunked. He dealt with the normal things any seaman did. The rains came, as did fair breezes and gales, as the ship sailed steadily to the east across the Tasman Sea. They passed a dead sperm whale on April 26. That would be the only glimpse he would get of one up close. Howell spotted rights and humpbacks and did not deign to give chase. He ordered the boats lowered to hunt a pod of sperm but came up empty. At least Ambrose did not have to work the pumps. The repairs at Sydney held. They took on water and wood along the way, and a few men ran off. "Cursed is he," Howell declared on May 21, "that gives it a thought." A few days later, one sailor fell from the yard on deck and died "without a groan." Such was life for society's expendables.

Though the *France* was not heading back to the United States, it did have to resupply from time to time. To load up on barrels of food and water, it was heading to another critical hub in the global whaling business: the Bay of Islands on the north island of what is now New Zealand.

"New Zealand," in fact, did not yet exist as a formal colonial entity. Herman Melville called it a "small English settlement" where Māori lived and which now attracted Europeans. As they closed in on the settlement, a later visitor would recount, they passed a rocky promontory called Cape Brett. Finally, they reached the "Bay of Islands, four in number, with very large rugged rocks cropping out of the sea, on port side."[30] It was beautiful. A visitor to the region at the time concurred: "The Bay of Islands is surrounded by lofty and picturesque hills, and is secured from all winds. It is full of lovely coves, and a safe anchorage is to be found nearly all over it; added to this, a number of navigable rivers are for ever emptying themselves into the Bay, which is spotted with innumerable romantic islands all covered with perpetual verdure."[31]

The chief settlement within the bay was known by its Native name: Kororāreka. It was an open society, a place ruled and fought over by vying Māori tribes. They were struggling with one another, no doubt, because British statesmen and their merchant minions provided some with guns at the expense of others. The locals welcomed the whalers. They grew potatoes and raised pigs that they sold to whalemen in exchange for muskets, ammunition, tobacco, and tools. They also sold sex and alcohol. Traders and craftsmen had moved in as well, all to refit and supply the growing number of ships that came and went. In total, about three thousand visitors a year came to the small and increasingly bustling settlement.[32]

Kororareka in the Bay of Islands, New Zealand, George Clayton, 1845. (Alexander Turnbull Library, Wellington, New Zealand)

In 1839, just the year before Ambrose's escape, seventy-one British, fifty-nine American, twenty-one French, one Portuguese, and two Tahitian vessels arrived in the Bay of Islands. Where once the British had dominated, the Americans were catching up. And now the French were coming, too. It was quite a scene for such a little anchorage, with much of the traffic coming or going via Sydney.[33] Europeans traveled here for "flax, timber and whales; seals, sex and souls."[34] But it was strategically important, especially because of whale oil. The Bay of Islands tied two networks together. One was imperial and centered in this part of the world in Sydney. The bay was a satellite of Sydney, with so many ships coming and going. It was also so clearly a key Pacific node in the global whaling network.

Kororāreka was intensely democratic and egalitarian, befitting the new age that had arisen from the age of revolution. It was a free trade, free movement, free labor zone.[35] With openness came cultural mixing and a great deal of conflict as well. Tribe fought tribe, European coerced Māori. Merchants, whalers, and escaped convicts eyed one another with suspicion. Catholics railed against Protestant missionaries, who proved more than eager to return fire. All preyed upon one another. Kororāreka was likened by missionaries to Sodom and Gomorrah. It was a place where European men took Natives as wives for a few weeks. In exchange, the Māori demanded guns and gunpowder, which the Māori used against each other. This was a place beyond the line, like the Caribbean of old. Also like the Wild West in America, a place where Billy the Kid would be at home.[36]

The Bay of Islands has been called the "Cradle of New Zealand." But in 1840, it was known as the "Devil's Playground" and "Blackguard's Beach."[37] Just a few years earlier, Charles Darwin had stopped over on his ship HMS *Beagle* on the way to the Galapagos and the visit that would transform the intellectual parameters of the world and give us that most modern of ideas, the "survival of the fittest." In the animal kingdom, but increasingly in the world, this phrase summed up the condition all beings seemed to have to negotiate with their wits and with their brawn. And his thoughts on the whalers, ex-convicts, and Māori he saw? The Bay of Islands was, he intoned, "the hell hole of the Pacific."[38] It seemed to him a "rum and blood drenched place." Fighters but few others would have been at home, especially in the many grog shops that dotted the waterfront.

Others confirmed what Darwin said. "There is still a third class of our countrymen to be met with here," wrote a draftsman who traveled along with Darwin on the *Beagle*, "whose downcast and sneaking looks proclaim them to be runaway convicts from New South Wales." He noted, "These unhappy men are treated with derision and contempt by all classes; and the New Zealanders, being perfectly aware of their state of degradation, refuse all intercourse with them. They are idle, unprincipled, and vicious in the extreme, and are much feared in the Bay of Islands; for when by any means they obtain liquor, they prove themselves most dangerous neighbours." It seems all noted that escaped convicts caused trouble.[39] In fact, such people at the Bay of Islands specialized in taking in Omoos like Ambrose. They were called "crimpers." Crimpers lured whalemen off their ship, proceeded to get them blind drunk, and then sold their services to a needy master whose ship was undermanned.

Lord Palmerston, the British foreign secretary of the time and one of the most powerful men of the age, worried that the settlement could destabilize much of Britain's Pacific vision. "The nearness of those islands to the penal settlements of New South Wales and Van Diemen's Land," he wrote to a British naval commander in the region the same year Ambrose was on the lam, "has also led to their being resorted to as an asylum for fugitive British convicts, and such persons, having associated with men left in New Zealand by whaling ships and other vessels have formed a society which indispensably requires the check of some controlling authority."[40]

The British had good reason to worry. The rival French had built a church staffed by missionaries who arrived in 1839 and saw to the spiritual needs of whalers and of natives. More importantly, the mission gave France a presence in a place that was vital to global trade. Americans, too, realized they had a stake in the site. The government hired on a consul named James Clendon. The consul was charged by the secretary of state to keep track of American shipping in the port, send reports back to Washington, and to look after America's economic interests in the region and to protect the seamen who were so critical to them. Clendon kept the secretary of state up to speed on what was happening in such an important port. He worked closely with British officials who helped him return deserters and to keep the peace. Sometimes they clashed, as in the summer of 1839, when sailors from Sag Harbor suspected some British seamen of crimping a young shipmate. The men, "armed with pistols and cutlasses," attacked the house that they thought he was held in and tore it down, despite a local missionary asking them to desist. As they tore away walls and ceiling, they "unfurled the United States flag in front of the House." Quite a scandal in a place used to scandals.[41] Clendon saw the same things Palmerston did. In 1839, he reported back to Washington that this vital town of Kororāreka was a "lawless" place run by ex-convicts from New South Wales. These often would "decoy" seamen to jump ship and then get an advance for their services from another ship that was "distressed" by desertions. Often, just as in Moreton Bay, Natives were hired to capture deserters, only exacerbating tensions.[42]

No power controlled it. This made it an unregulated and unmediated part of the global capitalist economy. It was a libertarian's dream, and a Darwinian Eden, we might add. It was perfect for an improviser like Ambrose. It was also, unsurprisingly, a site noted for fisticuffs, though Ambrose would not have time for a prizefight.[43]

And the moment the *France* arrived, the place was flooded with ships and seamen. A Frenchman went so far as to claim the bay looked like "a European port." He saw a dizzying number of ships. Ambrose hit it at its high point.[44] The 411-ton *France* dropped anchor there on June 14, 1841. On that day, Ambrose jumped ship, along with as many as six others.[45] In the meantime, while the rain fell and as the *France* left the bay to head north to whaling grounds, he sought out a new opportunity in Kororāreka. There were many lairs that would take him in.

And here we finally come to the meeting with Hand. Francis Ambrose bolted from the *France* just at the moment David Hand and his dismal ship lay in port at the Bay of Islands. The American consul reported that the place had become jammed when Hand arrived. So many sailors had deserted.[46] "It was however a great loss of time to the shipping," the consul informed the secretary of state, "when Desertions occurred for me to have to apply to the Police Magistrate for a warrant." Because of these delays and the fact that so many ships were pulling into port, giving men all sorts of choice and therefore leverage, "vessels have been detained many days I may say weeks before they could fill up their crews."[47] The *Hamilton* was suffering the most of all. Māori had tried to rob the ship of some of its boats. The consul had to cooperate with a British lieutenant governor to get the boats back. The British found a boat and had it returned. But desertions were doing the *Hamilton* in. It set the record that summer for the longest stay in port. It had been stuck there for about six weeks, not the standard two.[48] The ship could not secure enough sailors to leave.[49]

Hand needed hands. So, he had little recourse but to look to the desperate to get out. Ambrose, for his part, had to know where any ship he would try to sign onto was going. He did not want to go back to Australia. He also did not want to continue on a long whaling journey, as was the case with the *France*. As an escaped convict, he could not head back to Britain. He had to find a place where he would have no past. He had to figure all of this quickly, amid a sea of ships sitting anchored in the bay. Which one would fit? The *Hamilton* was the answer, as a later report would attest.[50] Ambrose did not have long to wait. He tarried there for only four or five days after absconding from the *France*. Hand was that desperate.

In Melville's *Omoo*, any master was "mortally afraid" of the "Sydney gentry" or a "bird" from Sydney. That is, escaped convicts. They were "in excessively bad odour," meaning that if any mutiny took place on board, they bore responsibility. "Ashore, these fellows are equally riotous," the master believed. One of his shipmates was what he called a "practised bruiser," who knew the rules of the ring, or what Melville calls "the art pugilistic."[51] They were, in a word, defiant. The system had made them that way. People like Ambrose were the perfect Omoo. And what choice did Hand have but to take aboard a character such as Francis Ambrose?

The time was propitious for Ambrose's arrival and these converging stories. This was an open port. Soon, it would be closed. The heyday of the Bay of Islands did not last long. The year 1840 proved to be key for the place. This was the year the global tales would intersect but also when they would cease. At very nearly the same time Ambrose was jumping from the *France* to the *Hamilton*, commissioners were in from Britain to meet the chiefs of a number of Māori tribes to sign a treaty.[52] In early February, the British delegation, missionaries including the French Catholic prelate, and Māori leaders convened with much official pomp and circumstance at a small Māori site called Waitangi, just on the other side of the bay. The Treaty of Waitangi is regarded as the foundational document of New Zealand, akin to the Declaration of Independence for the United States or, as some argue, the Magna Carta for England. But it did something quite different. It transferred sovereignty from the tribes to the Crown and made the Crown responsible for allocation and sale of lands and for law and order. British authority would unambiguously reign. The Māori would be regarded as subjects, whether they understood what this entailed or not. Those Europeans in Kororāreka hated it because it curtailed their freedom.[53] The treaty made the Bay of Islands and then all of New Zealand a dependent colony. Where the Western state existed, Omoos could not.[54]

What had been an open society—a place tailor-made for in-betweenness and for characters looking to remake themselves—began to close. In the coming years, there would be great resistance to what the treaty meant in the Bay of Islands. Māori would sack the town and drive out the foreigners, all to win the place back. In an act with an almost perfect sense of symbolism, they chopped down the flagpole on which the Union Jack flew above Kororāreka not once, not twice, but three times.[55] But it was too late. The British would control this place as tightly as they would Sydney before too long, making the openness that allowed Ambrose to escape a thing of the past. The whalers would stop visiting the settlement and begin looking elsewhere. "The British Government," the American vice consul observed, "have now assumed the entire Sovereignty of these Islands and have enacted laws and levied Imposts peculiarly harassing to our Citizens and most destructive to their Commercial pursuits, whilst they offer the most marked protection to their own commerce." The end result? "Our whaling and shipping interests are deeply affected by the loss of rights and privileges long enjoyed by those engaged in the lucrative undertaking," he lamented. Whalers would have to look elsewhere.[56]

As he boarded the *Hamilton*, he more than likely beheld quite a sight: "She turned out to be a small, slatternly looking craft, her hull and spars and dingy black, rigging all slack and bleached nearly white, and every thing denoting an ill state of affairs aboard." So wrote Melville when his protagonist first catches a glimpse of his whaler in *Omoo*. "Leaning carelessly over the bulwarks were the sailors," he went on, "wild, haggard looking fellows in Scotch caps and faded blue frocks; some of them with cheeks of a mottled bronze, to which sickness soon changes the rich berry-brown of a seaman's complexion in the tropics."[57] No sooner was he was on board than the ship weighed anchor. On June 18, four days after the *France* had pulled into the bay, it finally had enough of a crew to leave.[58]

During his brief, brief stay here, something else would happen. Francis Ambrose would more than likely lose his name. It had the convict stain now. He would begin to imagine how he would rechristen himself. We don't know what he called himself as he worked for his passage on the *Hamilton*. But we know that when he arrived on the other side of the world, he would embrace a new identity, a fitting act for an able shape-shifter, master improviser, and thoroughly modern man.

THE MIDDLE ROUNDS

ROUND 8

Sag Harbor

IN HERMAN MELVILLE'S masterpiece *Moby Dick,* the narrator and sometime whaleman Ishmael extols the epic role of the whaler in the world's development. Some claimed whaling was an "unpoetical and disreputable pursuit," he said. But to Ishmael, such a charge amounted to an "injustice" leveled by "landsmen." He conceded, "Butchers we are, that is true." But so were soldiers, Ishmael countered. And we honor them. In fact, as he argued, a soldier would shudder if he beheld a sperm whale. "For what are the comprehensible terrors of man compared with the interlinked terrors and wonder of God!" he declared. All the lamps that light the world "burn, as before so many shrines, to our glory!" The whalemen led the way in exploration and settlement, and the economies of so many nations depended on them: "Whaling is imperial!" Ishamel's paean to whalers suggests that they are worthy of a Homer or a Virgil, or even a Turner on the written page, and Melville styled himself as such.[1]

Whaling conjures images of a mythic fight between man and nature. In 1955, A. J. Liebling, the great midcentury writer for the *New Yorker* and boxing aficionado, compared the power-punching phenomenon Rocky Marciano to Moby Dick in his battle for the heavyweight championship with the smaller and cagier—and older—Archie Moore. For Liebling, Moore played Ahab in the drama. We know who won. If Ahab beat the whale? Well, as Liebling said, it would be "just another fish story."[2]

There was nothing Homeric or even Liebling-esque about the trip from Kororāreka, except for the suffering. He was now a man without a name; perhaps, though, he should have called himself Jonah. David Hand never mentioned the difficulties in the Bay of Islands. When he finally slipped out on June 20, 1840, he lamented he was "two men short." The delays had affected him. One day from the bay and he sighed, "For myself I never felt more unpleasant in my Life."[3] On the trip back, Hand hoped to fill his hold with oil. No luck. Day after day, a man standing watch on the mast scanned the horizon. He spotted some humpbacks but nothing else. The crew painted and sealed the boats, keeping them on the ready for the hunt. But they never left the ship. They had missed the season, no doubt because they were stuck so long in Kororāreka. On top of this, the weather bedeviled the crew. As they headed farther south, they encountered squalls, heavy rain, and then snow. The men had to shovel the decks. The weather never seemed to change. Day after day of "Dirty" weather and "Cold as the Duce."[4] Then there were the leaks. They grew nearly as bad as those that had plagued the *France*. The men, as Hand reported, furiously worked the pumps. Some days they labored for eight hundred strokes an hour. On bad days, the number grew to one thousand. With no whales in sight, the man who had been Francis Ambrose did his stint with the others belowdecks, keeping the rising water at bay. The *Hamilton* was cursed. "This unlucky ship," Hand lamented. He wanted off: "I wish I had never seen her."[5] Hand was Ahab.

The man who had been Ambrose lived a life of monotony on board the *Hamilton*. He did all the menial tasks, as the experienced men did the jobs that required skill. Pumping, tarring, painting, hauling, and heaving. Still, a leaky ship was a sight better than any stockade in Australia or the "hell on earth" that was New Zealand. Or the prisons and hulks of England. Or the riots and hunger of Bandon, for that matter. Working the pumps beat breaking rocks for roads. Sleeping in a forecastle, with dozens of grim, reeking men proved better than the hammock at Hyde Park Barracks. And even the good food aboard the *Bussorah Merchant* could not hold a candle to the "salt horse" and hardtack that was standard fare on the *Hamilton*.[6] At least he was heading to something. For the first time, he had chosen a path, however trying it proved.

The *Hamilton* made its way across the broad Pacific. The ship followed the swirling seas channeling it below Cape Horn and its howling winds, passing the cape on August 7. All of the power of the oceans is shunted into this narrow passage, creating a torrent of waves. The wind only amplifies them. Melville compared the passage to Dante's *Inferno*.[7] Hand agreed. These were "cold dull Times" on a "Leaky ship."[8] They pushed north into the Atlantic, then up the coast of South America toward the equator. On August 9, one of the pumps failed. They hoisted it out and found it "badly Cracked." They had no choice but to patch it up with cork and tar. "Hard times here," Hand noted.[9] On top of this, no whales appeared. The Atlantic had been overfished. Hand had to know he would find no joy on the way home. That meant shame and less profit. Maybe he would not be given another trip on the *Hamilton*. Investors cared only about barrels of oil. Then the ship entered the tropics. By September, Hand wrote the "Sun [was] hot anuff to melt 18 pound shot."[10]

Finally, on October 8, the crew could make out the Fire Island light. They then made their way into Sag Harbor. A local newspaper called *The Corrector* dutifully reported on October 8, 1840: "Arrived. 11th, ship Hamilton, Hand, 2600 whale and 300 sperm, to Mulford & Sleight," the no doubt unhappy ship owners.

For one who was not a working seaman, the man known as Ambrose had seen more of the world's oceans than nearly anyone else. He had crossed the Irish Sea, journeyed down the eastern Atlantic around the Cape of Good Hope, across the Indian Ocean to Australia, then over the Tasman Sea to New Zealand, before making this last trip around Cape Horn. He had nearly circumnavigated the whole earth, though he had done so mainly against his will. He had only failed to journey across the Atlantic from America to Europe.

He now beheld his new world. In truth, it did not look that different from the place he had left. Sag Harbor bore a striking resemblance to Kororāreka, minus the Natives. When Ambrose, or whatever he called himself, rocked up in Sag Harbor, the place was booming. It had always been a smaller whaling port, less prosperous than, say, New Bedford or Nantucket. Yet, it had been catching up. In 1837, more than thirty whalers had shipped out of the port to try what sailors referred to as "the greasy luck." It would reach its peak less than a decade later, and right about the time the crew of the *Hamilton* came ashore, with a fleet of more than sixty.[11]

By 1840, Sag Harbor served as an extension of a quickly industrializing New York. The oil brought in here would light the streets of a growing city, lubricate its engines and motors. More and more of it was needed, hence the capital invested by companies and the longer voyages to the Pacific. Sag Harbor was another place like the Bay of Islands, a nexus of global trade even if it was remote. The grim slaughtering and butchery necessary to make the world go round were hidden in places like this, just out of sight however important such work was.

But this did not concern Ambrose or whatever he called himself on board that cursed ship. What had to be clear is that he had now entered the United States. No passports were required. But the ship had to pass through customs. In fact, Sag Harbor had built one of the first customs houses in the United States, as this was considered the first port of call in the new republic. Main Street seemed a "forest of masts."[12] Just up from East Water Street, immediately east of the Long Wharf where the *Hamilton* pulled in, the area bustled with warehouses for oil, rope works, coopers, blacksmiths forging harpoons and lances, and the cheap lodgings that seamen needed, as well as the taverns and brothels they frequented. Above the din of the waterfront stood the stately homes of the financiers and investors with their widow's walks and picket fences.[13] This was little different from the Bay of Islands he had just left. Herman Melville's character Queequeg, in *Moby Dick,* intoned after he had seen this den of Christian iniquity that he would rather "die a pagan" than become as what he had witnessed at Sag Harbor. Sag Harbor prided itself, as the very names Washington and Madison Streets suggested, as being heir to a revolution that had created an orderly republic. The man who was once Ambrose was no longer in a colonial world.

This was less a place that was becoming than one that had self-consciously become. It had grown slowly at first, but with the end of the American Revolution, the resumption of global trade, and the first stirrings of an industrial revolution, whaling took off, and with it did Sag Harbor. But these days were coming to an end. Never again would so many ships venture out of Sag Harbor. A gold rush in the near future, the discovery of petroleum in Pennsylvania, diminishing yields in the whaling industry because of how far whalers had to travel to find their prey, were about to doom this industry that had been critical to worldwide industrial development. Though Sag Harbor had reached a high point, decline lay in its immediate future.

Maybe the man who had called himself Ambrose had been a Jonah after all. In all his time on a whaler, be it on the *France* or the *Hamilton,* he had never slaughtered a whale. Maybe Howell and Hand were the real Jonahs. On the *France,* right after Ambrose had jumped ship and in an episode that bore an eerie resemblance to the fate of Captain Ahab, Howell would die.[14] The good people of Sag Harbor would memorialize him on what is known as the Whalers Memorial. It stands in a local cemetery to this day. A marble snapped mast stands above a plaque that reads how John Howell died on July 23, 1840: "while engaged on the whale fishery in the Pacific Ocean, in command of the ship France." He "lost his life in an encounter with a sperm whale." He was twenty-eight years of age, one of six young "bold and enterprising ship masters" memorialized.[15] Lucky for Ambrose that he had not continued on with Howell. The *Hamilton* would meet an even worse fate. Hand was done skippering it after he returned. But the ship sailed on. On another voyage in 1845, the *Hamilton* went down off the coast of Brazil, by some accounts just as Ahab's *Pequod* would: rammed by a sperm whale.[16] It is not as far-fetched as it sounds. An international team of scientists claim an enraged sperm whale could lower its head and strike and sink a ship.[17]

What his experiences were in Sag Harbor are impossible to know. The records of much of the whaling—the crew lists, the pay lists, anything that might have a name or an alias—were burned up in the fires that would periodically devastate Sag Harbor. Alas, boomtowns, or quickly developing places, tend to burn, a fact that would haunt him in the future.

At this moment, though, fire did not enter his mind. He did not tarry. He headed down to New York City. He could have walked or taken a coach. More than likely, he boarded a sloop that would head out into Long Island Sound and sailed down to New York City. If he did so, the sloop was, no doubt, loaded with whale oil.[18]

As he pulled into a dock on the East River, he saw a city that did and did not resemble the London or the Sydney he knew. It certainly dwarfed Bandon, the Bay of Islands, or Sag Harbor. He was back in one of the world's developing nodes. At first sight, though, New York had to seem a disappointment. No doubt, the passenger sailing toward Manhattan beheld "a long line of shipping, and tangled thicket of masts along the East River," as Herman Melville described it. Up close, though, was a sight that was "a reproach and disgrace to the city that tolerates them." Even though the piers were handling more transatlantic traffic by the time he arrived in New York, they would have been wooden and shabby compared to London's. All the eye could see were "irregular, unsightly wharves."[19] Then

New York from Brooklyn, Thomas Horner, 1840. (Miriam and Ira D. Wallach Division of Art, Prints and Photographs: Print Collection, The New York Public Library)

again, London was an established connection point in an imperial system. New York was just beginning to develop.

Much more representative of what the area looked like when he alighted would have been what has most recently been called the Bridge Café. What is now the oldest wooden structure in the Seaport district, built in 1794, sits under the shadow of the Brooklyn Bridge on Water Street.[20] Back in 1840, it was a tavern, a haunt for "river pirates," a gambling den, and an Irish gang hangout called the Hole in the Wall run by a character named Gallus Mag. Margaret Perry stood six feet tall. She wore suspenders, hence the nickname "Gallus," and strapped a pistol and a club to her person. And she was not above using them to keep order in her bar. She even kept ears as trophies. She was, according to a chronicler, "the most savage female" the police had run across.[21] One wonders, since it lies on a corner, if it was a place known as "The Flashes," a sailors' bar where those flush after a voyage spent all their money. It certainly fit the bill.[22]

However ramshackle it appeared, this section of New York bore some resemblance to Wapping. All was utilitarian and made for traffic for trade. Herman Melville starts two novels where all the action for him started, right down by the piers and slips on the East River. He begins *Moby Dick* with Ishmael sauntering around Lower Manhattan. On the second page of the novel, Ishmael tells us about "the insular city of Manhattoes, belted round by wharves as Indian isles by coral reefs—commerce surrounds it with her surf." He tells the reader to take a stroll on a Sunday: "Go from Corlears Hook to Coenties Slip," and "What do you see?—Posted like silent sentinels all around the town, stand thousands upon thousands of mortal men fixed in ocean reveries." This place mattered because it connected New York to the Atlantic highway. In *Redburn*, an earlier novel, Melville recounts how a visitor on the East River would see "ranges of grim-looking warehouses, with rusty iron doors and shutters, and tiled roofs; and old anchors and chain-cable piled on the walk." "The long line of shipping, wharves and warehouses," he wrote, lay along the East River as far down as the Battery. On South Street and Fulton Street, open-air markets and stalls sold the goods sailors needed for the sea, behind which one found the boardinghouses on Franklin Square, brothels, and bars like the one run by Gallus Mag.

He more than likely settled right around here in a boardinghouse, or farther up along the East River, at this point. Many of these places sat next to taverns that sponsored gambling and prostitution. And blood sports. In fact, the oldest existing building in Manhattan, the Captain Joseph Rose House on Water Street, a few doors down from the Hole in the Wall, had fallen on hard times and become a boardinghouse and would in time turn into a venue that showcased rat killing. The neighborhood had declined with it into a "sea of wretchedness and sin" by the time the escaped convict visited the area.[23]

He purportedly began to fight as soon as he arrived. But he did so in a place where all of it was quite alien. We have to stress "purportedly." He is listed as having fought a fellow in New York called "Pat O'Connor."[24] However, no records of this O'Connor can be found.[25] A newspaper in Ireland recounted how he had taken on someone called "*Carbery*, who was in all probability an Irishman." Another source tells us that he put on an exhibition, with gloves, against a Bob Carbery in Boston on February 15, 1840. An exhibition would seem a stretch, especially for someone who enjoyed no reputation in a new place.[26] The dates are impossible, of course. He was working the pumps of the *Hamilton* then.

So, did he fight? He well might have. That said, the rituals, the rules, would have been pretty baffling to most New Yorkers. Americans did not have the long history with prizefighting that the Irish and English had. Part of this is simply due to timing. When most of the ancestors of the

New Yorkers came to America, fighting had not yet been ritualized. In 1709, we see the first mention of prizefighting in New York. It was regarded with curiosity and as an attempt by some of the provincials to emulate English ways. It gained no traction.[27] Americans only became acquainted with prizefighting and the rules of the ring when they were reimmersed in British and Irish culture as more and more immigrants arrived later in the eighteenth century. We see some evidence of Irishmen serving in the Continental Army during the Revolutionary War sparring with each other. But it struck those who witnessed such episodes as common men taking on aristocratic airs with this strange sort of dueling.[28]

Prizefighting just never took hold in the culture. The early American story is, in part as we have seen, a London story: of Bill Richmond and Tom Molineux. America, of course, had plenty of fighting. Americans in the backcountry engaged in what was called "rough-and-tumble," or frontier fighting. Men who were upset by slights and wounded honor punched and kicked and gouged. Fighters grabbed testicles and plucked out eyes and bit off fingers. These contests had no rounds and no rules.[29] Americans also had a culture of "Plantation fighting." In it, enslaved men engaged in combat in contests usually set up by masters. The fights often pitted the enslaved of one plantation against those of another. These were days of drinking and betting. Whiskey could be passed around to get fighters going and as a reward. Plantation fighting followed the conventions of the rough-and-tumble style. In these bouts, biting and kicking were not off-limits. The enslaved fought and wrestled until someone gave in. Winners could be rewarded with manumission in rare circumstances, as was the case—according to lore—of Tom Molineaux.[30]

So, a culture of early American prizefighting, as we would recognize it, did not really exist. After the Revolution, Americans in cities were not inclined to imitate what was regarded as a hated British custom. Some prizefighting did take place among the Irish who arrived and the English sailors who bought British goods, both increasingly entering port cities like New York. After the War of 1812, a few Americans engaged in pugilism. Right by the East River, on Cherry Street, a butcher named Jacob Hyer reportedly took on some English sailors in matches that followed the English prize-ring rules. The spectators, of course, bet on the outcome, and they argued over whether Americans or British were better fighters. But the practice did not take off. Most matches were localized and happened in only the most haphazard ways, even if they were following prevailing British rules.[31]

Some English fighters did visit. In fact, they wanted to make money, and America, with New York as its center, seemed the next great place where prizefighting would take off. James "Deaf" Burke, for instance, had killed a man in the ring and could not get a match in England. So, he arrived in America in the 1830s, hoping to attract enough attention to the craft to make a living from it. He called America "Yankeeshire." Burke fought a few bouts around New York City and one in New Orleans against an Irishman that devolved into a riot, but nothing really came of his visit. Perhaps his greatest claim to fame is the fact that Ahab compares Moby Dick the whale to Deaf Burke, vowing he would never dodge a fight with him should the two meet.

A few self-styled "professors of pugilism" arrived from England to teach sparring, or to try to entice young men with the craft. Soon, among the middle class in some places, "boxing" became more popular, even if prizefighting remained unpopular. That is, fighting as craft and as exercise had more appeal than the bare-knuckle variety which made one man a winner and the other a loser. Gloved exhibitions appealed more to the merchant class than to the working class, which favored zero-sum, winner-take-all contests with money and blood on the line, as in London.

It just did not capture imaginations. A British popularizer put it this way: "Brother Jonathan," the old English gibe for American, did not really care for "fair play," adding, "besides, the revolver, the bowie-knife, the knuckle-duster and the slung-shot were such popular weapons in the States that a contest with nothing more deadly than bare fists no doubt lacked the excitement necessary to secure popularity."[32] Things were a bit more complicated than that, but the observation rings true in one way: Violence in America had not been ritualized, outside of the duel and backcountry brawling.

New York seemed the most promising place for prizefighting to take hold. It appeared the most vibrant and the most closely connected to England and Ireland. But New York was not London. It had no critical pugilistic mass. It did not have enough capital and lacked the sizeable underclass needed to provide fodder for the ring. New York had no Fancy and could sustain no Fancy. It was still a polite and commercial town, not the developing maw that London had become. Moreover, it was not a frontier zone, like some areas around Sydney, filled with Irish who knew the customs of ritualized violence. It was something in-between.

But there were signs of change. The man once called Ambrose was one of a growing number of Irish heading to the city. The Irish had a long history in New York. They had journeyed there even before the American Revolution. After the Revolution, émigrés from the island, after the failed United Irish Rebellion, arrived in the city. Most of these who came just before and just after the Revolution tended to be Protestant. As such, they merged almost imperceptibly into the city. In a republican and democratic New York, these had found a home. Many came with skills. Some became trusted lawyers and physicians. More prospered as merchants. Some Catholics also ventured to New York, and they tended to be poorer. After 1815, their numbers began rising. The same pressures that drove the Ambroses from Bandon to London drove men and women from other parts of Ireland to New York. They came to labor. The same anti-Irish prejudice that the English embraced could be sensed in New York, the same seen and heard in the Rocks in Sydney, even if the poor Irish represented a small minority in the city. The working-class and Catholic Irish in New York acted, at this point, much like the beleaguered Irish minority in London. This did not mean they were polite. As in Wapping, they guarded their jobs against all competitors.[33]

The opening of the Erie Canal in 1825 had changed the complexion of New York and of the Irish in it. Before it, New York served as a trading town, with a hinterland reaching as far up the Hudson River as Albany. Trade came from around the world, to be sure, but its size and might could not match that of London. Or even Sydney, with a hinterland that now stretched to the fertile interior. New York's turn had come. The canal, built by Irish navvies, tied New York to the whole Midwest, giving it a hinterland that surpassed that of London and Sydney. The produce of a continent would now make its way on the canal to the Hudson and then downriver to a city that would soon be the commercial capital of what would be called with good reason the "Empire State." New York City was destined to become the center of a vast American empire stretching out to the West, and it would flourish because of it. And the Irish, as had been the case in London and Sydney, would help build it.

Soon, the city attracted more and more Irish looking for work. It proved an irresistible magnet for those whose labor was undervalued in Ireland. That's why the man known as Ambrose was there. One way or another, he was destined to work with his hands.[34] "The Irish labourers are found uncommonly handy and active," an Irish middle-class émigré wrote, "and for years have a large portion of their work on canals and turnpikes."[35]

By the time he left Sag Harbor and arrived in 1840, the Irish, mostly Catholic and working-class now, represented a minority, to be sure, but a sizable one, all because the nation was growing, just as the East End of London had and Sydney was. As in both of these other places, the Irish would not easily be pushed around. Bringing with them traditions of ritualized violence, they would make the best fighters in the exploding city.[36]

He had made it to the other side of the world and away from his trials in Ireland, England, and Australia. The days of being a victim, of being Francis Ambrose, were over. In New York, he would take on a new identity. And a new name: James Yankee Sullivan.

He never gave us a reason why. However, there are clues. Let's start with the surname. "Sullivan" was and still is the most popular surname in Munster and third in all of Ireland. It is a name especially associated with West Cork.[37] To be born a Sullivan there is like being a Jones in Wales or a MacDonald in Scotland. The name would allow for anonymity should he need it. Moreover, more and more people bore the name in New York at the time he arrived there. It might have been exotic in, say, the 1810s, but not anymore. With the canal, and with the demand for physical labor, Sullivans abounded. For an escaped convict, one who wanted to hide, Sullivan proved the perfect sobriquet. Finding a Sullivan in New York, just like in London or Sydney, would be like trying to find a needle in a haystack of needles.

But he had no intention of hiding. Sullivan also spoke to defiance. Think of the Sullivans who had intersected with his life. A James Sullivan was a neighbor in Bandon and maybe a kinsman. The boy with that name had been the godson of Francis's father, John Ambrose. The tough character who refused to ask for mercy after beating a beak in Whitechapel had the name James Sullivan. The boy with that name who also made the trek to Chatham and the hulk. Then there's the Irishman who killed the overseer in Moreton Bay, just before the fifteen-year-old from Bandon would arrive at the hellhole. He was called Patrick Sullivan. But also, apparently, James Sullivan. In choosing the name James Sullivan, he might have been making a statement, one that spoke to his multifarious and hard past but also to those who would not bend their necks. The name, in any event, suited him.

So too did Yankee. He had been in "Yankeeshire," as Deaf Burke would say, for all of a few weeks before he called himself Yankee. It took a great deal of "bottom" to do so, to use a contemporary colloquial term for gumption or heart. One reckons the New Yorkers must have had a laugh when they heard the man with the mixed-up West Cork, Cockney accent, tinged further in Australia, call himself Yankee.

Why Yankee? On the Bowery in those days, just a five-minute walk from the saloons and piers on Water Street on the East River, one could stroll to see any number of popular shows. The same was true of Chatham Street and Park Place, other popular destinations within easy walking distance of Water Street. These offered a mix of musical, monologue, comedy, and melodrama, and were designed for the workingmen and -women who lived in the teeming area. Many of these shows at this very moment featured a stock character called "the Yankee." In the 1830s and 1840s, Americans had a mania for "Yankee Theatre." Americans, and New Yorkers in particular, took the anti-British trope of the Yankee and turned it into a term of strength and endearment and a point of pride. The Yankee was anti-British to his bones and proud to call himself a republican and a democrat. He strutted on the stage, daring others to take him on. He was boastful, perpetually sporting a chip on his shoulder. He proved cleverer than any adversary. He believed in toppling kings and in the rights of the common men. He was an individual who could choose his destiny, a child of the revolutionary age when ordinary people grasped the opportunity to claim their God-given rights and challenge their overlords. And the Yankee was a fighter and certainly not a victim. Think of Natty Bumppo. He was a Yankee-like character, and writers like Cooper and Melville introduced Americans to this type of persona. The Yankee was an idealized version of what it meant to be an American. The ideal appealed especially to those who worked with their hands for a living. No man was better than them.[38] The name amounted to a rejection of all that had happened to Francis Ambrose.

At the very moment that the man who would call himself Sullivan was finding his way in the new city, an actor called George Hill was perfecting the Yankee character. Others took to calling him "Yankee" Hill. He traveled the Northeast, and even went to London a few times to perform, but New York had become his home base. He performed in all sorts of plays that cast him as a Vermonter, a New Jerseyite, a Mainer—all essentially the same part. The Yankee arrived in the big city as the epitome of American nationhood that was born through the age of revolution. Americans could not get enough of the Yankee; nor could the British, who eyed the upstart character with fascination. He was the new man of a new age.[39]

That Sullivan would call himself Yankee seemed almost overdetermined. A play called *Sam Patch, the Yankee Jumper* appeared just around the time the man who had been Ambrose landed in New York. It had toured the Midwest, where it became a smash hit. The play then arrived on the Bowery. It chronicled the life of a real-life folk hero who tossed himself down waterfalls. Sam Patch entranced the country and became a model for American democracy. In one rendering, Sam was picked out of the water by a whaling captain. Patch stood with the outcast and the disaffected. The persona Patch adopted was perfectly in line with that perfected by Yankee Hill.[40]

In an age that seemed to offer so much promise to common men, Francis Ambrose had known none of it. In Bandon, he was on the wrong side of history, a Catholic in an Ireland bound to the British Crown. His Protestant neighbors reminded him, despite growing opportunity, that he remained a croppy, and mobility and labor were the only tools he had. In London, he lived in a Britain before common people had any real rights. Democracy had not reached the East End by the time he was arrested. Australia? That goes without saying. Here he toiled as a convict, and the only freedom he tasted were the days when he was on the lam. Even on the whalers, his escape vehicles, he knew no rights. On these, captains ruled like kings, and a ship was a "monarchy in miniature," even if the men had some power through their ability to abscond. The age of revolution had not reached these ships.[41] Whatever the drawbacks, Yankeeshire seemed different than any place he had lived. Even an Irish Catholic was a man, a son of the promising age. Here he could be self-made and self-actualizing.

On the face of it, the name "Yankee Sullivan" had an incongruous ring to it. Earlier versions of Yankee plays on the Bowery could and did contrast the Yankee with Irishmen.[42] The name tied together an almost stereotypically Irish name to something unapologetically American. And yet he was really neither and both. Nevertheless, the name had advantages. It would allow him to work two proverbial sides of the street if he so desired, or along two registers, fashioning himself as he saw fit in a world that increasingly demanded that men and women define themselves as one thing and not another. The new man was too crafty for that. The years ahead would demonstrate his ability to shape-shift as his situation required.

So, fittingly, he took on a new persona in New York. Francis Ambrose had died. He was resurrected as James Yankee Sullivan. He was, like so many others, "the essential American," a man who was, as D. H. Lawrence observed, "hard, isolate, stoic and a killer." He would not take another name for as long as he lived.

Things looked so promising in New York. But he would not stay. Yet, that is. He had unfinished business to attend to.

ROUND 9

Liverpool

NO SOONER HAD he rebranded himself Yankee Sullivan in New York than he took off for England. The choice to return would appear puzzling. English authorities did not know James Sullivan, but to them Francis Ambrose had skipped out of Australia as an escaped convict. If the police recaptured him, he would be off in chains to Sydney again, then to be dispatched to yet another place like Moreton Bay. Did he want to take a chance and visit his family? Did he want to sink into anonymity in the East End of London and live in the shadows?

Well, he did not go to London. He left New York City after just weeks and perhaps a few fights with a new identity for the city of Liverpool. Police also patrolled Liverpool. But the common people there—as is the case now—did not really heed what officials said. The place teemed with expendables like him. It was a city of the defiant for the defiant. Tellingly, some Liverpudlians claim, even today, "We are not English, we are Scouse." The very term "Scouse," a term of derision to mock the poor of the city, is one Liverpool people embrace to define themselves.[1] So it was in 1840.

He was not heading there as a tourist. He was traveling of his own accord to Liverpool to train and to fight. New York at this point had little to offer Yankee Sullivan. England was still the center of the prizefighting world, and Liverpool had grown into a fight center in its own right. Liverpool provided an opportunity to take the raw skills he had acquired during his apprenticeship in Australia and refine them. He had a craft, and in the competitive world he moved through, it was the only saleable commodity he possessed. He headed to Liverpool to learn and to step onto the stage.

He also went for another reason, one much more prosaic. Liverpool was where the ships from New York headed. For a New Yorker, going to England entailed sailing to Liverpool. London had become the great port of the British Empire. Liverpool specialized in the Atlantic trade. Far west of London, it sat on a wide and navigable river, the Mersey, that flowed into the Irish Sea and thus directly into the Atlantic approaches. The trade from New York was becoming so critical for England that ship lines had established regular sailing schedules. This was new. Normally ships left when the hold and passenger manifests were filled. So a traveler could wait days or even weeks before leaving the docks on the East River. But trade between the two was growing in importance, and because global finance and business depended on reliability, set sailing schedules were demanded. Now ships that could sail quickly were plying the route. Packet ships were the Concordes of the day, making the run from New York to Liverpool and back again at an astonishing speed. The fastest were doing the route in fifteen days, though they almost all did it fewer than thirty, about half the time of regular crossings.[2]

Time on this route was money. The Black Ball Line, so called because the pennants on its ships featured a large black dot, started running a service while Sullivan lived in London. While he was plotting his escape from Australia, competitors, such as the Red Star Line, had already emerged to make the route even more regularized. The ships came and went from one of the wooden docks by Peck Slip. With the explosive growth of New York after the opening of the Erie Canal, the city had become the chief North American entrepôt. It bound not only the Midwest to the Atlantic, but with its shipping prowess, it also tied the South to the Atlantic. All of America, it seemed, was funneled into the shabby docks on the East River on the island of Manhattan, and increasingly the funnel emptied into the Atlantic and thence Liverpool.

These ships transported mail, but they also carried more precious cargo. In the holds went all sorts of products, but one mattered more than anything else: cotton. This product of the South was grown on plantations and picked by the enslaved in places from Georgia to East Texas. Planters sent the bailed cotton to New York, where it was held in warehouses and then loaded into ships, destined for Liverpool and finally the industrial mills of England's North, where it was woven into fabric. Few, if any, in New York reckoned with the human costs of this exploitative trade. Certainly not the men doing the hauling and stowing, most of them Irish. And not the masters of the Black Ball Line. They supplemented the shipping of cotton with the passenger trade. If someone wanted to go to London, they had to head first to Liverpool on these ships.

All Sullivan had to do was saunter down to the docks on the East River and procure a passage. He had his choice of ships.

He more than likely sailed on a ship called the *President*. Or rather sailed and steamed. The *President* was something new: a transatlantic steamship. It was one of the largest ships in the world and billed as one of the fastest. Sullivan left on November 11. Chances are he worked his way across, perhaps shoveling coal to stoke the engines. Of course, he would have had good experience working on a ship and heaving coal. The trip took sixteen days. Parenthetically, and once again confirming his status as a near-Jonah, a few months after his trip the ship would go down in a gale. All aboard would be lost at sea.[3]

Sullivan's trip, though, came off uneventfully. But even a year earlier, a passenger could find it tough going. A New York swell reported that the weather tended toward the "chilling and gloomy" on his crossing. One man was swept overboard. All complained of seasickness. And those were the good days. On the rougher ones, he reported a "wide and flashing thundering sea—the alternate roar and subsiding howl of the wind ringing in the ear like an unearthly knell—the creaking of the rigging, the loud and angry flapping of so many loose sails, the straining of the timbers and the abrupt and violent plunging of the vessel—all united to form a scene startling to the stoutest landsman's nerves." He sighed, "A man that has made but one voyage in a packet is as much to be avoided as the man who has read but one book." Then there was the tedium. "Cards—cards—cards—the alpha and omega of packet ship life," he lamented. The fellow passengers? "It would be easier to hang them," he deadpanned. Shipboard life made men equals. He preferred the "English to be English, Yankees, Yankees"—in other words, a world of clear boundaries. For all of his bellyaching, they made the crossing in twenty-one days.[4] Sullivan would have laughed at the traveler's complaints. He had seen much worse on a ship.

The journey represented a small step for Sullivan but a bigger step for humanity. He had accomplished something few, if any, ordinary men who did not earn their livings at sea had. He had now circumnavigated the globe. He did the first leg as a refugee from Ireland. The next legs came under compulsion, as a convict and as an escapee. Now he sailed the final one across the Atlantic as a free man, a Yankee. He chose this journey. In his most autobiographical novel, *Redburn,* Herman Melville wrote that "sailors only go *round* the world, without going *into* it." Sullivan had accomplished both.

He turned up in Liverpool, as early as we can tell, around the end of November 1840, just weeks after he arrived at Sag Harbor. He clearly was a man who knew what he wanted and who was making up for lost time. He was nearly twenty-eight years old, really getting on for a pugilist, even one who had done so much fighting inside and outside the ring. If he wanted to make a splash, he had to move. When he arrived, he came to a place that would answer his needs and that he was well prepared to appreciate. Liverpool distilled all of his previous experience.

It had the feel of London and New York. "This busy city," a visitor argued, "will in time rival London—in some particulars it is already superior—in the rapidity with which it can procure American and Indian goods." Liverpool was "Close and damp—and with more constant noise than I think has ever been in any town—How there can be such a constant supply of carts moving from six in the morning till eleven at night I can't imagine, but it is unceasing."[5] An American who paid a visit couldn't help saying, "The appearance of Liverpool has something similar to New York." The hustle and bustle but also the shipping reminded him of what New York was on the verge of becoming.[6] Maria Edgeworth, the Irish novelist, was amazed at the city. Through a window on her boat she had a "view of almost a fleet of sail vessels and steamers going out." On top of the ocean-bound traffic, canal boats, barges, and steamers were plying the Mersey, leaving every fifteen minutes to the opposite shore. "Man and woman are perpetual motion engines," she exclaimed. Here were goods and people "from all parts of the world."[7]

Melville agreed. He had traveled there when younger on a merchant ship. Much of what he recalled appeared in *Redburn.* In that novel, he compared Liverpool to London and New York. The Mersey had a feel of South Street in New York, especially all the warehouses. Looks, however, deceived. Liverpool had no shabby wharves. The docks he beheld "were mighty," akin to "a chain of immense fortresses." London envied Liverpool. "Even London," he declared, "was induced to copy after Liverpool."[8] Liverpool engineers had developed the world's leading dock systems. The docks worked like those basins built for trade on the East End of London, only on a larger scale. The docks could hold dozens of ships at a time, without concerns about tide.

Like New York and London, Liverpool was unsympathetically constructed for connection. It was a city made by the slave trade, and it transitioned easily to the industrial age. Men worked the docks at a frenetic pace, all to get goods and bodies in and to get them out.[9] New York was not as developed as Liverpool. London had to retrofit dock systems into established neighborhoods along the river. Liverpool just built and built the most innovative docks to handle more and more traffic. It was designed for one thing, and because of this, it was tailor-made for growth and innovation.[10] Farther and farther up the river with each new year docks were constructed. Along the Mersey, the viewer "beheld long China walls of masonry; vast piers of stone; and a succession of granite-rimmed docks, completely enclosed." The place bustled as thousands of laborers worked, men shouted instructions, and longshoremen went about their business on docks and in warehouses noted for "magnitude, cost, and durability." Everything here systematized movement.[11] With time, the wet-dock complex would extend seven miles down the Mersey.[12]

The connections to the global economy did not end there. A train line built in 1830 and specially made for the traffic took the cotton to mills in Manchester. With time the line would be tied into others eventually connecting to London itself and to other industrial hubs north of the capital. The dyad of Liverpool and "Cottonopolis," as Manchester was called, was built of the very stuff of modern industrial capitalism: worldwide oceanic networks; a well-connected group of entrepreneurs; a general spirit of improvement; new technologies; and a ruthless exploitation of labor both far away, such as the enslaved, and closer to home, such as the desperate, the opportunistic, and the uprooted. The energy that created and sustained the industrial revolution, and the railroad, tied these two places together and made them what they were.[13]

Liverpool served as the chief node that tied Ireland to Britain, because of its proximity to Irish ports on the Irish Sea, and to the broader

Atlantic. In fact, Liverpool was the most Irish city Sullivan had visited, at least up to this point in his life. Irish traffic abounded and moved through there, as would its people. The Irish who came as migrants arrived at Clarence Dock, which was going up just as Yankee arrived. The dock had been the first port of call for Irish seasonal laborers, who arrived in England to work on farms and then return home, akin to the migrant laborers who work in California's orchards today. Increasingly, though, many were using the dock as a stopover. They could head just a quarter mile to their right as they passed through the gates of the Clarence Dock and see the ships bound for New York at the newly built Waterloo Dock where Sullivan more than likely landed.

To survive entailed mobility, and Liverpool was the modern world's symbol of that. People here were continually on the move, coming and going, landing and leaving. The city served as the modern world's revolving door, connecting Ireland and part of England to the global economy. Routes had long existed tying Ireland to England, like the ones through Bristol that bound Cork to London. With the shift to free trade and the growth of empire, Liverpool amalgamated much of the work done by other ports. It became a port on an industrial scale to match a new age of political economy.[14]

The many pasts of Francis Ambrose intersected here. Liverpool buzzed with different peoples from different areas of the earth, but the Irish were overrepresented.[15] If he had been a regular Irish immigrant, Sullivan would have established himself in an Irish enclave by the Old Docks by Cleveland Square, very near the Albert Docks that would rise just after he left. Those Irish who stayed tended to perform the casual and menial labor needed to make this entrepôt function. They were served by the newly built St. Patrick's Chapel, filled with Irish in the pews and English Catholic priests on the altar. It was just a few years old when Sullivan arrived.

Liverpool shared a number of things in common with Bandon, most of which were brought over by migrants. Orange Lodges proliferated as more Irish came in, both Protestant and Catholic, especially during the 1830s. Their woes and animosities followed them. Sectarianism dogged them. Secret societies followed them, as did faction fighting.[16]

For all of its newness, Liverpool must have felt like Whitechapel to him. Here, once more, lay modernity's underbelly. However cosmopolitan Liverpool had become, it also was noted for its poverty, its beggars, and those who seemed to have alighted in the city only to die in its alleys and behind its warehouses. "These are haunts," Melville found, "in which cursing, gambling, pickpocketing, and common iniquities are virtues too lofty for the infected gorgons and hydras to practice." Sullivan must have been brought back to the days of Francis Ambrose on Petticoat Lane.[17]

One other aspect of Liverpool culture also had to resonate with him. Many of the men he had suffered with in Australia had also hailed from Liverpool. And many of these, in turn, were Irish Liverpudlians. These sorts would punctuate a great deal of his life to come, as we shall see. These, as much as Londoners or Irishmen, established the culture of Australia.[18] Sections of Liverpool had to remind him a great deal of the Rocks, in fact. Like the Rocks, as Irish numbers grew with the movement of people like Sullivan, this group became more assertive, certainly more so than in London.

All this was very creative and edgy, but it was also frightening and violent. Liverpool was a city that unapologetically was designed for what the world was becoming. Nathaniel Hawthorne, visiting in 1854, marveled at the sort of people this city produced. Liverpudlians, he wrote, possessed a "perfect coolness and independence."[19] Yankee Sullivan, in other words, fit right in.

Sullivan was in the right spot to fight. As even Margaret Thatcher would concede, Liverpool is a "city possessed with a particularly violent nature."[20] Such was certainly the case when Sullivan arrived. The chieftain of prizefighting in Liverpool was a former champion and Irishman named Jack Langan. Langan had enjoyed a great deal of acclaim in the 1820s, when Ambrose was young. He had fought and lost the championship to a terrific fighter named Tom Spring. As Maria Edgeworth reported, the loss stung Dublin, leading an old woman she encountered to wonder what would happen to "Paddy's Land."[21] Langan had left the fight game behind by the time Sullivan arrived in Liverpool. But he still loomed larger than life in the city. In fact, when Sullivan landed, one of the first things he would have seen across from the docks was a bar run by Jack Langan. Above the door, he had placed a statue of St. Patrick. He also speculated in cattle, which no doubt came from Ireland at the Clarence Docks outside his door, and he had a hand in the liquor trade, making him wealthy.[22] By 1840, Langan had become a fixture in Liverpool, where he styled himself a patron of St. Patrick's Chapel and of the Irish in the sectarian city.[23]

The form of fighting here could be rugged. Brutality marked it. Head-butting, nose-biting, and kicking were sometimes deemed within bounds. So too skulduggery.[24] Liverpool had for a long time been a fistic satellite of London; however, by the time of Sullivan's arrival, that was changing. The center of gravity was shifting away from London after a few boxing scandals, a more robust policing of the fight game, and the shriveling up of aristocratic patronage and the Fancy—along with the consequent difficulty of raising stakes. With the rise of evangelical piety and middle-class values, officials began cracking down on prizefighting, shunting it to the hinterland. In a few places, like Liverpool, where rural Irish were settling, the fight game still seemed to thrive. Liverpool had become "the metropolis of milling."[25]

Sullivan did not seek out the great Langan, though they had run into each other and knew one another.[26] He came here to work with another English Irishman closer in age and in experience to him, the great Jem Ward. Like Francis Ambrose, of course, Ward had grown up on the East End of London and whipped coal for a living. It was in the capital he made his reputation. Afterward, he moved to Liverpool, just as the mania for the fight game in London had begun to ebb.

Why take on Sullivan? He came to the metropolis of milling as an "unknown in the pugilistic circles," as a report in Britain's boxing bible, *Bell's Life in London*, put it.[27] But maybe not. The networks that brought convicts to Australia, and wool from Australia, also carried word of pugilism. Prizefighting, too, was bound into the imperial system. There were convict and pugilistic ties between Liverpool and Australia, especially in the person of Paddy Sinclair, an Irishman who fought in Liverpool before going Down Under.[28] Perhaps "Ginger" was known. But more than likely, he sought out Ward and told him who he was and what experience he had. One reckons that Ward put him through his paces in the ring and discovered he had a talent on his hands. And a hard man. Sullivan had to have impressed him. He, no doubt, played upon his East London connections with Ward and shared his many experiences. He certainly looked the part. Whatever the reason, Ward took him under his wing to join what amounted to a finishing school for fighting.[29]

Jem turned Sullivan over to train side-by-side with his younger brother Nick. Nick had just bested Deaf Burke in a controversial decision for fifty pounds a side at Oxfordshire and was scheduled to take on a giant named Ben Caunt for an English championship. Despite his record, Nick Ward was no Jem. Jem had "bottom," or heart. Nick possessed little of it. When it came to prizefighting, he proved a disappointment, once, for instance, walking away from a fight in the middle of it. As a sporting paper put it, "he has a very strong antipathy to punishment which can be avoided." Nonetheless, Nick was regarded as a first-rate sparrer. He had learned the finer points in sparring clubs in London before entering the prize ring. He knew how to defend and to move. He also understood ring strategy, even if he could not put it into practice himself.[30]

There was a great deal to absorb. Jem and Nick Ward specialized in the finer points. As Ginger, Sullivan had learned about the craft in the devolved world of the Rocks and the Australian frontier. One newspaper report suggested that he was made of good raw material but remained unrefined. Sullivan appeared "rough and ready, with a tolerable knowledge of the art of self-defence." The Wards—his "East End pals," as the paper put it—would fix that. His "fierceness and wildness," and certainly his evident bottom could be cultivated into craft through "his induction to the mysteries of the English ring."[31] Both Wards had learned at the center, and Jem had adopted the scientific style of Mendoza, only with a twist. The Wards were not above pushing rules and boundaries almost to the breaking point. Nick Ward would teach Sullivan not only the craft he had not been exposed to but how to take advantage of what the laws of boxing prescribed. For instance, one was not supposed to just drop to end a round. A round ended, of course, when someone hit the deck, but the rules presupposed that one fell after a blow or when one was flipped by a cross-buttock. Feigning to be hit, or to "slip" and fall, or to be pulled down by the momentum of one's punch, the Wards preached, was fair game. Doing this allowed the cagey fighter to dictate the terms of the fight and set the pace. Both Wards taught that fighting presupposed gamesmanship.[32]

Jem Ward owned a gym in Williamson Square, just steps from the docks and close to the chief Irish ghetto in the city and St. Patrick's Chapel. He hosted a stable of fighters there, and Yankee became one of them. Ward ran his fighters out of a pub on Williamson Square called the Star.[33]

Sullivan bopped between this and a place run by another disciple of the Wards, a fighter named Peter Taylor, "on the Cheshire side of the Mersey," that is, just across the river from Liverpool by Birkenhead, another Irish enclave and a shipbuilding center like Chatham. He would have been very much at home here. Taylor also had a public house on Williamson Square, so Sullivan found himself in the very heart of the Liverpool Fancy.[34]

Jem and Nick had worked their magic after only a few weeks. A sporting newspaper declared Sullivan in "excellent trim," having "trained with Nick Ward, under the able superintendence of Peter Taylor, of Liverpool." He was described by those who saw him train as "an out-and-outer." That must have been an understatement. Sullivan, it seems, had been in the best of hands.[35]

Still, the Fancy wondered who this Sullivan was. A "knowing cove" was someone who had the inside scoop. Knowing comprised a key aspect of the culture of pugilism. It also helped when it came to wagering. The coves were perplexed. *Bell's Life* reported that one of its readers asked if Sullivan was African American, like Molineaux or Richmond. The newspaper set him straight: "Sullivan, the Yankee, is not black." No one, outside his trainers, could guess anything more. "We know nothing of Sullivan's performances as a pugilist," the paper said, all of which he tried to keep quiet about. The less said about Australia, as far as Sullivan was concerned, the better. He was "described as a Yankee, but we suspect he dates his birthplace nearer home." At least they were right on that score. "He is an unknown in the London ring," the paper concluded.[36] Soon the world would discover what he could do. On January 24, *Bell's Life* wrote that Sullivan would be giving a benefit at Queen's Theatre, also on Williamson Square, in Liverpool. There, undoubtedly, he would spar. Jem and Nick Ward would assist him in the ring, and many of the leading fistic lights would turn out.[37]

Going to Liverpool may have seemed like stepping back into his past. But in the present, Sullivan was well served by training there. Yankee Sullivan had come to the right place to master the craft. It explains why, after having survived Australia, he left the evident promise of New York. All he needed now was a fight and some notoriety. The Wards could help with both.

ROUND 10

Crookham Common

IN 1841, THE MAN who had been Francis Ambrose exploded into the historical record as Yankee Sullivan. In that year, he emerged out of the shadows as fully formed. Now for the first time, he stepped outside of the bounds imposed by official records—census, criminal, vital, and a few snippets—and we can bear witness to what those years in Bandon, Whitechapel, and Australia did to him, as well as his stint in Liverpool with Jem Ward.

No longer furtive, he had a new name and had secured an identity, that most modern of appendages. He was a somebody after years of being the victim. He added to that a craft that had value in the worlds he moved through.

A fight accomplished all this.

The Wards connected him to members of the London Fancy, who had the ability to pull off a fight even when authorities were cracking down. Although Sullivan prepared for a bout in the Liverpool area, his appearance in the prize ring would be under the auspices of the London Fancy. The money wasn't what it used to be, but fighters still enjoyed a market. Jem Ward approached a matchmaker and promoter named Owen Swift, another Londoner, to get something arranged. Ideally, they were looking for "any eleven stone man in England," that is, around 150 pounds, to meet Sullivan.[1] Swift was the man to make a match. He had fought in the ring as a lightweight and was considered a man of "matchless science."[2] He then became a publican and ran a bar on Haymarket. The fight Swift proposed would be part of a twin bill. Before Sullivan's match, Nick Ward would take on Ben Caunt, a tall, lumbering fighter.[3] As an unknown, Yankee was on the undercard.

The opponent would be a fellow named John Lane. Lane was a "powerful" man and "terrible" fighter, meaning fearsome. He went by the nickname "Hammer," making him almost a product of the Industrial Revolution. Appropriately, he came from Birmingham.[4] Birmingham specialized in hard things like hammers and drop hammers, and in hard men like Lane. It was an industrial juggernaut of blast furnaces and mills, producing all sorts of things for consumers and for the building of infrastructure. Lane's father had worked, appropriately enough, in a foundry as "an iron-plate and hammer-maker."[5] Lane was known as a hard-hitter. So, he came by the nickname "Hammer" honestly. A "star of the Birmingham school," he "was regarded as a man of no common talent." He carried an almost perfect record. He weighed in at 150, ideal for a match. Even better, everyone in the know knew him. "His style of fighting [was] scientific and effective," and he was "popular."[6]

Most assumed Sullivan would be outmatched. Hammer was considered "one of the best of his weight." Sullivan? "It was thought that Sullivan would not have a shadow of a chance," a detailed account ran.[7] Still, the men who set up the fight knew what they gleaned from hearing about him and seeing him. "He is stated to be a Yankee," the paper covering the event wrote, "but we are inclined to believe he is an Eastender; like Jem Ward of Irish parents." His looks gave him away. "Although he may deny his parentage," the account continued, he appeared "very like a Connemara ram."[8] No mention was made of Australia, though the paper did say he had improved his craft "in foreign climes," before sailing to America for a short stay.

Next they had to set up a place for the fight. There was nothing easy about this, especially in the days when the fight game did not enjoy royal or aristocratic favor. With no protection, promoters had to search for places deeper in the country. The need to go to remote spots spoke of the changes to the fight game since Francis Ambrose had left London. Then, it was near its zenith; now, it had reached its nadir. As England became more developed, those pastimes that spoke to an earlier, more barbaric world had little place. Officials policed more vigilantly. The need to find something out of the way was heightened by the fact that the man running the show was Owen Swift. Swift had killed two men in the ring, leading to a reform of the old rules that governed boxing and that Francis

James Alias Yankee Sullivan, ca. 1846. (Library of Congress, Prints and Photographs Division, LC-DIG-pga-04356)

Ambrose had fought under in Australia.[9] Also adding disrepute was none other than Jem Ward, who had caused an uproar among the Fancy and the fight game's detractors for throwing a fight.

The promoters chose a distant place called Crookham Common. Crookham Common was in the middle of nowhere. And that was the point. It was a dark, isolated corner where even in progressive England the state would not have been able to reach and where police would not hound them. There were fewer and fewer spaces like it. It's not that the changing world had left it behind; rather, it had not yet really visited in earnest. It sat on the edge of a county, smack next to two others, a jurisdictional limbo, making it challenging for authorities to crack down on what transpired there.

That said, it could not be too far away. People still had to attend, and the terms of the fight dictated that it had to be held within striking distance of London. Thankfully, an expanding rail system allowed interested parties to get near the place. Most coming from London could take what would become the Great Western Railway to Reading, a length which had just been completed.[10] Men such as Sullivan and Lane, workingmen, had constructed both railroads and canals. The deeper and deeper these transportation lines reached into the country, that much more of the country was drawn into an increasingly integrated rail system. Nonetheless, Crookham Common still sat on the edge of that developing grid. From the rail station, they had to find coaches, and then had to walk up the heath. From Liverpool, the trip presented even more difficulties, one involving a limited amount of rail, perhaps a canal or two, a coach drawn by horses, and some walking. But it was immensely easier to get there than it would have been only ten years earlier. All roads, and increasingly railroads, led to Liverpool and to London.

The train, that new marvel, had quickly been adopted by the Fancy to bring fights to far-off places. The first rail-fights took place just around this time. And this one at Crookham Common would be among the first.[11] That said, the choice of this hard-to-reach, but not-too-far-off spot suggests how prizefighting and civility were in a race, with the railroad as the chief vehicle. Behind the iron horse came civilizing influences and reform, as well as organized police forces.[12] Prizefighting seemed to represent a barbarous past that needed to be pushed farther and farther away and that, hopefully in the eyes of the middle class, could be done away with. Ironically, in this brief window of time, pugilism now relied on that very symbol of a new industrial age to remain viable in Britain.

On the open heath in Berkshire, near Buckinghamshire and Oxfordshire, Sullivan was a long way from Yankeeshire, and the oddsmakers made him the underdog. The London Fancy had turned out in force, if not for this match, at least for the first one. Nick Ward beat Ben Caunt on a technicality. Ward claimed Caunt hit him while he was down, a disqualifying foul, but a result that somehow smelled.

On the day Lane and Sullivan met, snow lay on the ground, and the first fight and the rising temperatures had mucked up the ground. Then Sullivan and Lane came into the ring. The two followed the prescribed rituals to a T. They threw their hats in. The combatants entered, followed by their seconds. Next came the colors. This was something new, a part of the "New Rules" they would fight under.[13] The colors said something vital about the fighter. They had to be tied to a post holding up the ropes of the ring.

The *New York Times* would later remark how in one of his fights in England, Sullivan "went into the ring with the American flag wrapped around his loins."[14] Such a move on Sullivan's part would have made some sense. But evidence suggests that he did not do so on the day of the fight. This would be his only English prizefight, and commentators at the time made no mention of an American flag, though they certainly called him Yankee. Maybe he brought American flags into sparring sessions and exhibitions. That could have been the case. If Yankee had come in brandishing the flag during a spar, it would have served his purposes. He needed and wanted to be noticed, and waving the Stars and Stripes would help promote the bout and stir interest. Boasting and preening were part of the culture of the ring, as well as how common men found voice. More importantly, being an American made him a perfect foil. The United States and Britain did not yet enjoy a "special relationship." More often than not, their diplomats clashed over foreign policy and over tariffs. Claiming himself as an American probably earned him a shot in a big fight against Lane. The flag would have allowed him to stress the American side of the name.

For this fight—his lone venture in the ring in England—the Stars and Stripes did not make an appearance. He chose something a bit more conventional and tending toward the Irish end of the name spectrum. Sullivan tied his colors to a post, "a green throttle-squeeze," or a scarf, "with yellow spots." Lane chose purple with a yellow border.

The Hammer seemed happy-go-lucky, laughing and chumming it up with the onlookers, displaying "a playful, devil-may-care confidence." Sullivan appeared angry and severe, "as grave as a mustard pot" and "as fierce as a deviled kidney." Little did they know that his look matched his persona.

Then they stripped. The newspaper covering the event made no remarks about the marks on Sullivan's back from his many floggings. No mention was made of the tattoos, but they had no doubt faded. Still, "Yankee looked a very ugly customer indeed," a popularizer put it later, at five foot ten and "in first-rate condition." Moreover, "his face was a thorough Irish one, not handsome but indicative of dogged and almost savage courage." This writer claimed that Sullivan impressed the crowd when he took off his shirt. Nonetheless, a contemporary report read that the odds changed in the moments before the fight from 2 to 1 for Lane, to 5 to 3, and even 3 to 1. Lane's jauntiness and reputation probably account for this, as well as the fact that he was skilled, experienced, and a known commodity. Maybe the oddsmakers mistook Sullivan's trapped anger for nerves.[15] He was ready, whatever the odds suggested.

It started at 4:22 p.m. From the get-go, Sullivan was the aggressor. He threw a left, which Hammer "prettily stopped." Hammer countered with a one-two, a left jab followed by a right cross. Sullivan blocked both. Sullivan, then, waited for Lane to come to him. They exchanged some blows, but none with great effect. The first round revealed a great many things to the onlookers. "There was nothing novice in his pretensions," they saw. Sullivan was counterpunching from the start, seeing what Lane threw and adapting to it. He started the match with his arms up, in a defensive, almost turtle-like position. Years later, the great trainer of Mike Tyson, Cus D'Amato, would call this the "peek-a-boo" style. He did not at this point employ the tactics of the Wards. He was fighting straight-up, all to show his skill and his toughness, and with poise. He was not rattled.

In the early rounds, Sullivan demonstrated defensive abilities. He was adept at blocking punches. He also drew first blood, as evidence by the "claret" from Lane's mouth. Sullivan's punches had smashed Lane's lips into "his ivories." Still, Lane had skills as well. He was using his left to great effect, popping out a quick jab which Sullivan sometimes caught and which sometimes caught him. By the fourth round, "the dials of both were painted." Sullivan tried to get in close to use uppercuts. Sullivan also prided himself on his wrestling abilities. Hammer, though, proved the physically stronger of the two.

The tide began to turn with an accident. On one throw, Hammer fell and caught his arm under Sullivan. He had injured this same arm in an earlier bout. Within a few rounds, it was apparent he was hurt. The injury worsened when Sullivan blocked two punches with "the points of his elbows." Lane could no longer throw his right. In a few rounds, it hung uselessly down by the side of his body. "The bone called the *radius,* was completely fractured," he learned later. Gamely, Lane continued, peppering Sullivan with lefts. Two, three, or even four at a go. Sullivan could not stop them. These must have been demoralizing, and Sullivans's face bled and swelled up. But he kept coming at Lane, making him fight off of the back foot. Still, Lane laughed as he went back to his corner as the rounds ended. His corner asked if the fight should be stopped. Lane refused, believing "he could lick him with one hand."

But it had to become clear that he would never finish the task. Sullivan seemed too determined. More importantly, the Yankee had adopted a strategy of enduring the punishment to get in close and hit Lane where it hurt. "Sullivan hit short at the lame arm," doing what his backers were screaming for him to do. He was putting up with the stiff lefts to get close to the hanging arm and then to hammer it.

Sullivan's East End pals bayed for blood, telling Sullivan to get in and finish the injured man. Sullivan, apparently, obliged. By the tenth round, Lane was going down to avoid punishment, while Sullivan was "boring in." It was clear there was no way that Lane could win as a one-handed fighter against an aggressive and determined Sullivan. The attacks were wearing Lane down. "Go in and fight," Sullivan's corner yelled, "he's got but one hand." Sullivan was biding his time and letting the injury do the work for him. In the eighteenth round, Sullivan stoned him with a shot to the left eye. The next round, Sullivan popped him again, and down Lane went again. He could not come to scratch for the twentieth.

The words became heated as well. "The manner in which Sullivan endeavored to inflict additional punishment upon Lane's disabled arm was strongly commented on," one account alleged.[16] Some charged, at this point, that Sullivan was spitting in Lane's face and mocking him. The spectators "laughed and jeered at the agony and gesticulation of Lane," a critic of the fight and of pugilism noted. "Such is the conduct of the professors of the manly art, which is to induce a generosity of feeling into the brawls of Englishmen," the critic added.[17] He had a point. Jem Ward was looking for a fight, and the rest of the Liverpool Fancy were intimidating the crowd. They engaged in "ruffianly conduct" and had come "armed with 'life protectors,' or rather 'destroyers.'"[18]

That Lane stood the hammering for that long is remarkable and testament to his bottom. "A more extraordinary display of British bravery never signalized the doings of the ring," the paper said in saluting Lane. Some claimed that if Lane had not broken his arm, he could have taken Yankee. Perhaps. But such counterfactuals could not obscure the fact that Sullivan was a legitimate fighter. He knew how to be cruel and insolent in a pursuit that rewarded both. In addition, he realized the advantage he had and proved willing to endure punishment to see it through. No one would doubt Sullivan's bottom, or his skill, for that matter. The onlookers came away with an appreciation for his abilities as an "adept," meaning someone who could devise tactics to suit the situation in real time. This required a calm and cool demeanor and great deal of confidence.

After the fights, the assembled trudged from the soggy, snowy heath to coaches that took them to Reading, where they could catch the new train to London, arriving just after 9:00 p.m. A number also took a circuitous route back to the capital, maybe to evade the "beaks of Hampshire" and the "badgers" of Berks. In any event, they went miles and miles out of their way to Bishop's Stortford before catching a train to Vauxhall. They were, no doubt, none the worse for wear after the visit. Bishop's Stortford had more breweries than nearly any other English town.[19]

The Fancy in Liverpool and in London had taken notice, and Sullivan's exploits made headlines. That is what he had hoped for. In newsprint and by word of mouth, the victory of Sullivan over Lane would travel by coach, and railroad, and by packet ship to those places in the world filled with men like Sullivan. It even made it to whaling ships. The London sporting press covered pugilism in Australia, in "Shamrockshire," and increasingly in "Yankee-land." New Yorkers had no real Fancy, no urban critical mass of workingmen, no real infrastructure for prizefighting. "The British Prize Ring," a popular wag put it, "did not take kindly to American soil."[20] But more and more were eager to learn what was happening in London. Yankee Sullivan had accomplished his mission. This fight against Lane appeared in the sporting press in London, still the center of global pugilism, and that round-by-round coverage made its way verbatim to New York.

After the fight, Sullivan took a chance, playing on his moment of celebrity to see family in London and to go to Ireland. He did not stay long in London, bolting the city even before he could collect his prize money at Young Dutch Sam's, the son of Dutch Sam and an excellent East End prizefighter in his own right.[21] Maybe he visited old haunts in Whitechapel. One supposes he spent time with his mother, father, and brothers. Reports circulated of how he attended a benefit in Liverpool—that is, a boxing exhibition—and that he did the same in Dublin, staying in a tavern right around Grafton Street. Maybe he drank at one of the bars the great Dan Donnelly had owned.[22]

Should he stay or should he go? Well, the choice was easy. He was on the lam, and word would get out about his past. His "East End pals" certainly knew of his history. Others would as well. The Fancy lived on knowledge, and if he were to stay, the "foreign climes" would become less fuzzy and appear for what they were. Should he fight again there, he would be known as the Yankee who beat Lane and who had, as rumor had it, slipped away from Sydney. He could not stay ahead of the law for long should this news spread, as it surely would.

Perhaps even more significantly, he had missed his moment in England. The golden age of prizefighting looked to be part of a rapidly receding past. Yes, more fights were taking place. But the police were cracking down, just as deep-pocketed patrons were finding other ways to spend their time and money. The industrial world demanded new habits on the part of the working class, and evangelical preachers hit this point hard.[23] Time, moving as if on a rail line, was passing it by. In America? Well, at least it would be safer in Yankeeshire, and the future of his craft looked brighter. Things there had not become quite so refined. So, from Dublin he traveled back to the entrepôt of Liverpool. He said his goodbyes to the Fancy there, and the men who helped him learn the finer points of the craft, and set out once again for his New World. New York would become the home of this Yankee, but he had accomplished what he wanted to on the trip across the Atlantic. He ventured back across the ocean as a celebrated prizefighter.

ROUND 11

The Five Points

In New York, Yankee Sullivan met his moment. So, too, did prizefighting. He, it, and the city arrived together. As New York was transitioning from a seaport to a global hub—that is, a behemoth on a London-like scale—interest in prizefighting exploded. Sullivan proved instrumental. New York in the 1840s suited Sullivan better than any place he had been. Perhaps more significantly, Sullivan suited New York. He seemed made for this place-in-time.

What follows is a tour of Sullivan's New York. Woven into the fabric of Yankee's New York were not only the man but also his craft. It's no coincidence that Sullivan and prizefighting hit the big time at the same moment. Sullivan arrived on this stage when the Irish stepped out of the shadows and became forces in the city, even before the Famine but accelerating with it. The trickle that grew into a flow went hand in hand with subtle shifts in how people organized work, just as it informed rivalries and tensions in New York. These entangled dynamics drove the creation of an emerging and vibrant—and violent and exclusionary—democratic urban culture. Prizefighting tied this tapestry together.

Yankee Sullivan reigned over it all. The Lane fight gave him credibility and a modicum of celebrity among the working class, which provided a platform for power just as New York reached the urban and cultural critical mass for prizefighting to take off.

He first had to figure out where to settle. Doing so did not prove difficult. There was only one place for the likes of him: the Five Points. The neighborhood sat just a short distance from the East River docks where he arrived once more, no more than a five- to ten-minute walk up Ferry

Street from Peck Slip. His first address was on Water Street, 316 to be exact, in the southern end of what was called the Ould Bloody Sixth, that is, the ward the Points fell within. It sat right under what are now the approaches to the Brooklyn Bridge, blocks away from the Hole in the Wall.

Sullivan knew this world. The Five Points bore a striking resemblance to Whitechapel. The Points had the same perplexing and enlivening mix of peoples and cultures. It also had about the poorest population in New York. As was the case with the East End of London, the better-off leveled the same sorts of criticisms at the denizens of the Points. "No decent person walked through it; all shunned the locality," a firefighter said. All were jammed into wooden tenements, living in filthy conditions. To outsiders it seemed a vice-ridden area of "tumbling and squalid rookeries."[1] It was, in short, another modern slum with all of its attendant ills. It was infested by what critics called "wharf rats" and "river pirates" and sinners of all descriptions. Children were neglected, and people lived hand to mouth.[2] Here was yet another place where the adjective "notorious" colored every description.[3] Sullivan caught sight of the same sorts of evangelicals looking to convert and remake the poorer sort in London and in Sydney. One, a Methodist woman, proclaimed just around the time he was there, "If there is a spot in the crowded city where vice reigns unchecked, surely all will

The Five Points, after George Catlin, 1827. (New York Public Library Digital Collections)

admit it to be in that vicinity." She asked, "Who can think of the hundreds born in sin, nurtured in misery, with no earthly prospect but the prison and the gallows, without a deep, unutterable yearning to snatch them from the fearful fate." Another lamented how New Yorkers faced the "herculean task of uplifting the wretched people at the Five Points." Needless to say, exactly as had been the case in London and in the Rocks, the denizens there "scorned" reformers.[4]

The same sorts of patronizing voices, in other words, that decried the "slums" of London characterized the Points as a den of iniquity. The neighborhood stood as the antithesis of the middle-class world that surrounded it, and the fact that it existed in close proximity to the police, the press, and the homes of reformers made it their favored target. Of course, the truth is more complex, and the Five Points consisted of men and women doing their best to live purposeful lives on the margins of the global capitalist economy. Even if this was another underbelly of the networked development that was now tying centers together around the world, the sort that Francis Ambrose had navigated in his earlier life, people still managed to get along and even thrive, despite the evident vice around them. It was, as much as the Rocks and Whitechapel, a complex place.[5]

When Sullivan returned triumphantly after the Lane fight, Dickens toured New York, and he saw the working-class neighborhood with middle-class eyes. London and New York struck Dickens as exactly alike, especially what he regarded as the slums. He saw the same mixture of people, the same poverty, and the same dysfunction. "A vast amount of good and evil is intermixed and jumbled up together," he found.[6] The Points was "the world of vice and misery," the home "of all that is loathsome." He was appalled by "these narrow ways, diverting to the right and left, and reeking everywhere with dirt and filth." He knew such places well and had spent nights touring them as a flaneur back home. The "bloated faces" he described he had seen before in London. He likened the people to walking pigs that should be grunting instead of talking. The mixing of Black and white in the area troubled him.[7] And here the Irish predominated, just as in London. Without the Irish, he argued, "it would be hard to keep your model republic going." In New York, he wondered, "Who else would dig and delve, drudge, and do domestic work, to make canals and roads, and executing great lines of Internal Improvements!"

All of this had taken shape quite suddenly just before Sullivan and Dickens landed. In forty years, from 1800 to 1840—just a year before Sullivan was to settle here—New York's population had jumped by 500 percent. It now reached over 300,000, all crammed into the southern tip of Manhattan.[8] The Five Points, the cheapest place to live, surged in numbers as well. Once, long before Sullivan arrived, the neighborhood had been an idyllic pond. As population grew, the pond had been contaminated by breweries and tanneries. The Collect Pond was then drained into the Hudson, via what would be called Canal Street. The land stank and was marshy, making it the least desirable place to live in Manhattan. The first people to live there in great numbers were African Americans, many of them the recently emancipated enslaved. Thereafter came the poor Irish. In 1830, over 17,000 Irish had called New York home. Within fifteen years, that number jumped to more than 90,000. Sullivan represented only one in a vast movement taking place before the Famine. With this substantial pre-Famine migration, the numbers of Catholics in New York also surged. The lion's share of these were the poor Irish.[9] Those who gravitated to the Five Points effectively made it an Irish Catholic ward.

Sullivan came to a part of the city that had just experienced convulsive riots. In the mid-1830s, a series of disturbances shook the Five Points. Devotees of rival political parties took to the streets to stake their claim to the Points. Whigs tore into supporters of Andrew Jackson and his Democrats in riots around election day. Many of the targets were Irish. But true to form, they fought back with ferocity. The violence of one of these riots, centering on an election and on keeping the Irish in their place, exceeded anything seen in New York before. A few months later, around Independence Day in 1834, a more serious series of riots destroyed much of the Five Points. The same Whigs attacked abolitionists and African Americans and more or less tore apart a church on Chatham Street, just a stone's throw from the Points, leading to a Black exodus. The disturbances may well have stemmed from fears of racial mixing and of how an impressive Black community had taken root in the area. The Irish, necessarily, were in the middle of this exodus, even if the anti-Black pogroms that marked the Points in 1834 were perpetrated predominantly by those native to the United States.[10] The Irish filled the vacuum of the Points. By the time Sullivan was walking its streets, the population of African Americans in the area had declined to 6 percent, half of what it had been before the riots of 1834. It would drop even further, to only 4 percent, while he was there.[11] Whether wittingly or unwittingly, the Irish were the beneficiaries of and accomplices to what we could call racial cleansing. The Blacks Dickens saw, and whom Sullivan lived around, were the remnants of what had been a vibrant community.

The difficulties that afflicted the neighborhood had been heightened in the years before he arrived. In 1835, a fire devastated the city, demonstrating once again how places constructed quickly and on the cheap were especially vulnerable to fire. Then, in 1837, the city experienced a financial panic. Banks failed as cotton brokerages in New Orleans went out of business and could not pay what they owed to New York merchants. A depression settled on all of the United States, but New York was hit especially hard. Bank collapses played against a backdrop of surging food and coal prices. Manufacturing stalled. With few social safety nets, those in places like the Points suffered more than most. Many of the poor had to enter almshouses. Some could not feed themselves. All of the work that the Irish and others in the Points were needed for dried up. "The Irish immigrant leans against his shanty, with his spade idle in his hand," an observer noted, "and starves." By 1841, things were rebounding, but the Panic of 1837 left an uneasy mark on marginalized areas of the city, especially the Points.[12]

Because so many poor settled here, many with traditions of collective action, and because of the hardships of these years, gangs played privileged roles in the Points. The tenements housed groups with colorful names like the Dead Rabbits and Plug Uglies—the whole panoply that filled the pages of Herbert Asbury's classic *Gangs of New York* on which Martin Scorsese based his film of the same title. The young men in gangs lived close to each other, hung out together, and protected one another in a competitive crucible.[13]

If people preyed on each other here, they also prayed with each other. As much as uneven development created the conditions for poverty, it also encouraged people to band together. Here the Irish soon had their own church, Transfiguration. Transfiguration was an apt name for the Ur-church of the Irish in New York. Originally, a church by this name stood on Chambers Street, on the southwest corner of the Sixth Ward. Catholics had purchased what had been a Scottish Reformed Presbyterian

Church there. Then, with the growth in the numbers of Irish in the Points, a newer one was needed. What would become the new Transfiguration had served as a Protestant church before being sold to Catholics as soon as the place became an Irish-dominated neighborhood. It still stands. With time, after southern Europeans came streaming into New York, it would be repurposed into an Italian parish, and finally a Chinese one, with masses now offered in Cantonese and in Mandarin.[14]

Did Sullivan darken its doors? Probably not. At least no more or less than his Irish neighbors did. Just as was the case for his family in London, life's transitions and occasions were marked in the church. In New York, Sullivan probably married in the church. In 1841 or 1842, he wed a woman named Margaret, born in Ireland, more than likely in Transfiguration Church. We know little about her beyond this bare fact, not even her maiden name.[15] More on Margaret later. The upshot is that the Irish in the Points, almost all of them excluded from the historical record, relied on community, and Transfiguration served as its most visible manifestation.

The Five Points served New York's ceaseless demand for growth. These people worked hard and had to be entrepreneurial. The Irish appreciated how to do what the modern world demanded. New York was blessed with two rivers, supplying plenty of dock work. The East River piers handled the growing global trade. Many of those working the docks there walked from the Five Points. So, the Points were to the East River what Whitechapel was to Wapping. The Irish also did most of the unskilled work associated with building New York, and the city seemed to have an endless need for human muscle. The women did what women did in places like London or Sydney. They took in boarders, they toiled as domestic servants, they did piecework, they ran groceries, and they sold goods on the street. This was a world of Irish work Sullivan would have recognized when he called himself Ambrose. "Look at yonder poor Paddy," Ralph Waldo Emerson pointed out in 1849, "whose country is his wheelbarrow." The Points was filled with "Paddies" and barrows and Irish Bridgets on the streets hawking wares and food, just as they did in London and the Rocks and Liverpool.

Even if the Irish did the most thankless work and had to contend with the seedier aspects of a growing city, they knew how to get ahead in this world. These were not uprooted peasants unable to cope in urban environments. Scholars have done all sorts of work trawling through the bank records of the Emigrant Savings Bank just a few blocks from the Points and right next to Transfiguration Church on Chambers Street. Irish immigrants established the bank to help individuals from the community support themselves. Even those with the meanest jobs—men doing day labor and women doing domestic work—saved money to build nest eggs. Perhaps these Irish were ready-made for a world of competition, prepared, as Ambrose had been, by the changes gripping Ireland before they left. The evidence suggests that these were savvy, upwardly mobile, and adaptable people—the sort just like Sullivan.[16]

Did Sullivan save? Probably not. Though the Emigrant Savings Bank records yield more than one hundred James Sullivans, many from other towns in West Cork, none appear to be him. The same with depositors with the names Murray and Ambrose. None of the possible names fits. There's a good reason why we don't find him saving. The bank opened in 1850, nearly a decade after he had established himself in the Points.[17]

If we scratch beneath the surface, a complex picture emerges. The Points, like the Rocks, was a place of extraordinary creativity. In this neighborhood where global cultures collided and where Black and Irish subcultures mixed and melded, tap dance was created. New York's distinctive accent came into being. American popular culture had its birth here. And working-class swagger ruled. The Points fostered, and perhaps demanded, fusion, invention, and reinvention. It's no accident that Francis Ambrose could restyle himself, of all things, Yankee Sullivan here.[18] The Five Points was colorful, right down to the same sort of "flash" language one heard in Whitechapel. "Coppers" were, well, cops because of the badges they wore. The term originated in the Points at this time. Here "autumn divers" picked pockets. A "bludget" lured men into dark alleys to mug them. "Groaners" attended charity sermons to rob the congregants.[19] To live here was to be thrilled, with the good and the bad that goes along with it. The Points seemed tailor-made for a prizefighter, a man who had to stand alone in the ring. In other words, Sullivan was in his element.

The last place Sullivan lived in the neighborhood sat on the corner of Centre Street and Franklin, the western edge of the Five Points, just a block from tony Broadway. This was where the then newly built Tombs stood. Modeled on an Egyptian mausoleum, this was New York's prison complex. It was designed to hold 350 prisoners, but soon it was bursting at the seams with inmates.[20] His place was also next to the tenements of Cow's Bay, so named because back in the day when the Collect Pond still existed, farmers led their cows down this alley to drink. When Sullivan moved here it was a mixed Irish–African American area with tenements named "Brickbat Mansion" and "the Gates of Hell." As a visitor put it, right at the time Sullivan lived there, "for misery, degradation, filth, and multitudes" the tenements there "cannot be exceeded." No doubt, this description smacks of typical middle-class prejudice; and it obscured deeper realities. Cow's Bay was the home of the poor and marginalized, yet, people here, Sullivan especially, knew how to scramble to get ahead.[21] New York's elite detested such streets. But here, too, beyond the purview of the refined classes, could be found the complicated mix that also marked Whitechapel and the Rocks.

In between his stays on Water Street and Centre, Sullivan became an entrepreneur, running a succession of saloons in and around the Five Points. Each of these he called the "Sawdust House."[22] The celebrity status he had gained beating Lane and returning to New York as a champion gave him the leg up he needed to open such places. The Sawdust House moved from place to place while he lived in the Points. He placed one, by some accounts, on the corner of Walker and Division Streets.[23] It sat right on the northwest corner of what is now Canal Street and Forsyth. He also ran saloons on Cherry Street, Madison Street, and two on Chatham Street. He would later open his Sawdust House on the corner of Franklin and Centre Streets. An image from the period of Chatham Street gives us a sense of what the front of the Sawdust House would have looked like in Sullivan's time. It shows a line of buildings between two and six stories tall, each with canvas awnings above the sidewalks. Horses and omnibuses ply the road, while pedestrians saunter and loiter in front of the buildings.[24]

Inside was another world. New York's directories list him as running a "porterhouse," a "tavern," or selling "liquors."[25] Each was called the Sawdust House because of the sawdust on the floor. Barmen strew sawdust on all barroom floors, to soak up spilled ale and tobacco juice, as well as blood, one supposes. You can still see and smell sawdust at the famous bar—and New York's oldest one—McSorley's.[26] Saloons had important functions to fill in the Sixth Ward where so many lived close to the edge. Here men looked for work. Here they could find guidance. "The liquor dealer is their guide, philosopher, and creditor," someone at the time noted. The barman built a bond of trust with the clients.[27]

At Sullivan's they found more. In creating the Sawdust House motif, he borrowed from the London and Liverpool sporting house model, the same places that inspired the men of Sydney to build such saloons. Owen Swift, the Wards, Jack Langan, Tom Cribb, and of course the great Mendoza all owned public houses. So had Dan Donnelly. New York had a tavern culture, but not a prizefighting one, so Sullivan set out to combine the two. Here, the men of the neighborhood gathered on a Saturday night and, "over their well-filled glasses, would sing and talk of the exploits of the daring Sullivan, who couldn't be beat."[28] They also gambled here, giving his bars an air of excitement, as they watched men fight and spar. Sullivan billed the Sawdust House as a place to drink, smoke cigars, bet on dog and cock fights, and learn "the Art of Self-Defense taught in a few lessons."[29] Again, beating Lane had given him the notoriety he needed.

We see in the places of violence, and those run by Sullivan, the costs of city-making. Here men would drink. And the emphasis was on men. As historians would say, this represented the ideal site to find a "bachelor subculture," in which wives had no place and where the drinks were rough-and-ready.[30] Ale featured because it was easy to brew and to store, and it happened to be the favored drink of workingmen. Alcohol took the edge off their marginalization in the city and the alienation many felt. They drank to ease the pain and to find conviviality in such difficult straits. Saloons enabled men living on the margins to plant a stake in a new land. They seemed to root peripatetic men. Here men could find relief. But places like the Sawdust House did more. They allowed the Irish to claim space in a way that scandalized and infuriated the people who set themselves up as their betters. Public drinking sounded a note of defiance.

Sullivan also sparred in his tavern and in others like it. He did so, as well, in what we would call gyms or exhibition spaces. He boxed at Chambers and Broadway, where once stood the headquarters of the *New York Sun*, a newspaper.[31] He ran a gym on Frankfort Street, right by the Hole in the Wall, and just across from City Hall Park and what would become the headquarters of the Democratic Party in New York, Tammany Hall. He was playing on his notoriety in beating Lane to sponsor sparring sessions. "Those who are studying the 'science of self-defence,'" a report lauding him as the conqueror of the Hammer read, "have now a good opportunity to take a lesson."[32] He delivered some of these lessons at Monroe Hall at 514 Pearl Street, an address that now exists as Foley Square, the headquarters of the NYPD. Once again, when it comes to Sullivan, history has a profound sense of irony.

The Sawdust House allowed Sullivan to make a living while tapping into the demographic change that was remaking the Five Points. More and more men from Ireland were pouring into the place, many wanting drink and action. Now it had a people arriving who were as steeped in fighting culture as the Ambroses had been when they set sail from Bandon to London or when the Rocks was dominated by larrikins. Sullivan stood a good chance of heading up a working-class Fancy, one that was egalitarian and antiauthoritarian, attributes right in line with Jacksonian democracy.[33] He was sitting on top of the world.

He was also sitting on top of a volcano. The Sawdust House testified to the fact that New York had achieved critical urban mass. New York had a great deal of kindling and tinder, the combustible sort of social tensions that seemed to define global cities and that made for great matches and terrific violence. These—some socioeconomic, some historical, and some ethno-religious—were multilayered. And they could be complex and even contradictory and interweaving.[34]

Older tensions still pertained here. As a postrevolutionary nation, Americans hated the British. Americans had shed British blood to gain their independence. They saw themselves as a people destined for progress because they had embraced enlightened ideas about self-government. The British epitomized the aristocratic airs that American egalitarians had banished, in theory, from their shores. In the War of 1812, a war that amounted to a second American battle for independence, New Yorkers had become noted for their vocal patriotism. The lower sort especially were proudly nationalistic and virulently anti-British.

Layered on top of this anti-British sentiment, and related to it, was a good bit of class animus. The poor eyed the "better sort" enviously and suspiciously, especially in the years after the Panic of 1837. The wealthy, those connected to the global system of trade, had prospered with the Erie Canal and with growing ties to British trading networks. Working-class people thought their erstwhile betters aped the British too much.

The men who owned warehouses and ships had cozy relationships with Britain, and these were the sort who could manage the ups and downs of a market economy, while working people found themselves out of work. The anglophiles seemed to be gliding along as New York grew by leaps and bounds, while others languished.

Then there were shifts in the political economy and in labor. Yankee Sullivan landed in a city right in the middle of the same sort of transition that gave rise to bitter disputes in Liverpool. Increasingly, New York was moving from an artisanal labor system, which valued craft and proprietorship, to one defined by wage labor. While this shift conferred some autonomy and fostered mobility, it also ushered in troubling changes. The artisanal system had given workers pride in the products they created and had provided some semblance of support and some control over their working lives. Wage labor, much of it unskilled, could mean grueling work; it also heralded more freedom to choose an employer but less security. The lower sort in the emerging system worked without the typical safety nets of the artisanal system. Wage labor could often make for faceless and anonymous work. New York needed backs and arms to build the city that globalization was creating. Skill was not at a premium. A whole swathe of working New Yorkers felt isolated and vulnerable with the transition. They worried that the future lay with the unwashed and the unskilled. They fretted that their independence was coming to an end.[35] As New York was shifting from seaport to global node, and as older ways of work were falling by the wayside, opportunities abounded for the unskilled, but it caused grave difficulties for those established.

Enter the Irish. As more of the Irish poor came in, just pouring onto the docks and streets near Peck Slip in an unregulated way, they did so as harbingers of the shift away from skilled labor. Those settling in the Five Points seemed to undercut established workers and to keep wages low. The presence of so many working-class Irish only increased competition. Or so those invested in the older system argued. On top of this, these Irish seemed alien. Far from the Irish who came earlier, that genteel, educated, and middle-class group, many of these newcomers seemed to come from another world. Those heading to the Points had little education, few skills, and tended to be poor and Catholic. Most of the new Irish appeared as an alien other. Working-class New Yorkers, many angry and feeling threatened, saw in the Irish a challenge to their very way of life.[36]

Just around that time, in 1844, New Yorkers elected a Know-Nothing mayor. The Know-Nothing Party, or Native American Party, wanted to drive the Irish out or at least make their lives as miserable as possible, hoping to make New York what it had, in their idealized vision, been before. In that year, the Know-Nothing candidate only won because Nativists threatened the Irish to keep them away from the polls. In years thereafter, the level of support for Nativist candidates would drop, but 1844 represented a high-water mark. The Irish must have wondered, given the brutal reception some of them received as they transited through Liverpool, if they would ever escape sectarianism.[37] And in this regard, they would be right. Nevertheless, the city needed the Irish to build, perhaps making people hate them all the more.

Such swirling tensions are what Sullivan had to bob and weave around. But he was well prepared to do so. This was, after all, a place designed for improvising and fighting. In New York, men settled disputes with violence, much as they did in Liverpool and in Sydney. New York also specialized in shape-shifters.[38]

Yankee Sullivan would meet the moment with his fists. Fortunately, setting up prizefights was becoming easier because of these tensions and because of the presence of all of the Irish. Irish forms of collective violence did indeed make their way to America, just as they did to Australia, and merged into prizefighting. Take gang violence, for instance. The very term "Dead Rabbit," the name of the chief Irish gang in the Points, meant something akin to a prizefighter. A rabbit was flash language for a "rowdy," and a dead one was an especially athletic fighter, sort of like Sullivan.[39]

Moreover, he had foils. Nativists, like Bill the Butcher, were also in their element. In the film *Gangs of New York*, Daniel Day-Lewis plays a character named Bill "the Butcher" Cutting. In real life, he was an equally nasty piece of work called Bill Poole. He indeed worked as a butcher, a skilled working-class profession under threat from the arrival of the unskilled Irish horde, as he would have argued. He considered himself an authentic American handy with his fists. The Irish hated him. He epitomized, for them, Nativism and Know-Nothingism.

In this combustible cauldron, the Irish rallied around Sullivan. They saw him "as a bright sample from the Emerald Isle," and they "were in extasies on account of his defeat of the great Hammer Lane." An Irishman had beaten the English at their own game. His reputation preceded him. Before long, Sullivan increasingly came to be seen as the champion of the Irish.[40] Sullivan fought a succession of fights that only embellished his reputation as the finest fighter around and that allowed him to channel New York's many tensions productively. He chose his adversaries well.

In 1841, he set up a fight with an Englishman named Vince Hammond in Philadelphia. The Nativists in this city made New York Know-Nothings seem tame by comparison. A few years hence, they would burn down a few Catholic churches in a series of pogroms. Sullivan and Hammond met on a site south of the city. It was no contest. The most dramatic aspect of the fight was who would draw "first blood." Sullivan told his cronies to bet all they could on him. Alas, Hammond caught him in the mouth early on, and Sullivan could feel his lips begin to bleed. He sucked them in and then gashed Hammond, claiming the prize with "delight." He then fought a "clever" fight. The bout took only ten minutes and went eight rounds. Hammond "was nothing in the hands of Sullivan." It was "child's play."[41]

From Hammond he graduated to someone he could really hate. In January 1842, he took on a New York Nativist. Tom Secor, a big strapping man outweighing Sullivan by more than twenty pounds, came from that stratum of New York that detested the Sullivans of the world. Secor was a working-class Protestant, a man who stood for the sort of labor that was fading away. The fight came off close by, on Staten Island, right by the Narrows and next to Fort Tompkins. Before two thousand spectators who had made their way there from the Points and the neighborhoods around it by boat, Sullivan gave Secor an out-and-out hammering. This one seemed personal. Apparently, Sullivan would be remembered for being the first to spit tobacco juice into the eyes of an opponent.[42] Following the new rules established in London, the fighters brandished colors and tied them to the ring. Sullivan chose black, almost like a pirate putting up a black flag. It was a fitting choice.

In the fight, the dark arts of the Wards were on full display. Throughout the match, Sullivan employed the Ward tactic of hitting and going to ground "to avoid the return." In this way, he could exploit the rules and deprive Secor of any counterattack. He hit quickly and then fell. Round after round went thusly. All the while, Sullivan "pointed tauntingly" at Secor and "made faces" at him. He did this by design, to exasperate Secor. Throughout the bout, he targeted the nose, the soft part of the head, and before too long Secor was gushing. By the twenty-second round, Secor was coming to scratch with his arms down, exhausted by the beating. He had hardly touched Sullivan. Two rounds later, "it was now apparent to every body that Secor with his bold, straight forward mode of fighting, could not contend successfully with his wily and active adversary." Sullivan's apprenticeship in scientific and crafty fighting and gamesmanship stood him well. Still, the fight went on, all through the sixty-fifth round. By this time, Secor could hardly stand as he received "blow after blow in the face." Sullivan extended his hand to Secor to end the fight. The beating had gone on just over an hour. The Nativist, however, would not surrender. Finally, two rounds later, his seconds refused to allow Secor to come up to scratch. Sullivan dominated, but people complained. They thought his "dropping system" broke the rules. In fact, Sullivan was on the cutting edge of the craft. One of those in the know explained that "the practice was introduced by the Wards in England, and practiced particularly by Nick of that name."[43]

Sullivan oozed a confidence verging on cockiness. The lopsided nature of his victories revealed that Sullivan knew a great deal more about the craft than his neighbors. The early fights revealed something else. The win gave his supporters, largely Irish from the Points, "renewed encouragement." They "were in raptures with the fighting abilities so bravely displayed by the cunning Yankee." He was proving himself cunning indeed, both in and out of the ring.[44] After Yankee had beaten Secor, as a report breathlessly put it, "The fighting spirit was now in the ascendancy, and as the friends of Secor were determined to 'take down' the Irishman, they cast their eyes about the pugilistic circle to find a man capable of holding up the honor of the Stars and Stripes against the encroachment of the Green Flag of the Emerald Isle."[45] But no one could stand up to Sullivan.

Next up was an even less able foe. Nativists thought maybe an English-born professor of pugilism from Brooklyn could do it. Now here was someone everyone in the Points could hate. The "City of Churches," as the borough was called, had plenty of Irish there, but it had a reputation as the anti–New York, a hive of Protestant uprightness that stood apart from the metropolis across the East River. A fellow named William Bell represented that world. He had reputedly "been teaching the good people of Brooklyn how to defend themselves against the 'wily influence of foreign encroachments.'"[46] The two met on August 29, 1842, for three hundred dollars a side at Hart's Island, an overgrown unoccupied island north of the city on Long Island Sound.

Bell looked the part of a "gentleman." He never stood a chance against this new kind of fighter, who chose blue for his colors. Sullivan played with him throughout. Once he asked for quarter, pleading with Bell that he was ready to give in—only to hammer him in the ear with a right after Bell fell for the ploy. Another time, Sullivan came to scratch slowly and wearily. Bell went in for the kill, and Sullivan turned on him in an instant. "Luk at the divil," the Irish cheered. Bell's polite pugilism "could not successfully contend against his experienced adversary." It went thirty-eight minutes and lasted twenty-four rounds. Throughout the match, Sullivan demonstrated his abilities to use the whole ring and command the space. He knew how to work Bell into corners. In this bout Sullivan did not employ Ward tactics at all. He did not have to.[47] And anything went, as far as he was concerned. Allegedly, he told Bell after the fight, "All's fair in war!"[48]

This succession of fights, in fact, brings Muhammad Ali to mind. When he was called Cassius Clay, he was reviled as an upstart, a man who thumbed his nose at convention and at the power structures of the day during a period of profound transition. He came from a beleaguered group, one looked down upon by society, and he represented their arrival. And perhaps their mastery. Sullivan captured the zeitgeist of an age every bit as disconcerting and dynamic as the 1960s. The parallels don't end here. He used the ring like a Clay. He could move like the butterfly and sting like the bee. He taunted.[49] Like Clay and then Ali, he could back up his talk.

In New York, Sullivan could change identities as gracefully as Clay/Ali would. He could be Irish when it came to contesting Nativists; or he could play the Irish American versus a British foe. Or just be the American. He could be the Yankee; he could be Sullivan. He could be both. It was the perfect time and place to be Yankee Sullivan. He realized this and played upon it. For his colors, he had tied black or blue to the ring posts. The choice suggested ambiguity, but there was little need to be explicit. The Irish knew who he was. And playing with ambiguity or in-betweenness suited his purposes. Sullivan left it to his supporters to decide who or what he was. This was a world designed for someone with the shape-shifting name—and abilities—of Yankee Sullivan. The time-in-place was made for a man used to navigating in-between places.

The mania for prizefighting reached new heights with Sullivan's wins.[50] Before Yankee, "boxing was practically an unknown art on this side of the water," the great ring historian and publicist Nat Fleischer declared.[51] After Yankee? "The fighting spirit took a sudden start," a writer put it at the time. It may well have been "stimulated and produced by the arrival in this country of the famous James, alias Yankee Sullivan."[52] With him, a whole infrastructure began to take shape for fighting, and the Five Points became a hatchery for prizefighters.[53] In this way, neighborhoods filled with the Irish were part of a pugilistic hinterland. Their bodies, hardened by work, were perfect stuff for the craft. Money was also involved, as boxing was bound to gambling. We have seen this all before, of course. The New York fighting world, however, differed from the one on display in England. There was no aristocratic Fancy. In New York, fighting was a working-class pursuit with a great deal at stake; bouts took place not as spectacles per se, though they were that. Rather, prizefighting revolved around status and power. Fighters like Sullivan learned to appropriate the honor culture that so entranced the upper class—the code duello—and to apply it to the competitive nature of working-class life. Because it depended on tensions and potential violence to sustain it, prizefighting grew quickly to epic proportions.

What he was doing captured the attention of people not normally interested in fisticuffs. In one letter, for instance, from 1843, a woman named Elizabeth Gage from Stamford, Connecticut, asked an acquaintance for news from New York. The letter starts with a few words about "Yankee Sullivan the boxer" and how men around the Five Points "have desperate fights every night." Another woman charged with drunkenness went so far as to call herself Yankee Sullivan. A note in a newspaper a few years later reported how Sullivan had arrived in Troy, New York, to set up a fight there. While there, he "was severely *whaled* by a boatman named Hubbard." One doubts the veracity of the account. A whaler taking down Sullivan seems rather outlandish. Nonetheless, he was now a headliner for newspaper readers.[54]

He also proved instrumental in the growth of a sporting press. In 1845, the New York *National Police Gazette* began publishing lurid tales about the city. The editors also covered what many took to be the base pursuits of the working class. These made good copy, and the readership was growing. Prizefighting featured. Sullivan's fights, and all they tapped into, proved irresistible to promoters and writers. Men who published sporting rags sat down with him in his bar to get the skinny and to learn whatever he decided to tell them about his life story. Sullivan tended to glide past his time in Australia. His enemies emphasized it. It all made good reading. These writer/popularizers aped the London papers that they read and where they first learned about Yankee Sullivan in any event. At the same time, coverage in the press increased the interest in fighting to a fever pitch.[55] Theaters on the Bowery, which had staged Yankee plays, now held benefits for prizefighters. The same one that hosted Charles Dickens in 1842 held a boxing exhibition between an "English champion" and an "American giant" to put on a "display of self-defence."[56] Another called the Arena held sparring sessions most nights now. Indeed, it was opened, according to a critic, "for the avowed purpose of exhibitions in Pugilism."[57] New York's pugilistic public sphere even reverberated beyond the city across the Atlantic. The fight against Secor was covered by the London sporting press, which took to quoting *The Flash*, a New York rag that highlighted prizefighting. It hailed Sullivan as the conqueror of Lane and as a disciple of the Wards. In London, the "American Fancy," especially Sullivan, made news. As early as 1844, a London sporting newspaper reported on a Black entertainer from Sheffield who kept audiences in "a continuous roar," billing himself as "Yankee Sullivan."[58]

This all added up to something quite extraordinary. Sullivan could not just take advantage of a well-heeled Fancy that existed. He had to create his own proletarian version, with his Sawdust House serving as its temple. He soon became a darling of the press he helped bring into being. "We have been accused of partiality towards Mr Sullivan in our accounts," wrote one newspaperman, but Sullivan was news. Moreover, "a few have gone so far as to say that the cause of this partiality is fear of his friends." The writer probably had a point, but his observations spoke to how Sullivan had become a celebrity.[59]

He certainly looked the part. According to a report, he appeared on the streets as if he had stepped out from a scene in *Gangs of New York*. He

Yankee Sullivan in the 1840s. (Author's collection)

wore his hair close-cropped, like a fighter, and had a thick neck. He had a fierce look about him, with "glaring green eyes" and high cheekbones. His hair was still reddish brown. For clothes, he wore a "close-fitting, bottle green velvet cutaway coat, tight-legged corduroys, high cut vest, spotted scarf." Sullivan sported a diamond pin and favored a "protruding shirt collar and straight broad-brimmed plug hat." He seemed the "beau-ideal of the fighter." And the Five Pointer.[60]

As a "blood sport," fighting, as in Britain and in Australia and in Ireland, had been suited to the rural life whence it came originally. But it only took off because New York had reached a stage of development that London had graduated from and that Sydney was also caught in the grips of. The old, honor-bound rituals of prizefighting flourished amid the seething tensions that made the globalized connected city. Those tensions differed from place to place. But they were variations on a theme. It seems that somehow prizefighting was bound to city-making in the English-speaking world. Men like Sullivan built these cities. They needed champions, too. If he did not exist, someone would have had to create Yankee Sullivan.

No doubt Yankee Sullivan had participated in what seemed the last gasp of great prizefighting in London. As he arrived, New York would take over that mantle. Yankee served as catalyst. As a London sporting paper put it, he "gradually raised a desire among the Americans to rival their brethren of the Old Country in the fistic art." He was deemed the "oracle."[61] Meanwhile, the Nativists in the city wondered who would or could "'take down' the Yankee."[62]

New York offered something the fight game in London never could: a path to power. New York was not only a republic. It was also a burgeoning democracy. Men like Sullivan could vote. They had a voice. He seized this opportunity. One boxing writer called Sullivan the head of an "Irish brigade, an organization that flourished at the time and combined pugilism with politics." He was right. Famously, Sullivan served as a "ward heeler" and, more to the point, "shoulder-hitter" and "zealous electioneer" for others, doing what needed to be done to win votes and secure elections. The job could entail kicking over ballot boxes, breaking ribs, splitting heads, beating police, and even invading homes, all of which he did. His "political influence" made him a valued friend and a feared enemy, as a paper put it. The Sawdust House gave him an ideal venue for his many activities.[63]

So, too, did another institution. Much of this political work was also accomplished through fire companies. Volunteer fire companies proliferated in the Five Points. These served as centers of association and of identity. Sullivan became a leader of the Spartan Fire Company on 49 Chrystie Street, Engine Company Number 15, right near where he owned a few saloons. "Spartan Hall," in fact, became yet another Sawdust House for a while. Fire companies and saloons attached themselves to political factions in the Points. Sullivan never ran himself, though he did garner one vote for the city's assembly in 1842, but while a member of a firehouse, he worked for a number of Democratic factions in the ward.[64]

The Spartan Fire Company included a great many Irishmen, like Sullivan. It was also tied into gang networks and operated like an Irish secret society. The so-called Dead Rabbits, for instance, were really a Democratic faction made up of firemen, rowdies, and other hangers-on from one corner of the Points.[65] Rockites would be right at home here. Fire companies, and the gangs that filled them, played a mediating role between the young men on the streets and the Democratic Party chieftains who relied on their support for votes and for intimidation. Democracy was undiluted here, and gangs and companies embraced the causes that workingmen would find amenable. Sullivan had found a true home with the Spartans. The Spartans opposed convict labor and whipping. And they hated those, like abolitionists and Nativists, who disliked the Irish. On this score, Sullivan relished beating Whigs.[66]

Only a gang or a company could handle the many tensions animating the Points. Politically, it was an intensely competitive, faction-addled place. To be political in the Ould Bloody Sixth Ward did not mean the aspirant fought only Nativists or Whigs at the polls. Things were more elemental. One fought all comers. The savvy politician had to improvise and adapt, even at times going against the interests of one's followers and cooperating with the perceived enemy. Here Irish took on Irish, Catholic clashed with Catholic. At issue were precious jobs and the ability to deliver them. Lives and livelihoods hung in the balance. From the bits we know, intramurally—that is, within the Sixth Ward—Sullivan was all over the map. The alliances were dizzying and often kaleidoscopic, and they broke down and regrouped time and time again. Sullivan fought with barmen like him, he sided with Cork men, he could work with Irish Protestants from the south of Ireland who lived in the Points, he allied himself with those from specific areas within the ward, he got behind conventional Tammany men, he cast his lot with radical workingmen known as "Locofocos." In 1849, he was in the middle of a nasty dispute between two Irish politicians, after he tried to punch one in a bar. Then he turned on Tammany, in one instance instigating a dustup in a Tammany Hall bar. More often than not, Sullivan allied himself Mike Walsh of the Spartans, whom they called "our Napoleon." Walsh billed himself as a working-class champion. He supported anticapitalist causes. He also was a proslavery advocate. Earlier on, Walsh was anti-Catholic. He was Irish, but Protestant. Later, when he saw which way the winds were blowing, Walsh courted Irish Catholics. At times, the Spartans stood apart from Tammany. At other times, they worked for Tammany. Sullivan, it was claimed, ran a Tammany-aligned "fighting committee" called the "White Eagles" for a bit while working for the Spartans. They claimed to be owned by no one, but they always vied for power. Sullivan and other Spartans used their fists against other Irishmen if necessary, even former Locofoco allies, to make their bid for power in the swirl of allegiances. This promiscuous approach did not, amazingly, lead to fixed positions and hatreds. Much was forgotten as alliances unformed and reformed. Sullivan served, in short, as an opportunistic fist for hire, mainly working for different factions of a divided Democratic Party in New York.[67]

When we think of democracy, we imagine that consent and reasoned debate lie at the heart of it all. But no one knew how democracy worked. In cities, especially, when common men had the vote for the first time, as they were competing for resources against the wealthier and against other workingmen with other allegiances, democracy was a blank slate on which the strongest could inscribe their wishes. Sullivan embodied that violent and aggressive but boisterous form of politics that was becoming the stuff of American urban democracy—before these sets of arrangements were systematized into something we would call a machine.

It's easy to assume that all was sectarian strife in the Points, that men like Sullivan, almost invariably a Democrat, only wanted to contest Nativists. But power did not work that way here. Yet, that is. Reaching across the seemingly unbridgeable divide did occur on occasion because competition among the Irish factions forced some to band with erstwhile enemies. In 1842, for instance, a massive election fracas broke out. Different Irish leaders were running for the position of alderman in the Sixth. They all claimed allegiance to the Democratic Party. And their followers savaged one another, even going so far as to break into houses to deliver beatings. At issue? On the face of it was a vote over Catholic education in the city, something one could figure they would all be behind. But the issue mattered less than the power it conferred. And even John Hughes, the archbishop, was not immune. Rioters, largely Irish, attacked his house when he got in the way of their rise to power and all the patronage it would confer.[68] Sullivan was part of a band that went over to the archbishop's residence and threw rocks through his windows. He claimed he did not march with some of the others to the residence, but there is little doubt that he got all the action going. He and a few other "bullies," in their cups naturally, did what Whigs had done in the past. They were "kicking over the ballot boxes" throughout the ward, and they went to war in the streets with a few rivals from another Irish gang. This was intramural warfare and rank intimidation, and Irish versus Irish. He and his henchmen claimed "political excitement and the spirit of party faction" caused the ruckus. But not them. Or so they said. Yet, Sullivan had backed the prelate a year or two earlier, even going so far as to support candidates for Hughes's so-called Carroll Hall party.[69]

Fighters featured on election days, at caucuses, and wherever a vote was cast. They did so most visibly at Dooley's Long Room in a local hotel where a final slate for the Democrats in the Sixth Ward would be determined. On these primary days, different factions brought in their muscle. It was accepted practice. Then again, democracy, they believed, had to be fought for. Sullivan became the paragon of what one historian called a "republicanism of the streets."[70] A reform committee argued that politics reached its lowest in primary season when "organized bands of unprincipled and reckless men . . . sell out their services to aspirants."[71] It was reported, with justification, that "the fighting men are all politically inclined, and serve their parties with fists and firearms."[72] There was little that separated prizefighting and politics, in form or in ritual. It is not an exaggeration to say that at this moment, prizefighting breathed life into politics, and politics animated pugilism. One was indispensable to the other in New York at this moment when New Yorkers were hashing out what democracy really meant, giving characters like Sullivan a status they would never have enjoyed otherwise.[73]

Yankee's world challenges many assumptions about democracy. A political actor had to feign and maneuver, to work with enemies and find new friends. All was defined by adaptation, not brute force alone or fixed ideologies. As in the ring, Sullivan read the moment, decided when to strike, and skillfully moved about from alliance to alliance. This was not because he was fickle, but because of how power worked in a democracy at this plastic moment. He did not prove the exception in this regard. His sensibilities were well suited to a place where only the fittest and most adaptable survived. The Points demanded it. This is, of course, how things were in New York, and London, and Liverpool. But in New York all was amplified because of popular sovereignty. To move, in and out of the ring, was to be a New Yorker.

Sullivan was a man of violence and a man of power, made ruthlessly so by the world he moved through.[74] He was part of a charter community determining how politics would function. He helped establish the cultural parameters of accommodating and also resisting, as practices congealed into system. If we view it this way, he and his ilk were cornerstones of New York's political culture. As the reformer Jacob Riis put it, after other groups had moved into the Five Points area, "The Irishman's revenge is complete. Victorious in defeat over his recent as over his more ancient foe, the one who opposed his coming no less than the one who drove him out, he dictates to both their politics, and [is] secure in possession of the offices."[75] And what drove New York also defined the nation. "New York

City," a near contemporary put it, "is really and truly the grand school and hot-bed of American democracy."[76] Sullivan had a role in this story.

In September 1842, around the time of the election drama, a New York newspaperman hoped a proper foe could be found. Watching Sullivan dismantle Secor and Bell, and listening to the lame excuses of their supporters, had only reinforced his belief "that Mr. Sullivan, in the Prize Ring, can conquer any antagonist who may come before him." Still, the "many friends of the American Prize Ring" were "anxious to produce some man who will pluck the laurels from the brow of Mr. Sullivan." People knew he had a good left and could grapple with the best of them. The fights demonstrated superior science, confidence, and a great right as well. His critics had to admit now that "Sullivan can fight a little." The writer, along with others who understood pugilism, stood "ready when he says the word to match him against any man in the United States, regardless of weight and size." This was a champion's boast. And Sullivan had earned the right to crow.[77]

The only thing that could stop him—at least for a while—was death. Just two weeks after his recent victory over Bell, New York's Fancy set up another fight just outside of New York, in Hastings on the Hudson. Sullivan did not fight, but he did take a leading part in the match. He arranged for the bout in the Sawdust House. It would pit an Irishman from Cork named Tom McCoy against a Liverpudlian named Christopher Lilly. The locals made their bets and then, on September 13, 1842, a Tuesday, made their way up the Hudson for what they figured to be an exciting day out in Hastings. Like so many other such bouts, this one involved personal enmity. It started as a "grudge" between the two that had begun over perceived slights during a sparring exhibition on the Bowery.[78]

This "Battle of Hastings" did not go as planned. Before the bout started, a local magistrate got wind of it. He approached Sullivan and asked if he was involved. Sullivan said "he had nothing to do with it." Sullivan warned the magistrate to leave if he knew what was good for him. Wisely, he took to a nearby hillside to watch the proceedings. Sullivan then took off his jacket and helped get the bout going.[79] It went longer than anyone could have imagined. McCoy, though battered by Lilly, gamely came out round after round. His seconds kept pushing him to the scratch. They had a lot of money riding on the outcome. Sullivan, who certainly had a financial stake in the bout, stood in Lilly's corner. It was Yankee who yelled "first blood," when Lilly hammered McCoy in the first round. He also mocked McCoy with "cries of 'Bah! bah!'" in the fourth. After the eighty-fifth, he went so far as to kiss Lilly on the head "in admiration of his prowess."[80] After a while it appeared McCoy could hardly stand. Or breathe. He was spitting up clotted blood. The match should have stopped.[81] After nearly three hours of fighting, and more than one hundred rounds, McCoy collapsed in the ring. In fifteen minutes, he was dead.

The event scandalized New Yorkers. His death, one published piece argued, was "no common one." It had "no redeeming quality in it." McCoy simply "died to gratify the fiendish propensity of the populace," as one report put it. Soon a whole mythology surrounded the fallen McCoy. He was a good man who had left Ireland with his mother and found gainful employment at the port, but soon became the "prey" of the likes of Sullivan. One such sharp was Lilly. "Lilly was from Liverpool; had acquired early habits of vice; was fond of sporting, boxing and sparring; and it is said, lived on the avails of these employments before he left his country," one report read. Sullivan had set up the fight and set McCoy up for an old-fashioned "sacrifice." With McCoy's death, magistrates tried to arrest Sullivan. He "defied" four of them to take him. They could not. The report concluded, "Foreigners are accused of introducing this sanguinary butchery among us." Sullivan was to blame.[82] To add to it all, a newspaperman wrote a piece claiming to quote the mother of the fallen McCoy. "Oh Sullivan! Sullivan!" she sobbed, "What have you done!"[83]

The police rounded up the culprits, or those they could find. Lilly skipped town. But Sullivan had too much at stake to leave. On September 25, authorities caught up with him and arrested what a paper called "the redoubtable cock of the New York Ring" on Staten Island by the Narrows, where he had been sailing with some friends, and dispatched him to the Tombs. Rumor has it that he was hoping to leave town and make his way down to New Orleans and thence Texas to escape punishment. Then they extradited him up to Westchester County for trial. Each day, overflowing crowds attended the trial. The jury there heard how Lilly "with both his fists" did "strike beat and bruise" McCoy. Blows to the head, neck, heart, belly, sides, and back had led him to die "instantly." Sixteen others, and Sullivan, were accused of "aiding, helping, abetting, comforting, assisting, and maintaining the said Christopher Lilly" in perpetrating the crime.

Sullivan was found guilty of manslaughter in the fourth degree "whilst engaged in a fight, commonly called a prize fight." In December 1842, a judge named Charles Ruggles sentenced two others to the county jail for a number of months, plus a fine. Sullivan, on the other hand, got two years "at the state prison at Mount Pleasant," in other words, the dreaded Sing Sing, an almost industrial-scale version of Hyde Park Barracks. On paper, he was not sentenced to "hard labor," as had been the case for much of his time in Australia, though he would work in the stone quarry. Why he received a harsher sentence was fairly clear. He had promoted the fight. He had become the embodiment of prizefighting in the Points. He was now served with his just desserts.[84]

All paused. This tends to happen when fighters die in the ring. In 1962, Emile Griffith gave Benny Paret a hammering at Madison Square Garden. Paret passed away ten days later. The very next year the featherweight Davey Moore died, prompting Bob Dylan to write a song lamenting how no one and everyone bore responsibility.[85] The great boxing chronicler Donald McRae decided to forgo writing about the "sweet science" after a "calamitous four months in 2019" when a spate of boxers lost their lives in the ring, followed by the inevitable anguish, hypocrisy, and finger-pointing.[86] Warren Zevon immortalized Ray Boom-Boom Mancini, from Youngstown, Ohio, who killed the Korean boxer Duk Koo Kim in the ring in 1982. As Zevon suggests, his death occasioned a period of introspection when the polite wondered if boxing could be countenanced in a civilized society.

The same happened in McCoy's case. Sullivan spent almost ten months in prison, but because he had become such a force in the city, friends arranged for New York Governor William Bouck to pardon him. The governor justified his decision by the fact that the sentence seemed too harsh, certainly when compared to those of the others convicted, as well as the fact that Sullivan had comported himself well. By the terms of his pardon, Sullivan was supposed to wash his hands of anything to do with the ring. That, of course, would not happen.[87] In no time, he was putting on exhibitions at Bowery theaters. The whole thing seemed fishy. A Sag Harbor newspaper put it this way: "Are Sullivan's services wanted in New York in preparation to the next election?"[88] The paper was probably not wrong.

For a period, newspaper writers, in venues like the *New York Times,* called for the abolition of prizefighting. With some justification, the wealthy sort and those apt to style themselves reformers feared that the growth of prizefighting represented the hold the lower classes now had on the city and how politics had devolved with mass participation. Critics and those who condemned Sullivan were on to something about the connection between the fight game and political culture. They were entangled with what the city had become.

What they did not appreciate was how the rise of Yankee Sullivan, and the violence implicit in it, revealed quite a bit about New York popular democracy and the culture that sustained it. Prizefighting and democracy gave common men like Sullivan a voice but at a price. First, there was the fact that politics and fighting in the Sixth had become so enmeshed in drinking culture. Sullivan was accused of drinking more than most. It seems there was more than a grain of truth to this. He could be vicious. And before shoulder-hitting or fighting in saloons, drink was generally taken.[89]

Second and relatedly, politics at the time privileged what sociologists today would call an almost toxic form of masculinity, again epitomized by Sullivan and prizefighting. Both pursuits empowered men who would have been emasculated by their betters. Both gave common men a stake, for the first time. But what did this mean for others? What of women? Sullivan, as we know, was married to Margaret. But we know nothing of his wife besides her name, the fact that she had been born in Ireland, and a description by a newspaper that called her "an interesting, pretty little women" who appeared committed to him.[90] The obscurity speaks volumes, of course, about the anonymous existences many working-class women led. They don't often appear in the records, and most often do only when they break laws or flout middle-class norms. In all fairness, we only know of Yankee because he had become a celebrity, earned by his fighting prowess. Most illiterate men also lived anonymous existences, much like Francis Ambrose before he morphed into James Sullivan. The same fate befell Margaret Sullivan. But at least through violence a man could make a name for himself. Not so for a woman, unless she gained notoriety for all the wrong reasons. A common woman could never be a champion. A common man could only assume such a title though violence.

Did Sullivan's violence extend to the household? Well, rumors circulated about how he treated Margaret, stories to which he took great offense, as we shall see. As for his fighting, firehouse, bachelor subculture, we know the awful things some could do to women. Among the gangster types in and around the Points, some dealt with women abominably. One Nativist leader named Tom Hyer, almost Sullivan's evil twin and one he was destined to fight in the future, killed prostitutes, and he and his henchmen gang-raped a woman at a brothel near the Points.[91] The New York sex trade, operating in what the flash language of the day called "lust holes," was flourishing as the city grew, with the Points as its epicenter, but so too was the misogyny that went hand in hand with it, all whipped up by the same popular press that was making Sullivan New York's cock of the walk.[92]

Women in the Points did not embrace bourgeois roles or anything like that. If only women had such leisure. They worked, and they could fight. We know that later on when Nativists would brawl with Irish gangs in the area, women would stand on rooftops raining down bricks and stones. In fact, Irish women were disproportionately overrepresented in prisons, courts, and police stations, especially in New York. Some of it had to do with poverty and their status in American society; some of it had to do with the fact that they were overpoliced.[93] Women embraced the flash fashion and argot of the Bowery every bit as much as the young men. But it was still a man's world, and a violent one at that.

Sullivan, so far as we know, did not violate women in the way that Hyer did, but this is the rough-and-tumble world he came from. Sullivan, as we now appreciate from a great deal of work on the subject, inhabited a world defined by masculinity and homosocial bonhomie. The ring, the saloon, the firehouse, and the polling place were the places of and for men. He and those who fought epitomized some of the most grotesque patriarchal attitudes of the day. Some of the men he fought saw women not only as second-class citizens, but as playthings beneath them that could be treated with contempt. Perhaps we could say that a burgeoning global system, centered on ports, demanded hard and physical labor that privileged the violent and the masculine. In this way, men on the very margins of that system, but indispensable to it, carved out a niche in cities and in a nation defined by patriarchy. Just as the ring ritualized the violence inherent in competing in places like New York, so it proved an all-too-tempting form of valorization.[94]

Then there was race. Democracy and fighting went hand in hand; they also, by their very nature, excluded. Much has been made of how the Irish "became white" in New York in these years. This notion revolves around the idea that when they first arrived, the Irish were regarded as inherently different, perhaps even subhuman, and to address this bigotry and to make a stab at power, they "sought refuge in whiteness," as a proponent of the theory argues.[95] They tried to scale the American ladder by using African Americans as rungs, when they should have forgone such racist attitudes and seen the logic of organizing along class lines.[96]

The truth is probably more complex. For a start, the Irish were always white in America. No one dared turn them away from the polls and from the city. Few wanted to. The city needed the labor. And they stepped right into America's preformed racial hierarchies and embraced racism.[97] Then there is context. The period when Sullivan lived in New York witnessed a time of political activism for African Americans. Far from passive, a Black elite in the city acted to protect fugitives from the Slave South and put an end to their second-class status. They sought to "strike the blow" against the society in which they found themselves. Yet, most of the common Blacks, the sorts that Sullivan was apt to rub shoulders with, "languished" in New York, as a historian explains, in these years.[98] At issue was more than whiteness. Nativists hated both the Irish and Blacks, and their idea of how to clean up what they characterized as a mess in New York can be summed up in a pithy phrase uttered by a nineteenth-century English historian and bigot: The United States might be great "if only every Irishman would kill a Negro, and be hanged for it."[99] Those who championed the rights of Blacks and also an end to slavery tended to look down their noses at Irish Catholics. The wealthier sort wished they did not come from Ireland to crowd their cities, just as they preached the virtues of human equality. Things in the Points were complicated.

The Irish and Sullivan reached the Five Points in numbers just as Blacks were leaving. They did so at a moment when being white conferred advantages, even to Catholic Irish. In other words, they stepped into a demographic vacuum in the Points just as they stepped into America's racist past. This, of course, was more or less Francis Ambrose's story in the Blue Mountains of Australia. He tended to arrive at a place just after the work of clearing out a people considered inferior and who haunted white imaginations. His timing tended to be impeccable. It gave him some cultural cachet in places he faced discrimination.

To be clear, the Irish, and by extension Sullivan, also embraced the racialized zeitgeist. To be white did confer power. And racism made American culture go round. As adaptable men and women, the Irish inhabited this sensibility, a way of seeing the world and of seeing others that would reach full flower later, when the Irish began to take over completely. They would not have apologized. It underscored how power worked. As much as the two groups might have found commonality, they battled for positions on the waterfront, and the Irish could treat Blacks cruelly. Racism ran through working-class culture by the time Sullivan arrived. Take the story of one man who worked with and against Sullivan for political power. His name was Isaiah Rynders. The son of immigrants from Germany and Ireland, in this case Protestant, Rynders ran the infamous Empire Club, a place fancied by prizefighters and by Democrats. He could turn out fierce men, the most notorious in fact, to get out the vote and keep Whigs away from the polls. A powerbroker in the Points, Rynders was also a bigot. He attacked Frederick Douglass at a speech he gave in New York, his "Men and Brothers" address of May 7, 1850. Douglass's famous question "Am I a man?" was, in fact, a retort to racist heckling from Rynders. Rynders was not Sullivan, of course, though he was a patron of Sullivan's soon-to-be bitter rival, the Irish-born fighter John Morrissey. But Rynders was a political animal who understood that his power rested on his ability to appeal to the Irish in the Points, and racism could do the trick.[100]

But even on this front, the Irish defied easy categorization. African American people, culture, and imagery were all around Yankee Sullivan. He lived, as we know, near Cow's Bay, one of the last refuges of Blacks in the Points. Minstrel shows on the Bowery, first appearing in 1843, speak to the pernicious side of mixing and merging. Thomas Rice, a white actor who had cut his teeth poking fun at the Irish, repurposed these barbs and caricatured Blacks by performing as "Jim Crow." He performed to large, raucous crowds on the Bowery. These racist performances, which the Irish applauded, also heralded something else troubling to New Yorkers. Some feared Irish and Blacks becoming too close. In fact, both the well-to-do and the working-class Nativists feared that Irish-Black unions would lead to the evil of "amalgamation," an idea that fueled a great deal of the anti-Irish and anti-Black feeling in the Points. Irish and Blacks amalgamated represented the collapse of a social order and the racial order that sustained it.[101]

So, this was a tangled world when it came to race. What of Sullivan? With Sullivan per se, there are precious few direct leads to follow. We know of one instance when Sullivan's election crew clashed with Blacks. They chased a young man through the streets on an election day. He got away.[102] That this young man might have been out to vote would have made him an outlier. While whites enjoyed universal suffrage, Blacks did not. According to the 1821 constitution, they needed property in order to vote. The Irish did not. Mike Walsh, Sullivan's Spartan crony, held many conflicting positions, but not when it came to race. On this issue there was little ambiguity. Walsh became a leading proslavery politician when he sat in the US Congress. He, like so many others, epitomized the seeming contradictions of this place-in-time. He stood for workers' rights. He was racist.

Tragically, among those like Yankee Sullivan in a hypercompetitive environment, exclusion made good sense. They proved adept at reading situations where power lay in the balance, and forcefully weighing in. Their adaptability proved a curse for African Americans. Men like Sullivan read the proverbial room, and they saw that perhaps in this instance they could grasp power within the rules of the emerging system. These rules not only allowed but rewarded violence just as much as they did exclusion.[103]

There is a lesson here about how American democratic politics came to be. It was not conjured ex nihilo. It was created. It was crafted by people who would and could use older, and often violent, ways of adjudicating disputes and dealing with difference. Prizefighting adapted these older ways to new urban challenges in a place-in-time in which republicanism was the coin of the realm. In this way, the Irish were well-suited to the Five Points and none more so than Yankee Sullivan. Sullivan, a globe-trotting prizefighter, helped create what has been called the "White Man's Republic," a form of democracy to which all leaders would have to defer. They had little choice, even if they tried to curtail some of its growth after the Lilly-McCoy tragedy.[104]

With time, Sullivan would make his use of Irishness much more intentional. He chose a fight against an Englishman to reveal what were becoming his true colors in 1847. Much had changed since the Lilly-McCoy fight, most especially the demographic makeup of the city. Think of the year: 1847, or Black '47 as it is mythically known in Ireland. Thousands of Irish were now washing up on the East River or trudging down to the city from Quebec, where their ships landed. These were Famine immigrants. In New York, they appeared as specters from another world, the very dregs of humanity. The moment represented a time when an ecological disaster struck obscure areas up to this point relatively untouched by the sorts of modern problems and opportunities that had hit Bandon a few decades earlier. The earlier and smaller crisis that had plagued Bandon led to all sorts of conflicts and to the decision of many, including the Ambroses, to leave. Now the crisis was a cataclysm on a different scale altogether. This moment of global immersion caused untold immiseration. For those leaving, New York represented a logical place to go. It was now part of the same global system that brought the blight. New York needed more labor, and these men and women would provide it. The Famine and the massive migration that stemmed from it were perfectly packaged modern phenomena.

The arrival of the immigrants only heightened enmities, and New Yorkers grew worried that they had little control over the tenor and future of their city. Imagine what New Yorkers, already concerned about their status and identity, felt when they beheld the men and women from Catholic Ireland in rags on the docks.

What did the newcomers think of Sullivan? A muscular Irishman who fought back? One who had not been emasculated by what the modern world threw at him? Sullivan was "strong, agile, quick, cunning, capable, a perfect master of his science." He was both physical specimen and "intellectual fighter."[105] He must have cut quite a figure for Famine immigrants. They came with nothing and were half-emaciated. He was all muscle and swagger, wearing the finest clothes. And he was Irish. Imagine, also, what prizefighting meant to them. They fought in Ireland and did not take their servile status lying down. Now they saw a champion of doing so. In the context of 1847, what would happen should the Irish-born Sullivan fight an Englishman?

That is just what he did. As they had exhausted any possibility to find him a suitable Nativist opponent, promoters understood that a British foe would also make good copy. Everyone hated the British. Chosen as his adversary was one of those English fighters who hoped to make a killing touring New York. And Sullivan knew him. His name was Robert Caunt. Sullivan had watched his brother, Big Ben Caunt, take on Nick Ward at Crookham Common. The younger Caunt was deemed to be a better, more scientific fighter than his big brother. Both came from a fighting English family. Perhaps this Caunt could put Sullivan in his place.

They could not fight around New York. Sullivan's previous fights, before the death of McCoy, had taken place right around the city. Prizefighting, though still illegal, had for a while become woven into the fabric of the city. The Lilly-McCoy fight had changed all that. So, they traveled to a place that knew next to nothing about fighting, a place that would soon know a great deal about other forms of fighting and that John Brown and his raid would make famous, Harpers Ferry. When it came to in-betweenness, it sat right between and next to a number of jurisdictions. Though in Virginia at the time, it lay across the Potomac from Maryland. The Fancy could make a quick getaway if necessary. It also sat right on the border of two counties. And next to a federal fort. This was the sort of place that prizefighting tended to visit when the heat was on. After the principals and about six or seven hundred others traveled down to Virginia by train, the curious soldiers came out to see what all the ruckus was about as a bunch of New Yorkers disembarked from boats with ropes and posts to set up a ring. The townspeople, who probably only knew of rough-and-tumble and numbered between two or three thousand, came out of curiosity.

The combatants tossed their hats in the ring, entered with the seconds, and did the obligatory handshakes. Then they tied their colors to the post. For the first time since he had fought in England, Sullivan chose green. Not the blue or black he had fought under before against the Know-Nothing fighters. And, in light of all the drama around 1847, consider what Sullivan's decision to wear green meant. It was a bet on New York's future for a man who knew how to improvise and to read situations. For over two years, the number of Irish had been climbing, and New York was their chosen destination. These people had landed right by Langan's in Liverpool, and through luck and guile, made their way to docks there that were sending ships to America. Many of these headed to New York because of connections between the two. Others were bound to places like Quebec, as the shipping system was overwhelmed with numbers. But these unfortunates also hoped to make their way to New York. It had become Ireland's chief city in a global system. And so Sullivan made his allegiances known.

The spectacle was akin to Clay/Ali's fights with Sonny Liston. The new was taking on the old at a febrile time when fighters stood as avatars for the issues bedeviling all. As with the bouts between Clay and Liston, this one at Harpers Ferry had global appeal. British punters, too, found the fight intriguing. For them, "it was confidently hoped that the younger Caunt would be able to wipe out the stain caused by the defeat of the great Hammer Lane." Maybe, in the person of Caunt, Britain could ascend to its rightful place once more as the global fistic capital. The bout was covered as far away as Sydney. In the first fight with Liston, Clay badgered the bigger, more powerful man relentlessly, hurling abuse as he did so. Then he went out and cut Liston down to size in short order. Caunt, an earlier version of the "big ugly bear," outweighed Sullivan by fifteen pounds. Like Liston, he did not stand a chance. Sullivan slaughtered him, popping him with "beauty destroyers" to the face. Sullivan landed hard punches; Caunt threw rights and lefts "that amounted almost to nothing." Between shots, Sullivan laughed at Caunt's appearance. Robert Caunt fought much like his lumbering brother, and he proved no match for the peerless Sullivan, who was at his "best and sharpest." It was butchery, and it was personal. An Irishman hammering a Brit, punching him "stupid," must have buoyed his supporters. The fight lasted all of twelve minutes. In the context of 1847, the victory had that much more meaning, most especially for the Irish. Quite understandably, just as would be the case with Clay's followers much later on, the win "naturally loosed an explosively triumphant degree of Hibernian crowing."[106]

Still, by fighting an Englishman, Sullivan was not above flaunting his American credentials. He was still Yankee Sullivan. "In this country," a report read, "the feeling was rather in favor of Sullivan, as he fought under the name of 'Yankee,' and thus enlisted the sympathies of the people." So what was he? American or Irish? The Irish stood in his corner. Without question. They were euphoric over the match.[107] To their opponents, this fight presented a dilemma. Ultimately, many ended up siding with the Yankee against Caunt, particularly because at this moment the United States stood on the verge of war with Great Britain over the fate of the vast section of the West known as "Oregon." Sullivan, whether he knew it or not, was participating in the drama of Manifest Destiny as much as he was in the struggle between Ireland and Britain.[108]

Yankee Sullivan tapped into quite a confused set of allegiances, all of which played to his strengths of being able to hedge. Sullivan could still appreciate that in his politico-fistic world playing both sides was smart. He would have known that even if he came home from Harpers Ferry as an Irish champion, he had to live in a city where switching allegiances still remained the path to power. The Irish were streaming in, but it would take years before they would dominate the city, if even he could conceive of such an eventuality. For the moment, they were a growing power base, but in a city that still boasted an anti-Irish majority. Remaining a Yankee, even if he could flaunt the Sullivan, made the most sense. For the moment at least.

The 1847 fight revealed one last change. Now fights were covered in real newspapers read by all, such as the *New York Herald.* A paper that could be all over the place politically, the *Herald* nonetheless enjoyed the largest circulation of any major paper in the city, topping the *New York Times* and Horace Greeley's *New York Tribune.* What Sullivan did was news. After all, he had threatened to make himself the champion of the downtrodden in an increasingly divided city that had to respect the voice and power of these newcomers. With his rise, as the *Herald* put it, a mania for prizefighting was shifting from the "dram shops" of the poor to "the domestic circle."[109] Prizefighting was growing in popularity with Yankee's rise. One of the sporting rags of the day began selling Pierce Egan's multivolume *Boxiana.*[110] What a change in so short a time. For this moment at least, he was the greatest.

ROUND 12

Still Pond Heights

THE YEARS 1848 and 1849 represented one of those moments when history turns. In Europe in those years, a revolutionary wave swept across the continent. All kinds of "isms" appeared on stage, and a generation fought over their merits. Liberalism, capitalism, nationalism, socialism, and undoubtedly a few more competed and collided to create the biggest conflagration that the world had experienced since the age of revolution. At issue was the fallout from that seismic set of events. The age of revolution created a new world of movement, trade, democratic participation, and nation-states. But it created a host of problems as well. Who could or should enjoy rights? What made nations? How to make sense of the industrial world and all that came in its wake? How to address the evident immiseration of cities and countryside in the wake of globalization?[1] In the storm, Europe almost fell apart.

The years 1848 and 1849 also stirred renewed hopes. In countries throughout Europe, the lower classes filled the street, decrying their lot under the emerging industrial order, but also pressing for a new future in which they would have political and economic rights. People united to create new nations and to try to break away from old, corrupt ones. These years presaged a new age of reform and perhaps revolution. It is no coincidence that Karl Marx and Friedrich Engels would cowrite their *Manifesto* in 1848, pointing out what dramatic transformations gripping many nations had wrought but also how change could be managed or perhaps harnessed. The invocation of "1848" suggested this mix of upheaval and hope.

These struggles centered in Europe, but they reverberated outward, spreading throughout the world and touching nearly all states. Except America. News arrived in March of what was happening an ocean away.

The *New York Herald* wrote that news of 1848 was "on every tongue and palpitating in every bosom of this great metropolis." But little happened. The many tensions that stirred 1848 in Europe were, as one scholar puts it, "filtered through American partisan alignments."[2] Americans seemed convinced that their revolution had achieved what it was meant to and perhaps even inspired what was happening an ocean away. They did not need another revolution. They inwardly focused on their own existential struggles over the institution of slavery, the arrival of immigrants to their shores, and the splintering of their political system. When it came to the external, they were focused on the outcome of a war against Mexico. In short, America slept in 1848 while the world around it reeled.[3]

Though the nation remained quiet, New York had its own version of 1848. New York's 1848 did not take place in New York. And it did not take place according to the script of European events. It occurred a year later in a remote location, far from the city, called Still Pond Heights in the Upper Chesapeake. The name suited the site. It was as sleepy as the world was boisterous. Nonetheless, at this place, a good bit about the soul of democracy in the city and nation would be decided. The isms here involved nativism, urbanism, perhaps socialism, and Catholicism. Whose city and, by extension, country was it? At issue were the meanings of Americanism, that form of nationalism that all were fighting to define in the wake of the American Revolution.

New York's 1848 could well have been a prizefight.

The fight had been brewing for years. It centered on two characters: Yankee Sullivan and the man he had been threatening to fight for some time, Tom Hyer, the so-called Champion of the United States. Hyer headed some of the Nativist gangs in the city and was the son of Jacob Hyer, who fought one of the first prizefights in the city a generation earlier. The younger Hyer, too, styled himself a fighter. He and Sullivan were not only "bitter pugilistic enemies, they were also keen political enemies," as Nat Fleischer, the great twentieth-century founder of *Ring* magazine, or the bible of the fight game, argued.[4] It was simple politics in the Five Points. "Sullivan goes for the Irish vote," a publicist observed, "and Hyer stands for the suffrages of the Native Americans."[5]

In 1848, Sullivan finally challenged Tom Hyer. They had had a drunken rough-and-tumble in Hyer's saloon, and Yankee had gotten the worst of it.

For a week after, riots were threatened. Saloons seethed. Yankee's hatred knew no bounds. For Sullivan, as a reporter put it, this amounted "to a sheer mania." "I am no Irish braggart," Yankee attested in daring Hyer to a real bout, "nor am I an 'Irish bully,' although I am an Irishman and am proud of it and believe I can show myself worthy of my country." He published these words in the *New York Herald* by way of a formal challenge. Hyer responded in the newspaper, saying, more or less, any place and any time, closing with the phrase, "I am his master." Hyer, a close friend of that great street fighter Bill the Butcher (not Cutting, but Poole), accepted the challenge from Sullivan for five thousand dollars a side. Raising this amount proved herculean, especially for the Irish, but for this they seemed up to the task.[6]

As talk of the fight surpassed even discussion of the war with Mexico, with even the "refined" in New York paying attention, the two trained like demons.[7] Sullivan worked out on Long Island, by a race track. He started before dawn, running miles around the track, after which he woke up his trainers and grabbed a few dumbbells for a bout of shadowboxing. At least five hundred reps for each arm. Then to sparring with his trainers and working on his grappling and wrestling. After this, he practiced combinations on the heavy bag, set to exactly the weight of his adversary, then finally he sat down to a breakfast of steak with English ale sauce. His morning routine finished, he rested, purportedly reading Pierce Egan's *Boxiana* to learn from the old masters. This is interesting given that he more than likely was illiterate. After relaxing, it was back to roadwork, perhaps running and picking up heavy rocks as he ran. And more ring work. And more steak. All the while, he abstained from tobacco and drink. He could only be with "Mrs. Sullivan" in "the Pickwickian sense," that is, platonically.[8] Adhering to that old bugaboo about sex and fighting, he was to live a monotonous, monk-like existence for weeks to prepare for the first great "fight of the century." Hyer did much the same. Only he meditated instead of reading Egan.

Sullivan won the toss to decide the field of battle. He knew he could not hold it near New York, with McCoy's death still shadowing all and in light of his conditional pardon. He demanded instead that it be held on a remote site in Maryland, far from authority, right between Maryland's, Virginia's, and DC's jurisdictional boundaries, somewhere along the Chesapeake. Sullivan knew the drill since the days of Crookham Common.[9] It would take place in February 1849. Meanwhile, both Hyer and Sullivan paid their installments of the five thousand dollars, with trusted officials stopping off at the Sawdust House on Chatham Street and Hyer's place on Park Row to collect the money. They sealed the deal by downing a bumper of champagne.

Preparations played out against a backdrop of big things being decided for the city in 1848. Politicians vied for power in local elections in New York, with all the drama associated with a political battle in the Points. Here, all politics remained local. A presidential election was also being contested. On the docket were slavery and democracy and the West. The war with Mexico had come to an end, with the Democratic vision of an open West now realizable. Texas, New Mexico, and California now belonged to the white republic of the United States. The continental vistas now open, of course, would supercharge the debate over slavery and nationhood, placing those New Yorkers who depended on the Southern economy for their jobs in a rather delicate position.[10] For the moment, however, the response was one of jubilation, for most Democrats anyway. General Winfield Scott, the American commander of the army, arrived in New York triumphantly when the Treaty of Guadalupe Hidalgo was signed. Much else involving the war caused confusion, especially when it came to the presidential election. Zachary Taylor, an American hero of the war, was running for president as a Whig. The Democrat's nominee stood little chance against someone running on a war record. To make matters worse for the Democrats, Martin Van Buren, the old working-class Democrat, had abandoned the party for a group that espoused abolitionism. He was running as well. The Irish in the Sixth Ward did not really have a national home in the election. In the same year, a Tammany man was elected as mayor, only beating the Whig by fewer than one thousand votes. The year before a Whig had won in a closely contested fight, and in 1849, the Democrats would be out again, as they split among themselves. Everything was close run in New York in these two years.[11]

These events fed into prizefighting. In a few brief years, from Sullivan's arrival back in the city only seven years earlier, New York had snatched the pugilistic crown away from England, and it would not give it back. New York had become the center of the fistic universe, and Sullivan was king. An editor even compared him to the famed conqueror of Mexico running for president of the United States. Sullivan, like Taylor, was a thoroughly self-actualized, self-made man, certainly not one of life's victims. "Both of them are great," a report read, "and both of them have achieved their greatness for themselves."[12] The same, of course, applied to Hyer. "Members of the pugilistic fraternity," a wag put it, had been captivated by the "grand set-to between Uncle Sam and John Mexico." But now the looming battle between Sullivan and Hyer captured imaginations. People feared warfare in the Points. Signs were ominous: "There was a bad feeling existing between the Sullivan party and the Hyer party." Daily skirmishes in the street could be breaking out, some feared.[13]

The prospect of the fight transfixed New York. For the first time, what had been a working-class pursuit, dominated by the Irish and gangsters in New York's slums, competed with great world events for attention. The middle-class tuned into news of the fight's preparations and turned out for exhibitions that both fighters put on with their cronies in theaters and venues on or near the Bowery. For these, those sparring wore gloves. Here was New York's new Fancy turning out in full force. Brokers, clerks, doctors, lawyers were rubbing shoulders with "hitters out," those democratic enforcers and hard men who ruled the Points. The *Herald* noted the "general contagion" for the fight game now, all because of this match.[14] The hype machine churned out story after story. Like those other great fights throughout history, it seemed to capture imaginations because it captured a moment. Ali v. Frazier; Tunney v. Dempsey; Jim Jeffries v. Jack Johnson; John L. Sullivan v. James J. Corbett. These pitted adversaries who represented something far larger than themselves, and the bouts usually lived up to the hype. Would this be a nineteenth-century "Thrilla in Manila"? New Yorkers hoped so.

Oddsmakers saw it as anyone's fight. In all, Americans wagered over three hundred thousand dollars on the match. But some who knew better worried. Sullivan was giving away a lot of weight. Then there was age. The seven years from his first real fights in New York, when he dominated, to 1849 were donkey's years for a fighter. Sullivan had started as a prizefighter at a later age because of his time in Australia. And then came the enforced hiatus after McCoy's death. The easy victory over the overmatched Caunt seemed to suggest he had cheated Father Time. But would this be the case? The knowing sort had questions.

They hoped to meet on Pooles Island in the Chesapeake, but Maryland authorities got wind of the plans and dispatched a steamboat to break up any attempted fight there. Marylanders worried about "her soil being desecrated by so foul and brutal [an] exhibition, which has drawn together the scum and villainy of all the Northern cities."[15] Two schooners carried the men to the island, doing their best to evade the police, with Yankee steaming down in one called, ironically, the *Whig*. Fans were venturing from as far as Philadelphia, including a "great number of blackguards."[16] With all the brouhaha, Hyer and Sullivan barely escaped being apprehended. While Yankee waited in a house on Pooles Island for the fight and for the Fancy to arrive, the police showed up. In a nice piece of skulduggery, Sullivan told a friend to jump out a window and bolt from the police. Yankee shouted, "Run, Sullivan, run, as if hell had kicked you!" The cops gave chase and nabbed the wrong man, as Yankee made his getaway.[17] He boarded again, spied Hyer's boat, and sought out a different site. They then chose the corner of a bend on the back end of a peninsula by a ledge called Rock Point at the mouth of Still Pond Creek. It was so called because of a creek leading into the pond that had never frozen over. How this led to "Still Pond" is anyone's guess. Here, a little-remembered skirmish had taken place during the War of 1812, its only claim to fame.[18] They chose it for a good reason. No one was apt to break up a fight here. These sorts of places were harder and harder to find. Nowhere was truly isolated anymore. The modern world intruded just about everywhere.

A friend from England, another fighter, gave Sullivan a piggyback ride from the boat to the beach. Hyer would similarly be attended to by a fellow named Dutch Charley Duane. They walked up three-quarters of a mile from the creek to a clearing by a farm. It was cold. Sullivan and Hyer made their way to a log farmhouse to warm themselves by fires on either end of the house. The owner of the house, a fellow named W. A. Gibson, was away at the time.[19] Only a small number made it to the obscure spot, maybe two hundred. They shoveled the snow off the ground, secured some wooden posts, grabbed some ropes—in this case the halyards from the *Whig*—and readied for the fight. Sullivan emerged from the house first. He threw his green hat in the ring. Sullivan's corners wrapped him in a blanket and brought a few hot bricks for him to warm his feet as he waited for Hyer to appear. Hyer then came out and tossed in his hat.

They would fight according to the London Prize Ring Rules, or "new rules," which, they knew, had recently been published in *Fistiana* in 1848, a compendium of fighting that now spanned the Atlantic. New York was growing in stature in the fight game, but the codes and the rituals still followed what had been established an ocean away, which had just been codified anew. They were not so new to Sullivan, who had fought Lane under these guidelines, as well as against some other adversaries in America. It was expected that Hyer also appreciated the rules. The same went for the referees, one of whom was chosen by each, and the umpire, whom the referees designated. They would be furnished with a copy of the rules.[20] Keeping their eyes on events would be two reporters from the *National Police Gazette* to certify the result.[21]

The combatants tied their colors to one of the corner posts: green with white polka dots for Sullivan, blue with white for Hyer, the ensign of the United States. In this fight, Yankee was the champion of the Irish, and this was as ethnically charged as any match in New York's history. Sullivan was playing a bit of a new role. He had managed New York's tensions up to this point by playing the shape-shifter. With the Famine, he was morphing into something else, the champion of the downtrodden Irish. What had been fluid relations before were becoming hardened, and he had to adapt. The choice of colors illustrated how he still could. "His admirers," a newspaperman at the time put it, "were only green disciples."[22] Tellingly, Mike Walsh was there. While many wore the colors of their champion, he declined to wear either. He was too good a politician, and too much was riding on this match. He wisely hedged his bets.[23]

The prefight rituals concluded, they now stripped and met in the center of the ring. It was 4:20 p.m.[24] They shook hands, though in a cautious way, and came to scratch. And Sullivan went right after Hyer. He "darted" and missed. Hyer countered with a right that hit Sullivan. Yankee then regathered himself and worked to get at Hyer's body. Most thought Sullivan was the better wrestler. Only Sullivan could not move him. Hyer instead took hold and flipped Sullivan, falling on top of him and lying on him for good measure.[25]

This more or less sums up the fight. Yankee's strategy revolved around taking the fight to Hyer, making it a "rushing fight."[26] He would not play according to the Liverpool convention of being the clever fighter. He wanted to defeat him with aggression and emotion. Alas, after Sullivan's first few attempts to get inside failed, a few had "an inkling that they had underrated their opponent." The next round the same thing happened. In addition, Hyer drew first blood. By round three, most knew Sullivan was in trouble. His plan had fallen apart; yet, he kept at the aggressive tactics, all of which Hyer foiled. Round after round, when Sullivan tried to get close inside, Hyer countered, inflicted some punishment, then wrapped Sullivan up and threw him. Each time, he landed on top, all of his weight crashing down. He generally used Sullivan as a prop to get back up, and he took longer and longer on top, allowing Sullivan precious little time to get to his corner to catch his breath. This wore on Sullivan. Then, the next round, Sullivan would initiate action "with the same reckless spirit and with the same desperate aim." He was fighting Hyer's fight. He had forgotten everything that had made him such a feared and scientific fighter. "Personal hatred," not calmness, drove him. By the eighth round, Sullivan was exhausted. Hyer now shifted tactics and went on the attack, trying to inflict damage quickly. All the while, everything a now desperate Sullivan did only wore him out more, creating more openings for Hyer, which he ruthlessly exploited. Hyer's shots found home, including a rabbit punch that landed on the back of Sullivan's head, stunning him.[27] Then there was the blood. It was flowing and clotting in Sullivan's nose. It covered Hyer's torso. By the fourteenth and fifteenth, Sullivan was losing his legs. To add to the pain, Hyer tied up Sullivan's arm and wrenched it. All knew it was over. A round later, in the sixteenth, Sullivan came to scratch in "a limpsey manner." Hyer rushed him to the rope, flipped him, and fell on him again. It was over. It had gone on for only seventeen minutes. It had been a "hurricane fight," that is, one that was action-packed from beginning to end.

Hyer left the ring. But before he did, he grabbed Sullivan's colors as a trophy.

Three things were at stake in the fight: "Ambition, Avarice, and Revenge." The fight would help determine power in the Points, in this crucible that was so evenly split and that seethed with anger.[28] These emotions, of course, made for a passionate fight, and this seemed to be Sullivan's undoing. But maybe something simpler was at work. In the ring, some old sayings always stand the test of time. No one beats Father Time. Fighters age quickly. And the beginning of a decline can be precipitous. Sullivan was years older than Hyer, and it showed. He could not beat Hyer at the young man's game of speed. And, as another adage goes, a good big man will beat a good little man every time. Hyer stood at six foot two to Sullivan's five foot ten. Hyer tipped the scales at 185, Sullivan barely made it to

155. Afterward, Sullivan claimed he weighed 144 to Hyer's 184. "The public (more especially those who are acquainted with the art of self-defence)," he argued, "will readily perceive the advantage which this superior weight gave him over me." Youth gave Hyer speed, and his muscle and size gave him power. Sullivan had tried to get inside him and beat Hyer at his own game. It was foolish to have done so. He was, as he conceded, "whipped."[29]

The bout at Still Pond Heights had a Homeric air about it, and it bore a striking resemblance to a fight that Homer chronicles. In the *Iliad,* the famed "god-like" Euryalus—the champion, not the hulk—had "worsted" a host of foes and then faced a heavy-hitting and taller adversary named Epeius, just as the "god-like" Sullivan, also undefeated up to this point, would confront someone whose abilities were just as estimable. Homer's fighters seemed evenly matched, in other words, when they squared off. Homer's bout would also prove quick and furious. "Their hands clashed together in heavy blows," the account reads, and "Dread then was the grinding of their teeth, and the sweat flowed on every side from off their limbs." Epeius spots a weakness and exploits. Then it is over. Like Sullivan, Euryalus's blood clots, and he cannot stand on his feet, and he would lose the cup, the honor usually associated with battle between armies.[30] As Homer relates, the fortunes of so many would shift because of what happened between these two men.

The 1849 fight, like Euryalus's, would mark a turning point or watershed.[31] Something in the city seemed to shift at this moment. On one level, what had been an underground activity of the vulgar caught the attention of men and women up and down the East Coast. At another level, what happened in the squared circle seemed to gesture to what was happening to and in New York and much of the United States. It offered clarity to many tangled tensions.[32] Even if Sullivan lost, his people were winning. The world belonged to wage labor, which they represented. It would belong to them demographically as well. But Yankee's time in the ring, when New York was becoming what it seemed destined to be and when so much was in flux, seemed to be ending, even if Hyer's victory was one of the Pyrrhic variety. Sullivan was made for transitions. Hyer came from a world now disappearing. Neither would graduate to that new world Sullivan was helping to bring into being.[33]

The fight, though Sullivan lost, would live on after this time. News of the bout made a splash in London and was covered in the sporting press.[34]

The Great Fight, Between Tom Hyer and Yankee Sullivan, for $10,000, James S. Baillie, 1849. (Harry T. Peters "America on Stone" Lithography Collection, National Museum of American History, Smithsonian Institution)

In Dublin, it also made news. A report claimed that the fight "caused a great deal of bad blood." It stirred up even more "native" feeling against the Irish who had "indiscreetly" backed Sullivan.[35] In America, it had a more pronounced impact. Nat Fleischer argued this episode represented "the first championship bout in American ring history." It was "as much an historic event in pugilism as was the signing of [Jack] Dempsey and [Georges] Carpentier almost 100 years later for the first million dollar gate."[36] A famous lithograph that was created at the time of the fight bears witness to its staying power. This image was widely reproduced and would eventually hang in Irish bars throughout the city. James Baillie, who drew it for the *New York Illustrated Times*, "the leading and Best Sporting Journal in America," as it billed itself, dedicated the piece to the patrons of the prize ring. Prizefighting, Baillie reckoned, was "an Antidote to the Knife."[37]

The lithograph captures a fleeting moment in time when Yankee Sullivan stood on top of the world. We enter the scene just before the fight is about to begin. The fighters are standing at scratch. A crowd sporting the colors of their champions anxiously waits for the action to start. One boy steadies himself on a wagon wheel to get a prime viewing spot. From his scarf we realize that he stands with Sullivan. A fellow sporting Hyer blue leans over to make a last-minute bet. As we look at the lithograph, we witness a moment of possibility. Then it all went down as it did.

But Baillie's point about the knife deserves some credit. Because of the fight, New York more than likely averted violence. Prizefighting did not only help in the transition to the modern and global. It was instrumental. It made the process manageable. New York was a combustible knot of dramatic changes, all of which fueled the rise of Sullivan. Prizefighting domesticated, channeled, and ritualized these tensions. As one historian writes, it gave meaning to mayhem. It did not so much offer a vicarious outlet to the real violence on the mean streets as much as it made so much of the chaos and uncertainty of common lives understandable. It gave the vicissitudes of life rules and champions. It gave debates that could become heated and even violent "a temperate and legitimate direction."[38] Common people could look to champions to fight enemies, almost like the role Euryalus played in Homer's *Iliad*. Though men "armed themselves" for combat in 1848 in the streets of New York, and many dreaded what could happen, nothing did.[39] "The pugilistic spirit" that could have "let off the fever of assassination, and the six-barreled pistols and murderous bowie knives" yielded to cheering on a champion, as a promoter argued. Prizefighting served as a "safety valve."[40]

The dog that did not bark in these years is more important than the dog that did. As opposed to a scene like the opening one in the film *Gangs of New York*, there was no large-scale violence, or "street slaughter," as had been feared and prophesied, in these years of great tension such as 1848.[41] The pressures and issues were there, to be sure. They just played out far away from the streets in Maryland.

The fight, a Washington, DC, newspaper put it, was one of "four great excitements" of the year. The bout was listed alongside such events as the discovery of gold in California. Unsurprisingly, it captured the attention of the nation, fascinating some Americans and appalling others. "The world must have retrograded alarmingly," one critic put it, if men such as Yankee Sullivan were regarded as "beacons." But for many working people he was.[42]

This story of prizefighting, the 1848–49 moment, and "beacons" brings us back to the anonymous whaler who did that bit of scrimshaw featuring Sullivan. It was undoubtedly the illustration that appeared in the *New York Illustrated Times* that inspired him to etch that image on the walrus tusk. Both Hyer and Sullivan strike the same pose as in the lithograph, though we have to scratch our heads at how he managed to misspell Yankee's name. That he used this image as a model should not surprise. The bout, as a paper would proclaim fifteen years later, "has become as familiar as the Declaration of Independence."[43] This was the whaler's fight as well, whatever side he stood with. Of course, he also carved Washington's name into the tusk. He might well have done so because this fight was part of that referendum over the experiment that Washington had brought into being. What sort of country would this be? What rights would common men on the margins enjoy? Could they, too, claim the republic as theirs, especially in light of the many changes transforming cities and inspiring migration from places far afield? Whose white man's republic was this? This fight was the scrimshander's 1848.

THE LATE ROUNDS

ROUND 13

Boston Corner

THE LOSS TO Hyer sent Sullivan reeling, triggering a series of whipsawing moves and setbacks. These would mark his life from this time forward. Sullivan returned to New York and seemingly took up where he had left off before traveling to Still Pond Heights. The old mystique, however, was missing. He threw himself into political work, supporting one of the Locofoco factions trying to take on the Tammany establishment in a Democratic primary in the Sixth Ward. Instead, he found himself slugging an alderman he had come out against, leading to an arrest. Then he brawled with Dutch Charley Duane, also as part of an intramural political fight. The struggles had not changed, nor the tactics—which still involved "a foot, a fist, or a brick-bat"—but Sullivan was no longer a nonpareil. In true Five Points fashion, both Duane and Yankee were intoxicated. Yankee got the worst of it. He also was concerned that the prizefight with Hyer ran afoul of the conditions of his pardon. For all these reasons, New York did not seem a good bet after Still Pond. So he left.[1]

In January 1850, he gave his friends "a grand blow-out" in the city before heading out on a new adventure. This time, he journeyed out West to try his luck. Maybe the move was not as radical at it seemed. He had secured a reputation that could travel along the networks he had helped fashion. The name Yankee Sullivan had become "a 'household word'" among the men who labored out West.[2] It seemed the ideal time to do so. With the discovery of gold in 1848, people from all over flocked to San Francisco. Perhaps here he could reinvent himself.

There were two ways to get to San Francisco from New York. One could go overland. But this was the harder route, the one only recently chosen by the ill-fated Donner Party. Most chose this way. Or there was going by ship. In the early stages, many from the East Coast boarded ships that would make the voyage around Cape Horn, exactly the way Sullivan had traveled, albeit in the other direction, when he was escaping New Zealand on the *Hamilton*. Some of these boarded on the North River by Chambers Street, just west of the newly opened Emigrant Savings Bank. Passengers paid $75 for steerage or $150 for a cabin. They stopped off in places like Rio in Brazil or in Callao in Peru. The trip around Cape Horn could take up to two hundred days.[3]

Sullivan chose a ship, but he took the much quicker route via the isthmus. In January 1850, he journeyed to Panama down the Atlantic on a US mail steamship called the *Cherokee* and traveled across the isthmus to board another ship, the *Oregon*, on the Pacific side. Both were owned by the same New York firm. The trip cost from $90 to $125 for cabins on the Atlantic leg, and $300 for a cabin up the Pacific. Steerage was less, but still more than the Cape Horn route. Then again, this route cut down the time substantially and was run on regular schedules.[4] A traveler could make it in fewer than forty days, if winds proved favorable. Still, the trip had its adventurous side. After disembarking on the Atlantic side, travelers had to make the "slow march" across to Panama City to board ships for the Pacific journey.[5] Sullivan, of course, was well used to roughing it. After brief stops in Mexico and in San Diego, he made it to San Francisco. The whole trip took thirty-six days.

As he passed through the Golden Gate into the great bay, he had to be reminded of the Narrows that opened into New York Harbor and of North Head and South Head that shunted ships into Sydney Harbor. Though a visitor at the time viewed the entrance to the bay as "novel and exciting," with each side of the passage framed with "high cliffs of rock" and sea lions frolicking, Sullivan had seen its like before.[6]

But this place differed. The gold that was found in the hills made it to the settlement now called San Francisco. The region had just been turned over to the United States after the war. Called Yerba Buena before, the Americans used the name of the old, humble mission of St. Francis, popularly called the Mission Dolores, that sat above on a hill overlooking the bay below. On the waterfront and creeping up the surrounding hills, buildings were going up quickly. Some ships that arrived did not bother to leave, but just sat in the bay, abandoned and repurposed as saloons, stores, warehouses, and even hotels. Pilots and crews beached them. They could not be bothered to head back to sea. A good example was the *Arkansas*, a ship that made a 178-day trek around Cape Horn from New York filled with men hoping to strike it rich. The *Arkansas* ran into trouble right by Alcatraz, then was grounded near the cove where Sullivan alit. A hole was cut into the bow to turn the ship into a saloon. The place was known for crimping, what San Francisco's early denizens rechristened as "shanghaiing." The *Arkansas* now rests beneath San Francisco's oldest bar, fittingly called the Old Ship Saloon.[7]

Fortune awaited in the gold fields. San Francisco was the epitome of the boomtown, filled with transients and jammed with shanties, canvas tents, and the goods miners needed—all to find gold, to sell it, to process it, and to transfer it. "The craze for the gold mines was in full effect," one sojourner recalled at the time.[8] The population exploded.[9]

Just like whale oil, gold made the world go round. Oil lubricated the machines and burned the lights that allowed the industrial world to march ahead. Gold did this for a global system of finance that would be based on credit and that needed a reliable monetary reserve. Gold served this purpose. The gold was mined in the hills of California, collected into Wells Fargo strong boxes that wended their way to San Francisco, then to ships bound to New York. From there, the gold could end up in London, paying off the debt New York bankers owed to their London peers. London served as the center of the network. Gold allowed for the city's further growth. The gold also greased the wheels of American expansion and global financial trade. It led to an explosion of commerce. It encouraged bonds to grow between the rest of the United States and California, especially in the form of railroads. It also enabled global connections to flourish. The gold could be poured into schemes for building infrastructure in the United States—again funneled through New York banks—especially for the push west. San Francisco was the key cog in the system, tying the gold fields to the banks in New York and then the rest of the world.[10]

San Francisco was a new Liverpool, only it developed at an accelerated rate. In no time at all, "the whole of the immense trade which we now witness with California, has sprung up." This entrepôt tied, as a New York newspaper declared, disparate regions of the world together in a length of time that it took other places, like Liverpool, "centuries" to accomplish. It remade the trade between Europe and China, and it promised to open Liverpool and London to Asia via New York. "For the last three centuries," it went on, "the idea of such a route between England and India has occupied men's minds; but it was reserved to the American people, in the first year of their possession of California, to start the movement."[11]

All eyes now turned to this remote settlement on the far side of the continent, one only really reachable by a long ship journey. And the government, as the British had done at Waitangi, now tried to bring this place under some semblance of control. Statehood, awarded in 1850, was the perfect form of appropriation.

The gold did not mine itself. It needed hard men willing to do the difficult work of extracting it from the earth. Those attracted were the sorts of men that Yankee Sullivan had run into all his life. The same networks that carried the gold throughout the world, and that were making San Francisco an entrepôt in the Pacific, spread news of the find, sustaining what was called "gold fever." The migrants to California in search of wealth and success by dint of hard work were called "Argonauts" by the American press.[12] They came initially from those places bound to the networks that San Francisco was a part of, and it was much easier to reach this settlement across the Pacific and up old, established Spanish colonial trails and then from areas proximate in the West. Miners and merchants came from other Pacific regions like China and Chile. News was heard in Hong Kong before it was back East. Some arrived from Mexico. They also traveled from regions farther north, like Oregon.[13]

Soon, as a minister who came to the city observed, San Francisco had developed into "a village of about 3,000 inhabitants, of whom about 1,000 were emigrants and sailors, of all countries and religions." In fact, this was a gross underestimate. As many as 25,000 lived there by the end of 1849. Many, many more lived in the mountains doing the hard work of mining and came and went from the city.[14] As news traveled, they came from far afield, from areas back East in the United States and from Europe. A New Yorker declared, "The shipping was immense. A perfect forest of masts, outdoing N.Y., almost double." In the city, he saw "dirty tents and wooden shanties" through the spars, as well as "people of all kinds." The people were as diverse as what he had seen in New York. "Traveling to and from this are Sandwich Islanders, Chinese, South Americans, Indians, Californians, Poles, Irish, Russians, German, French, Mexicans, Dutch, and Americans," he found.[15] San Francisco quickly became the most diverse city in the United States.[16]

But, in truth, San Francisco became a colony of New York. Word took longer to reach New York, but when it did, it set off a frenzy. Ships were setting off filled with the kind of men who drank in the Sawdust House. The discovery of gold spurred the development of more docks and warehouses in New York. It even initiated discussion of extending Canal Street to the East River to tie the increased traffic on the Hudson to the infrastructure for trade already in place. The Pacific Mail steamers, which transported goods and people up from Panama in the Pacific, were financed by New York corporations. "The California fever," a newspaper gushed, was binding New York more tightly to the American empire in the West. The small boomtowns that emerged through the gold rush, then, were the farthest tendrils of a global system, all threaded through New York, that was supplying money and muscle and connections to London banks.[17] This, then, was the sort of world Sullivan could appreciate.

This motley mix did not always get along. Old enmities traveled along the networks of movement and trade. For instance, Irish from the Points and from the Old Country, most coming via New York, flooded into San Francisco. The Irish represented the largest ethnic group in San Francisco. Most of these did what they did in the Points, working as longshoremen and as unskilled laborers doing construction. They now lived again in a place eerily like New York, Sydney, or London, in sections of the city filled with "drinking-saloons and gambling houses." Just as they did in all of these places, they did their best to get along and survive.[18] Here, they met their avowed enemies, as they had in Bandon, in London, in Sydney, and in New York. Reports flew that a gang called the Hounds, a New York volunteer unit raised during the Mexican-American War, was robbing Chilenos and Mexicans and, purportedly, shooting some of them as well. A later chronicler claimed they aimed to "exterminate" Chileans and Mexicans, all in the cause of white nationhood. Many of the Hounds embraced the same Nativist, Know-Nothing attitudes seen in the army and espoused by Hyer and Poole. It's as if the Bowery Boys had reestablished themselves in California.[19]

Australians and Omoos, too—the sort Francis Ambrose had known in the Rocks and in New Zealand—made the journey. In fact, Australians learned about the discovery of gold before New Yorkers did. They were bound into Pacific trade and communications networks that tied the West Coast of the United States to China. Much of this ran through the

Kingdom of Hawaii, a stopover point for shipping that Westerners referred to as the Sandwich Islands. News of gold reached Sydney from Honolulu. And as soon as they heard, men with tickets to leave and many without boarded ships bound for California. Broadsides pasted to walls around the very place Francis Ambrose had bolted from in Sydney announced, "GOLD, GOLD, CALIFORNIA." Merchants there who were struggling with a recession and a glut of goods, just like their peers in New York, also hoped to make a killing. By mid-1851, about eleven thousand Australians had ventured to California, most from Sydney, after American whalers, who were in and out of Pacific ports, reached Sydney with the talk of gold.[20] Adding to this mix were men sailing from Kororāreka, as well.[21]

The Australians settled in one section of the booming city, an area called "Sydney-Town," just south of the slopes leading to Telegraph Hill on the waterfront butting up against neighborhoods filled with Chileans and Mexicans. It became known before too long as an area of vice and of grog shops, what a contemporary called "hives of dronish criminals, shabby little dens with rough, hangdog fellows hanging about the doorways."[22] Collectively, the denizens were known as the "Sydney Ducks." The name had a few meanings. Those coming to Sydney-Town were migrating like ducks from another part of the world. They were seabound creatures as well. They tended to float up where opportunity presented itself. Maybe the term had to do with the waddle-like walk of many from having irons affixed to their ankles. And they also took the name from another term for larrikins. It meant, then, a Sydney gangster, sort of like a Dead Rabbit of the Rocks. Unsurprisingly, more than 40 percent of these were Irish-born.[23] Rumors flew of how the Ducks set fires to plunder and pillage. True to form, the *San Francisco Herald* declared that the settlers in Sydney-Town had "acquired a reputation little better than the Five Points of New York or St. Giles of London."[24]

It's almost as if the past lives of Francis Ambrose and Yankee Sullivan converged in one place at one time. Hounds, ducks, and rabbits. And gold. San Francisco was an unregulated sort of space that Ambrose and Sullivan had known so well.[25]

Just as the first waves arrived, prizefighters chose to come. It's little surprise they did. As the most adaptable masters of improvisation, as champions of the working class, and as political animals, they were attracted to this world. A good example would be John Morrissey. A big, brash fellow, and also an immigrant from Ireland and then New York, Morrissey traveled here to challenge anyone he could find to make a name for himself. Here was opportunity to earn a reputation, particularly because so many were drawn to California. Older fighters, too, headed to the area, like the Liverpudlian Chris Lilly who killed McCoy in the ring in Hastings. Tom Hyer also ventured to California. Here was new possibility just as New York seemed to be closing up and becoming more respectable. As institutions and practices were becoming set in New York, here again was a plastic place, a site that could be molded. Fighters came, too, from Sydney. The fight game was at its height in the Rocks in 1849, when gold fever struck. With the boom in San Francisco, prizefighters and the Fancy left with all the gold hunters. Here was the future. With their exodus, the mania for prizefighting in the Rocks died down, and officials there clamped down on the practice.[26]

Here, then, was a Fancy that straddled the globe. Like the global credit system, and like the whaling industry, it, too, rose and fell with supply and demand and proved sensitive to fluctuations. The modern Fancy proved a fluid system that mapped onto the world of open and free movement that defined the age. It, too, traveled in the ships that brought the laborers and the goods. New York served as its center, but the press ensured that it was tied to Sydney, London, and now San Francisco. Prizefighters, therefore, learned of opportunity just as gold seekers did.

Sullivan did his best to re-create his life in the Five Points. In that regard, prospects looked promising. Things here were playing out about as they had in Dooley's Long Room. Democrats were running for office, and this place was as competitive as the Points was. Here, too, Whigs and Know-Nothings abounded. He could still work with some of them as need be, but with so many Australians from the Rocks and New Yorkers from the Points coming in, the smart money was on Democrats. The question was which faction to support, or, more to the point, which ballot boxes should be stuffed and which shoulder hit.

But first things first. Picking up where he left off in New York, he opened a saloon. He did so with Lilly. On the east side of Portsmouth Square, right where the Chinatown Hilton now stands, he operated out of the United States Hotel. This place, just streets away from the port, was a gambling house that also offered bowling. Spars took place upstairs as well.

From New York, he ordered a "show-lantern" made of brass, stained glass, and crystal and measuring twelve feet in height by four wide. It purportedly cost three hundred dollars, as even readers from as far away as Alabama learned. The United States was a fancy hall, with a bar on one end and gambling tables throughout. Another place next door was frequented by Mexicans, Chileans, "and a sprinkling of Chinese." All were betting. The same went for Sullivan's place. Sullivan was preparing to make a go of it in this Western Five Points, still styling himself an entrepreneur.[27]

Beginning at the end of March 1850, he threw himself into promoting fights and sparring in saloons and theaters, putting on exhibitions of "the manly art of self-defence." He charged five dollars for admission.[28] Everyone knew Yankee Sullivan, even the Australians who entered. News of his exploits and his fights reached around the world, a phenomenon he had helped create. He did not enter the ring; however, he did manage to train up some fighters who were coming of age. The most famous of these was a young man named John Heenan. With time, he too would enter the political world Sullivan brokered in New York. The son of Irish immigrants, Heenan came from the tough town of Troy, New York. He reckoned that the future lay in California. Heenan worked in the town of Benicia. The "Benicia Boy" labored in the yard of the Pacific Mail Steamship Company, the line that sailed from and toward New York, swinging a hammer. He did heavy labor there during the day, just as he caroused and looked for opportunities to fight in the evenings. Such possibilities were now abounding. Sullivan took a special shine to him because they came from a similar world and had the same aspirations, even if Heenan was twenty years younger. He and Sullivan appeared in theaters together to put on some boxing exhibitions.[29]

He also worked with Australian "milling coves." They found fights soon enough, some of which, as an Australian paper put it, were organized by Yankee Sullivan, whom a report still called "Ginger." He and his fellow ex-convicts were putting on exhibitions at his United States Tavern in Portsmouth Square, now a gambling center in the city. Sullivan even encountered "his antagonist John White" there. This must have been the White he fought in Australia.[30]

The London paper that thought he was a catalyst for American boxing alleged that he did the same for Irish migration to California. He and "Knights of the Knuckle" paved the way for "emigrants from 'the Old

Countrie.'" Yankee aimed to become nothing less than "governor-general of that delightful part of the World." The newspaper was not overstating the case. These prizefighters, as had been the case in New York and in Sydney, acted almost as urban frontiersmen, in this case scouting out opportunities and exploiting them.[31]

The mixture of New Yorkers and Australians and Irish—with prizefighters as their storm troopers—made for a combustible environment. In 1850, when Sullivan decamped, "the condition of things here was exceedingly rough." One of those living in San Francisco argued "there was a very dangerous class of men here at that time; robberies and assaults were frequent." No doubt, all was not chaos. But he, for one, carried a pistol out at night. The Australians frightened him. So did the New Yorkers. These sort "made themselves prominent as rough men."[32] As was the case, of course, with Sullivan.

Something happened in San Francisco that never could have in New York. Anti-Irish and anti-Australian factions, led by those merchants profiting from the connections gold conferred, were able to band together and make a concerted effort to drive out what they perceived to be corrupt influences. The more respectable sort decided in 1851 that something had to be done. Leading merchants and officials formed what they called a Vigilance Committee to take law and order into their own hands. They particularly focused on the Ducks, who were wreaking havoc in the city. They did not want a Rocks-like culture to emerge here. They also banished the Hounds.[33] The members of the Vigilance Committee rounded up some miscreants and hanged a few. William T. Coleman, one of the leaders, considered what was happening in the city a contest between "the best people" and "the Hounds." By "Hounds" he meant not only the New Yorkers but much of the rest of what he considered riffraff. "Among the new immigrants," he believed, "unfortunately, was a quota from New South Wales and other English colonies." They were "the worst element of the world." The committee took shape "to vigilantly watch and pursue the outlaws and criminals who were infesting the city, and to bring them to justice, through the regularly constituted courts, if that could be, through more summary and direct process, if must be."[34]

The "Spirit of Lynch Law," a California newspaper declared, was raging.[35] The first to be hanged was John Jenkins. An ex-convict from Sydney, he had stolen a safe. Much of the crowd gathered, the established sort, was happy to see him dispatched. The committee strung him up at Portsmouth Square. By doing so, it was sending a signal. This, the site where Sullivan had established his bar, was what its members regarded as the epicenter of vice. Jenkins died with the "incorrigibility of the impenitent sinner." The Vigilance Committee members expected attacks from "the roughs." But none came. They let his body hang there overnight.[36] They hanged a few more, including one Australian named English Jim who, when asked on the scaffold if he had any final words, said, "This is a damned tiresome business. Get it over with."[37] All told, in the summer of 1851, the vigilantes lynched four men. They called ninety-one men before the committee, most Australians. They ordered fourteen deported, and a good number were encouraged to leave. Things seemed to quiet down in San Francisco. At least for a while.[38]

Rumors flew of how Sullivan was part of the roundup. A report even circulated of how he, too, had been killed at the hands of the Vigilance Committee. He was, after all, better known than nearly everyone there, a true celebrity. A story also made the rounds throughout the country and was "repeated all over the Union," as if a great man had perished, of how he had been shot dead in Sacramento after he assaulted someone. But such was not the case. "Yankee Sullivan is not dead," Americans learned. Sullivan had already moved on. He had stayed there less than a year.[39]

The likely reason for his departure is more dramatic and more prosaic at the same time. At 4:00 a.m. on May 4, 1850, a fire broke out at the United States Hotel. Arson was suspected. Specifically, authorities thought Australians set the blaze. This was San Francisco's second great fire, the first occurring just months before. Boomtowns, built quickly of wood, tend to be susceptible, as New Yorkers and citizens of Sag Harbor knew. On this night in May, eight square blocks went up in flames. Rioting and looting followed. No one was convicted. For the record, Sullivan was not suspected. But it is clear his investment had gone up in smoke. So he had left his base in Portsmouth Square well before Jenkins swung.[40]

If his first move after the hammering by Hyer proved explicable, Sullivan's next series were head-scratching. A California newspaper declared, near the end of 1850, that "Yankee Sullivan has returned to New York from California, out of health and out of money." Someone from New

York let them in on something: "He is a mere wreck—disease has broken him up, and he has evidently 'fought his last fight.'" California, apparently, had broken him. The account added, "We are not aware that morality or human happiness will be the sufferers by the above event." For the record, he was not a "mere wreck," though he had been ill. This sort of over-the-top reporting on the condition of prizefighters would prove par for the course from this time on. Fighters would ever be on the brink of collapse but would miraculously rise again. The story of the great John L. Sullivan comes to mind. This Sullivan regularly appeared unhealthy and on his last legs as a fighter, only to come back. The same would be said of Jack Dempsey, Muhammad Ali, and, more recently, Tyson Fury. Each of these heavyweight champions had let themselves fall out of condition, but extraordinary athletes all, they rebounded to defy expectations. At this moment, Yankee Sullivan found himself at the low ebb, but he was hardly finished. The report, though, did get one thing right. He had indeed returned whence he came. He came back to see if he could reprise his old life in New York.[41]

New York was not what it was when he reigned. It had changed dramatically in just the short span from right before the Hyer fight to his return from California. Yankee Sullivan, in fact, entered the wilderness in the ever-expanding city. He still cut a grand figure in the Points and had not lost his appeal. But he was low on cash. And growing older in a young man's fight world. The times, moreover, were changing. More and more Irish poured into the Five Points and, now, areas in Manhattan farther afield. If anything, the process accelerated while he was out West. The whole city seemed Irish, and it had almost happened overnight. Around this time, one-third of New York hailed from Ireland. The population of the city was surging. Germans, too, were entering in large numbers, and a whole German neighborhood had grown up right to the northeast of the Ould Bloody Sixth called Kleindeutschland.

New York was bursting. The docks ran up the East River past Corlears Hook. The culture of the Points was moving with the city as it grew. Poor, working-class areas were popping up in new parts of the city. Docks extended now along the North River, that is, the southern section of the Hudson separating Hoboken and Jersey City from Manhattan. As this happened the relentless move to the north of Manhattan continued apace, as poor displaced wealthier folks trying to stay a step or two ahead of the lurch north. Sullivan had come from an earlier New York, one growing to be sure, but one in an earlier stage of transition. He was not of this moment.

The Five Points remained as competitive as ever, and in what was clearly becoming a Darwinian place—even anticipating Darwin's grand thesis about to be published—and only those willing to enter the ring could survive. Sullivan held fast to the conventions that had allowed him to rise in the city: adapt, improvise, and move. For the 1852 election cycle, he chose for his drinking partners those most likely to back winners, and these happened to be Hyer and Poole. The trio, it was reported, sauntered around town in "drunken orgies," which led to violent encounters, such as one on Mercer Street and another on Broome Street, at which Sullivan shot a man in the arm. Carousing, politics, and fisticuffs were still merged in Sullivan's world, only now the entanglements led him into alliances with former enemies. To these men, all politics was still local. They set themselves against the Empire Club faction run by Tammany chieftain Isaiah Rynders, a man Sullivan had backed before. By 1852, they had fallen out. Reports made the rounds that Hyer and Sullivan also appeared together in Baltimore while the Democratic Party convention was taking place. One reckons they made their presence known outside the convention in the streets. By one account, Sullivan was up to his old tricks there, and he was involved in a street fight, one in which he was caned. But something new was evident in Baltimore as well. It seemed Sullivan had made quite a turn and "left the democrats and joined the whigs."[42]

As New York was becoming more Irish, this proved a questionable decision. The Irish, his old base of support, would find little comfort from Whigs, even if Sullivan relished drinking with them. He and three others tried to suggest otherwise to "Citizens of Irish Birth." He cosigned a letter decrying some newcomers to the city, presumably Irish, who were arguing that the Irish could and should only vote for Democrats. Those who "are neither citizens nor voters" should not make so bold as to "dictate to us, older, and as we presume, quite as well informed residents of this Metropolis." The letter continued that Sullivan and his cosigners would "vote for General Winfield Scott," the Whig, in his race against Franklin Pierce, the Democrat. For the Irish, the case could be made. Scott, the letter went, had "advocated for Ireland." In the minds of the letter writers, Pierce was the bigot. The plea did not sway the Irish of New York.[43]

The rules were beginning to shift. The Irish had more and more muscle each day, as more and more of the Irishmen who did all the building and hauling as New York inched northward demanded their rights and their piece of the pie. They did not need to tap into dizzying debates about shifting alliances. They needed a champion. And there were plenty of men willing to try to play that role. Until the Hyer fight, Sullivan had assumed this task. Now others would try to do so. In the process, it would become evident that the Five Points and politics in New York had changed in the short period of time since Sullivan had reigned supreme.

The main challenger throwing his hat in the ring to serve as champion of the Irish in New York's Five Points was the same John Morrissey who had tried to make a name for himself in California. To appreciate this chapter of Yankee Sullivan's life means understanding a bit about Morrissey. Like Sullivan, Morrissey was born in Ireland, but nearly twenty years later. Instead of to London, his Tipperary family fled to Troy, New York, a tough industrial town tied to the Erie Canal and to New York City. Morrissey worked industrial jobs in Troy and ran with a gang. He was known to be a rough street fighter, and he had done time in jail for "disorderly conduct." He even did one stint in an Albany Penitentiary at the same time as his mother, who was arrested for "beastly intoxication." From a young age, a report ran, he "inherited a strong will, great tenacity of purpose, a courageous disposition, and the natural love and aptitude for pugilistic controversies," which, the author added, "is a characteristic of the nation from which he sprang." He took some instruction in boxing. But it didn't stick. He brawled.[44] He then took what skills he had to New York. Morrissey found a job as an immigrant runner. This entailed working down by the docks on the East River with characters with names like "One-eyed" Daly, greeting Irish immigrants as they disembarked, helping some, fleecing others, and trying to enlist all as good Tammany Democrats. He then set his sights on becoming a fighter and a man of stature. For this he needed a reputation.

One day he swaggered into the Empire Club—a power base within the Points that Yankee had frequented and now was turning his back on. By this time, Rynders was going all in with the Irish, so given the evident demographic changes in the city, Morrissey was picking what he regarded as a winner. He was looking to find Dutch Charley Duane, the man who had carried Hyer on his shoulders into the ring when he fought Sullivan and who later gave Yankee a beating when he was drunk. If Morrissey could take him down, he would start making a name for himself. Alas, Dutch Charley was not around. He then announced, in a way that only the great John L. Sullivan would be able to pull off, that he could lick any sonuvabitch in the house. Challenge accepted. The hard men in the Empire Club pummeled Morrissey, laying him out with a spittoon. Undaunted, he returned. His moxie and bottom impressed Rynders. "There wasn't a man in New York," an English boxer who witnessed the beating reckoned, "who could lick Morrissey with a hickory stick in half an hour."[45]

He took up saloon fighting. As one story ran, perhaps apocryphal, at Sandy Lawrence's Pistol Gallery on Broadway, after a fellow by the name of Tom McCann had cheated Morrissey in a game of cards, Morrissey challenged him to a fight. As he was taking off his coat, McCann threw him into a potbelly stove, scattering hot coals across the floor. McCann pinned Morrissey to the floor and began bludgeoning him. When his back began burning, smoke ascended. "Old Smoke" had been born. He now had a nickname that would stick.[46] He then beat McCann "insensible." Morrissey was the sort to challenge anyone. And so Rynders set him to work as a shoulder-hitter. He was quickly coming to do the work that Sullivan once had performed. Like Sullivan, he set up in a saloon on Broadway called the Gem, right where the Woolworth Building stands and just around the corner from New York's first Catholic church, St. Peter's.

But he wanted more. Unable to rise above his station immediately in New York, as we know, he caught "gold fever" and headed out West to make his fortune. He found fights instead. He tended to win them. Even if his supporters drew pistols and knives to let his adversaries know Old Smoke could not lose. Like Sullivan, the ring would provide his way out and up. Gambling, as well. Morrissey embraced the sporting culture of the period. He had also "earned a 'rep' as a digger of gold with a pack of cards or a roulette wheel," wrote a later newspaperman. He might have added faro, the game he specialized in.[47] The young Morrissey, in other words, apprenticed in California.

With these new skills in and out of the ring, he returned to New York. He itched for a big fight. In the first few years of the 1850s, he tried to take on Hyer, but Hyer's price was too high. Another champion would do, if even an Irishman. In 1853, he chose Sullivan, who was now cavorting with Hyer and the Whigs.

This should not surprise us. This is what good fighters do. They fight each other. And they often come onto the scene in bunches. This is how "eras" come into being. Think of the "Four Kings" of boxing in the 1980s: Roberto Duran, Sugar Ray Leonard, Marvelous Marvin Hagler, and Thomas Hearns. They more or less round-robin-ed one another, realizing that only by taking the others on could they claim greatness. The same was happening in these earlier years.[48]

But something more elemental was at work in the 1850s. Morrissey represented raw power and blind ambition. Years later, he remembered the anger that drove him. It was stoked by being an outsider. "Gentlemen," he was wont to say, "I will lick your crowd, and make you acknowledge me, if it takes me years." He had been "as poor as a wharf rat . . . but I kept on the wharves unloading steamers, working with longshoremen and getting beaten so often that I was hardly ever right well." He had believed that "as long as I was poor nobody would do me the favor to fight me in the ring." This was his only way to become a somebody in a city in which he stood on the wrong side of so many divides. Irish, unskilled, and Catholic, only his fists gave him a voice.[49]

Unlike Sullivan, he did not accommodate or adapt. Nativists could not stand Old Smoke. He once, or so the story goes, helped repel an attack on St. Patrick's Cathedral just north of the Points by a gang led by Bill the Butcher. Morrissey would never dream of tossing bricks through the archbishop's windows or consorting politically with anti-Irish Whigs.[50] More to the point, Nativists saw him as the young up-and-coming Irishman, the future that was leading the Famine-era tide turning their city green. Sullivan seemed to represent the past. Yankee switched allegiances with the wind, as guile was needed to survive politically. Old Smoke looked like a dreaded and implacable future.

Morrissey knew that Sullivan was his stepping stone to power. In 1853, he tried to entice Sullivan to battle, stalking him from public house to public house throughout the Ould Bloody Sixth and hurling insults. He crowed in his saloon the Gem that he could beat Sullivan in under an hour. But to no avail. Sullivan would not bite. As an experienced boxer, Morrissey knew he had to change his strategy when the first one failed. To this end, one evening, in his cups, he sauntered into the Sawdust House to challenge Sullivan yet again. They had words. Morrissey called Sullivan a "yellow coward." Men brandished weapons. Morrissey then hit right at his power base. He declared "that he was just as much an Irishman—though better, than Sullivan, he having been born at Templemore, Tipperary, in 1831, and not Troy, N.Y. as hitherto [is] generally supposed." The Bandon-born Sullivan must have laughed when he heard it, though the charge had to sting in the wake of Sullivan's conversion to the Whigs.

Then Morrissey allegedly went further still. He might have accused Sullivan of killing his wife.[51]

Now, there might have been some truth to this; however, the question is, which wife? We believe that Sullivan was married at this time. James Sullivan had more than likely wed an Irishwoman named Catherine Hurley, and the two were married at the time of Morrissey's charge. If so, they had probably tied the knot in Transfiguration Church. Catherine Hurley was a native of Bandon as well, and maybe their families knew one another there. We know nothing of her beyond the possibility of the Bandon connection and the fact that Sullivan was acquainted with her relatives in New York. There is also a possibility he had been wed before this time to Catherine Masterson, also originally of Ireland, in the mid- to late 1840s. She may have perished in the cholera epidemic of 1849. This, however, is pure guesswork. If men like Yankee Sullivan lived hard-to-track existences, the problem is amplified for women in this place-in-time.[52]

Morrissey did not have Hurley or even Masterson in mind; he was talking about an earlier relationship. Sullivan had, of course, married Margaret back in 1841 or 1842, just after he arrived in New York. We know from accounts that Margaret Sullivan, then only nineteen, perished in a fire in 1844 in Sullivan's old place on Madison Street. The story went that she was sitting in bed, mending some linens, when her clothes caught on fire from a candle nearby. Another account of the events said she fell asleep waiting for her husband to come home, and somehow the candle lit the bed afire in the middle of the night.[53] Some, though, whispered she was burned to death in her bed, that she and Sullivan were drunk and were arguing, and that he pushed her onto the bed, tipping a lamp onto it as well. Perhaps Sullivan in a drunken rage threw a lamp on the bed while his wife slept and got off the hook because of his political connections, an accusation that would appear much later but the one that Morrissey may well have uttered as well.[54]

We have no idea what to believe. Deaths by fire were common enough in a part of the city where most of the ramshackle housing was made of wood. But was Sullivan to blame? An incident that had recently occurred might well have served as a template. In 1843, a woman was accused of burning a few people to death. It became a New York sensation. It was alleged she had worked as an abortionist and that she was having an affair. The penny press, the same press that was making Sullivan a celebrity, made her an anticelebrity. Her story scandalized New Yorkers, and it had to be on people's minds when Sullivan's wife perished.[55] But to many of his adversaries and even allies, the accusation that a violent, drunken Sullivan could do such a thing was believable. Whether true or not, these were fighting words.

What Morrissey charged, however taboo, made the rivalry an affair of honor. Sullivan had no choice but to accept the challenge and try to reclaim his stature. They set the fight for one thousand dollars a side, a relatively modest amount for a match of this stature. Sullivan needed money. The financial hit of the Hyer fight had "well high ruined" him. Adding to his burden, he had just moved the Sawdust House from the hurly-burly of Chatham Street to Centre Street, right next to the Tombs and Cow's Bay.[56] But the point is that he settled on a fight without a big payday when he could have used one. They would fight within weeks of the challenge. Sullivan had spent months preparing for Hyer. For Morrissey, he would not train for a long spell. He would tune up; he was not nearly as broken down as some of the reports from California suggested. The little time he had to prepare proved enough to get him into fighting shape. But, once again, such was and is not unusual for fighters still in their prime.

For all the vitriol, the protagonists would follow the strict conventions of the ring. They drew up "articles of agreement." Prizefighting followed its code duello, even if working-class men—and not aristocrats—were involved. Honor dictated as much. Sullivan and Morrissey agreed on the regulations to be followed, in this case "the new rules of the London Prize Ring" that had been used for the Hyer fight. Each side would deposit installments of the stake on a set of exact dates at select public houses. Winner take all. At the last deposit date, Sullivan and Morrissey would flip a coin, the winner to determine where the fight would take place. It had to be "within one hundred miles of the city of New York." The one who chose had to give notice within four days of the fight day, October 12. Doing so would ensure that the authorities would not get word, but that the Fancy could.[57]

The fight became the talk of the Points, largely because it led to some unexpected twists and turns. For a start, who would Tom Hyer or Bill Poole support? The matchup "led to great changes in the usual lines of popular partisanship, as both Sullivan and Morrissey had heretofore been considered (whether they were willing or not) as Irish or Irish-American champions. They were never to set their gaffs against each other." So said a wag.[58] Poole and the other Nativists hated Sullivan for quite a while; now they hung out with him. However, they detested the younger Irishman without reservation. He seemed more vicious and cockier. He also represented a rising consciousness in the Points that was more avowedly Irish and assertive and that suggested that through sheer numbers the Irish might come to dominate Tammany and then the whole city. Morrissey personified an existential threat. Sullivan had worked by the reigning democratic conventions, however violent they were. These were still based on competition. When Sullivan arrived, the Irish represented a minority, a vocal and visible one; however, they had to work within the political culture and arrangements of the day. Sullivan, to be sure, had to contest those who hated him. Doing so made him a champion. He also had to work with them from time to time. Doing so allowed him to remain a champion. Yankee thrived with fluidity and shape-shifting, skills that he had mastered in sites as they had been developing, places such as Bandon, London, Sydney, and Liverpool. Morrissey promised to introduce a new politics of domination, and an unapologetic one at that.

So, confusion reigned as New York seemed to reach a new democratic inflection point. But money still had to be bet. Sides had to be supported. Hyer cast his lot with his old nemesis Sullivan. Poole did as well, vowing to stand in his corner. Ultimately, a writer declared, "the sympathies of Hyer, Poole and others were with Sullivan." Sullivan still enjoyed his old support in the Points, but it was clear that if he lost, Morrissey would be the new voice of the Irish in New York. As for others, they thought Sullivan still represented Irishness. They had to assume Morrissey was American. "Many rural Americans," a booster of the fight game wrote, "who had looked upon Morrissey as the Irish champion, now gave him their support upon the ground that he was more of an American than Sullivan."[59] Insiders knew the real score.

Morrissey won the coin toss to determine where they would fight. He chose a place about one hundred miles north of the city, reachable from his old base of support in Troy. It was called Boston Corner. Admittedly, this is a strange name for a crossroads in the state of New York. Only it wasn't in New York, and that was the point. Technically, it belonged to Massachusetts, though it sat over the mountains from the rest of the state. The people there had asked to be brought under the jurisdiction of New York. Given its location, Massachusetts magistrates could not arrest criminals they would have to pursue through either New York or Connecticut. Criminals knew this. This bucolic slice of land between the Taconic Mountains and the Hudson River was "a no-man's-land." In 1855, it would become New York's. In 1853, no one ruled it. It epitomized in-betweenness. Boston Corner, a paper declared, had been "formerly part of Massachusetts, which State ceded to New York, but the cession was never ratified; and at present there is no control exercised over it of any kind. The ground was everything that could be desired." For fighters and miscreants, that is. Morrissey picked it for this reason. Like Crookham Common, it was "disputed territory" that sat between jurisdictions.[60] An 1878 history of Columbia County, New York, explained that "it became a sort of 'city of refuge' for criminals and outlaws of all classes, who fled to it to escape from the reach of the officers of the law." It also attracted prizefighters like Sullivan and Morrissey "who could here carry out their brutal and inhuman purposes secure from the interference of the authorities."[61]

And Boston Corner enjoyed another advantage. This sleepy place, with fewer than twenty-five homesteads and about sixty souls raising rye, corn, potatoes, oats, and buckwheat, was reachable. Investors saw the potential of tying New York to this area by rail. With rail, they could compete with rivals from Boston and with the steamship operators who plied the goods coming in from the Erie Canal and the West. New York bankers financed a single railroad line up from the Five Points—in fact, a block from the latest iteration of the Sawdust House and next to the Tombs—across the Harlem River right up to Boston Corner. It was among the first rail lines in the United States. A succession of peripatetic Irish laborers, living in shanties along the route, did the digging, blasting, and hauling to build the line through the 1830s and 1840s, finally reaching Boston Corner in 1852. They earned seventy-five cents a day and their board for the thankless work. The locals were "astonished" to see such men.[62] In 1845, a local magnate had built a smelting facility to produce pig iron on an industrial scale. In 1848, the ironworks spewed out four to six thousand tons a day. The raw product went by rail to a foundry close by that turned it into iron for guns, rail-car wheels, horseshoes, and carriage manufacturing.[63] The finished goods made their way back down the tracks to New York and to other industrial sites like Morrissey's Troy. Both devoured iron.

In just over three hours one could travel from City Hall to this hamlet. Cornelius Vanderbilt, the man making a mint from tying the world and nation together through rail and shipping, would purchase the line. He was wise to do so. The railroad represented the first moment that a substantial bridge that could support a train tied the city of New York to the mainland. Now goods could come and go without worries of rivers or canals freezing over. For the purposes of Morrissey and Sullivan, though, the New York and Harlem Railroad tied this limbo land of Boston Corner to their world. It was perfect.

Into this farthest verge of the industrializing world came the prizefighters. Imagine what the locals must have thought as three thousand gang members, with their flashy clothes and violent ways, jammed onto trains to venture to this place literally in the middle of nowhere. So many were coming up that the 7:00 a.m. train out of Manhattan had extra cars attached to it. The trains left Tryon Row, right by Sullivan's gym and across from City Hall and Tammany Hall, pulled by horses. Steam engines were not allowed downtown. At a depot on Thirty-Second Street, engines with iron wheels modeled from trains in Liverpool were coupled to the cars. Fights broke out between those in and those outside the train at the depot, as more and more people tried to jam in. Then it wended its way up Fourth Avenue, over trestles and through tunnels hewn from rock farther north in Manhattan, before crossing the Harlem River into sleepy Westchester. "The behavior of some of them while in the cars was not such as could be commended; and many acts of disorder, to use the mildest terms, were perpetrated," a reporter wrote in the *New York Herald*.[64] Few worried about tickets or paying. Of those who did, some paid in counterfeit bills or with slugs. The trainmen barricaded themselves in a mail car and unhitched the engine about a mile from Boston Corner. They wanted to get as far away from the passengers as possible.

Certainly a witness to the proceedings saw it this way. Harm Miller was but a boy in Boston Corner when the Five Points circus came to town. Years later, as an old man, he recounted what he saw. He and his brother Chaz had been playing around the blacksmith's shop "when all of a sudden in walked four burly looking chaps and asked how far it was to the next town." Harm pointed up the track and said it was "about a mile to Boston Corner." These were the gangsters just dropped off by the frightened trainmen. No sooner had they given directions than "in stalked six more rough lookers" hoping to find a place to bed down. The men informed Harm that they were going to see the fight the next day. This was the first Harm had heard of it, so closely guarded a secret it was. Next day, Harm and Chaz headed to Boston Corner after wrapping up their chores, "and by Jimminy-crack I never saw so many people. The square was black with 'em." These were "the roughest toughest gang" he had ever seen. He likened them to pirates. "They would walk right into the houses," he said, "and help themselves to anything they could find and walk right out and never say thank you." One fellow grabbed five loaves of bread cooling on a windowsill. The woman of the house asked him to at least spare her one. Morrissey, she pleaded, was staying there. He laughed and walked off. He, no doubt, had his money on Yankee. Pickpockets abounded. "They stole every chicken they could see," Harm said. They then "broke open the schoolhouse and cooked their plunder there." You couldn't find so much as an egg after the bout. Another witness told a tale of how an African American banjo player enticed the crowd while his buddies fleeced them of everything they had.[65] Here, men from the Points brought gambling accessories in their bags, setting up games of chance in open fields. Reports made the rounds of cockfights and dogfights. Women from all over strolled about. It was as if the Five Points had decamped in the wilderness. "A week of high life and heavy doings here in the spot nobody rules" was what was predicted.[66]

The field chosen for battle lay in a depression west of the mountains that formed a natural amphitheater. Just north of a schoolhouse, in Abram Vosburg's meadow and right next to the property of a fellow named John Allison, they would square off. Here, they formed two rings, with bouncers in between. The crowd stayed beyond the outer ring, all to ensure that the gamblers did not compromise the fight. As we shall see, it didn't work in this instance. For a moment, anyway, nowhere was becoming somewhere. In this somewhere the old would struggle with the new. For better or worse, Morrissey represented the future on Wednesday, October 12, 1853.

The seconds debated who would serve as the chief referee. They decided on someone named Charles Allaire. The problem was that no one was disinterested in this fight. All had something riding on it. Including Allaire. But a backer of Morrissey "took bets off his hands if he would serve, which was agreed to." How this would ever work, or how it would ensure Allaire was not crooked, was never explained. The early betting favored Morrissey 100 to 80. The English fighter who had marveled at Morrissey's ability to endure punishment said Sullivan was "the best fighter he ever saw." Morrissey, however, looked "herculean."[67]

Anywhere from three to five thousand people surrounded the ring. "Them old hickory trees there were more alive with men—every limb was bent," someone remembered. It "looked like a lot of turkeys gone to roost." Then, at 2:00 p.m., Harm Miller remembered, a hush fell over the throng. "It was the quietest crowd" he ever saw. "When they and their seconds came into the ring, it was so still you could hear a pin drop," he recalled. Morrissey entered first. He came out wearing a long scarf emblazoned with the Stars and Stripes, and his seconds tied his colors to a post. He played up the American side of his Irish American identity, but everyone knew he was fighting to be the champion of the Irish and to make America theirs. The American flag, he suggested, belonged to the Irish as much as anyone. Morrissey did not hide the fact that he was Irish and aimed to be their champion in a hostile new world.

Yankee Sullivan, a man whose very name allowed ambiguous identity and who had played up either one side or the other, had no such need to do so. He could be who he wanted in this fight against another from his tribe. Yankee threw his hat in the ring and tied his colors to the proverbial mast. He chose a black silk cravat, with black cords hanging down from it. This was a "very piratical and death-dealing signal."[68] The choice suggested that Sullivan would fight for "Death or Victory." As a Baltimore newspaper put it, he "mounted the black handkerchief to show that he was bound to win, or never strip for another fight."[69] The choice echoed the battle cry his father, John Ambrose, had screamed in Java about forty years earlier. In this context, however, it said something more. Yankee had purportedly used the Stars and Stripes, most visibly in early 1841 England before he took on Hammer Lane and tried to pass himself off as an American. Once he arrived in New York, whether he was beating Nativists or British fighters, he used black or blue. When he fought Caunt in 1847 and Hyer in early 1849 during the Famine years, he chose green. The green had been new. He was, as the Irish were streaming into the city, styling himself a champion for them. This choice reflected how the power calculus in the Points was beginning to change in the late 1840s. The Irish were just starting to consider themselves a political force, and ever the improviser, he recognized this new reality. The choice of black for the Morrissey fight suggested that he was reverting to ambiguity.

"They stepped up," Harm said, "and shook hands and then walked back." After coming up to scratch and posing in fighting attitude, they sparred cautiously. Each took the measure of the other. But they did not ease into the fight. Sullivan landed the first punch, a left on Morrissey's nose. Then "Bliff! And Morrissey lifted Yankee right under the right ear and sent him galleywest right under the rope not three feet from me," Harm remembered. "The fight was on." His seconds screamed at Yankee to avoid such shots or "he would be taken home in a box."

Sullivan heeded the advice. He displayed caution. Then he resorted to his left. Again and again. He focused on the nose. He wanted "first blood." Sullivan's seconds pointed to Morrissey's bloody nose and claimed it. Already Morrissey's was running with "claret." Morrissey charged, throwing a big right and a left, and Sullivan jumped back. As a rule, fighters should come into a punch to smother it, or move to the side and let it glide past—a move known as a slip. Leaning back is a trick that only a few could pull off. As Sullivan stepped back away from the punches, Morrissey missed. By doing this, Sullivan signaled that he thought Morrissey could not catch up to him, age be damned. He meant to embarrass and frustrate Old Smoke. As he pulled off the punch, he fell to the ground. The round then ended.

The first round said it all. He was not going to make the same mistakes he'd made in the Hyer bout. He would fight his fight. In using this strategy, Sullivan was demonstrating something he would do throughout the fight. He would fall rather than let the larger Morrissey fall on him. In this way, he wanted to set the tempo of the fight. He could tire Morrissey by bleeding him and take rests when he thought fit. He would also frustrate

Morrissey that much more. Sullivan controlled time and space. As one account put it, his supporters, those who had bet on him and his friends, "were in ecstasies." To sum it up, and all saw this right off, "the superior science of Sullivan was quite manifest."[70] In boxing skill, "Morrissey was a complete novice." Sullivan "threw himself into that easy London-school attitude, that bespoke the adept."[71]

Mike Tyson said that every boxing plan, as in any battle, goes out the window with the first shot to the mouth. But not this time. Sullivan kept his composure and fought his fight. "Yankee," Harm recounted, "had awful science; he kept pecking Morrissey right in the face." Morrissey would throw a haymaker, and the smaller Sullivan would slip, dodge, or parry. He had clearly learned from the Hyer loss. Keep away from the bigger man, be patient, pick your spots, and don't let him wrestle you down or take the big hit. This was textbook Mendoza, something right out of his *Art of Boxing*. And from the Wards. American newspapermen noted how Sullivan employed "the dropping system." Sullivan had leaned on the idea that he could use a tactic "in just repute" but not technically afoul of the laws of the prize ring. He had done so, of course, against Secor on Staten Island. He could claim, as he did then, that he slipped when throwing a punch or that a glancing blow had laid him out. He would drop when he chose to set the pace of the bout and then laugh, mocking both opponent and convention.[72] Throughout the fight, Morrissey's backers would complain of the use of the Ward tactic, "but on reference to the latest rules of the English ring," as a newspaper covering the fight put it, Sullivan's seconds "proved that Sullivan had a right to go down either in giving a blow or receiving one."[73] He "proved himself to be *au fait* to all the tactics of the Ring."[74] His time in Liverpool still bore fruit in the ring.

In the early rounds, Sullivan used straight rights and especially lefts to beat Morrissey to the punch. Morrissey swung. As he wound up, Sullivan let fly with quick piston-like shots to the face. Now, this tactic proved a bit unusual. Head-shots in bare-knuckle fighting can be dangerous. Hard foreheads break knuckles. And in fact, gloved fighting was instituted to protect hands, not heads. Sullivan, though, proved himself a sharpshooter, a sniper, who would wait, or feint, and let fly straight punches aimed at the nose and at times the eyes. After doing damage, he continued to go down "to avoid punishment." Only in the third round did Sullivan hurt his hands, splitting a knuckle as one of his punches found home again. This round, too, demonstrated Morrissey's strategy, if we can even call it that at this point. As Sullivan tied him up in a clinch, a classic move to stifle a big puncher, Morrissey bear-hugged him and threw him on the ropes. In this instance, Sullivan managed to slip below Morrissey, "and no damage was done."[75]

Yankee's left eye was bothering him, and it was swelling up. But beyond that, he was controlling the fight. Morrissey's face, though, "appeared shockingly mangled" by the fifth round. Sullivan shifted from the left to the right. These he threw, in textbook fashion, "straight from the shoulder." Morrissey's eyes swelled. His corner had to lance an eyelid and drain it so he could see. But they might as well have tried stopping the tide. Sullivan hit at will. By the eighth, the ring looked a shambles, literally, as Morrisey's cornermen were covered in his blood. Throughout, one writer reckoned, Sullivan landed five punches for every one of Morrissey's. By the eleventh round, Sullivan's seconds cautioned him to stay away from Morrissey. You "must surely win," they pleaded, by being "careful." He generally was, except when Morrissey was able to get him on the ropes. In a "fierce" or "truly desperate" fifteenth, Sullivan ran into some trouble when Morrissey tied him up, threw him against the ropes, grabbed the rope with both hands, and tried to squeeze the life out of Sullivan. Nonetheless, Sullivan "managed to extricate himself."

After this, Yankee kept the rounds short by falling when it suited him. The middle rounds went quickly by, sometimes with Sullivan landing a punch or two and then going to ground. The frustration set in. Then the trash-talking began. Morrissey began "derisively pointing at him" as Sullivan went down without getting hit to end rounds. After Sullivan dictated the action round after round, he started laughing at Old Smoke. Are you "now champion of America?" he mockingly asked. He then let loose three uncontested punches, two to the head and one to the body. By the thirtieth round, Sullivan's cronies were offering hundred-dollar and fifty-dollar bets on their man. The odds had swung 100 to 50 for Sullivan.[76] There were no takers.

By the thirty-third, Morrissey was losing his legs. The blood was "gushing in streams." The steady punishment had left him "in a shocking condition." His nose was "completely flattened and his face cut frightfully."[77] He was dropping his hands. His knees wobbled. His breathing was labored. He appeared "bewildered." No doubt the onlookers thought of McCoy. Yet Morrissey did not go down. Sullivan, too, was tiring, and though he was hitting Morrissey at will, the punches had lost their zing and their sting.

Years later, Morrissey would recall that "the hardest fight I ever had" was with Sullivan. "He was an artist," Morrissey recounted, "and he broke my nose, and cut me all to pieces." But the younger man would not fall. "I have always known that I could keep my legs and stand up until any of my opponents were worn out," he argued. Sullivan concurred. Allegedly he said later, "You might as well hit a brick wall as hit that man on the head."[78]

In the thirty-seventh round, things took a turn for the surreal. Accounts differ over what happened. Some say Morrissey was getting the best of Sullivan. Not a possibility. Others counter that Morrissey's minders were crying foul to bring the stalemate to an end and have their man declared the winner. So much was riding on the bout. Money, careers, power, the future. It probably went like this: Morrissey once again got hold of Sullivan and tied him up on the ropes. He lifted him off the ground as he did so, pinning him. This was the only way at this point Sullivan could lose, even if he could not finish Morrissey off. Sullivan's seconds knew it. Harm Miller saw things this way: "Finally Morrissey struck him a regular mule kick in the ribs and piled him over onto the ropes." By one account, Yankee could not break the hold. He dug his spiked shoe into Morrissey's shin. The seconds cried "foul" and ran into the ring. Or, to cite another eyewitness, Sullivan went down to a knee to wriggle free and illegally hit Morrissey. Or, alternatively, Yankee's men cut the rope to save their man. That's what Harm saw, after which Morrissey's men stormed the ring "and out come revolvers." Bowie knives, too, by one account.[79] A melee ensued. One tough nicknamed "Dublin Tricks" was duking it out with a fellow named "Awful" Gardner. Gardner was known to bite ears, much like Mike Tyson would do in a fight against Evander Holyfield in 1997. Awful tussled with Sullivan, and as one report put it, tried to get his teeth into Yankee's ear. He managed to mutilate Tricks's ear.[80] While the ring filled with maulers and brawlers, the referee kept time. He called the fighters to scratch. Morrissey made it. Sullivan was stuck outside the ring, mixing it up with one of Old Smoke's people. He did not make it back to scratch within the allotted thirty seconds. The referee gave the fight to Morrissey. It went fifty-five minutes.

Yankee Sullivan wuz robbed.

On the morning following the fight, the gangsters left as quickly as they had arrived, but hardly silently. After the fight, the hoods from the Points sacked a few towns on the way home. They ransacked farms, stole anything not nailed down, slaughtered hogs, and roasted them on the road.[81] The bout infuriated the authorities and the great and the good. The *New York Times* covered the fight and also ran an editorial. Even if the bout helped sell newspapers, the *Times* condemned the spectacle: "It is inexplicable, deplorable, humiliating that an exhibition such as the contest between Morrissey and Sullivan could have occurred." How to explain such "animal brutality" in what was becoming a civilized country? the Gray Lady wondered.[82] A paper from Albany decried the "revolting exhibition." "What right have we to boast of our 'intelligence' or 'Christianity,'" it asked, "when such scenes are allowed to go unpunished?"[83] But they all covered it. This was news. Sullivan went back to New York, but when Massachusetts officials got wind of what had gone on in territory they claimed but could not control, they issued a warrant for his arrest. He surrendered himself to a New York sheriff, who escorted him to prison in Lenox, Massachusetts. Tom Hyer, of all people, bailed him out for $1,500. They then went out on the town together, having "a good time."[84]

After he got out of jail, Sullivan was beside himself. "It is entirely unnecessary for me," he argued, "to state that I fairly and indisputably was the winner of our last contest." He added that 2,500 "disinterested persons" there would agree. Only ten "interested ones" argued otherwise. They had broken into the ring and broken up the fight, he believed, for Morrissey, money, and power. Sullivan challenged Morrissey to a rematch. He asked that instead of paying out the stakes to Morrissey, the money should go "to any charitable institution, viz: Fire Department Widows' and Orphans' Fund." This had to be a shot across the bow for Morrissey for alleging that Sullivan had killed his first wife in a house fire. Sullivan wanted to fight for real money this time, five thousand dollars. "Man and money ready at my house," he declared.[85] Morrissey did not accept the challenge. He did not need to.

Morrissey now succeeded Sullivan as the chief hard man of the Points and the one whom political chieftains would try to cultivate, "supplanting" Sullivan "as leader of Tammany's fighting forces," as Nat Fleischer would put it.[86] He, not Sullivan, was now the man to follow and to fear. True to his word that he entered the ring for "victory or death," Sullivan claimed to retire from prizefighting. From his new headquarters back at Chatham Street, he dictated out a letter to the *New York Clipper.* He still resented Morrissey and smarted over the loss. "Every one knows," he declared, "that this great, big, wooden man was no more in my hands than a shuttle-cock." Moreover, his followers had "the impudence to call me a braggadocio." In his retirement speech, he recalled his career in the city. "I have fought six battles in New York; five of which I won." He was always taking on opponents in what would now be called higher weight classes. He usually gave away at least twenty-five pounds. He also said that "no man on earth could have fought much longer than I did, nor harder" against Hyer. And Sullivan would know. He had fought in varied places around that earth. He counseled Morrissey to "hang up his fiddle." "For if he could not lick a man forty-one years old, thirty pounds lighter, and three inches shorter than himself," he should find another line of work. Sullivan signed off as "CHAMPION."[87]

The clash of styles evident in the fight reflected the clash of identities. In the ring on that day in 1853, Sullivan was improvisational, good on the give and the take, as well as the hit-and-run. He boxed cleverly. He fought as he lived, in a rootless and ruthless way. Morrissey was overbearing and aggressive. The bout could be likened to the famous series of fights between Sugar Ray Robinson and Jake LaMotta in the 1940s and early 1950s, a sextet that Martin Scorsese immortalized in his film *Raging Bull.* In the fights and in the movie LaMotta would have played Morrissey to Sugar Ray's Sullivan. Morrissey, like LaMotta, had one speed in the ring. And out of it. In the new New York that was coming into being, he could afford to take such an approach. In fact, it was smart to do so. Morrissey came to Boston Corner as the harbinger of a new world. The run-up to the fight and the bout itself demonstrated as much. So did its surprising aftermath.

Morrissey would become the champion of the Irish after the 1853 fight. In the summer of 1854, he still had a grudge against Hyer and challenged him once more after a run-in at the Abbey Hotel where pistols were drawn. It did not come off. "I never saw a bigger coward in my life," Morrissey declared.[88] He would take on Bill "the Butcher" Poole on the docks near Christopher Street. Poole had offered to fight with knives. Morrissey knew better. This would be a "rough-and-tumble," or a fistfight with no rules. Poole named the place, and he brought his gang with him. Morrissey survived a vicious kicking. But he always did just that: survive. As Sullivan had learned, he was indestructible. After the episode, one of Morrissey's friends would take out Poole with a pistol shot. Morrissey was fingered, but he beat the charges. Then "Old Smoke" went on to become, of all things, a New York state senator and a founder of the Saratoga Race Course. Word had it that he hobnobbed with the likes of Cornelius Vanderbilt. The Morrissey-Poole rivalry represented the last great hurrah of the *Gangs of New York* world that Old Smoke had arisen in. Now it was something quite different. His Tammany was run by the now-organized Irish, the great political force in this most democratic and Democratic of cities. It was a sophisticated machine, tailor-made for what New York had become. The Irish no longer lived in the shadows. They had become rooted. Morrissey styled himself "the pugilistic Trojan of the Tammany Hall" and its "raging bull," as Nat Fleischer put it, eventually becoming something no one could have imagined when Sullivan had arrived only a decade before the fight at Boston Corner: a two-term US congressman.[89]

As the new champion, Morrissey had made the transition with New York by making the leap to respectability, albeit with the patina of working-class swagger. As the old one, Yankee Sullivan could not. Men in the streets hailed Morrissey as their new political conduit to Tammany. Ballads of his fights with Poole and rough-and-tumble fighting appeared. A fantastical one of Morrissey's imagined "Glorious Victory over the Russian Sailor" also made the rounds. With this win, "St. Patrick's sons made the taverns roar, Flattering the Praise of Morrissey and Paddies evermore."[90] One popular song of the era was set to the tune of that newly written minstrel song by Stephen Foster "Camptown Races." "The Great Prize Fight" recounted a one-sided battle that made Old Smoke a mythic champion. It went:

> Sullivan made a match to fight, Du da, du da,
> With a man named Morrissey all so tight, Du da, du da, day.
> Yet Morrissey feared him not a bit, Du da, du da,
> But said he'd give him hit for hit, Du da du da day.

The song detailed Morrissey's "heavy blows, which reached Yankee's eyes and nose," as well as Sullivan's "tricks, by going down to escape the licks."[91] It ended by saying Morrissey won because Sullivan had hit him while down, a disqualifier.

That Morrissey beat a mythic Russian was neither here nor there. It just suggested that though from a small country and now in a great and up-and-coming one, he, and by extension the Irish in New York, could stand toe-to-toe against an Old World power. In an even more telling ballad, Morrissey stands for the growing number of Irish in New York and paved the way for outrages to occur later in New York's history. "Morrissey and the Black" starts with this line: "Come all you bold Irish and listen to me, I'll sing you the praises of John Morrissey." In the ballad, Morrissey takes on "Ned, the Black" for five thousand pounds. In most versions, Ned is fearsome, weighing over two hundred and towering above Old Smoke. Oddsmakers favored Ned 20 to 1. Morrissey did not care: "Here stands the form of an Irishman here," he boasts as he jumps into the ring, claiming to have "never been conquered by black, white, nor brown." Throughout he smiled at his Irish followers as he endured punishment. It seemed Ned had the better of him throughout, but Morrissey kept coming to scratch and eventually flattened "Black Ned with one powerful stroke" and "laid him for dead with five ribs of his broke."[92]

The line between this song and the Draft Riots was fairly straight, if not in its violence at least in the distinction it drew between the two groups. As more numbers came in, as the Irish began to channel their inner Old Smoke, they made the fight game theirs. They would not give it back to Nativist fighters, and from Morrissey a long line of Irish fighters in America would claim that lineage. That line always began with Morrissey. It would include successors who, unlike the mythical and conquering Morrissey, would refuse to fight any Blacks. The Irish would draw the "color line." The Irish would also rule the city by understanding that power depended on exclusion. Henceforth, they would make the fight game theirs in the same way. Old Smoke and his sensibilities had won out for the Irish. They would seek to dominate the city and the vulnerable around them. In this story, Sullivan is just the hapless adversary who lost.

Who or whatever was to blame, Yankee Sullivan had lost the battle, his objections to the contrary, and the war for New York. He proved prophetic, therefore, in choosing black and the theme of "Death or Victory" for his colors. He came to New York when the Nativists outnumbered the Irish, just as the stream of migration was beginning. His generation had to fight with guile to get ahead and had to build walls; but he and his peers had no choice but to construct bridges with their enemies now and again. Had he ever really left Bandon? The world Sullivan moved through, when global connections were being established and networks were coalescing and the Irish were a minority doing this work, demanded improvisation and shape-shifting. Morrissey's New York, when the Irish dominated, did not.

Sullivan had not finished moving, even after the failure in San Francisco and then the ill-fated return to New York. From this point forward Sullivan would be drawn back to his earlier experiences. The next rounds of his life brought him roving once more in search of places just like what New York had been when he had arrived flush with success from Liverpool in 1841. He was reverting to Francis Ambrose and the worlds he was accustomed to. He would, like Jay Gatsby, be borne "ceaselessly into the past," and become a tragic figure as Morrissey's star began to shine. Yankee Sullivan would disappear just as the world he created was vanishing.

ROUND 14

Nevada City

IN 1854 AND 1855, a Boston firm was commissioned to build a number of ships. The plan was to name two schooners after Daniel Webster. One would be christened the *Defender,* the other the *Expounder.* The great statesman had, after all, defended the Constitution and, more effectively than most, expounded on its virtues. When the builders were suggesting what to call them, someone argued that, perhaps, the *Expounder* should bear the name of Yankee Sullivan. He was then at the height of celebrity, and naming a ship after him—given his many sailing adventures and misadventures—was fitting. It was not to be. The shipbuilders stuck with Webster. Sullivan still had standing among many Americans, even as the defeats piled up, especially among workingmen. But he proved no match for a founding father figure like Webster.[1]

So it went for Sullivan after he lost to Morrissey. In late 1853, he was "re-arrested" in Westchester County for violating the terms of his pardon in the Lilly-McCoy event, though he was discharged under habeas corpus. It seemed he could not get out from under its shadow, suggesting how his window had closed in New York.[2] He, therefore, decided to leave again.

On January 31, 1854, the New York Fancy bid him a fond farewell. It seemed, this time, Yankee Sullivan would be gone for good. They pulled out all the stops to give him an evening to remember at the arsenal for the New York First Division on White Street just north of the Five Points and a block away from his old haunt on Centre Street.[3] More than one thousand people turned out for a boxing benefit and exhibition in his honor. "The assemblage was composed of all classes of society, from the dealer in fancy sticks in Wall street, to the dealer of faro in the Bowery," a report of the proceedings gushed. A bunch of young men sparred. These included some boxers from London and Liverpool. All of the performers tended to be "well acquainted with the 'arts and sciences.'" Sullivan capped the sparring, but he could only go through the motions. He had hurt his hand. He ended the evening by thanking the crowd. He hoped, as it was reported, "that his future conduct *out* of the prize ring would give as much satisfaction to his numerous friends and acquaintances, as his previous conduct had *in* it."[4]

Soon he set off, once more, for California. "The notorious pugilist Yankee Sullivan," a paper wrote, "arrived in the Yankee Blade," a ship coming from Panama. "This is his second appearance in California," it added.[5]

He entered San Francisco on July 1 and settled above a billiard saloon run by an Irishman at the corner of Pacific and Kearny Streets.[6] Once more, he threw himself headlong into life in the city. This time he started with politics. It seemed an ideal strategy. The vigilantes had been disbanded, and politics reverted to its competitive Five Points style. He allied himself, as he had in New York, with factions running for citywide and statewide office. Now he worked once more for Democrats. In doing this work, he was up to his old tricks. In 1854, as a witness put it, "Yankee Sullivan and others controlled the polls, and judges and inspectors of elections were not allowed to come in; the roughs constituting themselves inspectors." According to a California newspaper, Sullivan policed the vote. That is, after he "took possession of the polling place by force." One fellow from New York Sullivan worked for "was not a candidate for election," the witness alleged, "and I don't think he received a vote during the whole time the polls were kept open, four or five days; yet he was returned as elected from that precinct that he was not even a resident of, and served out his term of office as supervisor."[7] Another related that "Yankee Sullivan stuffed the ballot boxes in the twelfth district."[8]

At the next election, he was involved in more of the same. "Yankee Sullivan and some others of that stripe," a witness recounted, "controlled the precinct at the Presidio."[9] Sullivan served "as Judge of the Election," if that can be believed, during which some ballot boxes had false bottoms, all to make stuffing them a cinch.[10] If this did not do the trick, threats always worked. Terrence Kelly was charged with certifying returns. He signed when Sullivan told him to. He had no choice, he told authorities, because of "motives of self preservation." Kelly feared Sullivan would murder him.

Miraculously, the 150 votes to which Kelly was prepared to attest became 1,050 votes.[11]

Sullivan, therefore, slipped into his old life, hoping to re-create what he had lost in New York and earlier in San Francisco. He found some friends he had known in New York, and opened "a flash porter house" not far from the Old Ship Saloon and even closer to his place that had burned down, costing rent of six hundred dollars per month. In this venture, he partnered with a fellow ballot-box stuffer, Billy Mulligan. Mulligan was cut from the same cloth as Sullivan. Ten years younger than Sullivan, he came from Ireland while a small boy, settled in the Five Points, and did exactly the sorts of things Sullivan had. Mulligan operated as a gambler, shoulder-hitter, street fighter, and political operative. The warden of the Tombs, where he did time, called him "a professional blackleg." Thin and small, he had a reputation for ferocity, once even chasing the much larger Morrissey with a pool cue. One who feared him referred to Mulligan as a "demon in human form" who did not care a whit about the law. He had served with the army in the Mexican war, and he then went out West with all the prizefighters. He allegedly killed a man in a bar in Sonora in 1851. Mulligan comprised part of that movement of prizefighting political operators into the West, albeit the extreme and nasty version thereof. Sullivan and Mulligan called their place on Merchant Street "the Gibraltar," setting it up right off of Portsmouth Square in what is now an alley between Chinatown and the Transamerica Pyramid. This stood only steps away from the ill-fated United States Hotel in a building that had quickly arisen in the wake of the 1850 fire. The saloon, much like the Sawdust House and the United States Hotel, became the haunt of those interested in gambling, fighting, and politics. A report called the Gibraltar "the rendezvous of all the fancy reprobates about town." It catered to those "curious 'to see Sullivan.'"[12]

Sullivan sponsored some spars at theaters and taverns in the city. He even agreed to serve as a second for a duel, with pistols, that did not come off.[13] He spent much of his time shuttling between San Francisco and Sacramento doing political work, where on one occasion he was arrested for "discharging a pistol."[14] This was his redemption tour, though not redemption in the religious sense. This was him finding a fit in worlds he had proved adept at moving through.

In this case, things did not go according to plan. The politics turned out to be brutal. Factions proved dizzying, all this amplified by how the national debates over slavery were fracturing the Democratic Party. Infighting compromised any sort of unified effort to contest Whigs or, more to the point, Know-Nothings. Moreover, he had a falling out with Mulligan, his partner in the Gibraltar. They closed the bar. So, in September 1854, he headed to the hills, to the areas where men labored to find gold, far beyond the reach of any vigilantes, reformers, and Know-Nothings. Here he would give "exhibitions of 'the muscle.'" He had become a "professional vagabond."[15]

The gold-mining regions were a new avenue for self-creation. This is where so many young men found opportunity and hope. Sullivan as the runaway Ambrose had played this role before. Now he was once again; however, in this instance he came as a celebrity. More than likely, he did not travel by foot or by mule as the early 49ers did. By the time he visited the gold fields, a daily stagecoach ran between Nevada City, one of the most important towns for mines in the central area, and Sacramento, which was reached by boat from San Francisco. A trip cost fifteen dollars. At this time, despite the cost, the coach was, a miner reported, "always crowded."[16]

Though far from the centers of commerce and power, here was the world he knew so well writ small. He would encounter the same mix of people he had seen in urban spaces in London, Sydney, and New York. "There were people all from the South American States," a miner found, "China, the Sandwich Islands and Australia." Many of these, of course, had escaped from Sydney. New Yorkers abounded around the mines, as did men from Oregon. And, of course, the Irish.[17]

He toured the areas surrounding Sutter's Mill, northeast of Sacramento on the north fork of the American River and where California gold was first discovered back in 1848, initiating the gold rush. By the time Sullivan came, Placerville had supplanted Sutter's Mill as the site of the "Mother Lode." All the easy gold had been found, and now miners had to devise more ingenious and, in some cases, desperate measures to separate gold from rock. He traveled to Grass Valley, Nevada City, Diamond Springs, Placerville, and Mokelumne Hill—all prime mining areas where small settlements had sprung up to supply—and to entertain—the men in the gold fields.[18]

He had to have been reminded of the Blue Mountains when he arrived in the area. Indeed, the region was just as beautiful. But there was more there than met the eye. Just as the Blue Mountains were a widowed landscape, so too was this area. In the years before he arrived in these places in California, Native Americans had endured some of the worst violence in the tortured history between whites and Natives in America. Just as he had entered the Blue Mountains to build roads in the immediate aftermath of a racialized cleansing, so he did in California. With the first arrivals, Natives were enlisted as laborers.[19] In no time, many were being killed off.

Sullivan certainly visited areas where violence had been visited upon Native Americans. In these areas, as one who would know put it, during the "Indian Wars," miners saw all Indians "as their enemies" and referred to them as "Black devils."[20] Sullivan, the Fancy, the New Yorkers, and the Australians who ventured there were foot soldiers in what can only be described as a conquest. We have no evidence that Sullivan ever pulled a trigger. We do not know if he ever confronted a Native American. But he was part of the tide that allowed whites to dominate California. And we can be sure, given his experience with Natives in Australia, that he did not give as much as a thought to what was happening to California's Natives. He was a man of violence, not sympathy.[21]

In the very years that Sullivan headed to California for his future, just to the east of San Francisco, treaties were signed, as in New Zealand, to cede land to settlers in exchange for goods and protection. These were not ratified by the Senate. Most chillingly, as Sullivan sailed to San Francisco, a killing machine was coming into being. Settlers indulged in murder and terror to clear Indians off the land or to enslave them as laborers. State militias, government institutions, and federal forces conspired to displace the Indigenous people and then wage what was called a "war of extermination" against them. That war did not wipe Natives out. Many would survive, and their cultures would endure. Yet, these years proved extraordinarily traumatic.[22] This was an old American story, one played out in earlier periods and in other places. Only this time it was happening with frightening speed and with even more casualties because the global stakes were so high. Much of the gold that poured in went to New York and London, where financiers dreamed up ways to invest in the American West. And these dynamics only attracted more men like

Yankee Sullivan from all over the world. Natives, as had been the case in other places, got in the way.

The parallels between this American tale and his Australian experience are pretty compelling. A miner, when discussing the Natives he encountered, sounded eerily like the immigrants in Australia talking about the Aborigines. They were, according to his racist reading, "poor specimens of the human race—ill-looking, of low instincts, but harmless and cowardly."[23] In fact, settler colonialism defined much of Sullivan's existence, though he straddled different sides of the fraught equation. In Ireland, he was among those whose ancestors' lands had been colonized by settler and state. He participated in the process in Australia and California, if even by migrating to both places. In one context, Sullivan served as an unwitting agent of British imperial expansion and Native dispossession; in the other, as an active agent of an expanding United States. The Irish played the same role in both places. As much as miners, laborers, and dockworkers, they were dispossessors and "instruments of conquest."[24]

Natives were not the only ones who suffered at the hands of men like Sullivan. In both Australia and San Francisco, many Irish tormented the Chinese. They derided them as inferiors and as competitors for jobs. Later, just as they would with the Draft Riots, young Irish toughs in San Francisco assembled as a mob and attacked Chinese men and women and burned their homes.[25] The Irish in California acted in league with government, just as they did when it came to Native Americans. California passed a law prescribing fees for Chinese migrants ineligible for American citizenship. Officials tried their best to exclude them as well.[26] Only whites in the state could vote, just like in New York. California, too, was a white man's republic.[27]

Miners needed diversion. They lived dreary existences panning for gold. The method they nearly all used was called "placer" mining. Derived from the Spanish term meaning "sandbar," this form of mining entailed searching for gold bits, flakes, and even nuggets. If the adventurer found some evidence of gold by creek drainages, then he dug down to bedrock, right where placer gold was apt to be found. Then he dug horizontally, what was called "coyoting." The miners lugged up the dirt and sediment. Men worked by hand with simple equipment in small teams, set up aqueducts, and piled dirt and sand and hopefully bits of gold in troughs at the end of sluices. They then got out their pans, swirled, and saw if they had hit paydirt. More ambitious sorts built rockers which could do the separating more efficiently. The gold, if any were there, went right down to the bottom. All told, a small gang could shovel five cubic yards of earth a day. Teams of men could do the same work at a larger scale.[28] One veteran put it this way: "Gold hunting in California was no place for drones or epicures."[29] Men worked every bit as hard, or harder, than those who toiled "as day laborers upon a canal or railway excavation."[30]

After working at the digging, panning, and sluicing all day, miners wanted rowdy recreation, the sort that could be found in places like San Francisco, New York, London, Sydney, and Liverpool. A typical miner recorded in his diary how men tried anything to break the monotony and the drudgery. He noted, "Gambling going on everywhere as usual." He relished a trip to secure supplies. Moquelumne Hill, he wrote, had sixteen stores or groceries, scores of shops in the main town. Here, too, were watchmakers, jewelers, a dentist, "gambling and 9 saloons and preaching in one building." Killings proved a diversion also. In 1851, he reported a man named Campbell killed a Mexican. Campbell was convicted of "willful murder, but his brother gamblers would not suffer him to be hung."[31] These, too, were the violent types who did menial work in all of the places Sullivan had lived. These were the sorts attracted to prizefighting.

As a prizefighter, and as an attraction, Sullivan was sure to make money. On a number of occasions he visited Nevada City, a small outpost and market town in the Sierras that sprang up in the central mining district. This was not a civilized place. Nevada City, when he visited, was a manifestation of all the ills visiting the gold fields and early California. A miner working near Nevada City and coming in to the settlement regularly called the Mexicans he encountered "greasers." He discussed how one was whipped for a petty crime outside the jail that Sullivan would spend time in.[32] In Nevada County, right about the time Sullivan visited after the Morrissey fight, a white man shot a Chinese miner dead.[33] The Native Nisenan people had recently endured a program of extermination. In 1850, Natives attacked some men and killed one working on a sawmill in the area. Miners and US soldiers retaliated with fury, killing or running off the Natives. The closest mass killing around the time Sullivan arrived took place about forty miles away.[34]

Nevada City had been filled with saloons and brothels and gambling dens, making it one of the unruliest towns in California. Miners, who lived on the outskirts in log and canvas shanties, clamored for what the settlement offered.[35] The men wanted leisure, particularly on Sundays after six days of hard work.[36] Sullivan was playing this role. He was sponsoring prizefights, once promoting a match between Con Fitzgerald and Hugh Kelly that, purportedly, turned out four thousand spectators from the surrounding areas. He also put on exhibitions.[37] He was just one attraction for these men. In 1854, the local newspaper, the *Nevada Journal,* listed all of the new attractions. It said in October that on the same Sunday evening, "pleasure-loving people" that they were, they could hear a Reverend Douglas regale them with a talk on "where you will go when you die" and Yankee Sullivan "on the noble art of self-defence."[38] He was sparring and promoted bouts alongside bull and bear fights. These contests pitted a bull versus a bear in an enclosure very much like a ring. The men, of course, bet on the outcomes. Unfortunately, the animals had to be poked or prodded to get at it. But this is what he was competing against.[39] In fact, while Sullivan was in Nevada City, the local paper compared the "pugilistic affairs of Yankee Sullivan" to a dramatic run-in a local hunter had with a grizzly. Filed under "a bear story," it told of how a local hunter outran his enraged prey, tried to clamber up a tree, and was able to shoot the creature.[40]

Times, however, were changing. When Sullivan visited, the town boasted ten to fifteen thousand residents. In 1851, a newspaper announced that Nevada City was "a busy city, with its hurrying crowd of bustling life." A fire had just ravaged the settlement. Now all were rebuilding with purpose. Hotels, stores, and theaters dotted the main street. What had been crooked lanes were remade into straight avenues. In the town's theaters, edifying performances were taking place. Acting troops toured the mining areas and performed at the "Dramatic Hall." Circuses, minstrel shows, spiritualists all came through to entertain.[41] Respectability was fighting disorder.

Here, as in San Francisco, the voices of reason and civility condemned prizefights. In 1853, a year before Sullivan arrived, a group calling themselves the Sons of Temperance organized to root out the Yankee Sullivan types. The Sons did their best to close brothels and gambling houses and saloons. They wanted to get rid of bawdy entertainments. These evangelicals resembled the same sort that had tried to marginalize prizefighting in England earlier in the century. They knew what prizefights led to, and they recognized the world of immorality they sustained. As typical middle-class reformers, they tried to disentangle the settlements in the gold fields from what they regarded as corrupting influences. These "friends of good order" hoped to vanquish the uncivilized.[42]

Sullivan ran afoul of the new order. For sponsoring prizefights, he was placed in jail in Nevada City and appeared before judges a number of times. In late December 1854, authorities in Nevada City arrested him on a bench warrant "for his recent participation in a prize fight."[43] He was tried and escorted to the jail at gunpoint because, as a local lawyer remembered, Sullivan "was insolent" and the bailiffs feared him. Nonetheless, he was provided with food and whiskey while he was locked in his cell.[44] How the mighty had fallen. At least when he spent time in jails and prison earlier he was performing for more substantial things: for power, for status, for identity. But not in California at this moment. Up to this point in his life, prizefighting involved high stakes—material, ideological, and political. In Nevada City, there were no stakes. He was an entertainer. Nonetheless, as far as the better sort were concerned, there was no place for Yankee Sullivan. Hopefully, he would go the way of the bull and bear fights.

That moment when he and prizefighting thrived was quickly passing in Nevada City. It was not only reformers who bore responsibility. A dramatic change in how work was done in and around Nevada City also underwrote the transition. Entrepreneurs realized that, in principle, placer mining could be scaled up if water pressure could be increased. Some devised convoluted aqueducts and designed massive nozzles as the end of metal pipe systems, all to clear out gravel and sediment and do the work more quickly and at a much larger scale. About ten feet long, one of these nozzles could wash hillsides away with water to reveal the gold-flecked gravel below. Men dug reservoirs, then ditches as long as fifteen miles, and connected a series of pipes decreasing in width to concentrate water pressure. One ditch was being planned that would stretch twenty miles. In 1851, rival companies incorporated to hire the men to do the digging and the mining, the two most prominent being the Deer Creek Water Company and the Cayote Water Company. Demand for lumber soared, and more sawmills went up. Industrial scale had arrived to Nevada City. This method called hydraulic mining made for great efficiency. It was introduced just about a year or two before Sullivan arrived and when Nevada City was reaching peak boomtown.[45]

About the same time, companies formed to try to distill the gold found in quartz. Gold in veins could be found in the hard rock after all the placer work—the easy stuff—was done. The rock had to be quarried or blasted out, then pulverized. This process required machines. It also demanded capital. So, too, did the blast furnaces and the chemicals needed to extract the ore. The expense was far beyond the reach of any prospector or group of Argonauts. This method did not really take off in Nevada City, but it did in nearby Grass Valley.[46]

Men alone could not do any of this work, so heavy was the capital expense. Only companies could. The move to hydraulic mining represented a sea change. The common sort no longer ruled the roost, and they saw the wages they could expect decline precipitously as the transition occurred. Tellingly, this shift represented the moment when more and more Irish arrived, all to work for wages. This is what happened while Sullivan languished in jails for sponsoring prizefights.[47]

"The difference between mining in 1850 and 1853 was striking," a newspaperman wrote. Older ways of doing things looked "ridiculous." On top of this, the first brick building went up in Nevada City. "Civilized life" was coming.[48] The wildcatting days had gone. With the nozzles came the companies, more stores, the churches, and all the trappings of settled society. Methodists tried to convert souls. Others did as well. An Irish priest, John Shanahan, built a Catholic church, St. Peter's in 1853. It was a mission church, to serve the Irish coming in.[49] Civility and wage labor triumphed with the nozzles.

By 1856, about a year after Sullivan had left, a directory of Nevada City listed three Sullivans living there. One, C. L., was a grocer, which meant he was selling food and liquor. John and Michael worked as miners. They were doing so, no doubt, for a wage.[50] This was no place for Yankee Sullivan. At least what he had been. He returned to San Francisco after about six months of touring and entertaining.

Horace Greeley famously said, "Go West, young man." But Sullivan was no longer young. And though he had no fears of jail—and the log affair in Nevada City across from a simple courthouse could not have intimidated someone who had done time in Sing Sing, the Tombs, Hyde Park Barracks, and Newgate—his stays must have been sobering.[51] This was a small-time jail in an out-of-the-way place. He had hit all the big-time prisons before. Now he was languishing, over the age of forty, in a minor-league lockup. In New York, he had ruled the Points. Now he had to appear before judges ruling in settlements even far removed from San Francisco.

Sullivan's new misfortunes suggested that the moment-in-time when prizefighting and prizefighters flourished was coming to an end. This did not mean that pugilism was dying; rather, something else was beginning to supplant it. More and more of the wealthier sort, in fact, took up fisticuffs. They did so for exercise and to fight off what they regarded as the effeminizing influences of the modern world. Perhaps, as some suggested, they could become better Christians if they did so. In the 1850s, for instance, Christian proselytizers began popularizing what is known as "muscular Christianity." It was based on the idea that fighting and masculinity had a role to play in redemption. First devised in London, it soon spread to New York and became a new fixture of urban culture. "Boxing" with gloves to muffle blows began to grow in general appeal from this time on.

Prizefighters, of course, had boxed. Putting on gloved exhibitions, however, was more about promoting what really mattered. Prizefighters fought with bare knuckles, and they did so for money, power, and status. Now increasingly, middle-class men visited gyms and donned mufflers to try to learn the "manly art." This transition had taken shape in London a generation earlier. Now it gripped America.[52] Prizefighting corrupted. Sparring restored "vigor," of the man and the nation.[53] This shift was part of the process of turning something elemental into a "sport" or a "pastime" or a "craft." Prizefighting belonged to the past. Boxing to the future.

Sullivan made bail in Nevada after his most recent arrest. He then headed back to San Francisco. In the summer of 1855, he was rumored to be preparing for a prizefight of his own against a fellow named Joe Winrow. He even went into training, which caused all sorts of consternation for California's polite society, and planned to meet Winrow at a site for such encounters: Mare Island. He would put up two thousand dollars to Winrow's one thousand. But Sullivan backed out and forfeited the deposit, claiming that an injury to a finger was "preventing him engaging in the fight." The California paper that related the news added, rather drolly, "the public will be no losers."[54] In fact, it was speaking the truth. Sullivan was too old to fight in the ring. His former protégé John Heenan, looking to make a name for himself in the dog-eat-dog fight world, issued a challenge to Sullivan after he backed out of the Winrow fight.[55] Sullivan declined this invitation as well.

But this did not stop him fighting. In that same summer, he was in a tussle with his former partner at the Gibraltar, Billy Mulligan. It began at a cockfight in a joint that was run by none other than Sullivan's old friend and partner—and McCoy's killer—Chris Lilly. Mulligan took offense at something Sullivan said, and he called Sullivan a "Sydney thief." Fists flew. They decided to repair to a venue for a proper set-to. Whether Mulligan sucker-punched Sullivan is up for debate, but it seems he did pistol-whip him and gave him a kicking when he was down. Whatever happened, reports circulated that the fierce bantam and much younger Mulligan thrashed Sullivan and that the ex-champion was no longer the man he was when he was young. The *Daily Alta California*, a newspaper in San Francisco, reported that Sullivan appeared "much emaciated and enfeebled and not prepared for a fight." No doubt, his general incapacitation was much exaggerated. One suspects alcohol was the culprit.[56]

The problem in the West was that things happened at an accelerated pace, even for Yankee Sullivan. "California sped through decades of history overnight," a prominent historian writes.[57] The same dynamics of change that were transforming the East, and also other places that Ambrose and then Sullivan had lived, just took shape in shorter time spans. As he was getting older, time sped up. Sullivan would spend the rest of his life trying to catch up.

ROUND 15

Honolulu

In September 1855, after Mulligan laid him out in the streets of San Francisco, Sullivan still had amassed enough money through sponsoring fights and doing political work to move yet again and to reinvent himself once more. In that month, he picked up and left suddenly for Honolulu in the Sandwich Islands, sailing on board a packet called, appropriately, the *Yankee*. This ship, a clipper bark skippered by James Smith, plied the route between the two cities. It offered "every convenience and accommodation for passengers." It also carried the US mails and "freights taken at fair rates." It was akin to the Black Ball Line that ran between New York and Liverpool.[1] On this ship, too, came from San Francisco the sort of circuses and acts that so entranced the people in the developing mining communities. In 1855, the Lee and Marshall's Circus arrived, replete with ringmaster, acrobats, trick dogs, tightrope dancers, and a "North American Indian Chief." The next year brought the Great Western Circus.[2] Later on, it would be minstrel shows.[3]

This seemed a place Sullivan was suited to, given all of the different locales he had visited since his youth. The Sandwich Islands, or more properly Hawaii, served as a node in a connected world and was defined by in-betweenness. In 1855, these themes were especially evident. In that year, a new king had come to the throne. Born into the royal family as Alexander Liholiho, King Kamehameha IV had just assumed control of the Kingdom of Hawaii, taking over for his uncle, Kamehameha III, after he died in December 1854. He presided over an independent kingdom in the Pacific, in fact a constitutional monarchy.[4] The kingdom he inherited served as a crossroads between East and West, North and South in the Pacific. Hawaii was perfectly situated between China, Australia, New

Zealand, and the United States. Ships came and went all over the Pacific.[5] Its geographic location gave it many advantages, particularly with trade; it also threatened the kingdom's autonomy. Fears of colonization dogged the new king.

When he ascended to the throne, the young monarch had to engage in a great deal of diplomatic derring-do to maintain the kingdom's independence. Because of its location, Western powers tried to cozy up to the kingdom, with an eye toward amalgamating it into the informal empires they were creating. Americans, especially, saw the potential, as they imagined how a continental empire could possibly expand into the ocean. The empire of free trade that they imagined was destined for the Pacific, some believed. American missionaries had already established themselves in Hawaii. The British eyed the islands as a critical stopover on the way to their colonies in the Antipodes. They, of course, had been constructing a massive empire tying the Indian and Pacific Oceans to the center. The French realized the importance of the islands to contest what the British were up to in the Pacific. Their warships even attacked Honolulu at one point when they felt they were losing out to the British when it came to trade and that Catholics were not getting a fair shake. When Kamehameha IV assumed the throne, talk of annexation, which had reached a high pitch with his predecessor, had gone "sound asleep at the moment," the American consul to the islands learned, but all knew it would become a live topic with time.[6] The new king faced a tough dilemma.

Keeping his kingdom independent would require a great deal of statesmanship and steadiness. The American commissioner charged with the government to explore the possibilities of annexation summed it up this way: The Hawaiian Kingdom "was weak and insignificant, and could not stand without the good will of all the great powers."[7] The new king would try to stay that in-between course, playing one off of another as his predecessors had successfully done. Only now the task proved more difficult, particularly as so many places on the edge of the Pacific, like Sydney and San Francisco, were developing in almost double time. Hawaii was in media res. What seemed certain was that it would not remain as it was.

The same could be said of commerce. Early in the nineteenth century, the sandalwood trade fueled the economy. The fragrant wood was traded throughout the Pacific, and in Hawaii it grew in abundance. But Hawaiians had exhausted the wood, and this form of commerce stagnated.[8]

Then the whaling industry came to the fore. Since the first ships arrived around 1820, Honolulu had become a preeminent whaling center, and the number of ships entering the harbor skyrocketed.[9] In much the same way that the Bay of Islands had served the South Pacific, Honolulu was doing so for the North. More traffic came after the British seized control of the Bay of Islands, and as it went into decline as a whaling center. American whalers made Hawaii their favored port as they came to dominate the industry and as prime grounds shifted northward toward Japan.[10]

But even with whaling signs were ominous. The gold rush had sapped ships of their men, hampering the global trade. On top of this, inventive men had discovered that oil from the ground could do much the same as whale oil. It could heat, light, and lubricate. Petroleum, moreover, could be processed at a fraction of the price. For all the ships in the harbor, fewer and fewer of these were coming and going from whaling grounds. Though Hawaii took over the mantle of the Bay of Islands, it seemed that the high point of the Hawaiian participation had come and gone. Throughout the 1830s and 1840s, the numbers were growing, just as the Bay of Islands came under more thoroughgoing British authority. The peak had come for Honolulu in 1846. In that year, Honolulu registered 146 visitations, and Maui many more.[11] The numbers had been declining since then.

That said, new trade was opening up. Kamehameha IV and his advisors were hoping to encourage new industries on the islands. Sugar looked promising. Though in the first two years of his reign the amount exported did not really grow, the seeds were planted, with US capital investment, to ensure that sugar was a good bet for the future. The raw stuff in these years was sent to a refinery in San Francisco.

The kingdom was as networked as any place Sullivan had visited. Regular shipping schedules bound the kingdom to San Francisco. In 1855, just as he came to the throne, a dispatch line was established. Honolulu and San Francisco were separated by about 2,080 miles, but the trip could be made in less than two weeks. Regular sailings also took place to Australia and New Zealand.[12] These connections had already been taking off with the discovery of gold and the to-ing and fro-ing it engendered. Goods and people came and went within this network. Regularized services were yet another set of threads of global networking. Honolulu was also a place where imperial lines and ambitions between the Americans, the British, and the French entangled, but also commercial lines as well.[13]

For all of the worries about in-betweenness, the new king's greatest anxieties centered on his physical ailments. Most troubling was a serious case of asthma. A bad attack could end the life of even a king. None of his predecessors after the man who had united the Sandwich Islands in the first place, Kamehameha I, had lived well into adulthood.[14]

As Sullivan alighted from the *Yankee*, he had to realize that he had been here before. Not literally, of course, but to this sort of place. The harbor of Honolulu had to have reminded him of the many hubs he had visited, trained in, lived in, and fought in. Honolulu was not a well-developed place, certainly by New York or London standards; however, he had to have been brought back in his mind to the Bay of Islands—and no doubt a shiver went down his spine—when he saw the whalers sitting in the harbor. Here was another place now with all the hallmarks of a whaling town. Its streets housed the same variety of boardinghouses, saloons, and brothels he had known in every one of his stops. In Honolulu, the area where these places could be found was called Cape Horn. Whalemen broke the laws he was accustomed to seeing broken. They even engaged in a riot with locals in 1852, precipitated by "drunkenness, fast riding, and quarrels," as the marshal of the islands put it.[15] Only Honolulu sat in a sovereign nation, with its own court and government. It had embassies, consular offices, hotels, and merchant houses. It was no "hellhole."

Yankee Sullivan still enjoyed celebrity status because of what he had achieved in just these sorts of places. When the bark *Yankee* made Honolulu on Monday, October 22, 1855, an American there recorded the passengers arriving, culminating with "'Yankee Sullivan' the noted Prizefighter."[16] San Francisco newspaper readers awoke one morning to a report snipped from a Honolulu paper called the *Polynesian* and carried on the return trip of the ship Sullivan took there that "the King returned to Honolulu after making the tour of his dominions." The British had sent a sloop-of-war there as well. The newspaper saved the best for last. "It appears they have murderers and robbers there as well as in California," it read. "Yankee Sullivan, professor of the *noble* art of self defence, is there at present," the paper continued. He "proposes opening a gymnasium."[17]

Aside from the snide swipe about prizefighting, the newspaper's account contained more than a grain of truth. In fact, Sullivan wanted to make a fresh start of things and open a gym. In doing so, he was tapping

Yankee Sullivan from the daguerreotype by Abraham Bogardus, ca. 1850s. (Rare Books and Special Collections, Hesburgh Libraries, University of Notre Dame)

into the growing mania for sparring and boxing. Maybe in this time-and-place he could find himself once more.

It wasn't out of the question. He seemed to come hoping to make himself respectable. He had married once more in California, and he journeyed to the kingdom with his new wife and her stepfather, a former ex-convict from Sydney named John Lamb.

Well, respectable might be stretching it a bit. A German priest in San Francisco performed the ceremony in 1855, the same year they left for the Sandwich Islands.[18] Emily Mae Brittain, her maiden name, had come to the city from Australia. So, they had much in common. But there was a problem. Sullivan had, in fact, married a bigamist. Emily was still legally wed to a man named Charles McElroy of San Francisco. On top of this, by marrying her, he himself had become a bigamist. When Sullivan bolted from New York, he left a wife behind on Chatham Street. We have no idea what happened to her, but it seems he had no intention of going back or bringing her out West. This Katherine, of course, was his second or third wife, after the first had perished in a fire that he might have set off in a drunken rage. Now he had moved onto wife number three or four—only this latest union was illegal.[19]

The bigamy, more or less, summed up his time in Hawaii. The return to California after he had lost his power in New York smacked of desperation and had ended up in his taking a beating at the hands of Billy Mulligan. Now he was grasping at straws. He had become a celebrity, to be sure, but one who appeared to be a has-been and little more than a curiosity.

That said, things had a promising start. Emily gave birth to a baby girl while in Hawaii in December 1855. Yankee Sullivan was a father. They named her Catherine. Maybe he was settling down.

Moreover, the newly crowned king was thrilled that Yankee Sullivan of all people had sailed to Honolulu. A newspaper in Honolulu would claim the kingdom was "honored" with his visit.[20] More than that, he "managed to ingratiate himself into the good graces of His Majesty King Kamehameha."[21] He asked Sullivan to give him lessons. Wells Fargo, the company that sent all that gold back East, dashed off a report to a paper in Sacramento that "'Yankee Sullivan' is basking in the sunshine of Royalty!" He was giving "private lessons in the 'manly art of self-defence' to the Royal family." If the paper thought that was too much to believe, it added he was "bottle companion and body-guard to the King in bar rooms and billiard saloons." He was packing them in, also, in public exhibitions. He quickly became a sensation.[22]

It is amazing that the young king befriended the notorious Sullivan. Kamehameha IV styled himself an urbane man. He wrote a well-rendered preface to the Book of Common Prayer. He considered himself a progressive reformer. He was an astute diplomat, keeping American annexation at bay while he courted the British. But he had good reasons to seek out the new celebrity arrival. Boxing could help relieve his asthma. For him, and for the rest of Hawaiians, Sullivan was "a new kind of missionary."[23]

The young king was reputedly improving with the help of his "teacher."[24] He had, under Sullivan's tutelage, "got to be a handsome scientific bruiser."[25] Like Byron and so many others after him, he hoped boxing would make him healthy. One way of thinking of the relationship was that Sullivan was playing John Jackson to Kamehameha's Lord Byron. Mentoring represented a new avenue for Sullivan. He had taught lessons in gyms and saloons before, but he had never before worked as a personal trainer. With Sullivan's arrival and with the king taking him under his wing, "his subjects follow the royal fashion and fisticuffs is the general amusement."[26]

He was also entertaining. One account from his time in Honolulu compared him to a performer named Catherine Hayes, an operatic icon of the age from Ireland who had toured the world, including the gold fields that Sullivan had visited, New York, San Francisco, and Sydney. She "pleased the semi-civilized inhabitants of the Sandwich Islands hugely, dividing the esteem of that public with Yankee Sullivan," a report read.[27] He was doing what he had done in Nevada City, in other words, just for a more august audience.

He spent a great deal of time in the court. Kamehameha liked having this sort of tough man around, and Sullivan enjoyed what looked to be access to power. Sullivan attended the king at court, and couriers noted how much the king was palling around with him. But this would not do. They worried, as the kingdom tried to navigate the tricky diplomatic world that Kamehameha IV had inherited, that carousing with a man who had been a prizefighter was not a good look. Reports leaked to the press of how Sullivan was inspiring some creative election work in Honolulu. Newspapers did not imply that he was participating, but they did note that while the king "employed himself in hunting, fishing, and boxing with the redoubtable Yankee Sullivan, and had become an accomplished amateur in the manly art," what it called "some excellent 'shoulder hitting' was displayed by the native 'short boys' at the polls during the election, at which a ticket half native and half foreign was chosen."[28] San Francisco newspapermen knew the score. "The Hawaiians," a San Francisco report ran, "must have taken lessons from their old visitor Yankee Sullivan, in the 'manly art' of ballot-box stuffing."[29]

The stories transfixed readers as far away as London and other British cities and towns. The king, one such report read, "pays no attention to politics." He was wasting time with his "inseparable companion" Yankee Sullivan.[30] It was clear that these stories were coming out of Hawaii and that people there were concerned. The young king, the coverage suggested, would be wise to disassociate himself from the likes of Sullivan. During such a challenging time for the islands, "King Kamehameha IV is said to have no higher pleasure than in boxing and keeping company with Yankee Sullivan."[31] He was "the constant companion" of the king "in boxing and good living." While the king was busy fiddling, as it were, the population of the Natives on the islands was dropping, a report ran, a steamship had gone down, and American sailors were running amok. Meanwhile, "theatricals were in great vogue at Honolulu."[32] Sullivan's "keeping company" was not helping him. "The King was very unpopular," and a correspondent from Honolulu wrote that some would not be shocked if "some day there should be a little revolution."[33]

Reports of what he was doing spread as far away as Australia.[34] Sullivan was putting on exhibitions. He sat in the royal box at the theater. Some of the reports also suggested that Sullivan was a favorite of "the ladies" at court. They were "accepting his company, at the opera, and other places of amusement."[35] There was even a rumor that he would be named "Envoy Extraordinary and Minister Plenipotentiary" from the king to Washington. Apparently, he declined the invitation "until he can bring a Treaty of Annexation with him."[36] This smacked of satire—a paper in Cleveland ran it under the headline "Don't Believe It"—but the reports of the outsized role he was playing at court seemed legitimate enough.[37]

Then there was his wife. Unsavory reports of her were also making the rounds. Newspaper readers in the United States learned of "a startling picture of affairs at the Hawaiian Court." Emily was sitting in the royal box when a circus was performing. The ambassadors of France and of England tried to join her. She refused to let them, creating a minor scandal in a kingdom that was trapped in a never-never land between these powers.[38] This story was covered by reporters all over the world.

Sullivan was supposed to be running a gym, but he was still getting into street fights. Most shockingly, one involved the young king. That episode took place on a Saturday night. On December 2, at about ten thirty, the king went to a bar at the "Commercial Exchange" to play billiards. Kamehameha was drunk. He had accompanied Yankee Sullivan's crew, including Sullivan's father-in-law. While at the bar, a fellow named Bessy, "partially intoxicated," as the American commissioner to the kingdom put it, sat down next to the king, "addressing him familiarly." The father-in-law took offense and "knocked him down," and then they dragged Bessy out of the room. The king and Sullivan left, but soon they returned. The barkeep would not let them in. "The party soon after broke in the door," the commissioner related, "and took possession, remaining a couple of hours." During this second round, someone else got into a scrap, at which another member of the Sullivan entourage "picked up a chair and knocked him down, breaking his jaw in two places." According to one account, the fellow Sullivan's crew attacked was named George Peoples, and he had arrived with a traveling circus from California. He was mistaken for another member of the troupe who had had words with Sullivan and his friends. The encounter left Peoples "badly bruised and . . . senseless."[39]

So it was with Yankee Sullivan. The king could not attend to government business for the next few days, so bad was his hangover. He also did not show up to meet the privy council. "He might be ashamed of the affair of last Saturday night, and reluctant to meet his ministers for fear they might speak of the matter," the commissioner believed. His "habits" for the last while "have been not of the best." The king "would do well to behave himself."[40]

The king could be forgiven. He had just reached the age of twenty-one. But Sullivan? Hard to believe that at his age, over forty, he was still acting like a juvenile delinquent in Whitechapel, and bringing a king down with him. The drinking and brawling worked when he was younger in times and places where this sort of behavior had a purpose. But not here and not now.

Sullivan's behavior initiated a war of words. A local minister of the Methodist Episcopal Church, the sort of pastor who decried dancing, had had enough. He began leaking accounts of how Sullivan was corrupting the king. They represented the king "to be the constant associate of Yankee Sullivan and of being a midnight brawler."[41] The government ministers around Kamehameha had had enough of Sullivan and his wife. This sort of press was not good for a king who had to navigate some precarious situations and daunting diplomatic challenges.

Newspapers in California picked it up and were writing on it. When these rumors spread, Sullivan struck back. In the *Polynesian,* he denied such accounts. "Respectable prints in California" were circulating reports of his behavior in Honolulu. They were "representing me as a midnight brawler, carouser, and using other choice epithets." It could not be because, as he put it, "I have all along held myself aloof from the society of those who use such phrases." He was right there. The word "epithet" had most likely never crossed his lips. But he most probably meant that he did not keep such company.[42] He condemned the "newspaper hacks" who ran salacious stories of him in Hawaii. They "frequent the barrooms in this place in the 'dull' season, for 'items.'" All to "make a paragraph to send abroad in order to gain a notoriety which they would fail to acquire by labor." All of what they reported "are gross exaggerations." He was what he was. "I do not feel ashamed to boast myself a teacher of the 'manly art of self-defence.'" He now had become a boxer and trainer and entertainer. "I am proud to say," he finished, "I will be supported by the most respectable residents in Honolulu."[43]

Such was the life of a modern celebrity. Newspapers from all over the United States—from New Hampshire to California, from Minnesota to South Carolina, and all points in between—covered his every move in Hawaii. Many reprinted what he allegedly wrote in the *Polynesian*. He was news.[44] Americans could not get enough of him. Fittingly, some of the very same newspapers reported on him reporting on the press. This, too, spread far and wide, pinging from one paper to the next via the same networks that carried the people and goods to Hawaii and around the United States.[45]

There was something else of note in his time in Honolulu, beyond the "Falstaffing it with Prince Hal of the Sandwich Islands."[46] Sullivan's behavior was clearly becoming more and more erratic. Drinking continued to present a problem for him, and even as he struggled to find respectability, he kept slipping into old ways, giving those in the press plenty to write about and those around a king facing real-world challenges much to note. A Five Points–beatdown might have worked in saloons and grog houses, when much more was at stake; they proved less acceptable around the palace of a king, when nothing for him really was. The king should be paying attention to affairs of state and the economy, it was noted in the papers, not spending his time with Sullivan and in idle pursuits. A respectable person in Honolulu, a Hawaii paper declared, condemned the visit on all of these grounds. The writer asked rhetorically, how could "this wretched man" be "on terms of intimacy with our young king?" He came near "to killing a foreigner," presumably the circus performer smashed with the chair. Only Providence preserved Hawaii. "The Lord graciously," he gushed, "saved the king and the nation from the influence of the vile man." He should, no doubt, fear "the vengeance due his crimes."[47]

For Yankee Sullivan the improvisational was now verging on the impulsive. The first two visits to California ended in disappointment, punctuated by his ill-fated comeback attempt in New York. Now he was clearly not strategizing like he used to. He was out of sorts and out of time. The same, of course, could be said of the Kingdom of Hawaii. It had thrived during the earlier periods, before Kamehameha IV took over the throne. But now the pressures were growing too great, particularly from the United States.

That shipping line from San Francisco was a harbinger of what would come. Over the next few decades, Americans would increasingly hem in the kingdom as they dominated the economy with their sugar plantations. As the nation-state developed a global strategy that began to center on the Pacific, Hawaii's days as an in-between place were numbered as well.

The American envoy in Honolulu noted that on March 5, 1856, "the 'Yankee' sailed at noon with the mail," adding "among its passengers were Yankee Sullivan." That he bothered to name Sullivan meant Yankee had left a mark in the kingdom, but not quite the one the prizefighter had intended. "This is a good riddance to the town," the envoy concluded.[48]

ROUND 16

San Francisco

WITH SCANDAL LOOMING over his time in court in Hawaii, Sullivan skulked back to San Francisco once more. Performing next to circuses and even Irish prima donnas was not really what he was cut out for. Nor was serving as a personal trainer. He was designed for other circumstances. A place like San Francisco, even if it did not work out the first time or the second, still seemed promising. It had an openness about it. It was growing into a major global hub. More men like him lived there. Perhaps he could make a mark before the forces of order closed a window.

Perhaps. In his corner were his experience and adaptability. He had remade himself, almost ex nihilo, so many times in so many places. He had proved himself as adept outside the ring as he did inside of it. By 1856, however, the smart money was on "perhaps not." He was like a character in a John Ford Western. In Ford's West, violent men had a place. Then they did not. In their wake came what we could call civilization. Prizefighters played similar roles, not on the frontier but with the places that tied the world together after the age of revolution.

There is a more prosaic reason to suppose he could not reinvent himself once more. He had been acting so oddly on a consistent basis. It was clear he was drinking and carousing more than even a younger Sullivan had been accustomed to. The *New York Times* claimed, "Drink made Sullivan insane." When in his cups, "he was furious against everybody, never distinguishing friend from foe."[1] When he decided to return to California, for a third go, many others were noticing he seemed to be out of step with his surroundings. A newspaper reported how he "had been drinking freely and insulting those with whom he was conversing." He was temperamental and agitated, leading a companion, on at least one occasion, to draw a pistol on him.[2] Granted, these voices showed little sympathy for him, but they did note that he was not quite the man he had been when he was a leader in the Five Points. He still thought of himself as such, but many no longer believed it. He still operated as if he could reclaim himself, but the world would not cooperate.

By the time he returned in the spring of 1856, San Francisco had matured.[3] It was no longer the boomtown. It was just a typically disorderly seaport city. In 1854, just as Sullivan was about to leave for Hawaii, the new Catholic cathedral, St. Mary's, was going up, not far from where he had set up the Gibraltar. Now it was done. It was sited up on the hill, above the din of the waterfront, standing taller than any other building. Soon the city climbed past it. In Sullivan's day, it represented the tallest structure in the city, and it could be seen from all vantage points. Its clock steeple each day admonished—and still does—all to "observe the time and fly from evil." Few in San Francisco heeded the call.

He returned to a city caught up in a complex drama partially of his making. San Francisco was alive with intrigue. Many of the Australians had left after being warned off or had decided to keep a lower profile. Only the seeming disorder had not come to an end. To those who formed the Vigilance Committee in 1851, the new threat looming was the many Irish New Yorkers, those just like Sullivan. They tended to support the Democratic Party, or at least a faction within it. They dominated the waterfront districts, and some had bought up valuable land there. They ran the gambling halls. Their ilk filled the pews of the Catholic churches that were arising in the city. To those steeped in Protestant evangelical values, and convinced the future of the city belonged to them as "Americans," these interposers seemed a threat to all they held dear. The New Yorkers were the new Ducks.

At issue were so many themes that had run through the life and experiences of Francis Ambrose and Yankee Sullivan. San Franciscans, most of whom had migrated to this part of the world, were struggling over land, commerce, politics, ideology, ethnicity, religion, and order. As the hoped-for Shangri-la promised by the discovery of gold never materialized, those who had ventured there found themselves fighting over control of the burgeoning city along these many fronts.

Portsmouth Square, San Francisco, 1855. (San Francisco History Center, San Francisco Public Library)

Sullivan had little alternative at this point in his life but to stake a claim here and try to use his skills and experience to his advantage. In April 1856, the "somewhat celebrated" Yankee was billed to be fighting at the American Theatre for one thousand dollars a side against Steve Simmons. The amount was believable, as he had achieved "world-wide celebrity." Announcements went up throughout the city, advertising the great event. Patrons shelled out two dollars for ringside seats. Fifty cents sent you up "by the gods." The place was packed, but the spectacle disappointed. Simmons "sparred with all the grace of a cow and all the science of a pumpkin." Though now over the hill as a competitive fighter, Sullivan hit the overmatched amateur whenever and wherever he pleased. The "glove fight" went seven rounds before Sullivan finished Simmons off. Sullivan, a report read, had a face that was "jammed and knocked as it has been in his various battles, [and that] looks like a big knot on a gnarled tree." He vowed after this "that he should never fight again."[4] One writer from the *San Francisco Herald* suggested such a course was wise, characterizing the sparring match with the greenhorn a "farce" and "the most extensive joke of the season."[5]

There was always politics. He certainly had meaningful experience. He went to work once more in this arena. Those on the ground reported that fighters were being used as bullies to stuff ballot boxes. "It was even vastly worse governed than New York," a contemporary noted, "and by the vilest politicians."[6] He knew this sort of open world, and Sullivan took up where he left off in San Francisco during his earlier stays. He allied himself with someone he had helped usher into office in an earlier visit to the city, an Irish New Yorker named James Casey. Casey served as an underling to a kingpin by the name of David Broderick, another one of these New York Irish who was hoping to attain statewide office. Like a Walsh, Casey knew how to read the winds. He was styling himself an antislavery Democrat. But he was also flirting with any and all.[7] Casey, in other words, had a past as checkered as Sullivan's. On Sullivan's return to San Francisco, he was running one of the wards down by the port, and he was seeking higher office and greater influence. He and the rest of the Irish there hoped to secure the local patronage machine.

They faced the same menagerie of Democratic rivals and their bitter opponents, the Whigs and Know-Nothings. Little differed from the Five Points, in other words. The competition was fierce within parties, and once again, he who could bring the muscle to the primaries stood a good chance of winning office. The sides were so evenly matched that in some years the Whigs ruled the city. The next year, almost invariably, it was the Democrats. Then came the Know-Nothings, who cut across some of these lines. Democrats divided into two groups. There were those who appeared more Northern in their composition, and the Irish tended to back these. Fittingly, they called themselves Tammany Democrats. Then there were some of a more Southern persuasion, steadfast supporters of slavery. The two wings, as was the case in the wider nation, could contest each other as fiercely as their traditional rivals.[8] Because the competition was so ferocious, Democrats could even court Know-Nothings to take it out on rivals within their own ranks.[9]

Sullivan was still enmeshed in local politics every bit as much as he had been in the Points. This was the same sort of unvarnished, almost unregulated democratic world of the Five Points. He and other toughs, as a critic claimed, were attempting "to rule the city."[10] In theory, Sullivan should have been right at home. In this place, though the Vigilance Committee had cleaned house a few years earlier, nothing was set, and so pugilists held sway.

His reentry, though, was hampered by a few issues. For a start, he struggled to control himself. One San Franciscan complained how Sullivan comprised part of a group of four drinkers, including another called "Cockney," who kicked down a door to a gambling house "swearing that they would gamble there—that their money was as good as anybody's." If they were not allowed in, they would break the place up. A police officer saw this. They "dared" him to "go out into the street to fight."[11] Another recounted how Sullivan beat a respectable San Franciscan "over the head and nearly deprived him of life." He grabbed the man's revolver and "shot off his pistol in the Street repeatedly." If this was not enough, Sullivan in another episode "stripped" the badge off a police officer's chest, shouting all sorts of obscenities as he did so.[12] With Sullivan and his cronies, San Francisco would never become all it could or should. "It was patent to everyone that the work of reform in our community," a witness to such behavior believed, "could not proceed while these men held high carnival, nor be effective while they remained in the state."[13]

Sullivan also returned to San Francisco in the midst of a recession, making stakes higher still. Banks collapsed. Trade had stagnated, and men who expected to rise were struggling to make ends meet. Miners were returning from the hills and rivers, looking for relief in the city, as their worlds were being turned upside down by capital-intensive mining. Many were stymied from buying lots near the docks. Meanwhile, many of the Irish New Yorkers could not find work. The Sydney Ducks were once more making their presence known. With so many unattached and frustrated young men hanging about a place already known for its violence, this was a recipe for social disaster.[14]

All it took was one eventuality to push the city over the edge. James Casey obliged. Casey was doing all he could to get elected, using any means fair or foul to clamber into office. He was employing Sullivan as his chief lieutenant. He was to hit shoulders, stuff ballot boxes, intimidate rivals, and encourage the lukewarm and fainthearted to vote the Tammany ticket. Casey figured having the notorious Sullivan in his corner could only help. Alas, he ran afoul of a newspaperman and failed banker with the unusual name of James King of William. King aimed to tell the truth, or so he claimed. This meant trying to make clear the ways and means some used to gain office. According to his friends, he "had undertaken local reform, and he was boldly assailing all evil doers, of every class and condition."[15] To his critics, he hated Democrats, Catholics, the Irish, and New Yorkers. Casey checked every box, and so King set his sights on him, particularly after the shenanigans of the recent elections, in which Sullivan had featured.[16] He ran pieces in his paper excoriating Casey's character. Casey took offense and dealt with it in the Five Points fashion. He shot King dead in the street.

The murder divided San Francisco and brought all of the tangled issues bedeviling the city to a head. Casey was, according to an anti-Irish rabble-rouser, a "Sing Sing bird and a tool of Broderick."[17] Sullivan's ilk believed the Whigs and Know-Nothings were out to erase them, and they would not go down without a fight. One rowdy declared that "he could take one hundred of the boys And run [out] all the damed Suns of Bitches, doefaced vigilant committees in San Francisco." He went on to warn that "if Casey Was hung the town would be burnt in less than twenty four hours."[18] Supporters of Casey showed a great deal of solidarity, for once forgoing some of their internecine squabbles over power to take on the anti-Irish and anti-Catholic foe. Their opponents now came to believe it was the New Yorkers, the Irish, the lower class, and Catholics who stood in the way of their advancement, their ability to secure prime land, and to hold sway in the city.[19]

The friends of King then resurrected the Vigilance Committee. One declared, "We must organize, protect ourselves, and save the country, or submit to further disgrace and ruin."[20] And organize they did, into a veritable army. One Irishman named James O'Meara, who stood on the fence, admitted that the institutions were "corrupted" because of what he derisively called the "boys."[21] This led to what newspapers called a "Revolution at San Francisco." Or, as O'Meara put it, echoing something that had been heard in Bandon in the 1820s, "these terrible troubles."[22] The governor called it by a simpler name: an "insurrection."[23] He was right.

The New Vigilance Committee proposed to do what the 1851 committee had failed to achieve. It would not only deal with a proximate problem, like the Ducks. It would reshape the city as it saw fit, the law be damned. Prizefighters and "rowdies," of course, sustained order of a sort, just not the type that could be recognized by the "better sort." Merchants and bankers did not thrive with openness and fluidity. They wanted certainty, and they would topple institutions to get it. The vigilantes formed themselves into companies and decided that the corrupt government, often run by the very men who besmirched the reputation of the city, had to go. Fittingly, they ended up organizing themselves at the local Know-Nothing hall on Sacramento Street.[24] The *San Francisco Herald*, the newspaper Catholics patronized, called it as most of the poorer sort saw it: a Reign of Terror.[25]

The committee also wanted to ensure that justice was meted out. And its members were "authorized by the law of civilization and Christianity."[26] None other than Billy Mulligan was in charge of the county jail. They knew that while figures like Mulligan determined right and wrong, Casey would never face his just desserts. The executive of the Vigilance Committee ordered the jail stormed. Casey and another Catholic by the name of Charles Cora who was imprisoned for a murder were taken out and transported to a new citadel bristling with cannon, guarded by a company of men, and surrounded by sandbags. It had been a two-story warehouse built on land reclaimed from the bay. Now, it stood as "a garrison in time of active war." In Fort Gunnybags, as it was called, the executive held a trial, passed judgment, and hanged Cora and Casey from a second-story window.[27]

On May 22, Casey's supporters staged a massive funeral cortege with eight hundred mourners and thousands more lining the route his remains would travel up to the old Mission Dolores church. They turned out to make their stand, much as they did in Still Pond Heights in 1849 when Sullivan fought Hyer.[28]

Herbert Asbury, a later chronicler of gang life in New York and in San Francisco, appropriately called the 1856 episode the "second cleansing." The committee collected information on all of the people they considered disturbers of the peace. Someone sent an anonymous note to the committee pointing out Yankee Sullivan as one of the culprits. It said that Sullivan was stuffing ballot boxes, that he had worked as Casey's man, and that he also was an escaped convict. The informant knew more. He had all of Sullivan's past. "Yankee Sullivan," he let the committee know, "went by the cognomen of Ginger in Australia." He had escaped on "an American whale ship, he being a convict for Life or fourteen years." The informer went on to say that "a reward of £50 Sterling is advertised for the apprehending of every convict payable by the British Government." The note was signed "one who knows."[29]

Who ratted on him? The list could have been long, but the informant had intimate knowledge of Sullivan's past. Maybe it was Mulligan. Could a personal feud have taken a political turn? Of course, they looked to be on same side in this fight, but he and Sullivan had had a falling out. And Mulligan knew him as a "Sydney thief." It could have been a political adversary of Casey's. It's a good bet that a member of a rival faction was using the committee to do its dirty work. It stood to reason. Politics here was a blood sport. In fact, the informer's letter smacked of Five Points politics.[30]

The note confirmed what the committee already knew. Sullivan was an enemy of the state, along with others who had been up to the same sorts of things. The executive drew up a "Black List." Near the top of it was Yankee Sullivan. He was deemed the epitome of all they saw wrong with their city. If only Yankee Sullivan could be purged, they might have peace. And have their way, of course. After the execution of Casey, the next step was clear. "The next most important work which presented itself to the attention of the Committee," its leader intoned, "was the needed action to be taken with regard to such notoriously bad characters as had been foremost in the disturbances of the country, noted as ballot box stuffers and general disturbers of the peace, prominent among whom were Billy Mulligan, Bill Lewis, Dan Alwich, Yankee Sullivan and others."[31] These were "a curse to the country."[32]

William Tecumseh Sherman certainly thought something was rotten. He had, at this point in his life, left the military and was in San Francisco hoping to make it as a banker. Sherman hated the vigilantes and was "decidedly opposed to the Committee." He condemned their seizure of power as "a regular coup d'état."[33] Sherman conceded that the shoulder-striker types, including Sullivan, were "notorious." Yet, he hated anything that smacked of irregular order. He also judged many of their charges of fraud and chicanery as "humbug." This was about power and who wielded it.[34] Empowered now to head up the local militia, he asked the Vigilance Committee to stand down. He tried to get the governor of the state to send weapons from US forces nearby. The weapons, intercepted by the vigilantes, did not make it.

In one fell swoop, the executive rounded up those on the Black List.[35] On May 26, Mulligan, Charley Duane—he who had hoisted Hyer on his shoulders in 1849—and Yankee Sullivan were arrested at night and thrown into rooms in Fort Gunnybags that were serving as jail cells.[36]

His arrest was notable. "A character whose sobriquet was Yankee Sullivan, a notorious hothouse politician, shoulder striker and ballot box stuffer, was arrested and incarcerated," a visiting physician remembered.[37] "What was to be done with them?" the executive of the committee asked. "They could not be hanged; they would be a source of expense and trouble; safe and satisfactory imprisonment was plainly impracticable," they reasoned. They would banish them for life, paying for first-class passage out of California.[38]

After his arrest, a few committeemen interrogated Sullivan in Fort Gunnybags. They claimed to have—and reprinted in heavily redacted form in newspapers—his "confession." In it, he named plenty of names, "implicating persons of high and low standing," and described how he and others took bribes to sway elections. It was clear he was muscle for hire to the highest bidders.[39] On each of these counts, of course, they were right. They also extracted what they believed to be his real name: Francis Murray. On this, of course, they were wrong.

The executive held a secret trial, and in it, Sullivan was found guilty. The judgment went like this: "Whereas, the evidence we have heard established conclusively that Billy Mulligan, Yankee Sullivan and Martin Gallagher have for years been disturbers of the peace of our city, destroyers of the purity of our elections, active members and leaders of organized gangs who have invaded the sanctity of our ballot boxes, and forever themselves pests to society—therefore resolved that William Mulligan, Yankee Sullivan and Martin Gallagher be transported out of the territory of the United States at the earliest possible moment, and that they be warned never to return to California under the penalty of death."[40]

Five days after their arrest, Mulligan, Duane, and the others were marched to the docks under military escort, and sent off on a ship called the *Golden Age* for banishment back to New York.[41] Sullivan would not be among them. Nor would he swing.[42]

Perhaps he could be sent back to Australia. One man in town said he could guarantee transport. The fellow in charge of the jail reported that he worked with a Johnson, who "was a special here for Wells Fargo & Co [and] . . . was on our police." Johnson, he claimed, "came as a detective from Australia. He got so well known by the thieves that he was compelled to leave the country. We took him as a detective."[43] Things did not bode well for Sullivan.

They threw him "in the blackest cell we have," as the vigilantes put it, "in a small cell under the stairway of the second story of Ft. Gunnybags." It measured twelve feet by six. It had no light. It was just feet away from where Casey had swung. All the imprisoned man could hear was the coming and going of guards and the interrogations. It was meant to inspire fear.[44] If Sullivan were returned to Australia as an escaped convict, he faced a future that looked very much like his past. He recounted for the inquisitors his experience in Australia. For his "bad conduct," he was "placed by the Government under a regimen of the severest kind," different from other convicts. Perhaps he would be sent once more to a site of secondary punishment.[45]

Reports leaked of how he was suffering in the cell in Fort Gunnybags. A physician who looked in on him each day said that "he manifested great apprehension as to his fate, recognizing, as he confessed to me, that he had done many things that he ought not to have done, and left undone many things that he should have done." He was ruminating. "Early after his incarceration, he became infected with the conviction that he would be convicted and executed by the Committee," the doctor went on, "under the impression that they were a band of strangers, rather than men who were actuated by correct and just motives and principles."[46] Sullivan asked for a priest, assuming he was to be hanged, but he was refused. He would not need one, a guard lectured him, because he was not to be executed. He asked for the British consul to intervene, as technically—as an Irishman—he was in some sense a British subject and had a claim to "protection." The British would not come to the rescue. To make matters unendurable for him, the jailers would not give him a drink, as had been the case in Nevada City. It's clear he was suffering from withdrawals. The guards let him see his wife, Emily. He seemed "frightened." She "tried to pacify him." He pointed to the diamond ring on her finger and said it was his first gift to her. Then he pulled out another one. He said it was to be his last gift to her. He said he had heard a guard saying he was to be hanged. She told him it was not the case. She left at midnight.[47]

The night after Emily's visit, late on May 30 and before sunrise on May 31, was hell. He had, as it was reported, awful dreams, of the footfalls of the jailers outside his cell, of the rope being put around his neck, of the drop. He was wracked by "anxiety and apprehension." He related all of

Death of Sullivan, from *Life and Battles of Yankee Sullivan* (Philadelphia: A. Winch, 1854). (The Reading Room/Alamy)

this to a guard the next morning at 5:30 when he asked for some water. The guard apparently reiterated that he was not to be hanged. He had committed crimes, but none of them of a capital nature. He was to be sent away. Sullivan, though, as the guard related, could not countenance this fate. He shot back that he would never return to Sydney. He wanted to head back to New York. He would repent. He would stop fighting and drinking. He would lead a quiet life in the country. Under no circumstances did he want to return on the same ship with his cronies who had also been arrested. They would kill him if they thought he had snitched in his confession.[48] The guard left.

Three hours later, at 8:30 a.m., on May 31, the guard opened the cell again. On the floor, he found a dull German-made knife and Sullivan lying in a puddle of blood. He rushed out to call the doctor. "I found him dead and cold," the physician reported, "lying on his bed, with an ordinary dinner knife lying by his side, partially clenched by his right hand, whilst at the end of his elbow at the left." He took a closer look. Blood had saturated the bed. "I discovered a deep gash or wound," he continued, "such as would be produced by such an implement, and which on examination

I discovered . . . to involve the brachial artery, which is the main vessel of the arm, and from which he had without doubt bled to death, there being a large pool of blood, sufficient to cause his death, upon the floor, immediately beneath the arm and elbow, which hung over the side of the bed." He had done quite a job on himself. The physician testified that Sullivan had severed the artery, as well as tendons of the biceps, and some of the ligaments. It would have taken him one hour to have bled to death, he figured. Rigor mortis had already set in. "The eyes were open, and there was no violence of struggling nor of violence upon his person, other than the wound alluded to, and hence the only inference to be drawn was that it was a case of self-murder," the doctor concluded.[49]

To stay aboveboard, the executive ordered an investigation. The guards were interviewed, and a physician was consulted.[50] It all pointed to a simple case of suicide. The inquest heard that fear of a return to Australia had driven him out of his mind. One witness related that Sullivan was suffering so much from withdrawals that he preferred to kill himself. The vigilante asserted, "He had fallen into a state of deep melancholy, produced probably by the denial of stimulants, to which he was accustomed." Normally, Sullivan was "constantly drunk, many witnesses putting his drinks at from fifty to eighty per day." Penned up "with nothing given him to drink but water, tea and coffee, his nervous system soon sunk to a low ebb, his circulation became sluggish, and his whole mental condition depressed and gloomy."[51] He had become a full-blown alcoholic. This witness argued that in the future, to avoid this sort of thing, prisoners should be given some alcohol to take the edge off. One of the jailers claimed, "At the time Sullivan killed himself, they hauled us over the coals. It was the fault of the guard for allowing the supper things to remain in his cell." He went on to admit, "After that we kept a guard to watch each prisoner."[52] Alas, it was too late for Yankee Sullivan. Whatever the rationale, whatever was going on his head, this was an open-and-shut case. And a welcome one to some. Sullivan, a critic of the rowdies wrote, "became a lawful target, and bid for bullets years ago."[53]

Some were not having it. His supporters claimed that Sullivan, in fact, was beaten to death. "Madam Rumor," a paper put it, "with her thousand tongues, at once began to circulate imagined causes of the death of Sullivan."[54] More than ten thousand saw the corpse. Between noon and 5:00 p.m.

that many people streamed through the coroner's office to see Sullivan and the wound.[55] A Democratic newspaper in Sacramento called it "murder." The committee reported the dream story, how it had alarmed him. "What?," a writer styling himself Junius asked, "Yankee Sullivan turned dreamer?" It was absurd, a "fiction."[56] One report flew how the deed was done by "a noted French thief" who had guarded his cell.[57] Charley Duane, the former enemy of Sullivan, claimed the suicide bit covered up what really happened. He asked two physicians, Bowie and Sawyer, to perform an autopsy. The knife he allegedly did the deed with proved too dull to cut flesh. It had to be a saber or a bowie knife. Duane claimed that a fellow named Edward Jessel, whom Sullivan had whipped in a street fight in New York some years earlier and who served as a guard in Fort Gunnybags, had inflicted the wound. Later that summer, Jessel was living in Jersey City and was beaten silly by a prizefighter in New York for how he allegedly did Sullivan wrong.[58] Nat Fleischer, the renowned ring historian, wrote that Sullivan had taken an awful beating after his arrest and had been left for dead.[59] Australians, especially, tended to believe he was "lynched" or strangled or beaten to death for not naming names, or shot.[60] He was, an Australian writer put it, "actually hanged, or, at all events, that he ought to have been."[61]

Catholics and the Irish, incensed by what they rightly regarded as an anti-Catholic purge in the city, thought the same. The New York Irish newspaper *The Citizen* claimed that Sullivan was done in by "terrorism." To extract a confession to stuffing ballot boxes, his handlers in jail suggested he was to be hanged. They refused to allow him to see a priest. And so he may have killed himself, but he "was done to death."[62] If indeed he took his own life, he did not do so in compos mentis. And it was clear that the bigots, those sorts he had endured in Bandon, in London, in Australia, and in New York, bore sole responsibility for his death.[63]

Emily, his wife, rejected the idea of suicide. At the inquest, where she was sworn in as a witness, she claimed that even though he was agitated the last night they met, the night before his death, "he did not seem to be much depressed in spirits, and was as cheerful as usual." Her husband, she argued "was always afraid of committing suicide." He had said just before his arrest that "he would never do so, as if he did he would not obtain the rites of the church, he being Catholic." When he was arrested, in fact, he had instructed her to pack their things, that they were leaving the state "for good" this time.[64]

Certainly his life story would not support a verdict of simple suicide. Consider how many jails had held him. He had done time in some of the most infamous prisons in all of the world. In fact, they comprise a litany of doom. Sing Sing, the Tombs, Hyde Park Barracks, Moreton Bay, Newgate, all the hulks, and sundry local jails all over the world where he was imprisoned for one thing or another. How could a place as ramshackle and modest as Fort Gunnybags drive a man to terror? A correspondent for Frederick Douglass's newspaper thought it implausible it would be suicide. "Poor Sullivan!" he wrote. "He did not appear to be the utterly degraded and abandoned character many might suppose." How could a man of such "physical or brute courage" end his own life over anxiety?[65]

Everything surrounding his death—the confession, informing, asking the British for help, the dread, the suicide—appears so out of character. Perhaps champions like Sullivan, men atop the world as fighters, are prone to act strangely. "The closer a heavyweight comes to the championship," Norman Mailer famously put it, "the more natural it is for him to be a little more insane." He "is either the toughest man in the world or he is not, but there is a real possibility that he is. It is like being the big toe of God."[66] A more likely explanation involves CTE: chronic traumatic encephalopathy—what we used to call the state of being "punch drunk." In modern parlance, Sullivan was exhibiting all the symptoms of someone who had spent too much time in the ring. Violent, unrestrained, verging into alcoholism: Those who had taken too many shots to the head often suffered from "dementia pugilistica," as it was called a generation ago.[67] Was Sullivan one such victim?

Going back in time and diagnosing is not as simple as it might seem. Granted, in a rendering of him drawn around this time, he has visibly aged, and he has a forlorn, vacant look to him. Neurologists, unfortunately, cannot tell if such an appearance suggests some underlying condition. But certainly his life journey points to such conclusions. A newspaper from California around this time proclaimed, "Yankee Sullivan is seriously addicted to ossification of the heart and liver." They were apparently turning into "bone." The reasons? "Sullivan had been thumped enough to be ossified all over," the paper quipped.[68]

Only lately have scientists begun to reckon with the costs of subconcussive hits to the head and what years of them do the brain. Prizefighters and boxers, as a rule, suffer from much higher rates of acute alcoholism than

"YANKEE" SULLIVAN.

An older Yankee Sullivan in the 1850s. (Rare Books and Special Collections, Hesburgh Libraries, University of Notre Dame)

the general population. Erratic behavior and heavy drinking go hand in hand with the holes in the brain caused by chronic jarring. How many hits had he taken over a long prizefighting life?[69] Such men simply lose their lives, or, as Mike Tyson puts it, the prizefighter ends up on Skid Row, "loses his mind," sometimes "goes insane," or falls prey "to the bottle."[70]

Alas, suicide is also par for the course. Compared to the general public, an inordinate number of fighters who exhibit the other behaviors take their own lives. Some years later, an Australian newspaper would opine that Sullivan died after taking too many shots to the head. "He went crazy from the injuries to his head he had received, and committed suicide," it read. His was a case study of "How Prize Fighters Die."[71] Patient Zero for a pioneering scientific study on CTE, a fighter named Paul Pender who beat the great Sugar Ray Robinson, started showing signs of cognitive decline and undue aggression right about the age Sullivan had. When researchers put his brain matter under a microscope, they could not believe what they saw. He was more than "punch drunk." His brain was filled with proteins and had the look of Swiss cheese. Another boxer named Randy Turpin, who also defeated Robinson, became paranoid and killed himself and tried to kill his daughter. Researchers now believe he was suffering from CTE.[72] The 2025 death of the English fighter Ricky Hatton is, alas, just one more example of the link between CTE, alcohol, and suicide.

Of course, we will never really know what happened to Yankee Sullivan. The only certainty we have is that the story of his demise became as complicated as his very life and that its timing fit the tragic arc of his life story.

All that was left was to claim the body. It was identified by his wife, Emily.[73] He left behind a five-month-old daughter.

Just as Yankee Sullivan's pasts caught up with him, San Francisco, a place that was becoming, had become. The Vigilance Committee saw to that. Four men were hanged, a number were banished, and hundreds were scared off.[74] And one killed himself. Or so they said. In the wake of the prizefighters, the miners, the adventurers, and the exploiters came more respectable people, such as the writers Mark Twain and Bret Harte. They saw the same diverse city but one more settled. It now was an established entrepôt. In their work, Harte and Twain looked back to just ten years earlier—the time of the "Argonauts of 1849"—and characterized it as a whole different era, one that had left its mark on the city but one now gone.[75]

New York had changed in Sullivan's lifetime, from its almost frontier-like days, when things were open and plastic and when he ruled the roost. Australia, too, was becoming more respectable. Even Nevada City. In fact, change seemed to accelerate throughout his life, and he was only to stay half a step ahead of it as he moved, trying to find his place.

He had helped create a global pugilistic culture, and that world took notice of his death. His passing was covered all over the United States, as men and women could not get enough of what had happened to this prizefighter. Many, reprinting the same story, said it was the work of "Judge Lynch."[76] Others accepted the inquest's findings of suicide. Everyone knew "the notorious" Sullivan, another term bandied about in dozens of reports across the country. Papers in Australia issued reports. The British and Irish learned of his death as well. Even Hawaiian-language news stories came out about what had happened to him.[77] In death, he had become news in every place he had touched.[78]

They laid out the body "in a plain but handsome coffin" and brought it three miles up the hill to the old mission of St. Francis Assisi. To reach it, the cortege traveled up the hills and over the sand along a plank road over marshes and swamps that had just been built as a toll road.[79] It would have taken the better part of a day just to reach it. It is now called, appropriately, Mission Street. Around it, Irishmen had squatted and set up taverns, so it was a fitting place for Sullivan to be conveyed.[80] The priest who served as pastor was an Irishman from Kilkenny named Richard Carroll. Carroll was described as "a scholarly young Irish priest," and he ran the seminary with fifteen students that stood close to the Mission church. He also was sickly, and the damp adobe structures did not help his condition. What a contrast to the man he was burying.[81]

Mission Dolores lay a world away from Fort Gunnybags. It had been established by St. Junipero Serra as the northern point of the El Camino Real and of the mission system, right next to a Yelamu Ohlone village of about one hundred people called Chutchui. The mission took its more popular name from a body of water nearby named after Our Lady of Sorrows. The first mass was said there on June 27, 1776, just weeks before the Declaration of Independence was signed a continent away. The Natives it ministered to were long gone, pushed out with the relentless expansion of the city and the many peoples who propelled its growth. Its plastered adobe walls were flaking and cracking when Sullivan's body was conveyed to the church. The priest said the blessing in the narrow and simple church before an elaborate Mexican altar with St. Michael brandishing his sword. Our Lady and St. Anne looked on, as did other saints associated with the missions.

In the church's eyes, Sullivan was no suicide. The priest would not have been able to say a funeral mass or bury in consecrated ground the body of a man who had taken his own life. This was murder. In the simple, poor, and neglected church, the priest said a requiem mass, and then Yankee Sullivan's remains were carried into the mission's graveyard surrounded by a rickety old picket fence and lowered into the grave.

The tombstone said he "died by the hands of the V.C." It was fitting that the money for the grave marker was given by a fellow named James Mulloy. He, no doubt, comprised part of a migratory and pugilistic culture that spanned the Atlantic and the Pacific, one Sullivan had helped bring into being. Mulloy had been born in Liverpool.[82] From here he went to Australia, and from that place he traveled to San Francisco with the gold rush. He, too, was investigated by the Vigilance Committee. One fellow fitting his description and whom officials called "James Malloy" resided on the Plank Road leading to the Mission at a bar called "the Grizzly." He, too, was enmeshed in election fraud and in brawling. Officials regarded him as "a most desperate villain" who "kept a low brothel," which he ran with a refugee from New South Wales, Sophia McInnes. Their place was a "devil's hole."[83] Mulloy or Malloy, in other words, was cut from Sullivan's cloth, and the words he chose to memorialize Sullivan hit the mark. On the headstone, an "anthem" adapted from the Penitential Psalms was carved below the claim about the Vigilance Committee, one that reveals a great deal about the world Sullivan helped create:

> Remember not, O Lord, our
> Offences, nor those of our parents,
> Neither take thou vengeance of our sins
> Thou shalt bring my soul out of
> Tribulation, and in thy mercy thou
> Shalt destroy mine enemies.

The stone listed the dead Sullivan as a "native of Bandon, Ireland," a world away from San Francisco. This was the sort of place, in a period of time just before Mark Twain arrived and started cataloguing life there, that required both the ability to seek out those to support and those to hate. These were comfortable worlds for both Francis Ambrose and Yankee Sullivan, or at least worlds he was suited for.

Perhaps the prizefighter had finally found rest.

Epilogue

YANKEE SULLIVAN DID not enjoy one afterlife, but many. These proved as mottled as his complicated life. That story starts and ends with his grave. A tale, probably apocryphal, made the rounds after Sullivan's death. When Mulloy's tombstone was set to be fixed over the grave, a gravedigger opened up the plot to ensure the stone would stand on the right spot. He wanted to identify the remains before he placed the marker. The sexton worried. Sullivan still enjoyed a reputation in the growing city, and there were rumors of souvenir seekers about. He fretted about "resurrectionists," that is, body snatchers or grave robbers. The now-decomposed corpse had no value as a cadaver for surgeons to study anatomy, as had been a practice in the old days that gave birth to the story of Frankenstein. More likely, a, say, Sullivan arm could be quite a trophy and fetch a good price. As soon as the diggers finished their work and reinterred the remains, the sexton waited in the shadows and watched. Sure enough, the "ghouls" came. The sexton laughed to himself. They had arrived too late.[1] Though one story did surface that suggested he was not scrupulous enough. One barman in Philadelphia, years later, claimed to have the skeleton hands of Tom Hyer and Yankee Sullivan "on exhibition." One reckons he invented this tall tale to sell whiskey and beer.[2]

Sullivan would be remembered in nearly all of the places he lived, though only insofar as he could be incorporated into stories about national distinctiveness. In Ireland, Yankee Sullivan was regularly listed as one of the early great fighters. But so many of them were Irish that he hardly distinguished himself in lore. He just appeared as one of many, an interesting curiosity in a nation that once prided itself on producing fighting men. Such is no longer the case, and accordingly, he is now all but forgotten in Ireland.

In Australia, on the other hand, he would enjoy a posthumous reputation. He was part of the tangled fistic line that led to some of Australia's greats. Sullivan defined Australia's gritty past. In popular memory, he is usually remembered as someone who had spent time as a convict before hitting it big in the fight game in the United States, another settler society, which became the global center of boxing.[3]

He did, however, enjoy another Australian afterlife that speaks to the multifaceted nature of legacies. For example, an old-timer remembered witnessing a fight involving a "Ginger Sullivan," who "was afterwards a champion in America." He was not alone. Another fellow who could recall convict days told of how "'Ginger' Sullivan, the famous English champion and 'scientific fighter,'" triumphed over a local fighter. Neither of these Ginger Sullivans would have been Francis Ambrose. He never used the name Sullivan while serving as a convict. And, in fact, a number of fighters later on took the name Ginger Sullivan, decisions which probably had nothing to do with Ambrose.[4] Still, Ginger was remembered and misremembered in Australian lore, both for what he did and for what he became. He could be incorporated into a national narrative that started with the convict past, whether that was one that brought shame—the "convict stain"—or pride. "When the legend becomes fact," as the saying goes, "print the legend." So it should be with Ambrose, Sullivan, and Australia.

In England? He was all but forgotten, perhaps only a footnote because of his victory over Hammer Lane, but nothing more than that. Sullivan was not part of this boxing story, one that centered on the idea of British nationhood. In this regard, the great Tom Cribb eclipsed all others, even Daniel Mendoza. This is hardly surprising. After all, Francis Ambrose had just missed the heyday, and even had he stayed and fought in Britain, as an Irishman, he could have been nothing more than a lesser luminary or a foil, the role generally played by Irish, Jewish, and Black boxers.

It was in the United States where he enjoyed the most complex set of afterlives. Many remained fascinated with Sullivan because of the larger-than-life role he played in American pre–Civil War culture. He had been a celebrity, one of America's first, in the city that was coming to define the nation. Here's just one example: In 1862, his former friends—and even a few enemies—put on a boxing exhibition in his honor. John Morrissey, "the old antagonist" of Sullivan, led the cavalcade of stars who would spar. They did so to support, believe it or not, Sullivan's mother. Mrs. Ambrose, born Catherine Murray in Bandon, left London after her husband, John Ambrose, died. She headed to New York. In 1862, she was "a very old lady (over 70) and incapable of helping herself." At a theater on the Bowery, a star-studded cast of fighters—now all associated with Tammany—did what the organization did best: look after one of its own. Yankee Sullivan had played the role of political soldier. Now New York was paying him back.[5] These were his cronies and fellow professionals, those who knew Sullivan, warts and all.

For others, he offered an antimodel of Americanness. In American lore, he and the prizefighters with political ties remained a byword for political corruption, a bogeyman of sorts and reminiscent of the bad old days to which no one wanted to return. Or he epitomized the Tweed-like corruption that some insisted still afflicted American cities. Progress had taken care of him. But he still haunted the imagination, suggesting that American democracy was fragile and that backsliding presented a constant threat.[6]

That haunting took some bizarre directions. In the years after his death, for instance, Sullivan became an object of intense study for phrenologists. This quack science took the Western world by storm in the early nineteenth century and then became a popular obsession even as its scientific reputation was flagging. It posited that one could tell everything one needed to know about the character of a person by understanding the shape and size of certain parts of the head. It was a strange variant of the scientific world that Charles Darwin had helped create. For phrenologists, Sullivan offered a gold mine of information on one aspect of human behavior.

A series of manuals and studies used Yankee Sullivan to explain the rudiments of phrenology. Though they could not measure his skull, the manuals provided drawings of him and from them intuited its size and shape. Sullivan's skull revealed a large "propensity." Such people, one study went, "have strong animal desires; and that selfishness that takes care of number one; are strongly attached to this world and its pleasures; and with great activity, use vigorous exertions to accomplish worldly and personal ends." These traits were supposedly "liable to their depraved and sensual manifestation," as had been the case with Sullivan. That said, people like Sullivan "have great force, energy, and determination," even if in his case these proclivities were misdirected.[7]

Another said that in Sullivan "we see an iron temperament and the elements of endurance that are rarely surpassed. He had a low, broad head, indicating a predominance of the organs of the animal propensities over those of the moral, the former of which are located above the ears, the latter situated in the top-head." The detail captured was extraordinary. "His head," the manual went on, "had the appearance of large mechanical organs; sense of property, talent for figures, and for order in his affairs." There was more. "He had great secretiveness," the manual read, "which made him remarkably acute and cunning, combined with large Cautiousness, which led him to be guarded and safe in his actions," virtues for a prizefighter to be sure. "His Mirthfulness appears to have been large," it concluded, "hence he perceived the ludicrous and the witty and enjoyed fun highly, though with his temperament and general organization, he was sarcastic rather than playful in the use of his Mirthfulness." The manual made one last point: "His reasoning and perceptive organs appeared fairly developed; hence we infer that he was quick to gather knowledge and able to plan quite successfully."[8]

Yankee Sullivan was the perfect specimen for this "science." "Perhaps no characters in community furnish a better illustration of Phrenology, or evince in a stronger light the influences of training and education, than this same class of fighting men," the report gushed. "Organized by nature for pugilism, either in contests with single combatants or for war in the army, or for contending with rough life in some industrial pursuit," it found, "if they fail in the latter to find a safety-valve to which to work off the steam of their animal propensities, they gravitate towards such conditions as will give them an opportunity for their gratification." A character like Yankee Sullivan was the sort of man to frighten those respectable people apt to find solace in the sort of quackery that rationalized their status in society and demonized those below. The phrenologists, of course, got some things about his nature right—in the same way a horoscope does—but they left little room for nurture, and Sullivan had had his share of nurture.

So, Yankee Sullivan still fascinated Americans after his death. His name turned up everywhere. Fighters called themselves "Yankee Sullivan," as did two-bit criminals from Chicago, Cincinnati, and Jersey City and even an engineer from Pittsburgh who died in an act of rail sabotage, as well as an American who swam the English Channel.[9] In the decades after his life ended, Americans recounted his battles, and others reprised his sordid exploits in urban politics. A woman in San Francisco, on visiting a medium and threatening to tear the place up during a séance, even claimed to be possessed by Yankee Sullivan's ghost.[10]

Then, poof, he was gone. After the period of macabre fascination with Yankee Sullivan that lasted into the 1880s, Americans forgot about him. With the passing of those "sporting men" who knew him or fought him, he became little more than a byword for bygone. Prizefighting gave way to boxing, and he became one of the "pioneers."[11] After his time, reformers transformed fisticuffs into a sport and an entertaining diversion. They changed the rules. They based rounds on time. The old rituals went by the wayside. No more throwing the hat into the ring, for instance. Fighters now donned gloves when they fought for purses. These new guidelines were called the Marquis of Queensbury Rules. They fit the world better. Time was the chief commodity of the fully blown industrial world, and how people organized their lives. Before this, prizefighting perfectly suited the world of becoming. It meshed the timeless with the timed. It took an older, pastoral blood sport, something from the premodern world, and affixed the thirty seconds to get to scratch, something more in line with the burgeoning world. It was the in-between avocation made for an in-between world, when so much for common workingmen was at stake. No more.

John L. Sullivan—no relation—represented the last champion to earn a title with the rules Yankee fought under, and the first under the new sets of rules. In the 1880s, he stood on top of the prizefighting world. This Sullivan towered as an American fighting champion and as the most famous man in the world. When Yankee fought, prizefighting existed beyond the law and on society's margins, as the passion of those men who were regarded as menaces. He was ending his fighting career just as prizefighting was morphing into something else. With John L., boxing emerged from the shadows to become America's pastime, something embraced by all, even by his bosom buddy Teddy Roosevelt. Americans, Roosevelt included, characterized John L. Sullivan as the very paragon of American manhood.

What a change in so little a time. But no wonder. By the time Yankee Sullivan had left the stage, the world he had helped craft had fully come into being. The networks he traveled as a pioneer had cohered into the very sinews of modern trade and movement. These now were the lifeblood of all of those places he had lived just as those places were transitioning. By then, Yankee Sullivan's time had ended. Those who had benefited from the world he and other common men like him helped build had no desire to remember him and his ilk. And from this moment on, he would be as forgotten as a bit of scrimshaw languishing in an archive, perhaps living on as merely "notorious."

With time, in America, the story of Yankee Sullivan became one less of myth than nostalgia. Yankee Sullivan lived on among those who still did the hard thankless work of making a city grow. He did so most visibly with that famous image carved by the whaleman. In a "Ghost Story," written just around the time of Sullivan's death, the author set the story in a bar, and in it the men drink beneath the same image that the scrimshander copied.[12] George Washington Plunkitt, that sage of the mature Tammany Hall machine, told of how some bars in New York City featured the print, including one on the waterfront where "boatmen drink their grog" and that had as its only ornaments "a three-cornered mirror nailed to the wall, and a chromo of the fight between Tom Hyer and Yankee Sullivan."[13] To such workingmen Sullivan was akin to a Tom Joad, a vanished figure from a bygone era who once raised a fist to the world.

Nowhere is the nostalgic more prevalent than in New York City's iconic Irish bar, McSorley's. Joseph Mitchell, who wrote for the *New Yorker* and covered all aspects of New York City life in the mid-twentieth century, described McSorley's as an almost hallowed place "opposed to change." And he claimed the print was there. But to see it, you have to know where to look. In the back of an alcove to the left, just as you enter, a nook or cranny in the most awkward spot in the saloon to get to, Sullivan is about to fight Tom Hyer still, just when he ruled the city and the moment before his fall. Few, if any, drinking there would even know who Sullivan was or what he represented. But the image adds to the atmosphere of a place that stands as an homage to an old and lost New York.

Sullivan lives on in one more way, under the category of notorious. The California band Primus recorded a song about him called "Fisticuffs" in 1997 on their *Brown Album*. In the song, they seem enamored with the bare details of his life, moving backward through it from his death in California, a stint in "Botany Bay atoning for his sins," a fight in England, to his life on the Bowery, where he reigned as "a prince of lawless times." Of Sullivan's origins, the band has no idea, except that no one knew his name. But they were certain on one point: His death "drained him down to Hell."

The songwriter, Les Claypool, had been watching UFC (Ultimate Fighting Championship)—that is, the form of no-holds-barred fisticuffs most reminiscent of bare-knuckle fighting, the sort Sullivan specialized in—when he wrote the lyrics. The tone of the music was meant to create an industrial, urban soundscape, what Claypool imagined to be Sullivan's context.[14]

Then there is whiskey. In 2017, a new brand of whiskey called "Prizefight" began appearing on the shelves of American liquor stores. On its label are the images of two old-time fighters with their names beneath: John Morrissey and Yankee Sullivan. The problem is these are not Sullivan and Morrissey. The label, in fact, features illustrations of Tom Sayers, an English fighter, and John Heenan, the fellow Sullivan trained and then ducked in California. Sayers and Heenan fought not in 1853 but in 1860. The figures on the whiskey bottle came from a sketch by Thomas Nast, the artist who gave us the popular image of the bearded grandfatherly Santa Claus and many of the most anti-Irish caricatures of the mid-nineteenth century. It appeared in the *New York Illustrated News*. There is no image of the Sullivan-Morrissey bout—though Morrissey attended the 1860 Sayers-Heenan fight, pulling for, believe it or not, the Englishman. But that's another story.

What is intriguing about the whiskey is how it is made, distilling a great deal of Yankee Sullivan's lived experience. The makers of the brand bill the whiskey as a transatlantic enterprise. A distiller in West Cork turns the grain into alcohol. He then ages the raw spirits in American rye barrels from New Hampshire. The makers on both sides of the ocean hope to pay homage to the Irish as transatlantic fighters. More interesting is the fact that the Irish contribution to Prizefight is made in a place called Skibbereen. The town lay just to the west of Bandon where Francis Ambrose was born, less than an hour's drive today on the N71. In fact, in the 1820s, some Ambroses lived right next to it. Perhaps Yankee's grandfather even came to Bandon from this region.

The distiller, Flor Prendergast, saw his vision could be realized when he met Steven Grasse. "I always laugh that Irish whiskey was the vodka of whiskey," Grasse told a reporter. "And it would be great to do something more interesting with it. So we came up with the idea of sending spent rye barrels from America to West Cork and having them finish their Irish whiskey in those used casks. I was surprised it hadn't been done before." We are far from the rotgut world of Sullivan, even if, as the partners argue, the transatlantic whiskey honors those Irish who boxed and "who came with nothing and fought for everything."

The story of Prizefight speaks to our era of globalization, one consciously cultivated by today's cosmopolitan elite. The actual prizefight that Prizefight whiskey draws inspiration from, the 1853 Morrissey-Sullivan bout, was the product of a very different sort of globalizer, featuring men who came from the margins when they were places to leave and not destinations. These men did not discuss palate or color or nose when they drank. For them, whiskey was, as an Irish comedian today puts it, "anger trapped in a glass." Grasse, to his credit, understands that as well. Why Yankee Sullivan? Irish whiskey finished in American rye barrels, he explained, had an "Irish-American vibe." And Yankee Sullivan offered a "great backstory." "Brand mysticism" is what drew him to Sullivan. The idea is simple. "Taking risks and developing authenticity" sells whiskey. Sullivan offered both. Grasse did not want to go for "what is trendy." He saw going back to the 1850s, to the era of "badass," a term he used, as offering a way to do so. He is not alone. The prizefighter also appears on beer bottles, inspiring a beer called "Sullivan Hazy Pale Ale." It is listed as "Punchy but friendly." Apparently the brewer only knew part of the story.[15]

As Grasse suggests, for both Primus's song "Fisticuffs" and for the whiskey Prizefight, Yankee Sullivan was resurrected as an anti-type of modernity. He represented—and still does—the quality he started out with as Francis Ambrose: defiance. The same could be said for how he is recalled in McSorley's—with the hard edges of the word sanded off and lacquered with a patina of Irish American sentiment. The same idea resonates in Australia, as his image brings men and women back to convict days, before Australia was a polite society and when prizefighters held sway.

Yet defiance does not work when it comes to narratives of what it means to be American. In this regard, Sullivan's afterlife offers lessons as well. Let me return to the decade after Sullivan's death, when he still enjoyed a vestigial celebrity status, to understand what Sullivan said and says about American sense of self. In 1877, on the occasion of the death of Cornelius Vanderbilt, the *New York Times* dedicated page after page to the "Commodore." The coverage was fawning, maybe verging on mythical. This was the Commodore, after all, the man who, like Alexander Hamilton and

DeWitt Clinton, possessed vision and means and who did all he could to tie New York to the world. Now, this was the man who had to have created New York.

But one little piece on the Commodore featured Sullivan. The story goes like this: In 1844, the Democrat James Polk and the Whig Henry Clay were facing off for the White House. Vanderbilt decided to host a parade of horses in New York to get the vote out for Clay—and presumably demonstrate his support. Having a friend in the White House, after all, would never hurt. He led out five hundred men on horseback, and the cortege happened to pass near City Hall Park and Sullivan's bar on Chatham Street. Inside with his cronies, Sullivan heard all the fuss. As if the readers had to know, the *Times* reminded its readers that Sullivan was—in scare quotes—a "Tammany worker." He also "boasted that he could 'whip any Yankee Whig in sight.'" But not this day, apparently. As the parade passed, he looked to "take the Commodore down." He seized the reins of the horse and pulled. Ah, but Vanderbilt got the best of Sullivan. He pulled out his whip and struck Sullivan on the back. Vanderbilt then jumped down off his mount and—as the *Times* put it—"so badly beat him that his friends took him away in a nearly senseless condition."[16]

Absurd.

This could just have been a man-bites-dog tale—Sullivan, after all, was at the very height of his fighting prowess and could have beaten any man in the world. But there's more than meets the eye here. To be sure, Yankee Sullivan epitomized all that the *Times* and its readership would have loathed: Catholic, Irish, Democrat, pugilist, Tammany man. He hit every mark. But, to be fair, this story of how Vanderbilt whipped Sullivan had much broader appeal and was reprinted as far away as San Francisco.[17] The reason why the story made the news is simple. Americans were and are more comfortable believing that it's the great men, the founders in the national narrative, whether hailed or decried, who move great events, dynamics, and processes. But not the unwashed masses. And Sullivan was their champion. Americans struggle to admit him into the panoply of those, like Washington or like Vanderbilt, who helped fashion the modern world with all of its complexities. Americans cannot reckon with the complicated idea of globalized modernity that Sullivan represents. Admitting as much makes us take on board not only the good but also the less savory. In fact, one cannot be disentangled from the other. And Sullivan reminds Americans of that simple yet troubling fact.

Yankee's afterlife conjures one final paradoxical lesson of the shaping of our world. Obscure men like him fit into a violent system that needed brute labor to instantiate the global, a system that increasingly allowed for mobility and democratic participation. These sorts seemed perfectly suited to places caught in flux, as was much of the Western world after the age of revolution. Yankee's shape-shifting adaptability and his endless creativity help explain why he proved so adept during moments of becoming and their concomitant plasticity. Such places-in-time truly belonged to him and his ilk, the flotsam and jetsam of the world. They were well-suited for the promise, crass competitiveness, opportunity, and exploitation that defined their age. They were perfect moderns and connectors.

There was always a cost, and Yankee bore it, as did many others. The window of time for the Yankee Sullivans of the world, this time of "becoming," was brief, and outliving the moment made for tragedy. Yankee Sullivan managed to survive a number of the places in transition that attracted and needed the likes of him. He even flourished for a bit. But he did not survive the last. In fact, he died just as his task was done and as they had "become." Moreover, these places-in-time were ruthless and remorseless. Adapt or die were their watchwords. As were exploit or be exploited. And, in truth, grinding poverty and short, hard lives would be the lot in life for most of these shape-shifters.

After their brief walk out onto the stage, these men sank back into obscurity. Only notables like Sullivan lived on, and only as bogeymen or badasses.

We are apt to see figures such as Sullivan as the "deracinated," or the unfortunate uprooted. This word misses the mark. Though he died as he was born, under unclear circumstances and with another name, Yankee Sullivan was neither victim nor survivor. Agency be damned. This is the frightening sort who made our world—brick upon stacked brick, load after heavy load, punch by brutal punch. We would rather forget them, and they don't fit our tidy narratives, and they disappeared as quickly as they came; but they were our unlikely, unwelcome, and complicating founders—with all the mix of promise and perdition this phrase entails.

After years of tracking him around the world, I had to pay Sullivan a visit. So, on my last research trip, this one to San Francisco, I stopped

Yankee Sullivan's grave at Mission Dolores Cemetery, San Francisco. (Photo by the author)

by the mission church dedicated to St. Francis to see his grave. Today, it is part of an oasis in the lovely Mission District. It sits beside a massive church, now a minor basilica, that was built after the earthquake. The original mission church survived the quake, making it the oldest building in San Francisco, fitting, of course, as the whole city takes its name from this humble structure. After chatting with the parish priest about the history of the mission, I entered the graveyard. I spotted Sullivan's grave immediately. It is a beautiful and peaceful setting. Around him rest Italians, what a monument calls "Faithful Indians," Mexicans, Frenchmen, a Scot, American-born men and women, and a great number of other Irish, nearly all of whom wanted to tell visitors which county they had come from. Thousands of Natives, whether faithful or not, lay buried on the mission grounds, unacknowledged after Europeans came in droves and took over the graveyard. It is, in a word, a diverse place but one shaped by the long-forgotten colonial narrative, just like the city then and now.

For Sullivan, they chose a gravesite right next to the church, as if he needed the most intercessory help. His headstone is oriented eastward, so that he might face the rising sun.

In the quiet of a drizzly morning, I took out a flask I brought with me, filled with Prizefight Irish whiskey. And we shared a drink. As I sipped and then poured the whiskey onto his grave, I thought that the prizefighter's tale had come full circle to a fitting and proper conclusion. Francis Ambrose, the fighting man who was born with a name befitting a priest or a poet, was now buried in the graveyard of his patron saint's church. It all fit.

Until it didn't. Just after my visit, I reached out to the curator of the Mission to discuss Sullivan. I wish I hadn't. He let me know that the gravesite I visited, the one that looked so perfect, was not, in fact, the place where Yankee Sullivan lay. "Sullivan's grave location that you viewed is not where he is actually buried in our Mission Cemetery," the curator told me. His grave marker and the fencing were moved to the current location when the back part of the cemetery was closed and turned into a schoolyard. Sullivan's body, he said, was not relocated. They pulled up Sullivan's headstone and the wrought-iron fence around it, and squeezed them in right next to the church. They did not disinter the body. It lay somewhere beneath the asphalt where I had seen schoolchildren playing. Lord knows who I shared my whiskey with.

I was staggered. Sullivan had foiled me once again. Even in death, he proved elusive and, perhaps, defiant. The prizefighter, after all, had not found rest.

ACKNOWLEDGMENTS

This book covers a lot of ground and all sorts of things. I needed expert support. The following scholars and friends answered my questions and offered tangible and intangible help in all sorts of ways throughout the process, including encouragement. Here goes: Beth Bland, Tom Bartlett, Ted Beatty, Jake Lundberg, Michael Hoppen, Lisa Caulfield, Ian Kuijt, Richard Waterhouse, Mike McDonnell, Brian Ó Conchubhair, Grace Karskens, Bill Miscamble, Simon Fennell, Tom Bowsher, David Astorr, George Rugg, Guy Collender, Richard Doctorow, David Mulkins, Enda Delaney, Carlo Rotella, Rob O'Sullivan, Peter Hession, David Dickson, Paul Buser, Kevin Kenny, Breandán MacSuibhne, Niamh Gallagher, Ian McBride, Eugenio Biagini, Christa Dierksheide, Grantlee Kieza, Claire Connolly, Nick Guyatt, Frank Shovlin, and Peter Boyle.

I was helped by the research staffs at the following archives: Cambridge University Library; the Bodleian Library at Oxford; the British Library; the Public Records Office, Kew; the National Archives, Dublin; the Cork City and County Archives; West Cork Historical Society; East Hampton Library; Sag Harbor Historical Society; New York Historical Society; New York Public Library; Notre Dame Special Collections; Mitchell Library of New South Wales; the Russell Museum, New Zealand; the Huntington Library; the Bancroft Library at the University of California, Berkeley; and the Hawaii Historical Society. The work on this book could not have been done without the people who created ancestry.com; historical newspaper databases for the United States (America's Historical Newspapers), Britain (the British Newspaper Archive), and Australia (Trove); and the Digital Panopticon, which allows the user to track convicts. These sorts of resources are amazing when trying to find an elusive character.

I have given talks on aspects of this project at the following places: the Irish History Seminar at the University of Cambridge; Santa Clara University; Hertford College, University of Oxford; the Hamilton Center, University of Florida; Glucksman House, New York University; the University of Virgina; Boston College; the Royal Irish Academy; the

University of Edinburgh; University College Dublin; the University of Liverpool; and Notre Dame's History Department.

Katherine Fynes, David Carlson, and Liam Kelly provided research support. They were all great.

I was lucky to tour a number of the places in the book with some terrific human beings. Martyn Powell hosted me when I visited Bristol. Tom and Marra Richardson did the same on my treks to Bandon. Dan Sternberg and Rich Rosenzweig drove me around Boston Corner. Rich turned out to be a generous font of knowledge. Mark Dunn took me on an extraordinary pub crawl through the Rocks in Sydney. Stan Alost and I explored and mapped out the Five Points for the better part of a day. I dragged my daughter-in-law Sarah Griffin on a trawl through the broader Lower East Side. Fabian Hilfrich, Frank Cogliano, and Colin Barr walked the East End of London to discover Ambrose's world. Frank, Simon Fennell, and I went in search of boxing history in London, just as the project was getting under way. Later on, Tom Healy took the trek with me from rag fair to rag fair in Whitechapel. Greg Quiery took me on a fun-filled and sobering tour of Irish Liverpool. David Astorr introduced me to the wealthy present and laboring past of Sag Harbor. Guy Collander and I spent a wonderful day traipsing through Chatham. Brian Dorini and I surveyed Sullivan's San Francisco. My daughter Maggie Griffin went in search of the 1849 print in McSorley's. She found it after I had missed it. I learned as much from all of these people as I did from visiting Sullivan's many haunts.

Gary Gerstle and the Cambridge American Seminar played a critical role at a critical moment in the life of this project. I was unsure of a next book project when I was invited to give a paper at the seminar. I decided on Sullivan and New York. The talk was received warmly, and a few of the participants urged me to make global Sullivan my book.

Two friends started me fighting and trained me and encouraged me to write this sort of book. Awful cruel men that they are, they should have helped me; but they punched instead. These are Nate Walker and Neil MacDonald. It's an honor to spar with the likes of them, two of my best friends who taught me so much. Fittingly, they worked the corner when I fought at Gleason's Gym in New York. They also happily went drinking afterward at McSorley's.

A number of scholars helped me keep my faith in the profession and the craft, largely through dark humor and friendship. I am privileged to do so much with Frank Cogliano, Lige Gould, and Brendan McConville. Their way of seeing the past helped me see the possibilities of re-creating Sullivan's world. Tim Breen, another of my closest friends and an especially skilled craftsman, read a good chunk of the manuscript and helped me discover the best way to frame it. Colin Barr loved chatting about the project, or at least pretended to, and helped me maintain my sanity. Robert Ingram listened over pints at some of the more interesting pubs in London.

It sounds pompous to say "my agent," but there you go. I have an agent. George Lucas read and reread drafts of the proposal and generously commented on each. He was and is terrific to work with.

Then there is Nadine Zimmerli. She is a crack editor. As a rule, she does not suffer fools. But she found an exception in me, it seems. She showed confidence in this project from the get-go, and she expertly helped me navigate the process and the reviewers. She is tops. I learned one of the reviewers was Warren Hofstra. A great scholar and a terrific guy, he gave me a needed shot in the arm with his comments on the manuscript. I discovered later that Kevin Kenny was a reader for the proposal. He similarly helped me a great deal with his review. I did not know the other two reviewers. One was from Australia I would wager, and he/she really helped me get up to speed with the literatures and with the nuances of the convict-era Down Under. I am most grateful for that intervention.

I started this when I was Harmsworth Professor at the University of Oxford. The Rothermere American Institute was a wonderful and supportive place to write and think. In that year, I was lucky enough to hang and work with Adam Smith, Dan Rowe, Uta Balbier, Nick Cole, Stephen Tufnell, Justin Jacobs, and Peter Thompson.

I finished the book at St. Edmund's College at Cambridge. Three people offered consistent inspiration (and slews of conviviality!): Vittorio Montemaggi, Josh Copeland, and Chris Young.

I owe a special thanks to a number of people, expert in boxing history and/or images, who shared their knowledge and resources with me. They did so unstintingly. These are Tony Gee and Pierre Spake, two princes among men. They have forgotten more than I know about the early fight game, especially Tony, who set me straight on a good number of details. Pierre kindly permitted me to reproduce one of the images he owns of the famous 1849 Hyer-Sullivan fight.

You will note this book has two dedications. Let me explain. I have listed Kenneth J. Lamb as someone who assisted with the research for the book. It is wonderful and fitting to recognize Ken's contribution in a formal way. Ken is a descendant of Yankee Sullivan and has long been fascinated with his shady ancestor. I was knee-deep into the research for the book when I first heard something about Ken. I was at Bandon, at the West Cork Historical Society. The archivist there recalled someone from Australia phoning in about Sullivan, but he could not remember anything about the caller, including his name. Sometime later, Katherine Fynes, a research assistant trawling through Irish records, discovered Ken for me. I then reached out to him. An undaunted researcher, Ken has done extraordinary investigation into the life of Sullivan, assembling copious notes and drafting a series of sections and appendices, replete with excerpted primary sources, for a genealogical study. The scholar Nancy Taniguchi let Ken know I was legit as a historian and that perhaps I could do a good job with what he had unearthed. Ken then offered to share his notes with me and told me I could use whatever of his I found useful. I crafted my narrative and wrote up a draft using what I had discovered. Then I turned to Ken's notes to confirm my storyline. We had relied on a great many of the same sources. Nonetheless, a number of things he had found were news to me, particularly on the family. Ken had dug up some amazing material that added a great deal to the story, such as the street on which Sullivan's family likely lived in London, details of his misadventures in Australia, and the name of the ship on which he probably escaped from Sydney. Finding this sort of stuff is not easy and requires exhaustive searches through online sources. You will see how I point out in the notes all of the important details of the story that Ken found through his work. Some of this source work he organized into chapters, the sum total of which he had provisionally entitled "The Life (and Battles) of 'Yankee' Sullivan"; other pieces of evidence are more stand-alone bits he hunted down. I cite all under the heading "Lamb MSS." I make special mention of these particulars because I would like to give credit where credit is due. And it is giving due credit to a friend. I visited Ken and his wife, Heather, in Canberra, and we spent a lovely day going over gaps in the story, some of which Ken was able to clear up. Later, as I was completing the study, I asked Ken to undertake some additional research on a few more holes that I needed to fill (the citations for these are labeled as "Lamb MSS, Misc. Notes" along with the sources). Though the writing, the arguments, the archival research, and the interpretation are mine, Ken's generosity animates this book. It has been a true joy to meet someone who cares about the details as much as I do and who is so kind.

As for the second dedication, well, that speaks for itself. Pride of place in this section goes to my family. They are the reason I do what I do. With them, my treasure lies. So, here's to Mary Hope, Michael, Sarah, Eileen, Liam, Bri, Frankie, Maggie, Annie, Joan, Reagan, and Cailin. This book—and this life—are dedicated to each of them.

NOTES

Introduction

1. Powder Horn 008, Massachusetts Historical Society. The piece was a gift of Katharine Gordon Lewis, who left no record of how she acquired it (see "Gifts to the Society," *Proceedings of the Massachusetts Historical Society* 45 [1911]: 185). My thanks to Anne Bentley for her help on this score.
2. One, a fine piece in a huge collection at the New Bedford Whaling Museum, has a fighter named John Heenan on the panbone of a sperm whale. Heenan fought an epic match with the great English brawler Tom Sayers in 1860. For a sense of the diversity of carvings, see Alan Granby, *Wandering Whalemen and Their Art: A Collection of Scrimshaw Masterpieces* (Cahoon Museum of Art, 2021).
3. Eric Jay Dolin, *Leviathan: The History of Whaling in America* (Norton, 2007), 278–79.
4. See, for instance, David Milne, *Worldmaking: The Art and Science of American Diplomacy* (Farrar, Straus and Giroux, 2015).
5. There are a number of perspectives on these phenomena. But of late they have been characterized by boom and doom. For the former, a more optimistic take on the world of growth this period helped usher in, see Joel Mokyr, *A Culture of Growth: The Origins of the Modern Economy* (Princeton University Press, 2016). The latter is summed up by novelist Paul Kingsnorth and what he calls the "Machine," or the hyperconnected world of the modern liberal industrial, and dehumanizing, global order we live with today (see *Against the Machine: On the Unmaking of Humanity* [Thesis, 2025]).
6. Donald McRae, *The Last Bell: Life, Death and Boxing* (Simon & Schuster, 2025), 233.

Round 1. Bandon

1. "Thormanby [W. Wilmot Dixon]," *Boxers and Their Battles* (R. A. Everett, 1900), 224.
2. I discovered the name with the help of an Australian novel: David Whish Wilson, *The Sawdust House* (Freemantle, 2022). The one newspaper to get this right was one from Washington, DC, in a section dealing with trivia and gossip. It named him "Frank Ambrose" (see *Daily Critic*, 16 September 1875).

3. Will and Ariel Durant, *The Lessons of History* (Simon & Schuster, 1968), 24.
4. Edward MacLysaght, *The Surnames of Ireland* (Irish Academic Press, 2012), 5.
5. These findings are based on tithe applotment books. Tithe applotment books for land that various Ambroses farmed and where they lived are held in the National Archives of Ireland. They can be found at https://titheapplotment books.nationalarchives.ie.
6. Ballymodan and Kilbrogan Baptismal Registers, Representative Church Body Archives, Dublin.
7. "Matrimonial Register of the United Parishes of Ballymodan, Kilbrogan, and Desert Serges," National Library of Ireland, accessible through https://www .nli.ie/. My thanks to Edward Wallace for finding this reference.
8. Baptism Record of 19 February 1791, Cork & Ross (RC) Records, Cork SS. Peter and Paul, National Library of Ireland, accessible through https://www .nli.ie/.
9. Contingencies for East India Parties, Southern (Ireland) Depot, British Army Muster Books and Pay Lists, 1817; Disability and Out-Pensions, Admissions, 21 August 1817, Royal Hospital Chelsea Pensioner Admission and Discharge Records, National Archives, Kew, accessible through ancestry.com.
10. On this battle and siege, see Alan Harfield, "Cavalry Units in Java, 1811–16," *Journal of the Society for Army Historical Research* 81 (2003): 243–63; Harfield, "The Siege of Meester Cornelis, Java, August, 1811," *Journal of the Society for Army Historical Research* 72 (1994): 133–41; Tim Hannigan, *Raffles and the British Invasion of Java* (Monsoon Books, 2013), 94–102; and Maj. William Thorn, *Memoirs of the Conquest of Java* (London, 1815), 55–68, 168.
11. Sujit Sivasundaram, *Waves Across the South: A New History of Revolution and Empire* (University of Chicago, 2020), 230–35; "The Siege of Meester Cornelis, Java, August, 1811," *Journal of the Society for Army Historical Research* 72 (1994): 133–41.
12. Hannigan, *Raffles and the British Invasion of Java*, 200.
13. Disability and Out-Pensions, Admissions, 21 August 1817, Royal Hospital Chelsea Pensioner Admission and Discharge Records.
14. Contingencies for East India Parties, Southern (Ireland) Depot, British Army Muster Books and Pay Lists, 1817; Disability and Out-Pensions, Admissions, 21 August 1817, Royal Hospital Chelsea Pensioner Admission and Discharge Records. John Ambrose still revered the Fifty-Ninth. Just before he was mustered out, the Second Battalion of the Fifty-Ninth suffered one of the worst seaborn tragedies in British military history. A troop transport called the *Seahorse* went down off the coast of Ireland. It was returning from the famous victory of Wellington over Napoleon at Waterloo and heading to Cork. John,

of course, was not on board; nearly all the men were lost. When money was raised to create a memorial to the tragedy, John gave five shillings, a significant sum of money for a laborer who could expect to earn that much in a week (see https://theseahorseshipwreck.blogspot.com/p/the-sea-horse-monument.html). On the tragedy, see J. P. Entract, "The Tramore and Kinsale Tragedies, 1816," *Journal of the Society for Army Historical Research* 46 (1968): 225–34.

15. Contingencies for East India Parties, Southern (Ireland) Depot, British Army Muster Books and Pay Lists, 1817; Baptism Record of 15 February 1798, Cork & Ross (RC) Records, Bandon.
16. "A Description of Bandon, 1835," Local History Forum, 2016, West Cork Historical Society.
17. For the history of Bandon and much of what follows, see Patrick O'Flanagan, *Irish Historic Towns Atlas no. 3: Bandon* (Royal Irish Academy, 1988).
18. "A Description of Bandon, 1835," Local History Forum, 2016, West Cork Historical Society.
19. West Cork Historical Society Exhibition on Bandon; Frederick Stoven to John Sweet, 3 July 1829, CSORP/OR/1829/681, National Archives, Dublin.
20. West Cork Historical Society Exhibition on Bandon.
21. "A Description of Bandon, 1835," Local History Forum, 2016, West Cork Historical Society.
22. George Bennett, *The History of Bandon, and the Principal Towns in the West Riding of County Cork* (Cork, 1869), 520.
23. *Southern Reporter and Cork Commercial Courier*, 30 August 1855; Frank Keohane, *The Buildings of Ireland: Cork City and County* (Yale University Press, 2020), 244–53.
24. Frank McNally, "Out and Proud: Frank McNally on the Many Irishtowns of Ireland," *Irish Times*, 16 March 2023.
25. Padraig Hamilton, "The Lismore Papers and Nineteenth-Century Bandon," *Bandon Historical Journal* 3 (1987): 32.
26. For Chapel Lane, I am relying on the Baptismal Record of Thomas Ambrose, 15 February 1798, Cork & Ross (RC) Records, Bandon. On language, a report commissioned by the Royal Irish Academy in 2003 to study the language did not even bother to study Bandon. See Pat Crowley, "West Cork Decline of Irish and Poets and Scribes," www.academia.edu/37972239/West_Cork_Decline_of_Irish_and_Poets_and_Scribes_docx; and Garret Fitzgerald, "Irish-Speaking in the Pre-Famine Period: A Study Based on the 1911 Census," *Proceedings of the Royal Irish Academy* 103 (2003): 191–283. On 1851, see the map in Gearoid O'Tuathaigh, *Ireland Before the Famine: 1798–1848* (Gill Books, 2007), 142.

27. 1841 map of Bandon in O'Flanagan, *Irish Historic Towns Atlas no. 3: Bandon.*
28. See Baptismal and Marriage Records, Cork & Ross (RC) Records, Bandon; Baptism Record of James Sullivan, 22 June 1809, Cork & Ross (RC) Records, Bandon.
29. O'Flanagan, *Irish Historic Towns Atlas no. 3: Bandon,* 6.
30. I know a great deal about the Ambroses because of what the records don't say. The 1821 rent roll for the Earl of Bandon, held in the Cork City and County Archives and which included land held on Chapel Lane, included no Ambroses. The Ambroses did not make the cut or appear in the records of any estate, it seems. See also O'Flanagan, *Irish Historic Towns Atlas no. 3: Bandon,* 5; Bennett, *The History of Bandon,* iii.
31. Lindsay Proudfoot, *Urban Patronage and Social Authority: The Management of the Duke of Devonshire's Towns in Ireland* (Catholic University of America Press, 1995), 75.
32. Proudfoot, *Urban Patronage and Social Authority,* 200–201.
33. See, for instance, Proudfoot, *Urban Patronage and Social Authority,* 160; and Padraig Hamilton, "The Lismore Papers and Nineteenth-Century Bandon," *Bandon Historical Journal* 3 (1987): 36.
34. On this, see Enda Delaney, *Making Ireland Modern: The Transformation of Society and Culture* (Oxford University Press, 2026).
35. "Military Regiments Stationed in Bandon," Bandon-geneology.com/Military-regiments-stationed-bandon.htm.
36. James Huston to Robert Eedy, 24 March 1826; Wills and Elydia Anstis, 29 July 1827, Eedy Letters, Cork City Archives; O'Tuathaigh, *Ireland Before the Famine,* 106.
37. O'Tuathaigh, *Ireland Before the Famine;* Proudfoot, *Urban Patronage and Social Authority,* 29, 117.
38. Ian d'Alton, "From Bandon to . . . Bandon: Sectarian Violence in Cork During the Nineteenth Century," in *Crime, Violence, and the Irish in the Nineteenth Century,* ed. Kyle Hughes and Donald MacRaild (Liverpool University Press, 2017), 178.
39. Andy Bielenberg, "The Irish Economy, 1815–1880: Agricultural Transition, the Communications Revolution and the Limits of Industrialisation," in *Cambridge History of Ireland,* vol. 3, ed. James Kelly (Cambridge University Press, 2018), 179–203; Malcolm Campbell, *Ireland's Farthest Shore: Mobility, Migration, and Settlement in the Pacific World* (University of Wisconsin Press, 2022), 71.
40. James Donnelly, *Captain Rock: The Irish Agrarian Rebellion of 1821–1824* (University of Wisconsin Press, 2009), 111–12. For Ned Kelly and the emulation of dress, see Peter Carey, *True History of the Kelly Gang* (Vintage, 2001).

41. Donnelly, *Captain Rock.*
42. D'Alton, "From Bandon to . . . Bandon," 177.
43. "Violence, Protest and Melees: Hurling in Pre-Famine Ireland," Maynooth University Spotlight on Research, www.maynoothuniversity.ie/research/spotlight-research/violence-protest-and-melees-hurling-pre-famine-ireland.
44. See the work of people like Breandán MacSuibhne, *The End of Outrage: Post-Famine Adjustment in Rural Ireland* (Oxford University Press, 2017); and Paul Roberts, "Caravats and Shanavests: Whiteboyism and Faction Fighting in East Munster, 1802–11," in *Irish Peasants: Violence and Political Unrest, 1780–1914*, ed. Samuel Clark and James Donnelly (University of Wisconsin Press, 1983), 64–93.
45. James Donnelly, "Factions in Prefamine Ireland," in *The Uses of the Past: Essays on Irish Culture*, ed. Audrey Eyler and Robert Garratt (University of Delaware Press, 1988), 113–30. The Ambroses are mentioned on page 316.
46. On this nature of violence, I am indebted, in part, to the work of Gemma Clark, especially the new project on arson in the nineteenth century. Seminar presentation on 27 April 2022, Hertford College Irish Seminar, Oxford; and D'Alton, "From Bandon to . . . Bandon," 179–90.
47. Bennett, *The History of Bandon*, iii.
48. Richard Tresilian to Charles Grant, 10 July 1820, CSORP/1820/1249, National Archives, Dublin.
49. Armiger Sealy to Charles Grant, 13 December 1821, CSORP/SC/1821/1369, National Archives, Dublin.
50. Petition of Jonas Sewall and Jonas Sealy to Richard Wellesley, Lord Lieutenant, n.d. [1822], CSORP/1822/502; W. S. Currey to Alexander Mangin, 7 March 1823, CSORP/1823/622; Petition of inhabitants of Kinsale to Lord Lieutenant, n.d. [1822], CSORP/1822/3364, all in National Archives, Dublin.
51. Bennett, *The History of Bandon*, 531–37.
52. Joseph Jervois to Charles Grant, 22 October 1821, and accompanying testimony, CSORP/SC/1821/163, National Archives, Dublin.
53. For the battle I rely on Joseph Jervois to Charles Grant, 1 October 1821, CSORP/SC/1821/780, National Archives, Dublin; Bennett, *The History of Bandon*, 531–37; Bandon-geneology.com/riots-1821.htm; Frederick Stoven to John Sweet, 3 July 1829, CSORP/OR/1829/681, National Archives, Dublin; D'Alton, "From Bandon to . . . Bandon," 179.
54. Bennett, *The History of Bandon*, 531–37.
55. George Bellett, *Memoir of the Rev. George Bellett* (London, 1889), 65.
56. A Calendar of Prisoners in the Custody of Henry Green Barry, Esq. High Sheriff of the County of Cork, at Summer Assizes, 1821, Cork City Archives.

57. Arminger Sealy to Charles Grant, 5 May 1821, CSORP/SC/1821/1312, National Archives, Dublin.
58. Armiger Sealy to Charles Grant, 13 December 1821, CSORP/SC/1821/1369; Arminger Sealy and others to Henry Goulburn, 30 December 1821, CSORP/SC/1821/1387, both in National Archives, Dublin.
59. Letters and attachment from Joseph Jervois to Henry Goulburn, 27 December 1821, CSORP/1821/206, National Archives, Dublin.
60. Joseph Jervois to Charles Grant, 26 December 1821, CSORP/SC/1821/205, National Archives, Dublin.
61. Arthur Keily to William Gregory, 19 June 1823, CSORP/1823/1387, National Archives, Dublin.
62. Donnelly, *Captain Rock*, 65–69.
63. Donnelly, *Captain Rock*, 143.
64. Donnelly, *Captain Rock*, 311.
65. Donnelly, *Captain Rock*, 51.
66. Report of Richard Griffiths on the Southern District of Ireland, 1823, CSORP/1824/1551, National Archives, Dublin.
67. Proudfoot, *Urban Patronage and Social Authority*, 170.
68. James Huston to Robert Eedy, 24 March 1826, Eedy Letters, Cork City Archives.
69. Relief Committee Report and Subscription, 1830, CSORP/1830/1369, National Archives, Dublin.
70. Bennett, *The History of Bandon*, 372.
71. Grahame Farr, *West Country Passenger Steamers* (T. Stephenson and Sons, 1967), 2–7; William Barry, "History of Port of Cork Steam Navigation, 1815–1915," *Journal of Cork Historical and Archaeological Society* 23 (1917): 6.
72. Or, they could have sailed on a brig such as the *Fame*, which plied a route between Cork, Bristol, and the docks in Wapping in London. See Voyage Accounts, Sept. 1812–Feb. 1813, Written by John Armstrong, Captain, HLN/56/22, National Maritime Museum, Caird Library and Archive, Greenwich.

Round 2. Whitechapel

1. Proceedings of the Old Bailey, 6 December 1827, https://www.oldbaileyonline.org/record/t18271206-122?text=ambrose.
2. *Public Ledger and Daily Advertiser*, 4 December 1827. Ken Lamb brought this as well as Keys's role to my attention (Lamb MSS, chap. 1).
3. Newgate Prison, London, Register of Prisoners, 3 December 1827, UK Prison Commission Records, 1770–1951, National Archives, Kew, accessible through ancestry.com.

4. Charles Dickens, *Nicholas Nickleby* (London, 1839); Peter Clark, *Dickens's London* (Haus, 2019), 86.
5. Charles Dickens, *The Adventures of Oliver Twist* (Chapman and Hall, 1866), 71, 427–32.
6. Lyn Lees, *Exiles of Erin: Irish Migrants in Victorian Britain* (Cornell University Press, 1979), 51, 86, 152; Sheridan Gilley, "The Roman Catholic Mission to the Irish in London, 1840–1860," *British Catholic History* 3 (1969): 124–25, 127.
7. Raphael Samuel, "The Roman Catholic Church and the Irish Poor," in *The Irish in the Victorian City*, ed. Roger Swift and Sheridan Gilley (Routledge, 1985), 278–79.
8. Graham Davis, *The Irish in Britain, 1815–1914* (Gill and Macmillan, 1991), 5–11, 55–56.
9. David Barnett, "The Structure of Industry in London, 1775–1825" (Ph.D. diss., University of Nottingham, 1996), 44.
10. John Darwin, *Unlocking the World: Port Cities and Globalization in the Age of Steam, 1830–1930* (Penguin, 2020), 316–17.
11. Peter Stone, *The History of the Port of London: A Vast Emporium of All Nations* (Pen and Sword History, 1988), 97–104.
12. Matthew Green, *London: A Travel Guide Through Time* (Penguin, 2015), 273; Stone, *The History of the Port of London*, 116–22.
13. Barnett, "The Structure of Industry in London, 1775–1825," 50.
14. Sarah Palmer, "Port Economics in an Historical Context: The Nineteenth-Century Port of London," *International Journal of Maritime History* 15 (2003): 27–28.
15. Stone, *The History of the Port of London*, 118–19.
16. "A new map of London and its environs: from an original survey extending 8 miles east and west, 6¼ miles north & south, in which all new and intended buildings, improvements, &c. are carefully inserted/drawn by Mr. Thompson" (https://collections.lib.uwm.edu/digital/collection/agdm/id/382/).
17. Peter Guillery, *Survey of London*, vol. 54: *Whitechapel* (Yale University Press, 2022), 10; Barnett, "The Structure of Industry in London, 1775–1825," 45–47; Jerry White, *London in the Nineteenth Century: A Human Awful Wonder of God* (Bodley Head, 2007), 132.
18. Lamb MSS, chap. 1; F. H. W. Shepherd, ed., *Survey of London*, vol. 27: *Spitalfields and Mile End New Town* (Athlone/London County Council, 1957), 237–41.
19. Dan Cruikshank, *Spitalfields: The History of a Nation in a Handful of Streets* (Random House, 2016), 204.
20. Graham Davis, "Essay in Bibliography: The Irish in Nineteenth Century Britain," *Saothar* 16 (1991): 130.

21. Clark, *Dickens's London*, 91.
22. "Petticoat Lane Market," in *Survey of London, Whitechapel*, vol. 1.
23. This is based on Ken Lamb's trawl through census records. See 1841 Census for Middlesex, HO 107/710/13, 14, National Archives, Kew (Lamb MSS, chap. 1, appendix B).
24. Shepherd, *Survey of London*, vol. 27: *Spitalfields and Mile End New Town*, 237–41.
25. Oskar Cox Jensen, *Vagabonds: Life on the Streets of Nineteenth-Century London* (Duckworth Books, 2024).
26. Thomas Beames, *Rookeries of London* (London, 1850), 2.
27. Cruikshank, *Spitalfields*, 1–4.
28. This is per Ken Lamb's readings of family connections and Old Bailey Proceedings, February 1817 (Lamb MSS, chap. 1). See also Edward MacLysaght, *The Surnames of Ireland* (Irish Academic Press, 2012), 67.
29. Robert Topinka, *Racing the Street: Race, Rhetoric, and Technology in Metropolitan London, 1840–1900* (University of California Press, 2020), 71–72.
30. White, *London in the Nineteenth Century*, 328.
31. *Adventures, Memoirs, Former Trial, Transportation, and Escape of That Notorious Fence, and Receiver of Stolen Goods, Ikey Solomons* (London, 1829).
32. Cruikshank, *Spitalfields*, 422.
33. Green, *London: A Travel Guide Through Time*, 266.
34. Charles Booth, *Life and Labour of the People*, vol. 1: *East London*, 3rd ed. (London, 1891), 66.
35. Charles Dickens, "A Nightly Scene in London," *Harpers*, April 1856.
36. Charles Dickens, "Spitalfields," in *Household Words*, 5 April 1851.
37. Henry Mayhew, *London Labour and the London Poor* (Penguin, 1985), 108. Unless otherwise noted, subsequent citations for Mayhew refer to this edition.
38. These points are covered in Jensen, *Vagabonds*.
39. Jensen, *Vagabonds*, 71–77, 218–19.
40. St. Mary Moorfields Baptisms for Joannis Ambrose (1823) and Eduardus Ambrose (1826), Archdiocese of Westminster Catholic Records, accessible from findmypast.co.uk. The brothers were originally found by Ken Lamb (Lamb MSS, appendix B).
41. Beames, *Rookeries of London*, 19, 26; Davis, *The Irish in Britain*, 54.
42. G. O'Tuathaigh, "The Irish in Nineteenth-Century Britain: Problems of Integration," in *The Irish in Britain*, ed. Davis, 149–50; Green, *London: A Travel Guide Through Time*, 263–64.
43. See Reports of the Bible Association, BSA/F1/London/4, Cambridge University Archives, Cambridge University Library.

44. Michael Slater, ed., *Dickens' Journalism*, vol. 2 (Cambridge University Press, 2014), 360–65.
45. Mayhew, *London Labour and the London Poor*, 473–74.
46. Richard Kirkland, *Irish London: A Cultural History, 1850–1916* (Bloomsbury, 2022), 3–4, 21, 36–37, 45. The classic statement of these immigrants and their mindset is O'Tuathaigh, "The Irish in Nineteenth-Century Britain: Problems of Interpretation." On adaptations, see Lees, *Exiles of Erin*, 17–18.
47. This is based on Enda Delaney's reading of the Irish in the period. See *Making Ireland Modern: The Transformation of Society and Culture* (Oxford University Press, 2025).
48. *A History of St. Mary and St. Michael's Parish, Commercial Road, East London* (Terry Marsh, 2007), 13–23.
49. Lamb MSS, appendix B; St. Mary Moorfields Baptisms for Joannis Ambrose (1823) and Eduardus Ambrose (1826), Archdiocese of Westminster Catholic Records, accessible from findmypast.co.uk; Denis Evinson, *Catholic Churches of London* (Sheffield Academic Press, 1998), 29–31; Gilley, "The Roman Catholic Mission to the Irish in London, 1840–1860," 126.
50. Samuel, "The Roman Catholic Church and the Irish Poor," 274; Gilley, "The Roman Catholic Mission to the Irish in London, 1840–1860," 125.
51. Petition for Clemency, 21 April 1828, HO 17/35/85, National Archives, Kew.
52. *Dictionary of English Furniture Makers* (Leeds, 1986), www.british-history.ac.uk/no-series/dict-english-furniture-makers; Barnett, "The Structure of Industry in London, 1775–1825," 176–79.
53. See Mayhew, *London Labour and the London Poor*, the chapter titled "The Street-Buyers," https://www.gutenberg.org/files/60440/60440-h/60440-h.htm.
54. See Mayhew, *London Labour and the London Poor*, the chapter titled "Casual Hands," https://www.gutenberg.org/files/60440/60440-h/60440-h.htm.
55. *Bell's Life in Victoria and Sporting Chronicle*, 17 July 1858.
56. Davis, *The Irish in Britain, 1815–1914*, 5; Mayhew, *London Labour and the London Poor*, 492.
57. Jerry White, *London in the Eighteenth Century: A Great and Monstrous Thing* (Harvard University Press, 2013), 242–44; Stone, *The History of the Port of London*, 116.
58. Charles Dickens, *The Uncommercial Traveler* (London, 1861).
59. Jeff Jones, *East End Born and Bled: The Remarkable Story of Boxing in London* (Amberley, 2020), 23; White, *London in the Nineteenth Century*, 185.
60. Jones, *East End Born and Bled*, 23.
61. Mayhew, "Labour and the Poor, 1849–50," Letter IV, 30 October 1849, The Dictionary of Victorian London, https://www.victorianlondon.org/mayhew/mayhew04.htm.

62. John Strachan, "Poets and Pugilists," *History Today*, 1 January 2009; David Snowdon, "Dickens Serves out the Chicken: A Misleading Character Portrayal Taints a *Boxiana* Hero" (2020), www.academia.edu/35785608/Dickens_Serves_Out_The_Chicken_A_Misleading_Character_Portrayal_of_a_Boxiana_Hero, 1–15; Margaret Reynolds, "'In Chancery' Again: Dickens and Prize-Fighting," *Dickens Studies Newsletter* 14 (1983): 48–50.
63. See David Snowdon, *Writing the Prizefight: Pierce Egan's Boxiana World* (Peter Lang, 2013).
64. Snowdon, *Writing the Prizefight*, 235, 239.
65. *Fistiana; Or, the Oracle of the Ring* (London, 1841), 271, British Library.
66. Adam Chill, *Bare-Knuckle Britons and Fighting Irish: Boxing, Race, Religion, and Nationality in the 18th and 19th Centuries* (McFarland, 2017).
67. Snowdon, *Writing the Prizefight*, 153.
68. Pierce Egan, *Boxiana, or Sketches of Antient and Modern Pugilism*, vol. 3 (London, 1818), 74.
69. Tony Gee, *Up to Scratch: Bareknuckle Fighting and Heroes of the Prize-Ring* (G2 Entertainment, 2001), 16.
70. *New York Clipper*, 7 June 1884, as per Lamb MSS, chap. 1.
71. *Fistiana; Or, the Oracle of the Ring*, 135.
72. See, for instance, Daniel Mendoza, *Memoirs of the Life of Daniel Mendoza* (London, 1826); and Gee, *Up to Scratch*, 35.
73. Randy Roberts, "Eighteenth Century Boxing," *Journal of Sports History* 4 (1977): 256.
74. Lewis Edwards, "Daniel Mendoza," *Transactions* (Jewish Historical Society of England), 15 (1939–45): 86; Gee, *Up to Scratch*, 40.
75. For a look at Mendoza's geographic footprint, see Ronald Schechter's map entitled "Mendoza's London," in *Mendoza the Jew: Boxing, Manliness, and Nationalism* (Oxford University Press, 2014).
76. Edwards, "Daniel Mendoza," 90.
77. "Big Hitting, Hard Drinking Dutch Sam," https://abeautifulbook.wordpress.com/2018/04/09/big-hitting-hard-drinking-dutch-sam-petticoat-lane-whitechapel/; Jones, *East End Born and Bled*, 30–31.
78. William Page, ed., *A History of the County of Middlesex*, vol. 2 (Oxford University Press, 1911), 292–95; Jones, *East End Born and Bled*, 34–37; Dennis Brailsford, *Bareknuckles: A Social History of Prize-fighting* (Lutterworth, 1989), 73, 87–91; Pierce Egan, *Boxiana*, vol. 4 (London, 1824), 221, 602–4.
79. *Charles Booth's London: A Portrait of the Poor at the Turn of the Century Drawn from His Life and Labour of the People of London*, ed. Alfred Fried and Richard Elman (Hutchinson, 1969), 57–64.

80. Mayhew, *London Labour and the London Poor,* 19, 60.
81. White, *London in the Eighteenth Century,* 156–62.
82. White, *London in the Eighteenth Century,* 526.
83. Church Lane Whitechapel, IOR/L/L/2/1297, British Library.
84. Peter Guillery, *Survey of London,* vol. 54: *Whitechapel* (London, 2022), 35.
85. Alessandro Albano, "The Artful Dodger Free House: A Natural Old East End Way," *Medium,* 15 February 2016, https://medium.com/@alessandroalbano/the-artful-dodger-free-house-a-natural-old-east-end-way-385d6119a490.
86. Mayhew, *London Labour and the London Poor,* 852.
87. Jensen, *Vagabonds,* xv–xviii.
88. Jensen, *Vagabonds,* 71–77, 220–21.
89. *Public Ledger and Daily Advertiser,* 4 December 1827; Jensen, *Vagabonds,* 70–71.
90. Heather Shore, "Transportation, Penal Ideology and the Experience of Juvenile Offenders in England and Australia in the Early Nineteenth Century," *Crime, History, and Societies* 6 (2002): 85.

Round 3. Chatham

1. Report of Lieutenant Walter Pike on Board the *Euryalus,* 29 November 1805, MB.59/065, Caird Library, Royal Museums Greenwich.
2. Plan of the Battle of Trafalgar by an Officer (Jonas Toby) purser on board the HMS *Euryalus,* 1805, M/125, Caird Library, Royal Museums Greenwich; Pages from the Log-Books of HMS *Prince, Euryalus,* and *Naiad* relating to the Battle of Trafalgar, MS Facsimile 323/2, British Library.
3. Report of Lieutenant Walter Pike on Board the *Euryalus,* 29 November 1805, MB.59/065, Caird Library, Royal Museums Greenwich.
4. Franny Moyle, *Turner: The Extraordinary Life and Momentous Times of J. M. W. Turner* (Penguin, 2016), 381–86.
5. On how prisoner labor fed imperial aims even at naval installations, see Clare Anderson, *Convicts: A Global History* (Cambridge University Press, 2022). My thanks to Cian McMahon for bringing this book to my attention.
6. W. Branch-Johnson, *The English Prison Hulks* (Christopher Johnson, 1957), 147.
7. "A Phantom Burglar and the Hulk," British Library *Untold Lives* blog, 31 October 2012, https://blogs.bl.uk/untoldlives/2012/10/a-phantom-burglar-and-the-hulk.html; Branch-Johnson, *The English Prison Hulks,* 147.
8. Quarterly Returns of Prisoners in Hulks, 1828, HO 8/17, 286, National Archives, Kew; Lamb MSS, chap. 1.

9. Charles Dickens, *The Uncommercial Traveller* (Boston, 1890), 347–48.
10. For a glimpse of the labor of convicts, see Philip MacDougall, *Chatham Dockyard: The Rise and Fall of a Military Industrial Complex* (History Press, 2012), 126–30.
11. Andrew Lambert, "'The Chief Arsenal of the Royal Navy and of Great Britain': Chatham, the Royal Navy and the Wider World," in *Chatham Historic Dockyard: World Power to Resurgence*, ed. Neil Cossons (Historic England, 2021), 25.
12. John Sell Cotman, "Three Sketches of Hulks on the Medway, c. 1828," The Cotman Collection, Leeds Art Gallery, https://cotmania.org/works-of-art/43615.
13. Branch-Johnson, *The English Prison Hulks*, 119, 121.
14. Branch-Johnson, *The English Prison Hulks*, 131.
15. Branch-Johnson, *The English Prison Hulks*, 150.
16. This is based on Ken Lamb's search through these Home Office Papers. See Prison Hulk Registers, HO 9/2, 123–24; and Criminal Warrant Books, HO 15, 171–80, National Archives, Kew (Lamb MSS, chap. 1).
17. "A Phantom Burglar and the Hulk," British Library's *Untold Lives* blog.
18. "Convicts in the Dockyard," *Chatham Dockyard Historical Society Research Paper*, no. 2, 5–6; Branch-Johnson, *The English Prison Hulks*, 155–56.
19. Branch-Johnson, *The English Prison Hulks*, 152–54.
20. Heather Shore, "Transportation, Penal Ideology and the Experience of Juvenile Offenders in England and Australia in the Early Nineteenth Century," *Crime, History, and Societies* 6 (2002): 82–84.
21. Shore, "Transportation, Penal Ideology and the Experience of Juvenile Offenders in England and Australia in the Early Nineteenth Century," 86, 90.
22. Branch-Johnson, *The English Prison Hulks*, 123.
23. Euryalus Register, Chatham, 1828, UK Prisons Hulk Registers and Letter Books, 1802–1849, National Archives, Kew, accessible through ancestry.com.
24. *Bussorah Merchant:* Deck Log, 24 May 1825 to 22 December 1825, IORL/MAR/B/63A, British Library.
25. *The Sun* (London), 10 March 1828; "39th (Dorsetshire) Regiment of Foot," National Army Museum, www.nam.ac.uk/explore/39th-dorsetshire-regiment-foot#:~:text=This%20infantry%20regiment%20was%20raised,to%20form%20The%20Dorsetshire%20Regiment. My thanks to Guy Collender for digging this up for me.
26. *Public Ledger and Daily Intelligencer*, 10 March 1828. For these dates and numbers, I am indebted to Ken Lamb (Lamb MSS, chap. 1). On the open boat, see "General Remarks" of the Journal, *Bussorah Merchant*, Convict Ship, by Robert Dunn, the Surgeon, February to September 1828, UK Royal Navy Medical Journals, 1817–56, National Archives, Kew, accessible through ancestry.com.

27. Charles Bateson, *The Convict Ships, 1787–1868* (Brown, Son & Ferguson, 1959), 252; "General Remarks" of the Journal, *Bussorah Merchant,* Convict Ship, by Robert Dunn, the Surgeon, February to September 1828, UK Royal Navy Medical Journals, 1817–56, National Archives, Kew, accessible through ancestry.com.
28. *Bussorah Merchant* Convict Journal by William Maybury, 1828, Caird Library, Royal Museums Greenwich.

Round 4. The Rocks

1. M. E. Yapp, "The Establishment of the East India Company Residency in Baghdad, 1798–1806," *Bulletin of the School of Oriental and African Studies* 30 (1967): 323–36.
2. Charles Bateson, *The Convict Ships, 1787–1868* (Brown, Son & Ferguson, 1959), 68–78. For the details that follow about the trip, I rely on the diary kept by Maybury (*Bussorah Merchant* Convict Journal by William Maybury, 1828, Caird Library, Greenwich Royal Museums). See also Phillip Knightley, *Australia: A Biography of a Nation* (Vintage, 2001), 32.
3. *Bussorah Merchant,* Ship, Taken into Service, particulars respecting, consignment, E/4/931—Madras Dispatches, 12 January to 20 July 1825, British Library.
4. This is how Knightley (*Australia: A Biography of a Nation,* 33) puts it. For a study of convicts and empire-building employing the idea of "punitive mobility," see Clare Anderson, *Convicts: A Global History* (Cambridge University Press, 2022), 7.
5. Lamb MSS, chap. 1; Anon., Journal Written on Board the Convict Transport *Commodore Hayes,* During a Voyage from England to Australia, 22 May to 3 August 1823, ML MSS 6272, Mitchell Library, State Library of New South Wales.
6. Robert Hughes, *The Fatal Shore: The Epic of Australia's Founding* (Vintage, 1986), 144–45.
7. Bateson, *The Convict Ships, 1787–1868,* 55–67.
8. Journal, *Bussorah Merchant,* Convict Ship, by Robert Dunn, the Surgeon, February to September 1828, UK Royal Navy Medical Journals, 1817–56, National Archives, Kew, accessible through ancestry.com.
9. *Bussorah Merchant:* Deck Log, 24 May 1825 to 22 December 1825, p. 120, IORL/MAR/B/63A, British Library.
10. *Sydney Gazette,* 27 July 1828 (cited in www.freesettlerorfelon.com/convict_ship_bussorah_merchant_1828.htm); Hughes, *The Fatal Shore,* 156–57.
11. Muster Role of Convicts, Bussorah Merchant, 15 September 1828, New South Wales Convict Indents, State Records Authority of New South

Wales, accessible through ancestry.com. On this, see Hughes, *The Fatal Shore*, 155. Ken Lamb brought this to my attention.

12. Bateson, *The Convict Ships, 1787–1868*, 298–99.
13. Bateson, *The Convict Ships, 1787–1868*, 252.
14. *Bussorah Merchant* Convict Journal by William Maybury, entry for 26 July 1828, Caird Library, Greenwich Royal Museums.
15. Muster Role of Convicts, Bussorah Merchant, 15 September 1828, New South Wales Convict Indents, State Records Authority of New South Wales, accessible through ancestry.com.
16. Zoe Alker and Robert Shoemaker, "Convicts and the Cultural Significance of Tattooing in Nineteenth-Century Britain," *Journal of British Studies* 61 (2022): 842–43.
17. List of Prisoners, with occupations and arrest details, on the *Bussorah Merchant*, Convict Records, https://convictrecords.com.au/ships/bussorah-merchant/voyages/219.
18. Lamb MSS, chap. 1; Sir Thomas Brisbane to Michael Bruce, 31 December 1823 and 30 January 1824, MS. Facs.d.302, Bodleian Library, Oxford.
19. Maria Edgeworth to Charles Edgeworth for Black Castle, 8 February 1828, MS.ENG.Lett.c.703, pp. 162–64, Bodleian Library, Oxford.
20. Maria Edgeworth to Mrs. Bannatyne for Black Castle, 9 February 1828, MS.ENG.Lett.c.720, pp. 191–93, Bodleian Library, Oxford.
21. Christina Eliza Brooks Diary, 29 June 1825 to 8 March 1829, entries for 9–17 March 1827, MLMSS 4661, Mitchell Library, State Library of New South Wales.
22. Grace Karskens, "Revisiting the Worldview: The Archaeology of Convict Households in Sydney's Rocks Neighborhood," *Historical Archaeology* 37 (2003): 34.
23. "Convict Discipline . . . By Them That Were There," vol. 2: "The Evidence of Ernest Augustus Slade," comp. Brian McDonald, p. 12, Mitchell Library, State Library of New South Wales.
24. Grace Karskens, *The Colony: A History of Early Sydney* (Allen & Unwin, 2009), 212–24, 9; John Izzard, "A Nation Begins," *Quadrant* (2010): 67.
25. Extracts from the Diary of James Scott, ML MSS 2906, p. 35, Mitchell Library, State Library of New South Wales.
26. Grace Karskens, *Inside the Rocks: The Archaeology of a Neighborhood* (Sydney, Hale & Iremonger, 1999), 109.
27. This reading of the Rocks is based on the extraordinary book by Grace Karskens entitled *Inside the Rocks*.
28. Karskens, *Inside the Rocks*, 49; Grace Karskens, "Revisiting the Worldview: The Archaeology of Convict Households in Sydney's Rocks Neighborhood," *Historical Archaeology* 37 (2003): 50.

29. Jane Lydon, "Archaeology in The Rocks, Sydney, 1979–1993: From Old Sydney Gaol to Mrs. Lewis' Boarding-House," *Australian Historical Archaeology* 11 (1993): 36.
30. Karskens, *Inside the Rocks*, 46–47.
31. This is based on Ken Lamb's readings of 1828 census and on the accounts in *Sydney Gazette and New South Wales Advertiser*, 26 September 1829, 1 October 1829 (Lamb MSS, chap. 1).
32. Karskens, *Inside the Rocks*, 55–56; New South Wales Convict Indents; *Sydney Gazette and New South Wales Advertiser*, 31 March 1828; Entry 693, 1828 NSW Census, https://mhnsw.au/guides/1828-census/, as per Lamb MSS, chap. 1.
33. An image of the church that stood at the time appears in *Australian Town and Country Journal*, 28 January 1888.
34. "Colonial Census: A Transportation to 1828," *Sydney Morning Herald*, 17 September 2007.
35. Karskens, *Inside the Rocks*, 77–78; Sign of St. Patrick mentioned in *Sydney Herald*, 15 April 1846; https://convictrecords.com.au/convicts/baker/sarah/116890.
36. *Sydney Gazette*, 15 January 1824.
37. R. Therry, *Reminiscences of Thirty Years' Residence in New South Wales and Victoria* (London, 1863), 40.
38. Karskens, *Inside the Rocks*.
39. For this, I am indebted to Ken Lamb and his reading of Colonial Secretary's Correspondence in State Records of New South Wales (Lamb MSS, chap. 1).
40. Richard Waterhouse, "Bare-Knuckle Prize Fighting, Masculinity and Nineteenth-Century Australian Culture," *Journal of Australian Studies* 26 (2002): 101–10. See also Grantlee Kieza, *Boxing in Australia* (NLA, 2015), 10–12, 20–21; Grantlee Kieza, *Australian Boxing: The Illustrated History* (Gary Allen Pty, 2021), 11.
41. This is Ken Lamb's theory as well (Lamb MSS, chap. 1). Accounts that list or recount the fight are Ed James, comp., *The Life and Battles of Tom Hyer* (New York, 1879), 21; Ed James, *The Life and Battles of Yankee Sullivan* (Philadelphia, 1854), 10.
42. Karskens, *Inside the Rocks*, 187.
43. J. B. Hirst, *Convict Society and Its Enemies: A History of Early New South Wales* (Allen & Unwin, 1983), 53–54, 102–3, 108–9.
44. Lamb MSS, chap. 1; Sydney Gaol Entrance Book, 4 July 1829, New South Wales, Australia, Gaol Description and Entrance Books, 1818–1930, State Records Authority of New South Wales, accessible through ancestry.com.
45. Christina Eliza Brooks Diary, 29 June 1825 to 8 March 1829, entries for 29 June and 18 August 1825, MLMSS 4661, Mitchell Library, State Library of New South Wales.
46. Bateson, *The Convict Ships, 1787–1868*, 210–11.

47. Beverley Earnshaw, *The Larrikins of Lavender Bay: The Story of the Phoenix Hulk*, 1996, North Shore Historical Society, Cammeray, NSW, N994.402 37, Mitchell Library, State Library of New South Wales.

Round 5. Moreton Bay

1. See, for instance, A. G. L. Shaw, introduction to Thomas Cook, *The Exile's Lamentations* (Library of Australian History, 1978), v. Robert Hughes, *The Fatal Shore: The Epic of Australia's Founding* (Vintage Books, 1986) provides a pretty bleak picture of the early years. Australia, it suggests, had its birth in state-sponsored coercion and oppression, bringing out the very worst in human nature. Australia began with human degradation. Of all the books on the early days of Australia, it is the most dramatic and, frankly, the best. Still, since then, people have pushed back to say things weren't all that bad, and it seems these critics of the "fatal shore" thesis have a valid point. It stands to reason that people who experienced grave injustices and coercion would regard the exceptional as typical, believed tales told that reinforced how they saw their predicaments, and were prone to exaggeration.
2. Jennifer Harrison and J. G. Steele, eds., *The Fell Tyrant* (Royal Historical Society of Queensland, 2003), 2–3.
3. Lamb MSS, chap. 1; *Sydney Gazette and New South Wales Advertiser*, 13 August 1829, and 20 August 1829; and a reading of Transcription of Moreton Bay Convict Records by Ken Lamb, Queensland State Archives, www.publications.qld.gov.au/dataset/transcription-of-moreton-bay-convict-records.
4. Harrison and Steele, *The Fell Tyrant*, 54.
5. Susanna and Jake de Vries, *Historic Brisbane: Convict Settlement to River City* (Boolarong, 2013), 10–12.
6. *Sydney Monitor*, 14 August 1830.
7. Per index of Moreton Bay Convicts compiled by Marilyn England in 2014 (see https://harrygentle.griffith.edu.au/rare-books-and-documents/).
8. "The Convicts," Paul Budde History, Philosophy, Culture, https://paulbuddehistory.com/convict-history-of-brisbane/the-convicts/; Harrison and Steele, *The Fell Tyrant*, 40; de Vries, *Historic Brisbane*, 17.
9. The best account of Moreton Bay, and one this work relies on, is Hughes, *The Fatal Shore*, 441–55.
10. Harrison and Steele, *The Fell Tyrant*, 1.
11. *The Fell Tyrant, or The Suffering Convict* (London, 1836), 19–23, courtesy of the Mitchell Library, State Library of New South Wales.
12. *Sydney Monitor*, 14 August 1830; Harrison and Steele, *The Fell Tyrant*, 8.

13. See, for instance, Spicer's Diary, or "Book of Public Labour, 1828–1829," Queensland State Archives; and Marilyn England's compilation of statistics in Spicer's Diary, Griffith University Rare Books and Documents Digitized Versions of Documents, 2013.
14. Harrison and Steele, *The Fell Tyrant,* 46.
15. Hughes, *The Fatal Shore,* 115.
16. Regulations quoted in A. G. L. Shaw, introduction to *The Exile's Lamentations,* by Thomas Cook (Library of Australian History, 1978), vi.
17. Hughes, *The Fatal Shore,* 454–55.
18. Diana Paton, "A Tread-Mill Scene in Jamaica," in *Victorian Jamaica,* ed. Tim Barringer and Wayne Modest (Duke University Press, 2018), 61.
19. *Sydney Monitor,* 14 August 1830; Harrison and Steele, *The Fell Tyrant,* 60; de Vries, *Historic Brisbane,* 18.
20. Hughes, *The Fatal Shore,* 270–71.
21. Mamie O'Keefe, "The Runaway Convicts of Moreton Bay," *Journal of the Royal Society of Queensland* 10 (1976): 52–53.
22. Lamb MSS, chap. 1; Transcription of Moreton Bay Convict Records by Ken Lamb, www.publications.qld.gov.au/dataset/3595fe09-05aa-4463-b1f1-f8d983e85d77/resource/a7bb95ae-0064-4884-828b-a8d4e0e50a50/download/ggp-collections-access-bnecollections-and-accessrowenaken-lamb-recordsconvictsmoretonbay5abscon.xlsx.
23. O'Keefe, "The Runaway Convicts of Moreton Bay," 53–55.
24. Hughes, *The Fatal Shore,* 279–80, 447, 453.
25. O'Keefe, "The Runaway Convicts of Moreton Bay," 56, 69.
26. Harrison and Steele, *The Fell Tyrant,* 37.
27. Lamb MSS, chap. 1; Register of Out-Patients Treated at Moreton Bay Penal Settlement Hospital, Queensland State Archives, Registers of Out-Patients Treated, accessible from https://www.archivessearch.qld.gov.au/items/ITM2858.
28. *Sydney Monitor,* 14 August 1830; Spicer's Diary, https://moretonbayandmore.com/2019/03/09/murder-at-moreton-bay-3-the-awful-entries-in-spicers-diary/.
29. *Sydney Gazette,* 21 April 1829.
30. This is according to Spicer's Diary (https://moretonbayandmore.com/2019/03/09/murder-at-moreton-bay-3-the-awful-entries-in-spicers-diary/).
31. *The Australian,* 21 April 1829.
32. Ed James, comp., *The Life and Battles of Tom Hyer* (New York, 1879), 21; Lamb MSS, chap. 1; Australian Convict Records (convictrecords.com.au). Ken Lamb compiled a list of Moreton Bay convicts accessible through the Government of Queensland, www.publications.qld.gov.au/dataset/3595fe09-05aa

-4463-b1f1-f8d983e85d77/resource/622ce7f9-549a-40e2-8cfb-81faeb783aa5/download/ggp-collections-access-bnecollections-and-accessrowenaken-lamb-recordsconvictsmoretonbay1origina.xls.

33. Ed James, *The Life and Battles of Yankee Sullivan* (Philadelphia, 1854), 10–11.
34. David Lester, Sydney, to Patrick Logan, 4 August 1829, Patrick Logan Family Archive of Manuscript Material, RP 9691, British Library.
35. Alexander McLeay, Government Order, Colonial Secretary's Office, Sydney, 17 November 1830, Patrick Logan Family Archive of Manuscript Material, RP 9691, British Library.

Round 6. The Blue Mountains

1. Or so says a popular print I found in the halls of the Royal Automobile Club in Sydney.
2. Ken Lamb has done an almost forensic investigation of his stints in and out of various prisons after Moreton Bay (Lamb MSS, chap. 2). His many run-ins with the law are captured in the official record. Much of this story relies on the records available online, as noted below, and on Lamb's findings.
3. Sydney Gaol Entrance Books, New South Wales, Gaol Description and Entrance Books, 1833, 1836, 1837, State Records Authority of New South Wales, accessible through ancestry.com.
4. Sydney Gaol Entrance Book, 28 September 1837, New South Wales, Gaol Description and Entrance Books, 1818–1930, State Record Authority of New South Wales, accessible though ancestry.com; New South Wales, Convict Records, Carters Barracks House of Correction, Register of Convicts, 1837, New South Wales Archives Collection, https://researchdata.edu.au/nrs-12217-house-registers-convicts/178422; Extracts from the Report of the Committee on the Subject of Tread-Wheel Labour, October 1825, p. 346, Mitchell Library, State Library of New South Wales.
5. *New South Wales Government Gazette*, 27 April 1836.
6. *New South Wales Government Gazette*, 2 August 1837.
7. New South Wales Criminal Records, Trial date: 1 November 1836, State Record Authority of New South Wales, accessible though ancestry.com; *Sydney Gazette and New South Wales Advertiser*, 10 August 1837.
8. Thomas Cook, *The Exile's Lamentations* (Library of Australian History, 1978), 36.
9. New South Wales, Convict Records, 1810–1891, Phoenix Hulk, Entrance Books, 1831–33, 20 February 1833, State Record Authority of New South Wales, accessible though ancestry.com.

10. *New South Wales Government Gazette*, 3 April 1833; New South Wales Criminal Court Records, 1830–1945, Trial date: 4 May 1836.
11. Helen Baker, *Hyde Park Barracks* (Angus and Robertson, 1965), pp. 27, 33, State Planning Authority of New South Wales, Mitchell Library, State Library of New South Wales.
12. New South Wales, Convict Records, 1810–1891, Phoenix Hulk, Entrance Books, 1831–33, 20 August 1834.
13. *Hyde Park Barracks*, guidebook (Museum of History New South Wales, 2020), 40–41; New South Wales Criminal Court Records, 1830–1945, Trial dates 28 April 1836; 4 May 1836; 1 November 1836. And 1837: Sydney Gaol Entrance Book, 28 September 1837, New South Wales, Gaol Description and Entrance Books, 1818–1930.
14. "Convict Discipline . . . By Them That Were There," vol. 2: "The Evidence of Ernest Augustus Slade," comp. Brian McDonald, pp. 20, 33, Mitchell Library, State Library of New South Wales.
15. Sydney Gaol Entrance Book, 18 May 1833, 6 May 1836, New South Wales, Gaol Description and Entrance Books, 1818–1930; New South Wales Criminal Records, Trial date: 6 May 1836.
16. Grace Karskens, "Defiance, Deference and Diligence: Three Views of Convicts in New South Wales Road Gangs," *Australian Journal of Historical Archaeology* 4 (1986): 19.
17. Grace Karskens, *Cox's Way: Historical and Archaeological Study of Cox's Road and Early Crossings of the Blue Mountains*, report commissioned by the Cox's Road Trust and Department of Lands, p. 6, Q994.45 48, Mitchell Library, State Library of New South Wales.
18. Karskens, *Cox's Way*, 5–8, 42.
19. Karskens, *Cox's Way*, 49–51.
20. "Mount Victoria Pass," *Lithgow Mercury*, 22 June 1914.
21. Karskens, *Cox's Way*, 51.
22. Lorraine Stacker, "Chained to the Soil on the Plains of Emu: A History of the Emu Plains Government Agricultural Establishment, 1819–1832," Nepean District Historical Society (2000), 7, 106; Emu Plains Agricultural Establishment Inquiry Statement by John Green, 1826, A2009, Mitchell Library, State Library of New South Wales.
23. "Discipline of Road-Gangs," *Sydney Monitor*, 17 January 1834.
24. Sue Rosen and Michael Pearson, "The No. 2 Stockade Cox's River—Its Life and Times: An Historical and Archaeological Investigation," (1997), p. 27, Mitchell Library, State Library of New South Wales.
25. Ollie Leckbandt, "The Mont Walker Stockade, Cox's River," Archaeological Report, p. 54, Q 994.4502, Mitchell Library; Rosen and Pearson, "The No. 2

Stockade Cox's River"; Clem Sargent, "Military Supervision of Convict Work Gangs: The Great Roads," *Sabretache* 44 (2003): 41–48.

26. *Sydney Herald*, 7 October 1833; *Sydney Herald*, 20 July 1835.
27. "Journal of an Excursion Across the Blue Mountains of New South Wales," November 1823, *London Magazine*, pp. 461, 464, Mitchel Library, State Library of New South Wales.
28. Rosen and Pearson, "The No. 2 Stockade Cox's River," 52, 57, 60.
29. A. G. L. Shaw, introduction to *The Exile's Lamentations*, by Cook, vi.
30. Cook, *The Exile's Lamentations*, 19–32.
31. Cook, *The Exile's Lamentations*, 29.
32. "Journal of an Excursion Across the Blue Mountains of New South Wales," 464–66.
33. "The Natives and the Outstations," *Adelaide Observer*, 16 May 1846.
34. James Greig to John Anderson, 11 November 1826, ML 2316, Mitchell Library, State Library of New South Wales; Mark Dunn, *The Convict Valley: The Bloody Struggles of Australia's Dearly Frontier* (Allen & Unwin, 2020), 156–58. On the concept, see Lorenzo Veracini, "'Settler Colonialism': Career of a Concept," *Journal of Imperial and Commonwealth History* 41 (2013): 313–33.
35. Dunn, *The Convict Valley*.
36. Lyndall Ryan, "The Myall Creek Massacre: Was It Typical of the Time?," in *Remembering the Myall Creek Massacre*, ed. Jane Lydon and Lyndall Ryan (University of New South Wales Press, 2018), 85–98.
37. Elizabeth Berry to Everina Wollstonecraft, 9 April 1841, MS. Abinger b.4, fols. 132–33, Bodleian Libraries, Oxford Archives.
38. Grace Karskens, "Defiance, Deference and Diligence," 17–19; Dunn, *The Convict Valley*.
39. Sydney Gaol Description Book, New South Wales, Gaol Description and Entrance Books, January 1836.
40. "Convict Discipline . . . By Them That Were There," vol. 2: "The Evidence of Ernest Augustus Slade," comp. Brian McDonald, Mitchell Library, State Library of New South Wales.
41. Sydney Gaol Description Book, New South Wales, Gaol Description and Entrance Books, Sydney Gaol, January 1836 and 1837.
42. *New South Wales Government Gazette*, 27 April 1836; *New South Wales Government Gazette*, 3 April 1833.
43. Richard Waterhouse, "Bare-Knuckle Prize Fighting, Masculinity and Nineteenth-Century Australian Culture," *Journal of Australian Studies* 26 (2002): 102.
44. *Sydney Monitor*, 12 November 1834; *The Australian*, 4 November 1834.

45. The New York account that appeared after his death and that mixed up Ireland with Australia and completely left out London made the claim that by this point Ambrose was "a Ring Fighter." He sparred at benefits, though one doubts this point. He "took plenty of exercise," though one reckons his regular duties saw to that. He agreed to fight Sharpless for one hundred pounds a side. Again, take this with a grain of salt (see Ed James, *The Life and Battles of Yankee Sullivan* [Philadelphia, 1854], 11).
46. *Bell's Life in Sydney and Sporting Review*, 15 July 1848.
47. *The Australian*, 23 August 1833.
48. *The Australian*, 23 August 1833; Waterhouse, "Bare-Knuckle Prize Fighting, Masculinity and Nineteenth-Century Australian Culture," 105–6.
49. James, *The Life and Battles of Yankee Sullivan*, 11.
50. *The Australian*, 23 June 1837. Thomas Brady is listed on the Bandon West Cork Heritage Center file for Yankee Sullivan as having been fought in Ireland. This is wrong, of course.
51. James, *The Life and Battles of Yankee Sullivan*, 11; Lamb MSS, chap. 1.

Round 7. The Bay of Islands

1. I am indebted to Richard Doctorow, the director of the Sag Harbor Whaling Museum, for the history of the ship.
2. Eunice Juckett, "Sag Harbor to Recall Days as Whaling Port," *New York Times*, 31 May 1964.
3. A. O. Scott, "Nobody Ever Read American Literature Like This Guy Did," *New York Times*, 29 July 2023.
4. *American Offshore Whaling Voyages, 1667 to 1927*, vol. 2: *Voyages by Master* (Old Dartmouth Historical Society, 2010), 161: "Christmas in a Landmark Village," *New York Times*, 22 December 1974; "Sag Harbor to Recall Days as Whaling Port," *New York Times*, 31 May 1964.
5. James Belich, *Making Peoples: A History of the New Zealanders from Polynesian Settlement to the End of the Nineteenth Century* (Penguin, 1996), 127.
6. Eric Jay Dolin, *Leviathan: The History of Whaling in America* (Norton, 2007), 205.
7. David Hand to His Father, 30 June 1839, East Hampton Library.
8. Rhys Richards and Jocelyn Chisholm, *Bay Islands Shipping Arrivals and Departures, 1803–1840* (Parramatta, 1992), no pagination, organized by date.
9. Hamilton Logbook (1043), master David Hand, New Bedford Whaling Museum Library.
10. Hamilton Logbook, 29 September 1839, New Bedford Whaling Museum Library.

11. Exhibition at New Bedford Whaling Museum on the sperm whale.
12. *Moby Dick,* quoted in Greg Grandin, *The Empire of Necessity: Slavery, Freedom, and Deception in the New World* (Picador, 2014), 85.
13. Amasa Delano, *A Narrative of the Voyages and Travels in the Northern and Southern Hemispheres* (Boston, 1818), 289, quoted in Grandin, *The Empire of Necessity,* 84.
14. Hamilton Logbook, 7 October 1839, New Bedford Whaling Museum Library.
15. Hamilton Logbook, 26 April 1840, New Bedford Whaling Museum Library.
16. *The Corrector,* 6 May 1840; Hamilton Logbook, 22 March 1840, New Bedford Whaling Museum Library.
17. *The Corrector,* 12 September 1840.
18. This is based on Ken Lamb's findings in official documents and newspapers (Lamb MSS, chap. 2). On the escape, see *New South Wales Government Gazette,* 11 and 18 March 1840.
19. Robert Hughes, *The Fatal Shore: The Epic of Australia's Founding* (Vintage, 1986), 210–12.
20. Belich, *Making Peoples,* 137–38.
21. Whaling Log of the Ship France, 1838–1840, entries for 23 December 1839, 24 December 1839, East Hampton Library.
22. Whaling Log of the Ship France, 1838–1840, entries for 1 February to 6 February 1840; 18 February to 24 February 1840, East Hampton Library.
23. Whaling Log of the Ship France, 1838–1840, entries for 21 March to 26 March 1840, East Hampton Library.
24. Anonymous Account of a Convict Escape, between 1840 and 1844, MLMSS 5536, Mitchell Library.
25. This is Ken Lamb's best guess, based on shipping records, of how Ambrose made it out. Much later, a report would suggest Ambrose had escaped Sydney on a ship called the *Citizen.* No ship bearing that name, however, was anywhere near Sydney at the time. The *Citizen* was plying the Atlantic with cargo. The *France* was the only American whaler leaving Sydney at the time of Ambrose's escape (Lamb MSS, chap. 3).
26. Whaling Log of the Ship France, 1838–1840, entries for 26 March and 27 March 1840, East Hampton Library.
27. Mary Phoebe Broughton Diary, 1839–41, MLMSS 4010, Mitchell Library.
28. On lays, see Elmo Hohman, "Wages, Risk, and Profits in the Whaling Industry," *Quarterly Journal of Economics* 40 (1926): 644–45.
29. Dolin, *Leviathan,* 223.
30. William Clark Taylor, *Jottings on Australia: with Remarks on the California Route to New York and Liverpool* (London, 1872), 110, New York Public Library.

31. Augustus Earle, *A Narrative of a Nine Months' Residence in New Zealand, 1827* (Whitecombe and Tombs, 1909), https://www.gutenberg.org/files/11933/1193-h/1193-h.htm.
32. Rhys Richards and Jocelyn Chisholm, *Bay Islands Shipping Arrivals and Departures, 1803–1840* (Parramatta, 1992), no pagination, introduction.
33. Shipping Intelligence Extracts from the 1840 newspaper *New Zealand Advertiser and Bay of Islands Gazette,* 2 July 1840, http://brind.co.uk/Brinddoc/world/newzeal/whaler/advertiser.html.
34. Belich, *Making Peoples,* 129.
35. Belich, *Making Peoples,* 130–31; exhibit at Russell Museum, Russell, New Zealand.
36. Richard Wolfe, *Hell-hole of the Pacific* (Penguin, 2005).
37. Wolfe, *Hell-hole of the Pacific,* 192.
38. Charles Darwin, *Voyage of the Beagle* (New York, P. F. Collier & Son, 1909), 421–25.
39. Earle, *A Narrative of a Nine Months' Residence in New Zealand.*
40. Lord Palmerston to Captain Hobson, R.N., Number 1, Foreign Office, 13 August 1839, *Historical Records of New Zealand,* ed. Robert McNab, vol. 1 (Wellington, 1908), 748.
41. James Busby and James Clendon, Report of Riot at Bay of Islands, 17 August 1839, in *Historical Records of New Zealand,* ed. Robert McNab, vol. 2 (Wellington, 1908–14), 609–12.
42. McNab, *Historical Records of New Zealand,* 2:608.
43. Wolfe, *Hell-hole of the Pacific,* 78.
44. Richards and Chisholm, *Bay Islands Shipping Arrivals and Departures, 1803–1840.*
45. Whaling Log of the Ship France, 24 June 1840; Richards and Chisholm, *Bay Islands Shipping Arrivals and Departures, 1803–1840.* It is listed as arriving on 16 June in this source.
46. McNab, *Historical Records of New Zealand,* 2:608.
47. James Clendon to John Forsyth, 3 July 1840, in *Historical Records of New Zealand,* ed. McNab, 2:614.
48. McNab, *Historical Records of New Zealand,* 2:615.
49. James Clendon to John Forsyth, 3 July 1840, in *Historical Records of New Zealand,* ed. McNab, 2:614.
50. On 30 June 1856, under a headline "Yankee Sullivan No More," the *New York Times* reported he made his escape on a ship called the *Hamilton.*
51. Herman Melville, *Omoo: A Narrative of Adventures in the South Seas* (Harper and Brothers, 1847), chaps. 23, 82.
52. Wolfe, *Hell-hole of the Pacific,* 56, 109.

53. Claudia Orange, *The Treaty of Waitangi* (Bridget Williams Books, 1996), 32–59; Trevor Williams, "Historical Revision No. XCV: The Treaty of Waitangi," *History* 25 (1940): 237–51.
54. Belich, *Making Peoples,* 198–99.
55. James Bleich, *The New Zealand Wars and the Victorian Interpretation of Racial Conflict* (Auckland University Press, 1986).
56. William Mayhew, Vice Consul, to Secretary of State, 21 February 1842, in *Historical Records of New Zealand,* ed. McNab, 2:620–22.
57. *Omoo,* chap. 1.
58. McNab, *Historical Records of New Zealand,* 2:615.

Round 8. Sag Harbor

1. Herman Melville, *Moby Dick,* chap. 24; Andrew Delbanco, *Melville: His World and Work* (Knopf, 2005), 122–28.
2. A. J. Liebling, *The Sweet Science* (North Point, 1949), 253.
3. Hamilton Logbook, entries for 20 June 1840, 21 June 1840, New Bedford Whaling Museum.
4. Hamilton Logbook, entries for 21 July 1840, 13 August 1840.
5. Hamilton Logbook, July 5, 1840.
6. Eric Jay Dolin, *Leviathan: The History of Whaling in America* (Norton, 2007), 259.
7. David Grann, *The Wager: A Tale of Shipwreck, Mutiny, and Murder* (Doubleday, 2023), 62–63.
8. Hamilton Logbook, entries for 6 August 1840, and 7 August 1840.
9. Hamilton Logbook, entry for 9 August 1840.
10. Hamilton Logbook, entry for 9 September 1840.
11. Sag Harbor Whaling Museum exhibit.
12. Eunice Juckett, "Sag Harbor to Recall Days as Whaling Port," *New York Times,* 31 May 1964.
13. Juckett, "Sag Harbor to Recall Days as Whaling Port."
14. *The Corrector,* 22 February 1840.
15. Kathleen Parrish, "'Behold Ye Living Passing By': The Ultimate in Booking Ahead," *New York Times,* 19 November 1989.
16. *The Corrector,* 16 April 1845. Floris Cash claims a sperm whale did it in "African American Whalers: Images and Realities," *Long Island Historical Journal* 2 (1989): 47. On other ships (not the *Hamilton*) that went down from being rammed by sperm whales, see Frederick Schmitt, *Mark Well the Whale* (Kennikat, 1971), 84.

17. "Science Shows How Moby Dick Could Totally Have Sunk That Whaling Ship," *Washington Post*, 7 April 2016.
18. It would come in 1844. My thanks to Richard Doctorow for pointing this out.
19. Herman Melville, *Redburn* (Penguin, 1976), 186.
20. John Leland, "You See Rubble and Garbage. She Sees New York's Next Great Park," *New York Times*, 27 July 2024.
21. "Gallus Mag," Lower Manhattan Historical Association web biography, www.historiclowermanhattan.org/criminals/gallus-mag.
22. Kevin Dwyer, "Blasts from the Past," *New York*, 31 May 2005; Irene Plagianos, "One Last Shot for a Historic Manhattan Bar," *Wall Street Journal*, 22 February 2020.
23. "The Rat Pit": Captain Joseph Rose House, Daytonian in Manhattan, 15 June 2010, https://daytoninmanhattan.blogspot.com/2010/06/rat-pit-captain-joseph-rose-house.html.
24. "Yankee Sullivan (James Ambrose) (alias Frank Murray)," www.cyberboxingzone.com/boxing/yankee.htm.
25. Other contemporary fight records that prove helpful in unearthing his battles in Australia make no mention of this fight, though one writer claimed they fought for five hundred dollars a side and that the fighting press in New York, as if there were one, declared him "the grandest fighter ever seen." No such report existed. See, for instance, Ed James, comp., *The Life and Battles of Tom Hyer* (New York, 1879); and "Thormanby" [W. Wilmot Dixon], *Boxers and Their Battles* (R. A. Everett, 1900), 224.
26. The account mistakes the date he came to New York. It also says he was transported to Australia for political reasons. So, we cannot be sure how much credence to give it. See C. J. Gannon, "Famous Irish Boxers, Their Lives and Fights," *Tuam Herald*, 26 September 1931, "Yankee Sullivan (James Ambrose) (alias Frank Murray)," www.cyberboxingzone.com/boxing/yankee.htm.
27. Carl Bridenbaugh, *Cities in the Wilderness: The First Century of Urban Life in America* (Ronald Press, 1938).
28. James Kirby Martin, ed., *Ordinary Courage: The Revolutionary War Adventures of Joseph Plumb Martin* (Wiley-Blackwell, 2013), 95.
29. Elliott Gorn, "'Gouge and Bite, Pull Hair and Scratch': The Social Significance of Fighting in the Southern Backcountry," *American Historical Review* 90 (1985): 18–43.
30. Sergio Lussana, "To See Who Was Best on the Plantation: Enslaved Fighting Contests and Masculinity in the Antebellum Plantation South," *Journal of Southern History* 76 (2010): 901–22.

31. For this and what follows on early boxing and prizefighting, see Elliott Gorn, *The Manly Art: Bare-Knuckle Prize Fighting in America* (Cornell University Press, 1986), 38–54.
32. "Thormanby" [W. Wilmot Dixon], *Boxers and Their Battles*, 220.
33. Paul Gilje, "The Development of an Irish American Community in New York before the Great Migration," in *The New York Irish*, ed. Ronald H. Bayor and Timothy Meagher (Johns Hopkins University Press, 1996), 70–83.
34. Kevin Kenny, *The American Irish: A History* (Routledge, 2000), 55–61.
35. Mathew Carey quoted in Peter Way, *Common Labor: Workers and the Digging of North American Canals, 1780–1860* (Johns Hopkins University Press, 1997), 90.
36. Way, *Common Labor*, 174–75, 194–95.
37. Edward MacLysaght, *The Surnames of Ireland* (Irish Academic Press, 2012), 280.
38. Francis Hodge, *Yankee Theatre: The Image of America on the Stage, 1825–1850* (University of Texas Press, 1964), 4–5, 41–45, 215.
39. Hodge, *Yankee Theatre*, 155–88, 211.
40. Paul Johnson, *Sam Patch, the Famous Jumper* (Hill and Wang, 2003), 93–95, 171–75.
41. Greg Grandin, *Empire of Necessity: Slavery, Freedom, and Deception in the New World* (Macmillan, 2014), 152; Eric Jay Dolin, *Leviathan: The History of Whaling in America* (Norton, 2007), 257. Or perhaps imperfectly. Melville's *Pequod*, after all, operated as a sort of American democracy writ small, expanding the idea of popular sovereignty wherever it went. Heedless of the cost. See Delbanco, *Melville: His World and Work*, 161, 164.
42. American Theatre Bowery, 15 January 1834, Program for "A Yankee Story by Mr. Marble," New York Public Library, Billy Rose Theatre Division, Bowery Theatre Programs, 1834–1842.

Round 9. Liverpool

1. Keith Duggan, "We Are Not English, We Are Scouse," *Irish Times*, 21 May 2022.
2. Herman Melville, *Redburn* (Penguin, 1976), 144.
3. This is the hypothesis of Ken Lamb, who reviewed all the likely passages from New York to Liverpool in the period in the *Morning Herald* of New York and the *Morning Post* of London for the fall of 1840, when he had to have sailed (Lamb MSS, chap. 4).
4. Isaiah Townshend, "Journal of a Voyage on Board the Sailing Ship Roscius from New York to Liverpool," 1840, Mss Col 3017, Rare Books and Manuscripts, New York Public Library.

5. Honora Edgeworth to Charles Edgeworth, 13 November 1827, MS.ENG. Lett c 739, pp. 57–59, Bodleian Library, Oxford.
6. Travel Diary of an American Gentleman on a European Tour, 1833–34, MS. ENG.e.3975, pp. 4–5, Bodleian Library.
7. Maria E. to Mrs. Edgeworth from Liverpool, 16 October 1830, MS. ENG. Let.c.700, fols. 26–28, Bodleian Library.
8. Melville, *Redburn*, 147, 186–87.
9. Simon Hughes, *There She Goes: Liverpool, A City on Its Own: The Long Decade, 1979–1993* (Decoubertin Books, 2020), 2–3.
10. Guy Collender, "Learning from the Nation: How Emulating Provincial Ports Led to an Interwar Renaissance for the Port of London," unpublished manuscript, 3–4. See also G. J. Milne, "Maritime Liverpool," in *Liverpool 800: Culture, Character, and History*, ed. John Belchem (Liverpool University Press, 2006). My thanks to Collender for a copy of the manuscript and the citation.
11. Melville, *Redburn*, 186–90.
12. Collender, "Learning from the Nation," 21.
13. David Gwyn, *The Coming of the Railway: A New Global History, 1750–1850* (Yale University Press, 2023); Edmond Smith, *Ruthless: A New History of Britain's Rise to Wealth and Power* (Yale University Press, 2025), 3, 324–25, 341–57.
14. John Belchem, *Irish, Catholic and Scouse: The History of the Liverpool Irish, 1800–1939* (Liverpool University Press, 2007), 28–31, 97–104, 188.
15. On this, see Malcolm Campbell, *Ireland's Farthest Shore: Mobility, Migration, and Settlement in the Pacific World* (University of Wisconsin Press, 2022), 8–9.
16. Raphael Samuel, "The Roman Catholic Church and the Irish Poor," in *The Irish in the Victorian City*, ed. Roger Swift and Sheridan Gilley (Routledge, 1984), 272, 280. On Irish assertiveness, as opposed to victimhood, see the work of Breándan Mac Suibhne, *The End of Outrage: Post-Famine Adjustment in Rural Ireland* (Oxford University Press, 2017). On numbers, see Belchem, *Irish, Catholic and Scouse*, 6–7; and Tom Gallagher, "A Tale of Two Cities: Communal Strife in Glasgow and Liverpool before 1914," in *The Irish in the Victorian City*, ed. Swift and Gilley, 107.
17. Melville, *Redburn*, 222.
18. Malcolm Campbell, *Ireland's New Worlds: Immigrants, Politics, and Society in the United States and Australia, 1815–1922* (University of Wisconsin Press, 2007), 12–13, 19.
19. Hughes, *There She Goes*, 4.
20. Hughes, *There She Goes*, 12–14.
21. Christina Edgeworth Colvin, "Two Unpublished MSS by Maria Edgeworth," *Review of English Literature* 8 (1967): 53–55. My thanks to Claire Connolly for bringing this to my attention.

22. *Fisitiana; Or, the Oracle of the Ring* (London, 1841), 61.
23. Belchem, *Irish, Catholic and Scouse,* 3–4; Adam Chill, *Bare-Knuckle Britons and Fighting Irish: Boxing, Race, Religion, and Nationality in the 18th and 19th Centuries* (McFarland, 2017), 124–30, 147.
24. David Snowdon, *Writing the Prizefight: Pierce Egan's Boxiana World* (Peter Lang, 2013), 154–55.
25. Dennis Brailsford, *Bareknuckles: A Social History of Prizefighting* (Lutterworth, 1989), 86, 119.
26. In *New York Clipper,* 7 June 1884 (Lamb MSS, chap. 1).
27. *Bell's Life in London,* 7 February 1841.
28. *Bell's Life in Sydney and Sporting Reviewer,* 5 August 1848. My thanks to Tony Gee for this reference.
29. Bob Mee, *Bare Fists: The History of Bare Knuckle Prize Fighting* (Overlook Books, 2001), 88.
30. Tony Gee, *Up to Scratch: Bareknuckle Fighting and Heroes of the Prize Ring* (G2 Entertainment, 2015), 113–16; Mee, *Bare Fists,* 102.
31. *Bell's Life in London,* 7 February 1841. My thanks to Tony Gee for bringing this to my attention.
32. Brailsford, *Bareknuckles,* 96.
33. The 1841 census, as per Ken Lamb (Lamb MSS, chap. 4); *Fisitiana* (London, 1841), 61, 262.
34. *Bell's Life in London,* 24 January 1841. I owe these points to Tony Gee.
35. *Bell's Life in London,* 31 January 1841; *Fistiana,* 270.
36. *Bell's Life in London,* 31 January 1841.
37. *Bell's Life in London,* 24 January 1841.

Round 10. Crookham Common

1. Ed James, *The Life and Battles of Yankee Sullivan* (Philadelphia, 1854), 11.
2. "Thormanby" [W. Wilmot Dixon], *Boxers and Their Battles* (R. A. Everett, 1900), 128.
3. Bob Mee, *Bare Fists: The History of Bare Knuckle Prize Fighting* (Overlook Books, 2001), 104.
4. "Thormanby," *Boxers and Their Battles,* 128.
5. "Thormanby," *Boxers and Their Battles,* 226.
6. *Bell's Life in London,* 7 February 1841.
7. James, *The Life and Battles of Yankee Sullivan,* 12.
8. *Bell's Life in London,* 7 February 1841. The rest of the account of the fight comes from this report. It is also reproduced, almost exactly, in James, *The Life and Battles of Yankee Sullivan.*

9. Tony Gee, "Fresh Light on the 'New Rules' of 1838," *International Boxing Research Journal* 152 (2021): 14–15. Some argue that Swift had killed three in the ring; Gee argues convincingly for two.
10. *The Great Western, Cheltenham and Great Western, and Bristol and Exeter Railway Guides* (London, 1839), 3–4; Samuel Barfield, *Thatcham, Berkshire, and Its Manors* (James Parker, 1901), 73.
11. Dennis Brailsford, *Bareknuckles: A Social History of Prizefighting* (Lutterworth, 1989), 108; David Gwyn, *The Coming of the Railway: A New Global History, 1750–1850* (Yale University Press, 2023), 316–19.
12. Brailsford, *Bareknuckles*, 108.
13. Gee, "Fresh Light on the 'New Rules' of 1838," 15.
14. *New York Times*, 30 June 1856.
15. "Thormanby" [W. Wilmot Dixon], *Boxers and Their Battles*, 231.
16. James, *The Life and Battles of Yankee Sullivan*, 15.
17. *The Statesman*, 7 February 1841. My thanks to Tony Gee for this reference.
18. *Bell's Life in London*, 7 February 1841.
19. *Bell's Life in London*, 7 February 1841.
20. "Thormanby" [W. Wilmot Dixon], *Boxers and Their Battles*, 220.
21. *Bell's Life in London*, 7 February 1841.
22. The postfight activities have been unearthed by Ken Lamb through his reading of newspapers (Lamb MSS, chap. 4).
23. Tony Gee, "The Demise of the (Bareknuckle) Traditional Prize-ring in Britain: A Brief Look at Some Pertinent Causes," in *The Boxing Yearbook, 2009*, ed. Barry Hugman (Mainstream, 2009), 45.

Round 11. The Five Points

1. Jay Dolan, *The Irish Americans: A History* (Bloomsbury, 2008), 39–40; Tyler Anbinder, *Five Points: The Nineteenth-Century Neighborhood That Invented Tap Dance, Stole Elections, and Became the World's Most Notorious Slum* (Free Press, 2001), 72–79. On Sullivan's address, I rely on Lamb MSS, chap. 5.
2. See Herbert Asbury, *The Gangs of New York: An Informal History of the Underworld* (Vintage, 1927).
3. *Second Annual Report of the Trustees of the Five Points House of Industry. Made to the Incorporators, March 1, 1856* (New York, 1856), 3, 21, New York Public Library; Lucy Sante, *Low Life* (Farrar, Straus and Giroux, 2003), 310.
4. William Francis Barnard, *Forty Years at the Five Points* (New York, 1893), 10–11, 16, New York Public Library.
5. On this, see Rebecca Yamin, ed., *Tales of Five Points: Working-Class Life in Nineteenth-Century New York*, 7 vols. (John Milner Associates, 2002). The

debate over whether all was vice or not is explored in Alan Mayne, "Tall Tales But True? New York's 'Five Points' Slum," *Journal of Urban History* 33 (2007): 320–31.

6. For this and what follows, see Charles Dickens, *American Notes*, vol. 1 (Leipzig, 1842), 110.
7. "Five Points Fury: Chaos Reigns in Lower Manhattan as Street Gangs, Police and Militia Clash," *NY Resident*, New York Public Library, 6 August 2001; Joshua Brown, "The 'Dead Rabbit'–Bowery Boy Riot: An Analysis of the Antebellum New York Gang" (master's thesis, Columbia University, 1976), 43, New York Public Library.
8. Dolan, *The Irish Americans*, 39.
9. Graham Hodges, "'Desirable Companions and Lovers': Irish and African Americans in the Sixth Ward, 1830–1870," in *The New York Irish*, ed. Ronald Bayor and Timothy Meagher (Johns Hopkins University Press, 1997), 110; James Trager, *The New York Chronology: The Ultimate Compendium of Events, People, and Anecdotes from the Dutch to the Present* (HarperCollins, 2003), 82–83.
10. J. D. Dickey, *The Republic of Violence: The Tormented Rise of Abolition in Andrew Jackson's America* (Pegasus Books, 2022), 38–62; Leslie Harris, *In the Shadow of Slavery: African Americans in New York City, 1626–1863* (University of Chicago Press, 2003), 194–98. On riots here, see Michael Feldberg, *The Turbulent Era: Riot and Disorder in Jacksonian America* (Oxford University Press, 1980), 3–7; Leslie Alexander, *African or American? Black Identity and Political Activism in New York City, 1784–1861* (University of Illinois Press, 2008), 85–86; and Anbinder, *Five Points*, 7–13.
11. Graham Hodges, "'Desirable Companions and Lovers': Irish and African Americans in the Sixth Ward, 1830–1870," and "Quimbo Appo's Fear of Fenians: Chinese-Irish-Anglo Relations in New York City," in *The New York Irish*, ed. Bayor and Meagher; Claudia Milne, "On the Grounds of the Fresh Water Pond: The Free-Black Community at Five Points, 1810–1834," *International Journal of Historical Archaeology* 6 (2002): 138; Anbinder, *Five Points*, 27–29, 46.
12. Trager, *The New York Chronology*, 76–77; Edwin Burrows and Mike Wallace, *Gotham: A History of New York to 1898* (Oxford University Press, 2003), 603–18, quotes from 613 and 617; Edward Spann, *The New Metropolis: New York City, 1840–1857* (Columbia University Press, 1981), 55; Anbinder, *Five Points*, 134: Daniel Levy, *Manhattan Phoenix: The Great Fire of 1835 and the Emergence of Modern New York* (Oxford University Press, 2021), 23, 54, 121.
13. Anbinder, *Five Points;* Asbury, *Gangs of New York*.
14. "Church of the Transfiguration," www.nycago.org/Organs/NYC/html/TransfigurationRC.html.

15. I could not gain access to Transfiguration Church records, despite numerous attempts. For his wife (and wives, in fact), I am indebted to Lamb MSS, appendix B.
16. On this, see Tyler Anbinder, *Plentiful Country: The Great Potato Famine and the Making of Irish New York* (Little, Brown, 2024).
17. Tyler Anbinder, "Moving Beyond 'Rags to Riches': New York's Irish Famine Immigrants and Their Surprising Savings Accounts," *Journal of American History* (2012): 741–70; Simone Wegge, Tyler Anbinder, and Cormac O'Grada, "Networks and Opportunities: A Digital History of Ireland's Great Famine Refugees in New York," *American Historical Review* 124 (2019): 1591–629. Emigrant Savings Bank Records can be found on Ancestry.com.
18. Anbinder, *Five Points*, 172–75.
19. Dennis Gildea, "The Language of the 'Fancy' in Print: Frank Queen's Clipper and Prize-Fight Coverage, 1853–1860" (Ph.D. diss., Pennsylvania State University, 1998), iii; "19th-Century Criminal Slang," Parks Department Tour of the Five Points, New York Public Library, 4 April 2004; Sante, *Low Life*, 236–37.
20. Sante, *Low Life*, 244–45.
21. Ed James, *The Life and Battles of Yankee Sullivan* (Philadelphia, 1854), 64; History Information Map of Chatham Square Area, c. 1825–c. 1850, Hand-drawn MS Map, Villages and Sections—Five Points—Clipping File, IRH-F, New York Public Library; Sante, *Low Life*, 28; Anbinder, *Five Points*, 91, 202.
22. Peter Gammie, "Pugilists and Politicians in Antebellum New York: The Life and Times of Tom Hyer," *New York History* 75 (1994): 274.
23. *New York Daily Tribune*, 6 July 1844; Nat Fleischer, "In the Bare Knuckle Days," MSS in Yankee Sullivan File, Notre Dame Special Collections; *American Fistiana* (New York, 1849), 1, Notre Dame Special Collections.
24. Gammie, "Pugilists and Politicians," 274; James, *Life and Battles of Yankee Sullivan*, 64, 34; *American Fistiana*, 3; "Chatham Square, New York," 1853–55, Daguerreotype, New York Metropolitan Museum of Art photographic collections, Gillman Collection.
25. New York City directories list James Sullivans as tavern owners at Mott Street, though other records do not suggest this is our man. In 1842/43, he is listed running a porterhouse at 218 Cherry. In 1844/45 and 1845/46, he is listed being at 41 Madison and running a porterhouse. In 1846/47, 1847/48, and 1848/49, he is at 9 Chatham Street in a porterhouse. In 1849/50, 1850/51, and 1852/53, James Sullivan is selling "liquors" at 11 Centre Street. He may have been back to Chatham Street sometime in the following year (82½ Chatham). These findings are available in New York Public Library's Digital Collections: https://digitalcollections.nypl.org/collections/new-york-city-directories#/?tab=about&scroll=70.

26. Joseph Mitchell, "The Old House at Home," *New Yorker*, 14 April 1940.
27. Dolan, *The Irish Americans*, 48.
28. Quoted in Elliott Gorn, *The Manly Art: Bare Knuckle Prize Fighting in America* (Cornell University Press, 1986), 70.
29. Gildea, "The Language of the 'Fancy' in Print," 77; *New York Evening Express*, 18 September 1845.
30. Gorn, *The Manly Art*, 141.
31. See James Delgado, ed., *Log of the Apollo: Joseph Perkins Beach's Journal of the Voyage of the Ship Apollo from New York to San Francisco 1849* (Book Club of California, 1986), 21, 63, Rare Books and Special Collections, New York Public Library.
32. *Bell's Life in London*, 22 August 1841. My thanks to Tony Gee for this reference.
33. Gildea, "The Language of the 'Fancy' in Print," 8.
34. For "empire city," I am indebted to a talk by James Belich ("Urban Colonialism in Global History," Global and Imperial Research Seminar, University of Oxford, 21 January 2022).
35. Malcolm Campbell, *Ireland's New World: Immigrants, Politics, and Society in the United States and Australia, 1815–1922* (University of Wisconsin Press, 2008), 21–23. On this theme, see especially Gorn, *The Manly Art*.
36. Sean Wilentz, *Chants Democratic: New York City and the Rise of the American Working Class* (Oxford University Press, 1984), 266–70.
37. Campbell, *Ireland's New World*, 24–25; Trager, *The New York Chronology*, 86. On the relationship between shifting labor regimes, the coming of the Irish, and the nativist backlash, see Elliott Gorn, "'Good-Bye Boys, I Die a True American': Homicide, Nativism, and Working-Class Culture in Antebellum New York City," *Journal of American History* 74 (1987): 388–410.
38. Gorn, "'Good-Bye Boys, I Die a True American,'" 388–410. On riots here, see Michael Feldberg, *The Turbulent Era: Riot and Disorder in Jacksonian America* (Oxford University Press, 1980), 3–7.
39. Gildea, "The Language of the 'Fancy' in Print," 54; Sante, *Low Life*, 199–200.
40. James, *Life and Battles of Yankee Sullivan*, 17.
41. *American Fistiana*, 1.
42. *New York Herald*, 12 August 1874.
43. The fight is covered in James, *Life and Battles of Yankee Sullivan*, 18–22; and *American Fistiana*, 4–6.
44. James, *Life and Battles of Yankee Sullivan*, 22.
45. James, *Life and Battles of Yankee Sullivan*, 22.
46. James, *Life and Battles of Yankee Sullivan*, 23.
47. James, *Life and Battles of Yankee Sullivan*, 25–27.
48. *American Fistiana*, 1.

49. Gorn, *The Manly Art,* 73.
50. Gorn, *The Manly Art,* 72.
51. "New York's Pioneer Rings," MSS in Nat Fleischer Papers, Notre Dame Special Collections.
52. *American Fistiana,* 1.
53. Gildea, "The Language of the 'Fancy' in Print," 5.
54. J. A. Westerwell to Elizabeth Gage, 2 September 1843, Pierre Spake Collection; *Daily Sentinel,* 17 August 1848; *Commercial Advertiser* (New York), 15 February 1845.
55. Trager, *The New York Chronology,* 88. On the rise of the prizefighting press in New York in these years, see Gildea, "The Language of the 'Fancy' in Print."
56. Bowery Theatre Program, 12 February 1842, Billy Rose Theatre Division, New York Public Library.
57. *Memoir of Thomas McCoy* (New York, 1842), 12, New York Historical Society.
58. *Bell's Life in London,* 27 February 1842. I owe this to Tony Gee. On the Sheffield story, see *Bell's Life in London,* 28 January 1844.
59. *The Great Fight Between Lilly and McCoy!,* broadside, New York Historical Society.
60. *New York Times,* 30 June 1856, cited in Kenneth Bridgham, "The Violent Life and Death of Yankee Sullivan," *Journal of the International Boxing Research Organization* 156 (2022): 22. My thanks to Tony Gee for this reference.
61. *Life of William Poole* (New York, 1855), 81, Notre Dame Special Collections.
62. James, *Life and Battles of Yankee Sullivan,* 28.
63. Richard K. Fox, *Prize Ring Heroes: Life and Battles of Tom Hyer, Yankee Sullivan, John Morrissey,* 18, Notre Dame Special Collections; *Spectator* (New York), 18 April 1846; *Connecticut Courant,* 16 April 1842; *New-York Commercial Advertiser,* 8 September 1845, 20 March 1846; *New York Evening Express,* 14 April 1846.
64. *Evening Post* (New York), 21 November 1842. Gammie, "Pugilists and Politicians," 274. On saloons, firehouses, and politics, see Anbinder, *Five Points,* 145–54.
65. Joshua Brown, "The 'Dead Rabbit'–Bowery Boy Riot: An Analysis of the Antebellum New York Gang" (master's thesis, Columbia University, 1976), 52–53, New York Public Library; Wilentz, *Chants Democratic,* 328.
66. Brown, "The 'Dead Rabbit'–Bowery Boy Riot"; Noel Ignatiev, *How the Irish Became White* (New York, 1995), 81–82, 90–93; *New-York Commercial Advertiser,* 30 September 1844; *Boston Daily Bee,* 29 June 1848.
67. Anbinder, *Five Points,* 156–60; Wilentz, *Chants Democratic,* 332–34; Brown, "The 'Dead Rabbit'–Bowery Boy Riot," 83–84; Gammie, "Pugilists and

Politicians," 270; Gorn, *The Manly Art*, 135; *New York Evening Express*, 20 May 1845; *New-York Commercial Advertiser*, 26 December 1845; *Hudson River Chronicle* (Ossining), 31 October 1848.

68. Dolan, *The Irish Americans*, 49.
69. Lamb MSS, chap. 5. This is covered in *The Sun* (11, 13, 14, 19, and 20 April 1842); *Connecticut Courant*, 16 April 1847; and *New York Aurora*, 15 April 1842.
70. Wilentz, *Chants Democratic*, 263.
71. Patrick McGrath, "Secular Power, Sectarian Politics: The American-Born Irish Elite and Catholic Political Culture in Nineteenth-Century New York," *Journal of American Ethnic History* 38 (2019): 45–46. The best account of this culture—and for election sports—is Tyler Anbinder, "Isaiah Rynders and the Ironies of Popular Democracy in Antebellum New York," in *Contested Democracy: Freedom, Race, and Power in American History*, ed. Manisha Sinha and Penny Von Eschen (Columbia University Press, 2007).
72. *Life of William Poole*, 49; Brown, "The 'Dead Rabbit'–Bowery Boy Riot," 83; Anbinder, *Five Points*, 150–51.
73. *Morning News* (New London), 12 July 1847. On Tom Hyer's political work, and the centrality of boxing to it, see Gammie, "Pugilists and Politicians," 265–96. On theater, see Bruce McConachie, "'The Theatre of the Mob': Apocalyptic Melodrama and Preindustrial Riots in Antebellum New York," in *Theatre for Working-Class Audiences in the United States, 1830–1980*, ed. Bruce McConachie and Daniel Freedman (Greenwood, 1985), 17–46.
74. He personified the "urban feudalism" that lay at the intersection of pugilism and politics. See Gammie, "Pugilists and Politicians in Antebellum New York," 268.
75. Jacob Riis, *How the Other Half Lives: Studies Among the Tenements of New York* (New York, 1890), 21.
76. Spann, *The New Metropolis*, 389.
77. *The Whip*, 13 September 1842, New York Historical Society.
78. James, *Life and Battles of Yankee Sullivan*, 78; Gorn, *The Manly Art*, 73.
79. *New York American*, 28 November 1842, Pierre Spake Collection.
80. *The Great Fight Between Lilly and McCoy!*, broadside, New York Historical Society; James, *Life and Battles of Yankee Sullivan*, 79–85. For "Battle of Hastings" and its aftermath, see Gorn, *The Manly Art*, 73–81.
81. *New York American*, 28 November 1842, Pierre Spake Collection.
82. *Memoir of Thomas McCoy* (New York, 1842), New York Historical Society, 1–8, 11, 20.
83. Gorn, *The Manly Art*, 78.
84. Lamb MSS, chap. 5; *New York Daily-Tribune*, 20 September 1842; *New York Express*, 26 September 1842; *New York Sun*, 26 September 1842; *New*

York Herald, 30 September 1842; "General Sessions, 28 September 1842"; "Transcript of Convictions, 2 December 1842," Court Records A0312(8)L, Folder 10, A0320(11)L, Folder 2, Westchester Country Archives; Gorn, *The Manly Art*, 76–77. On the stone quarry, see *New York Herald*, 16 April 1843.

85. Jonathan Coleman, "Death at the Garden," *New Yorker*, 24 July 2013.
86. Donald McRae, "I've Written My Last Book on Boxing," *The Guardian*, 1 March 2025. That book is the excellent—and aptly titled—*The Last Bell: Life, Death and Boxing* (Simon & Schuster, 2025).
87. *New York Herald*, 3 September 1843, 4 September 1843; *New York Herald*, 16 April 1843.
88. *New York Morning Courier*, 26 September 1843; *The Corrector*, 16 September 1843.
89. So claimed the *New York Times*. See "Yankee Sullivan No More," *New York Times*, 30 June 1856.
90. *New York Herald*, 3 December 1842.
91. Gammie, "Pugilists and Politicians in Antebellum New York," 269–70.
92. Patricia Cline Cohen, *The Murder of Helen Jewett* (New York, 1999); *The Great Fight Between Lilly and McCoy!*, broadside, New York Historical Society.
93. Elaine Farrell and Leanne McCormick, *Bad Bridget: Crime, Mayhem, and the Lives of Irish Emigrant Women* (Sandycove, 2023), 7–10.
94. See Gail Bederman, *Manliness and Civilization: A Cultural History of Gender and Race in the United States, 1880–1917* (University of Chicago Press, 1995), 1–3, 15.
95. Igantiev, *How the Irish Became White*, 111.
96. Igantiev, *How the Irish Became White*.
97. Charles Isherwood, "'Paradise Square' Review: The Civil War Invades a Bar in New York," *New York Times*, 7 April 2022. For the best critique of the paradigm, see Kevin Kenny, *The American Irish: A History* (Routledge, 2000), 67–71.
98. Leslie Alexander, *African or American? Black Identity and Political Activism in New York City, 1784–1861* (University of Illinois Press, 2008), 88, 95, 101–7.
99. Edward Freeman quoted in Peter Quinn, *Looking for Jimmy: A Search for Irish America* (New York, 2007), 23.
100. For the speech, see https://frederickdouglasspapersproject.com/s/digital edition/item/10291. This is covered in Spann, *The New Metropolis*; Oil-on-canvas painting, 1833, artist unknown, history exhibit of the Museum of the City of New York; Sante, *Low Life*, 80–81; Anbinder, *Five Points*, 142–44, 189. On the conversion of anti-Irish stereotypes into anti-Black stereotypes, see Edward Ayers, *American Visions: The United States, 1800–1860* (Norton, 2023), 87.
101. Harris, *In the Shadow of Slavery*, 247–52.
102. Anbinder, *Five Points*, 163.

103. See Joshua Lynn, *Preserving the White Man's Republic: Jacksonian Democracy, Race, and the Transformation of American Conservatism* (University of Virginia Press, 2019).
104. Lynn, *Preserving the White Man's Republic.* This is not a new interpretation. For an earlier iteration, see Anthony Gronowicz, *Race and Class Politics in New York City Before the Civil War* (Northeastern University Press, 1998); Spann, *The New Metropolis,* 326–29 (quote from 239).
105. *American Fistiana,* 8.
106. James, *Life and Battles of Yankee Sullivan,* 29–33; "New York's Pioneer Rings," p. 3, MSS in Nat Fleischer Papers, Notre Dame Special Collections; *Bell's Life in Sydney and Sporting Register,* 26 June 1847.
107. James, *Life and Battles of Yankee Sullivan,* 29.
108. Bernard DeVoto, *The Year of Decision: 1846* (Little, Brown, 1942), 5–6, 22.
109. Gildea, "The Language of the 'Fancy' in Print," 81.
110. Gorn, *The Manly Art,* 81.

Round 12. Still Pond Heights

1. Christopher Clark, *Revolutionary Spring: Europe Aflame and the Fight for a New World, 1848–1849* (Crown, 2023); Mike Rapport, *1848: The Year of Revolution* (Basic Books, 2008).
2. Clark, *Revolutionary Spring,* 698–701.
3. Clark, *Revolutionary Spring,* 698–702; Steven Hahn, *A Nation Without Borders: The United States and Its World in an Age of Civil Wars, 1830–1910* (Viking, 2016), 128–43; Daniel Walker Howe, *What Hath God Wrought: The Transformation of America, 1815–1848* (Oxford University Press, 2007), 792–96.
4. "The Great Prize Fight," MSS in Nat Fleischer Papers, p. 279, Notre Dame Special Collections.
5. *American Fistiana* (New York, 1849), 3, Notre Dame Special Collections.
6. See a nice little piece by Elliott Gorn, "The First American Championship Prizefight," *OAH Magazine of History* 7 (1992): 19–23.
7. *American Fistiana,* 22; Elliott Gorn, *The Manly Art: Bare-Knuckle Prize Fighting in America* (Cornell University Press, 1986), 83.
8. Ed James, *Life and Battles of Yankee Sullivan* (Philadelphia, 1854), 41. The preparations for fight are also covered in *American Fistiana,* 13–16.
9. On the use of borders, see David Snowdon, *Writing the Prizefight: Pierce Egan's Boxiana World* (Peter Lang, 2013), 4.
10. Hahn, *A Nation Without Borders,* 143.

11. James Trager, *The New York Chronology: The Ultimate Compendium of Events, People, and Anecdotes from the Dutch to the Present* (HarperCollins, 2003), 91–95; Edward Spann, *The New Metropolis: New York City, 1840–1857* (Columbia University Press, 1981), 134.
12. James, *Life and Battles of Yankee Sullivan,* 45.
13. James, *Life and Battles of Yankee Sullivan,* 33–34.
14. James, *Life and Battles of Yankee Sullivan,* 37; Dennis Gildea, "The Language of the 'Fancy' in Print: Frank Queen's Clipper and Prize-Fight Coverage, 1853–1860" (Ph.D. diss., Pennsylvania State University, 1998), 81.
15. Wallace Shugg, "'This Great Test of Man's Brutality': The Sullivan-Hyer Prizefight at Still Pond Heights, Maryland, in 1849," *Maryland Historical Magazine* 95 (1906): 54.
16. Shugg, "This Great Test of Man's Brutality," 52; *American Fistiana,* 22.
17. James, *Life and Battles of Yankee Sullivan,* 51.
18. Fred Usilon, *History of Chestertown, Kent County, Maryland, 1650–1899* (Chestertown, MD, 1899), 92–94, 138.
19. Shugg, "This Great Test of Man's Brutality," 55; *American Fistiana,* 22.
20. James, *Life and Battles of Yankee Sullivan,* 35.
21. *Spirit of the Times,* 17 February 1849.
22. *American Fistiana,* 1.
23. Walsh appears in the lithograph in the Pierre Spake Collection.
24. "New York's Pioneer Rings," MSS in Nat Fleischer Papers, p. 9, Notre Dame Special Collections.
25. The fight is covered in many publications. For the details, see James, *Life and Battles of Yankee Sullivan,* 54–58; and *American Fistiana,* 25–27.
26. "New York's Pioneer Rings," MSS in Nat Fleischer Papers, p. 9, Notre Dame Special Collections.
27. "The Great Prize Fight," MSS in Nat Fleischer Papers, p. 286, Notre Dame Special Collections.
28. James, *Life and Battles of Yankee Sullivan,* 59.
29. *The Spirit of the Times,* 29 March 1851 (Lamb MSS, Misc. Notes).
30. *The Iliad,* book 23.
31. On Homer, fighting, and representative moments, I am indebted to Kasia Boddy, *Boxing: A Cultural History* (Reaktion Books, 2008), 9–11.
32. On this, see Gorn, *The Manly Art.*
33. On the centrality of the fight for sporting culture and for broader changes in labor, see Gorn, "The First American Championship Prizefight."
34. *Bell's Life in London,* 11 March 1849, 1 April 1849.
35. *Freemans Journal,* 8 April 1851 (Lamb MSS, Misc. Notes).

36. Yankee Sullivan manuscript file, "The Great Prize Fight," p. 281, Nat Fleischer Papers, Notre Dame Special Collections.
37. Tyler Anbinder, *Five Points: The Nineteenth-Century Neighborhood That Invented Tap Dance, Stole Elections, and Became the World's Most Notorious Slum* (Little, Brown, 2001), 206. The quote comes from the lithograph I viewed in the Pierre Spake Collection.
38. *American Fistiana*, 4. On this, see Gorn, *The Manly Art*, 136–45.
39. James, *Life and Battles of Yankee Sullivan*, 34.
40. James, *Life and Battles of Yankee Sullivan*, 47–48; Gorn, *The Manly Art*, 87, 89.
41. James, *Life and Battles of Yankee Sullivan*, 37.
42. *The Republic*, 9 October 1850; *Cayuga Chief*, 13 January 1852.
43. Anbinder, *Five Points*, 206.

Round 13. Boston Corner

1. *New York Herald*, 21 May 1849; *New York Tribune*, 27 September 1849; *Troy Daily Whig*, 28 September 1849; *Onondaga Standard*, 24 October 1849; *New York Daily Tribune*, 22 October 1849 (Lamb MSS, Misc. Notes).
2. *Newport Mercury*, 12 January 1850. This is according to "Yankee Sullivan No More," *New York Times*, 1856; *New York Evening Express*, 16 June 1856; and *Alexandria Gazette*, 18 June 1856.
3. James Delgado, ed., *Log of the Apollo: Joseph Perkins Beach's Journal of the Voyage of the Ship Apollo from New York to San Francisco 1849* (Book Club of California, 1986), New York Public Library; Malcolm Rohrbough, *Days of Gold: The California Gold Rush and the American Nation* (University of California Press, 1997), 56–61; Daniel Walker Howe, *What Hath God Wrought: The Transformation of America, 1815–1848* (Oxford University Press, 2007), 816.
4. *New York Daily Tribune*, 4 January 1850, 15 February 1850, 8 April 1850; *Irish American*, 20 January 1850; *Daily Alta California*, 23 February 1850. His journey was covered in newspapers all over the country (Lamb MSS, Misc. Notes).
5. Francis Pinto, "Historical Facts and Incidents Relating to the First Regiment of New York Volunteers," BANC MSS 98/90, pp. 116–19, Bancroft Library, University of California, Berkeley.
6. Francis Pinto, "Historical Facts and Incidents Relating to the First Regiment of New York Volunteers," BANC MSS 98/90, p. 124, Bancroft Library, University of California, Berkeley.
7. As per historical marker outside the Old Ship Saloon.
8. Francis Pinto, "Historical Facts and Incidents Relating to the First Regiment of New York Volunteers," BANC MSS 98/90, p. 125, Bancroft Library, University of California, Berkeley.

9. John Mack Faragher, *California: An American History* (Yale University Press, 2022), 171; Benjamin Mountford and Stephen Tuffnell, "Seeking a Global History of Gold," in *A Global History of Gold Rushes*, ed. Benjamin Mountford and Stephen Tuffnell (University of California Press, 2018), 17–23.
10. Jonathan Tiemann, "Discounting Gold: Money and Banking in Gold Rush California," Case Study #22, *Oxford Global History of Capitalism Project* (2021); Simon James Bytheway and Mark Metzler, "Introduction: Bases of Credit," in *Central Banks and Gold: How Tokyo, London, and New York Shaped the Modern World* (Cornell University Press, 2016), 1–7; Jeremy Black, *England in the Age of Dickens, 1812–1870* (Amberley, 2021), 59–60; Steven Hahn, *A Nation Without Borders: The United States and Its World in an Age of Civil Wars, 1830–1910* (Viking, 2016), 152; Mountford and Tuffnell, "Seeking a Global History of Gold," 3–31.
11. *New York Herald*, 19 October 1849 (Lamb MSS, Misc. Notes).
12. Rohrbough, *Days of Gold*, 2–3; Hahn, *A Nation Without Borders*, 144–45.
13. Journal of John H. Cornelison, 1849–50, entry for 10 May 1849, Mss Col 675, New York Public Library; Mae Ngai, *The Chinese Question: The Gold Rushes and Global Politics* (Norton, 2021), 21–26.
14. Statement of Rev. Sylvester Woodbridge, Vigilance Committee Miscellany: BANC MSS C-D 202, p. 18, Bancroft Library, Berkeley; Matthew Graves, "Linked by the Sea: The Twinning of San Francisco and Sydney in Vernacular Tradition and Public Commemoration," in *San Francisco, a l'ouest d'Eden*, ed. Sophie Vallas et al. (Presses universitaires de Provence, 2020).
15. Journal of John H. Cornelison, 1849–50, entry for 12 November 1849, Mss Col 675, New York Public Library.
16. Edward Ayers, *American Visions: The United States, 1800–1860* (Norton, 2023), 193.
17. Edward Spann, *The New Metropolis: New York City, 1840–1857* (Columbia University Press, 1981), 281–87, 401–2.
18. Faragher, *California*, 195; Malcolm Campbell, *Ireland's Farthest Shore: Mobility, Migration, and Settlement in the Pacific World* (University of Wisconsin Press, 2022), 35–36, 68, 76–80, 95–96; James Belich, *Replenishing the Earth: The Settler Revolution and the Rise of the Anglo-World, 1783–1939* (Oxford University Press, 2009).
19. Statement of Hall McAllister, Vigilance Committee Miscellany: BANC MSS C-D 202, p. 14, Bancroft Library, University of California, Berkeley; Statement of Charles Gillespie on the VC, p. 5, microfilm CD 190, Bancroft Library, University of California, Berkeley; Herbert Asbury, *The Barbary Coast: An Informal History of the San Francisco Underworld* (Knopf, 1933), 40–42.

20. Jay Monaghan, *Australians and the Gold Rush* (University of California Press, 1966), 3–8, 74–75; Matthew Graves, "Linked by the Sea: The Twinning of San Francisco and Sydney in Vernacular Tradition and Public Commemoration," 81–92.
21. Sherman Richards and George Blackburn, "The Sydney Ducks: A Demographic Analysis," *Pacific Historical Review* 42 (1973): 20; Richard Wolfe, *Hellhole of the Pacific* (Penguin, 2005), 171, 176–77; Monaghan, *Australians and the Gold Rush*, 17.
22. George Kamiya, "When Derelicts from Down Under Overran San Francisco," *San Francisco Chronicle*, 21 July 2018.
23. Richards and Blackburn, "The Sydney Ducks: A Demographic Analysis," 21, 30–31; Robert Senkewicz, *Vigilantes in Gold Rush California* (Stanford University Press, 1985), 78–81; Ngai, *The Chinese Question*, 26; Monaghan, *Australians and the Gold Rush*, 34.
24. Asbury, *The Barbary Coast*, 50–51, 64–65.
25. William Armstead to George Armstead, 31 March 1851, William Armstead Letters, MS 76 B1, Bancroft Library, Berkeley; Benjamin Mountford, "The Pacific Gold Rushes and the Struggle for Order," in *A Global History of Gold Rushes*, ed. Mountford and Tuffnell, 88–89.
26. Richard Waterhouse, "Bare-Knuckle Prize Fighting, Masculinity and Nineteenth-Century Australian Culture," *Journal of Australian Studies* (2009): 103–4.
27. *New York Morning Express*, 20 March 1850; *Syracuse Daily Standard*, 19 April 1850; *Sandusky Register*, 17 June 1850; *Daily Alabama Journal*, 15 April 1850.
28. *Spirit of the Times* (New York), 8 June 1850 (Lamb MSS, Misc. Notes).
29. Some clamored for them to mix it up in a proper prize fight. But, apparently, Sullivan demurred, claiming he did not want to turn a protégé into an enemy. As he knew, so much was at stake in such affairs. *New York Herald*, 22 October 1859, cited in Kenneth Bridgham, "The Violent Life and Death of Yankee Sullivan," *Journal of the International Boxing Research Organization* 156 (2022): 24; Elliott Gorn, *The Manly Art: Bare Knuckle Prize Fighting in America* (Cornell University Press, 1986), 114–16.
30. *Bell's Life in Sydney and Sporting Reviewer*, 6 July 1850; *Bell's Life in London*, 1 December 1850 (Lamb MSS, chap. 2).
31. Asbury, *The Barbary Coast*, 20–21; *Bell's Life in London*, 13 April 1856. On this concept, see Belich, *Replenishing the Earth*.
32. Statement of William B. Watkins, on the Vigilance Committee in San Francisco, BANC MSS C-D 203, Bancroft Library, University of California, Berkeley.

33. Statement of Hall McAllister, Vigilance Committee Miscellany: BANC MSS C-D 202, p. 16, Bancroft Library, University of California, Berkeley.
34. Statement of William T. Coleman, BANC MSS C-D 181, pp. 2–18, microfilm, Bancroft Library, University of California, Berkeley; Doyce Nunis, *The San Francisco Vigilance Committee of 1856: Three Views* (Los Angeles Westerners, 1971), 28.
35. Senkewicz, *Vigilantes in Gold Rush California*, 82.
36. Statement of James C. L. Wadsworth, Vigilance Committee Miscellany: BANC MSS C-D 202, p. 24; Statement of William T. Coleman, BANC MSS C-D 181, pp. 19–23, microfilm; Francis Pinto, "Historical Facts and Incidents Relating to the First Regiment of New York Volunteers," BANC MSS 98/90, pp. 157–58; all in Bancroft Library, University of California, Berkeley.
37. Asbury, *The Barbary Coast*, 71.
38. Senkewicz, *Vigilantes in Gold Rush California*, 84–85; Mountford, "The Pacific Gold Rushes and the Struggle for Order," 98.
39. *Life of William Poole*, 82, Notre Dame Special Collections. The rumor was widely circulated. See, for instance, *New Hampshire Patriot and State Gazette*, 15 August 1850, and *Richmond Whig*, 16 August 1850. On lamenting the news of the "great" Sullivan, see *Plain Dealer*, 19 August 1850. On his not being dead, see *Vermont Christian Messenger*, 28 August 1850.
40. Lamb MSS, Misc. Notes; William Seacrest, *California Disasters, 1800–1900* (Word Dancer, 2005), 21–23; Samuel Dickson, *Tales of San Francisco* (Stanford University Press, 1947), 30–31.
41. See *Life of William Poole*, 82; *Daily Alta California*, 21 October 1850.
42. Peter Gammie, "Pugilists and Politics in Antebellum New York: The Life and Times of Tom Hyer," *New York History* 75 (1994): 287; Lamb MSS, Misc. Notes; *Public Ledger* (Philadelphia), 9 April 1852; *Times-Picayune* (New Orleans), 10 June 1852; *The Sun* (Baltimore), 5 June 1852, 28 August 1852, 30 August 1852; *Weekly Herald* (New York), 23 October 1852; *New York Herald*, 28 August 1852; *New York Times*, 8 April 1852; *Evening Post* (New York), 16 June 1852.
43. *New York Herald*, 23 October 1852 (Lamb MSS, Misc. Notes).
44. For Morrissey's life, see Ed James, *The Life and Battles of John Morrissey* (New York, 1879), 3–6, Notre Dame Special Collections. On his time in jail, see Lamb MSS, Misc. Notes; *Troy Daily Whig*, 9 November 1849, 18 February 1850; *Troy Budget*, 2 October 1850.
45. *New York Illustrated Times*, 2 February 1884, in John Morrissey manuscript file, Notre Dame Special Collections; Daniel Levy, *Manhattan Phoenix: The Great Fire of 1835 and the Emergence of Modern New York* (Oxford University Press, 2022), 195–96.

46. *Plain Dealer* (Cleveland), 19 April 1870.
47. "Doc Almy Recalls Ring Go at Boston Corners," n.d., manuscript from Nat Fleischer Collection, in John Morrissey manuscript file, Notre Dame Special Collections.
48. Gorn, *The Manly Art,* 82.
49. *New York Herald,* 2 May 1878 (Lamb MSS, Misc. Notes).
50. George Underwood, "Morrissey Preceded Tunney as Pride of New York's Greenwich Village," *The Ring,* December 1926, 14, in John Morrissey manuscript file, Notre Dame Special Collections.
51. "Famous Ring Battles" from the *National Police Gazette,* in John Morrissey manuscript file, Notre Dame Special Collections. For the charge, see "Doc Almy Recalls Ring Go at Boston Corners," n.d., manuscript from Nat Fleischer Collection, in John Morrissey manuscript file, Notre Dame Special Collections.
52. Intelligence on the alleged marriages relies on the dogged sleuthing of Ken Lamb (Lamb MSS, Misc. Notes). Once again, I could not gain access to Transfiguration Church records, which might unlock some of these details.
53. *New York Herald,* 20 April 1844; *New York Daily Tribune,* 20 April 1844; *Daily Troy Budget,* 20 April 1844; *New York Daily Tribune,* 20 April 1844 (unearthed in Lamb MSS, Misc. Notes).
54. Ed James, *The Life and Battles of Yankee Sullivan* (Philadelphia, 1854), 16. On the alleged lamp-throwing, see *St. Louis Republic,* 14 August 1898.
55. Alex Hortis, *The Witch of New York: The Trials of Polly Bodine and the Birth of Tabloid Justice* (Pegasus Crime, 2024).
56. James, *The Life and Battles of Yankee Sullivan,* 64.
57. James, *The Life and Battles of Yankee Sullivan,* 65.
58. James, *The Life and Battles of John Morrissey,* 6.
59. Richard Fox, *Lives of Tom Hyer, Yankee Sullivan, John Morrissey, and J. C. Heenan,* 39, Notre Dame Special Collections.
60. *New York Herald Tribune,* 14 October 1853; James, *The Life and Battles of Yankee Sullivan,* 65.
61. Captain Franklin Ellis, *History of Columbia County, New York* (Philadelphia, 1878); *Boston Semi-Weekly Advertiser,* Saturday, 15 October 1853.
62. Ellis, *History of Columbia County,* 403; Elijah Clarence Hyatt, *History of the New York and Harlem Railroad* (Mount Kisco, NY, 1898), 17.
63. "The Copake or Ancram Iron Works," *Merchants' Magazine and Commercial Review,* 1 October 1848, 19, 4.
64. Joseph Warren Greene, "New York City's First Railroad, the New York and Harlem, 1832 to 1867," *New York Historical Society Quarterly Bulletin* 9 (1926): 107–23; Gorn, *The Manly Art,* 111; Clay Perry and John Pell, *Hell's Acres* (Lee Furman, 1938), 276–79; *New York Herald,* 14 October 1853.

65. Interview by Colvin Card of the *Millerton Examiner;* and of Sidney Moorehouse of the *Amenia Union,* ca. 1905. My thanks to Rich Rosenweig for sharing these sources from his private collection.
66. Perry and Pell, *Hell's Acres,* 88.
67. *New York Herald,* 14 October 1853.
68. *The Life and Battles of John Morrissey,* 7; James, *The Life and Battles of Yankee Sullivan,* 66; "Lives and Battles of the Irish Champions," in John Morrissey manuscript file, Notre Dame Special Collections.
69. *The Sun* (Baltimore), 14 October 1853.
70. On the round-by-round account, I am relying on James, *The Life and Battles of John Morrissey,* 6–11, which repackages the coverage of the *New York Clipper.*
71. James, *The Life and Battles of Yankee Sullivan,* 6.
72. *The American Fistiana* (New York, 1849), 6.
73. *The Life and Battles of John Morrissey,* 11.
74. James, *The Life and Battles of Yankee Sullivan,* 69.
75. James, *The Life and Battles of Yankee Sullivan;* James, *The Life and Battles of John Morrissey.*
76. *Spirit of the Times,* 22 October 1853.
77. *The Sun* (Baltimore), 14 October 1853.
78. The two quoted in Kenneth Bridgham, "The Violent Life and Death of Yankee Sullivan," *Journal of the International Boxing Research Organization* 156 (2022): 23.
79. "Famous Ring Battles" from the *National Police Gazette,* in John Morrissey manuscript file, Notre Dame Special Collections; "Doc Almy Recalls Ring Go at Boston Corners," n.d., manuscript from Nat Fleischer Collection, in John Morrissey manuscript file, Notre Dame Special Collections.
80. Perry and Pell, *Hell's Acres,* 360; *Cleveland Daily Plain Dealer,* 21 October 1853.
81. Patrick Higgins, "The Battle of Boston Corners," *About Town: The Mid-Hudson Valley Community Guides,* 11 March 2014.
82. *New York Times* quoted in Gorn, *The Manly Art,* 112.
83. *Albany Journal,* 14 October 1853.
84. This was covered throughout the country. See, for instance, *Richmond Whig,* 18 November 1853; and *Boston Statesman,* 19 November 1853.
85. James, *The Life and Battles of Yankee Sullivan,* 70.
86. Nat Fleischer, manuscript notes on 1853 fight, Notre Dame Special Collections.
87. James, *The Life and Battles of Yankee Sullivan,* 71.
88. *Daily Picayune* (New Orleans), 28 June 1854; *Albany Evening Journal,* 26 July 1854.

89. Nat Fleischer manuscript notes on 1853 fight, Notre Dame Special Collections.
90. Pierre Spake Collection.
91. New York Public Library.
92. C. J. Gannon, "Famous Irish Boxers and Their Lives and Fights," *Tuam Herald*, 26 September 1931. There are many versions of the song, all more or less the same. I rely on the one from the University of Arkansas Folksong Collection found at https://digitalcollections.uark.edu/digital/collection/OzarkFolkSong/id/2953/.

Round 14. Nevada City

1. Arthur Clark, *The Clipper Ship Era* (Putnam, 1911), chap. 16.
2. This was carried in many national reports. See, for example, *The Sun* (Baltimore), 3 December 1853.
3. "Old State Arsenal at White and Elm Streets," New York Public Library Digital Collections, https://digitalcollections.nypl.org/items/510d47e1-2ce6-a3d9-e040-e00a18064a99.
4. *New York Clipper*, 4 February 1854 (Lamb MSS, chap. 12).
5. *Nevada Journal*, 7 July 1854.
6. *Daily Alta California*, 21 August 1855; *Sacramento Daily Union*, 22 August and 24 August 1855. The date of his arrival is based on Ken Lamb's reading of shipping advertisements (Lamb MSS, chap. 12).
7. Statement of Dr. William H. Roger, Vigilance Committee Miscellany, BANC MSS C-D 202, pp. 12–13, Bancroft Library, University of California, Berkeley; Nevada Journal, 15 September 1854; Pinto Memoir, BANC MSS 98/90, p. 167, Bancroft Library, University of California, Berkeley.
8. Statement of James Downs on Vigilance Committee, p. 4, microfilm CD 185, Bancroft Library, University of California, Berkeley.
9. Statement of George Frink on Vigilance Committee, p. 1, microfilm CD 188, Bancroft Library, University of California, Berkeley.
10. Pinto Memoir, BANC MSS 98/90, Bancroft Library, University of California, Berkeley, 180.
11. Statement of Terrance Kelly, San Francisco Committee of Vigilance, Papers Relating to Ballot Box Stuffing and Fraudulent Elections, 1854–56, Box 3a, Huntington Library, San Marino; Statement of Anthony Samsoni, San Francisco Committee of Vigilance, Papers Relating to Ballot Box Stuffing and Fraudulent Elections, 1854–56, Box 3b, Huntington Library, San Marino.
12. Lamb MSS, chap. 12; *Alexandria Gazette*, 18 June 1856; *Daily Alta California*, 19 October 1884; Herbert Asbury, *The Barbary Coast: An Informal History*

of the San Francisco Underworld (Knopf, 1933), 80–81; Joan Levy, "Meet Billy Mulligan from Our 1856 Election," *Daily Journal*, 15 May 2006; Statement of Samuel Samuelson, San Francisco Committee of Vigilance, Papers Relating to Ballot Box Stuffing and Fraudulent Elections, 1854–56, Box 3a, Huntington Library, San Marino.

13. *Daily Alta California*, 26 August 1854, 27 August 1854.
14. *Sacramento Daily Union*, 28 June 1855; *Daily Alta California*, 27 June 1855.
15. *Alexandria Gazette*, 18 June 1856. See also *New York Evening Express*, 16 June 1856 (Lamb MSS, chap. 12).
16. William Armstead to His Parents, 27 January 1852, William Armstead Letters, MS 76 B1, Bancroft Library, University of California, Berkeley.
17. Francis Pinto, "Historical Facts and Incidents Relating to the First Regiment of New York Volunteers," BANC MSS 98/90, pp. 135–36, Bancroft Library, University of California, Berkeley.
18. This is based on Ken Lamb's reading of the *Sacramento Daily Union* (Lamb MSS, chap. 12).
19. Francis Pinto, "Historical Facts and Incidents Relating to the First Regiment of New York Volunteers," BANC MSS 98/90, p. 127, Bancroft Library, University of California, Berkeley.
20. Alfred A. Green, "Life and Adventures of a 47er of California" (1878), p. 12, microfilm C-D 94, Bancroft Library, University of California, Berkeley.
21. Edward Ayers, *American Visions: The United States, 1800–1860* (Norton, 2023), 193.
22. All this is based on Benjamin Madley, *An American Genocide: The United States and the California Indian Catastrophe, 1846–1873* (Yale University Press, 2016). See also Daniel Walker Howe, *What Hath God Wrought: The Transformation of America, 1815–1848* (Oxford University Press, 2007), 810–11.
23. Francis Pinto, "Historical Facts and Incidents Relating to the First Regiment of New York Volunteers," BANC MSS 98/90, p. 130, Bancroft Library, University of California, Berkeley.
24. Malcolm Campbell, *Ireland's Farthest Shore: Mobility, Migration, and Settlement in the Pacific World* (University of Wisconsin Press, 2022), 46. See also David Emmons, *Beyond the American Pale: The Irish in the West, 1845–1910* (University of Oklahoma Press, 2010).
25. Campbell, *Ireland's New World*, 101–2; Mae Ngai, *The Chinese Question: The Gold Rushes and Global Politics* (Norton, 2021), 139–40.
26. Kevin Kenny, *The Problem of Immigration in a Slaveholding Republic* (Oxford University Press, 2023), 141–42.
27. John Mack Faragher, *California: An American History* (Yale University Press, 2022), 189.

28. See the National Park Service website for how it was done: www.nps.gov/yuch/learn/historyculture/placer-mining.htm#:~:text=Unlike%20hardrock%20mining%2C%20which%20extracts,a%20shoal%20or%20sand%20bar. Also John McPhee, *Coming into the Country* (Farrar, Straus and Giroux, 1977), 228.
29. Francis Pinto, "Historical Facts and Incidents Relating to the First Regiment of New York Volunteers," BANC MSS 98/90, pp. 127–29, Bancroft Library, University of California, Berkeley.
30. Vigilance Committees in San Francisco, Miscellany, BANC MSS C-D 202, pp. 356, 357, Bancroft Library, University of California, Berkeley.
31. Byron Nathan McKinstry, California Gold Rush Diary, 1850–1852, BANC MSS C-F 83, pp. 160–68A-B, microfilm, Bancroft Library, University of California, Berkeley.
32. George Townson, Nevada City, to Mary Townson, Brooklyn, MI, 27 March 1855, BANC MSS 2013/14, Bancroft Library, University of California, Berkeley.
33. Kenny, *The Problem of Immigration in a Slaveholding Republic*, 141–42.
34. Benjamin Madley, *An American Genocide: The United States and the California Indian Catastrophe, 1846–1873* (Yale University Press, 2016), 98–99, 220.
35. *Nevada Journal*, 19 April 1851; Aaron Augustus Sargent, *150 Years Ago: "A Sketch of Nevada County"* (Nevada County Sesquicentennial, 1998), 5–11; Mann, *After the Gold Rush*, 49–50.
36. Malcolm Rohrbough, *Days of Gold: The California Gold Rush and the American Nation* (University of California Press, 1997), 146–49.
37. *Sacramento Daily Union*, 11 November 1854, 15 November 1854; *Daily Alta California*, 11 November 1854 (Lamb MSS, chap. 12).
38. *Nevada Journal*, 27 October 1854.
39. Byron Nathan McKinstry, California Gold Rush Diary, 1850–1852, BANC MSS C-F 83, p. 172, microfilm, Bancroft Library, University of California, Berkeley; Sargent, *150 Years Ago: "A Sketch of Nevada County,"* 23.
40. *Nevada Journal*, 24 February 1854.
41. Sargent, *150 Years Ago: "A Sketch of Nevada County,"* 23; Ralph Mann, *After the Gold Rush: Society in Grass Valley and Nevada City, California, 1849–1870* (Stanford University Press, 1982), 36.
42. Mann, *After the Gold Rush*, 56–67.
43. *Sacramento Daily Union*, 11, 21, and 28 December 1854, 8 February 1855; *Daily Alta California*, 23 December 1854 (Lamb MSS, chap. 12).
44. George Rothwell Brown, ed., *Reminiscences of Senator William M. Stewart of Nevada* (New York, 1908), 97–98. My thanks to Megan Renoir for help finding this.

45. McPhee, *Coming into the Country*, 228; Sargent, *150 Years Ago*: "A Sketch of Nevada County," 16.
46. Mann, *After the Gold Rush*, 24–28; Erik Eklund, "Geology, Capital, and Company Formation on the Goldfields of the Industrial Age," in *A Global History of Gold Rushes*, ed. Benjamin Mountford and Stephen Tuffnell (University of California Press, 2018), 186–89.
47. Ralph Mann, "The Decade After the Gold Rush: Social Structure in Grass Valley and Nevada City, California, 1850–1860," *Pacific Historical Review* 41 (1972): 498–99; Rohrbough, *Days of Gold*, 202–3; Howe, *What Hath God Wrought*, 820.
48. *Brown and Dallison's Nevada, Grass Valley, and Rough and Ready Directory* (San Francisco, 1856), 33–35.
49. *Brown and Dallison's Nevada, Grass Valley, and Rough and Ready Directory*, 41; Mann, "The Decade After the Gold Rush: Social Structure in Grass Valley and Nevada City, California, 1850–1860," 491–92.
50. *Brown and Dallison's Nevada, Grass Valley, and Rough and Ready Directory*, 97.
51. For the location, see Robert Wycoff, *The Compleat Pedestrian's Partially Illustrated Guide to Greater Nevada City* (Gold Country Books, 1990), 46, at the Nevada City Visitor's Center.
52. Gail Bederman, *Manliness and Civilization: A Cultural History of Gender and Race in the United States, 1880–1917* (University of Chicago Press, 1995); Clifford Putney, *Muscular Christianity: Manhood and Sports in Protestant America, 1880–1920* (Harvard University Press, 2003).
53. Kasia Boddy, *Boxing: A Cultural History* (Reaktion Books, 2009), 93.
54. *Daily Alta California*, 18 July 1855, 26 July 1855, 21 August 1855.
55. *Daily Alta California*, 7 September 1855; *The Globe* (Sydney), 6 September 1913.
56. *Daily Alta California*, 18 June 1855.
57. Ayers, *American Visions*, 193.

Round 15. Honolulu

1. *Alexandria Gazette*, 18 June 1856. Even in 1859, it was still making the rounds. See Private Journal of Marshall W. C. Parke, entry for 15 November 1859, Hawaiian Historical Society; advertisement of 1 July 1856 in *The Diaries of David Lawrence Gregg*, ed. Pauline King (Hawaiian Historical Society, 1982), 300.
2. David Forbes, ed., *Hawaiian National Bibliography, 1780–1900*, vol. 3: *1851–1880* (University of Hawaii Press, 2001), 151–52, 165, Hawaiian Historical Society Library.

3. Private Journal of Marshall W. C. Parke, entry for 15 November 1859, Hawaiian Historical Society.
4. Noelani Arista, *The Kingdom and the Republic: Sovereign Hawai'i and the Early United States* (University of Pennsylvania Press, 2019).
5. Private Journal of Marshall W. C. Parke, entries for 31 August 1859, 27 September 1856, Hawaiian Historical Society; Steven Hahn, *A Nation Without Borders: The United States and Its World in an Age of Civil War, 1830–1910* (Viking, 2016), 396.
6. James Haley, *Captive Paradise: A History of Hawaii* (St. Martin's, 2014), 145–46; Charles Bishop to Joel Turrill, 13 April 1855, Joel Turrill Papers, Hawaiian Historical Society; *The Journal of Prince Alexander Liholiho: The Voyages Made to the United States, England, and France in 1849–50*, ed. Joseph Adler (University of Hawai'i Press, 1967), ix, xiv, Hawaiian Historical Society Library.
7. *The Diaries of David Lawrence Gregg*, ed. King, 225.
8. Ralph Kuykendall, "Early Hawaiian Commercial Development," *Pacific Historical Review* 3 (1934): 365–85.
9. Haley, *Captive Paradise*, 85.
10. Kuykendall, "Early Hawaiian Commercial Development," 365, 369; Richard Wolfe, *Hell-hole of the Pacific* (Penguin, 2005), 178; Eric Jay Dolin, *Leviathan: The History of Whaling in America* (Norton, 2007), 245.
11. Haley, *Captive Paradise*, 86; Ralph Kuykendall, *The Hawaiian Kingdom*, vol. 2: *Twenty Critical Years, 1854–1874* (University of Hawai'i Press, 1953), 135–40; Dolin, *Leviathan*, 353–54.
12. William Clark Taylor, *Jottings on Australia: With Remarks on the California Route to New York and Liverpool* (London, 1872), 173, New York Public Library.
13. *The Polynesian*, March 24, 1855; Kuykendall, *The Hawaiian Kingdom*, 2:140–41, 147, 168.
14. Haley, *Captive Paradise*, xv; William Parke, *Personal Reminiscences of William Cooper Parke* (Cambridge, MA, 1891), 54, Hawaiian Historical Society Library.
15. Dolin, *Leviathan*, 246–47, 279; Parke, *Personal Reminiscences of William Cooper Parke*, 35.
16. William Franklin Snow Manuscript Diary, 22 October 1855, Hawaiian Historical Society.
17. *San Francisco Bulletin*, 20 November 1855.
18. *Bell's Life in Sydney and Sporting Reviewer*, 13 September 1856.
19. On marriages and child, see Lamb MSS, appendix B, Misc. Notes; *Sacramento Daily Union*, 6 June 1856; *Daily Alta California*, 4 June 1856; *Daily Evening Bulletin*, 3 June 1856.
20. *The Pacific Commercial Advertiser*, 20 November 1856.
21. *Alexandria Gazette*, 18 June 1856.

22. *Daily Democratic State Journal,* 1 January 1856.
23. *Columbian Register* (New Haven), 9 February 1856. On asthma and the connection to Sullivan, see Ralph Kuykendall, *The Hawaiian Kingdom, 1854–1874,* 34.
24. *Elgin Courant,* 21 March 1856.
25. *Massachusetts Spy* (Worcester), 6 February 1856.
26. *Massachusetts Spy* (Worcester), 6 February 1856.
27. *Aberdeen Herald,* 21 February 1857; Basil Walsh, "Catherine Hayes," in *Dictionary of Irish Biography.*
28. *New York Weekly Herald,* 22 March 1856.
29. *San Francisco Bulletin,* 8 February 1858.
30. *Caledonia Mercury* (Edinburgh), 8 April 1856; *Daily News* (London), 7 April 1856; *Norwich Mercury,* 9 April 1856; *The Nonconformist,* 9 April 1856; *New York Herald,* 12 April 1856.
31. *Baltimore Sun,* 29 February 1856.
32. *New York Weekly Herald,* 1 March 1856.
33. *Connecticut Courant,* 8 March 1856; *Farmer's Cabinet* (Amherst, NH), 13 March 1856.
34. *The Age* (Australia), 20 May 1856.
35. *Alexandria Gazette,* 18 June 1856.
36. *Alexandria Gazette,* 7 March 1856.
37. *Plain Dealer,* 11 March 1856.
38. *Baltimore Sun,* 29 February 1856; *New York Weekly Herald,* 1 March 1856.
39. *Daily Democratic State Journal,* 1 January 1856.
40. *The Diaries of David Lawrence Gregg,* ed. King, 265–67, 271, 273.
41. *Daily Alta California,* 24 February 1856.
42. *The Polynesian,* February 1856, reprinted in *New York Weekly Herald,* 29 March 1856; and *Daily Alta California,* 24 February 1856.
43. *The Polynesian,* February 1856, reprinted in *New York Weekly Herald,* 29 March 1856.
44. The same or similar reports were recycled, for instance in the *Baltimore Sun,* 31 January 1856; *Connecticut Courant,* 2 February 1856; *Daily Ohio Statesman* (Columbus), 3 February 1856; *Portland Advertiser,* 5 February 1856; *Massachusetts Spy* (Worcester), 6 February 1856; *Cleveland Daily Plain Dealer,* 6 February 1856; *Columbian Register* (New Haven), 9 February 1856; *Report of the State Superintendent of Public Instruction* (Schenectady), 12 February 1856; *Daily Commercial Register* (Sandusky, OH), 15 February 1856; *National Aegis* (Worcester), 20 February 1856.
45. *New York Weekly Herald,* 29 March 1856; *Charleston Courier,* 31 March 1856; *Wisconsin Free Democrat,* 9 April 1856.
46. "Our New York Letter," *St. Paul Daily Pioneer,* 5 May 1856.

47. *The Polynesian*, 11 October 1856.
48. *The Diaries of David Lawrence Gregg*, ed. King, 296–97.

Round 16. San Francisco

1. "Yankee Sullivan No More," *New York Times*, 30 June 1856.
2. *Sacramento Daily Union*, 9 October 1855.
3. *Nevada Journal*, 4 April 1856.
4. *Daily Alta California*, 21 April 1856; *Daily Democratic State Journal* (Sacramento), 2 April 1856.
5. *San Francisco Herald* account carried in *People's Advocate and New South Wales Vindicator*, 12 July 1856.
6. Pinto Memoir (BANC MSS 98/90), pp. 188–89, Bancroft Library, University of California, Berkeley; Robert Senkewicz, *Vigilantes in Gold Rush San Francisco* (Stanford University Press, 1985), 104–5.
7. Nancy Taniguchi, *Dirty Deeds: Land, Violence, and the 1856 San Francisco Vigilance Committee* (University of Oklahoma Press, 2016), 30.
8. This is the interpretation of Senkewicz in *Vigilantes in Gold Rush San Francisco*.
9. Taniguchi, *Dirty Deeds*, 30.
10. William B. Watkins Statement on Vigilance Committee, BANC MSS C-D 203, pp. 1–2, Bancroft Library, University of California, Berkeley.
11. F. Collier Statement, San Francisco Committee of Vigilance, Papers Relating to Ballot Box Stuffing and Fraudulent Elections, 1854–56, Box 3a, Huntington Library, San Marino.
12. Statement of N. Proctor-Smith, San Francisco Committee of Vigilance, Papers Relating to Ballot Box Stuffing and Fraudulent Elections, 1854–56, Box 3a, Huntington Library, San Marino.
13. Statement of William T. Coleman, BANC MSS C-D 181, pp. 71–72, microfilm, Bancroft Library, University of California, Berkeley.
14. John Mack Faragher, *California: An American History* (Yale University Press, 2022), 198–99; Herbert Asbury, *The Barbary Coast: An Informal History of the San Francisco Underworld* (Knopf, 1933), 82; Jonathan Tiemann, "Discounting Gold: Money and Baking in Gold Rush California," *Oxford Global History of Capitalism Project*, Case Study #22 (2021), 10.
15. Statement of William T. Coleman, BANC MSS C-D 181, pp. 28–29, microfilm, Bancroft Library, University of California, Berkeley.
16. Statement of George Frink on Vigilance Committee, p. 1, microfilm CD 188, Bancroft Library, University of California, Berkeley; Taniguchi, *Dirty Deeds*, 36–37.
17. Senkewicz, *Vigilantes in Gold Rush San Francisco*, 168.

18. San Francisco Committee of Vigilance Papers, Unclassified Papers, 1853–56, Statement of H. M. Snyder, 17 May 1856, Huntington Library, San Marino.
19. Robert Senkewicz focuses on anti-Irish dynamics, whereas Nancy Taniguchi suggests that access to land was the issue. Ultimately, of course (and both would agree), it was about power and who wielded it. See also Doyce Nunis, *The San Francisco Vigilance Committee of 1856: Three Views* (Los Angeles Westerners, 1971), 22.
20. Statement of William T. Coleman, BANC MSS C-D 181, p. 30, microfilm, Bancroft Library, University of California, Berkeley.
21. Nunis, *The San Francisco Vigilance Committee of 1856: Three Views*, 76, 78.
22. 25 August 1856, *The Courier* (Hobart, Taz); James O'Meara, *The Vigilance Committee of 1856* (San Francisco, 1887), 20.
23. Faragher, *California*, 198.
24. Statement of William T. Coleman, BANC MSS C-D 181, p. 33, microfilm, Bancroft Library, University of California, Berkeley.
25. *San Francisco Herald* report carried in *Philadelphia Inquirer*, 2 September 1856.
26. Statement of William T. Coleman, BANC MSS C-D 181, p. 73, microfilm, Bancroft Library, University of California, Berkeley.
27. Nunis, *The San Francisco Vigilance Committee of 1856: Three Views*, 85; O'Meara, *The Vigilance Committee of 1856*, 18; Taniguchi, *Dirty Deeds*, 46.
28. Asbury, *The Barbary Coast*, 92; Taniguchi, *Dirty Deeds*, 57.
29. Statement of "One Who Knows," San Francisco Committee of Vigilance, Papers Relating to Ballot Box Stuffing and Fraudulent Elections, 1854–56, Box 3a, Huntington Library, San Marino.
30. Nancy Taniguchi, in *Dirty Deeds*, suggests how political rivalry could make politicians court all sorts of enemies (30).
31. Statement of William T. Coleman, BANC MSS C-D 181, pp. 71–72, microfilm, Bancroft Library, University of California, Berkeley.
32. Senkewicz, *Vigilantes in Gold Rush San Francisco*, 172–73; Nunis, *The San Francisco Vigilance Committee of 1856: Three Views*, 36.
33. William B. Watkins Statement on Vigilance Committee, BANC MSS C-D 203, p. 21, Bancroft Library, University of California, Berkeley; Faragher, *California*, 198.
34. Nunis, *The San Francisco Vigilance Committee of 1856: Three Views*, 54; Senkewicz, *Vigilantes in Gold Rush San Francisco*, 118.
35. As one writer put it, the match pitting Yankee and Simmons resulted in mayhem. Yankee had won, but many miners had lost a great deal betting against him. The Vigilance Committee took notice and sent police to arrest him in the middle of the night the following month. He injured five cops before they subdued him and gave him an awful beating (see Nat Fleischer, "In the

Bareknuckle Days, No. 4," p. 301, Nat Fleischer Papers, Notre Dame Special Collections). Another account argues he insisted on going to Casey's funeral. There he was arrested (see *Life and Battles of Yankee Sullivan* [Philadelphia, 1854], n.p.).

36. Taniguchi, *Dirty Deeds*, 59. *The Courier* (Hobart, Tasmania), 25 August 1856, says he was arrested on 28 June.
37. Statement of Dr. R. Beverly Cole on Vigilance Committee, BANC MSS C-D 180, p. 17, microfilm, 1877 statement, Bancroft Library, University of California, Berkeley.
38. Nunis, *The San Francisco Vigilance Committee of 1856: Three Views*, 37.
39. See *The Courier* (Hobart, Tasmania), 26 August 1856; Pinto Memoir, BANC MSS 98/90, p. 180, Bancroft Library, University of California, Berkeley.
40. Statement of William T. Coleman, BANC MSS C-D 181, pp. 76–77, microfilm, Bancroft Library, University of California, Berkeley.
41. Asbury, *The Barbary Coast*, 80–81.
42. Taniguchi, *Dirty Deeds*, 58–59, 71.
43. Vigilance Committee Miscellany, Statement of Aaron Burns, BANC MSS C-D 202, pp. 3–4, Bancroft Library, University of California, Berkeley.
44. Alfred A. Green, "Life and Adventures of a 47er of California" (1878), p. 50, microfilm C-D 94, Bancroft Library, University of California, Berkeley; *Bell's Life in Sydney and Sporting Reviewer*, 13 September 1856.
45. Nunis, *The San Francisco Vigilance Committee of 1856: Three Views*, 118; *San Francisco Bulletin*, 31 May 1856.
46. Statement of Dr. R. Beverly Cole on Vigilance Committee, 1877, BANC MSS C-D 180, pp. 18–19, microfilm, 1877 statement, Bancroft Library, University of California, Berkeley.
47. *Bell's Life in Sydney and Sporting Reviewer*, 13 September 1856; *Daily Alta California*, 28 May 1856.
48. *Daily Evening Bulletin*, 31 May 1856, 2 June 1856; *Daily Alta California*, 4 June 1856.
49. Statement of Dr. R. Beverly Cole on Vigilance Committee, BANC MSS C-D 180, pp. 18–19, microfilm, 1877 statement, Bancroft Library, University of California, Berkeley; *Daily Alta California*, 4 June 1856; *Bell's Life in Sydney and Sporting Reviewer*, 13 September 1856; *Weekly Butte Record*, 7 June 1856.
50. Vigilance Committee Miscellany, Statement of Aaron Burns, BANC MSS C-D 202, p. 6, Bancroft Library, University of California, Berkeley.
51. Statement of William T. Coleman, BANC MSS C-D 181, pp. 76–77, microfilm, Bancroft Library, University of California, Berkeley.

52. Vigilance Committee Miscellany, Statement of Aaron Burns, BANC MSS C-D 202, Bancroft Library, University of California, Berkeley, 3–4.
53. *Nevada Journal*, 6 June 1856.
54. *Daily Alta California*, 4 June 1856.
55. *Daily Alta California*, 4 June 1856.
56. *Daily Democratic State Journal*, 2 June 1856, 5 June 1856.
57. Taniguchi, *Dirty Deeds*, 66.
58. Kenneth Bridgham, "The Violent Life and Death of Yankee Sullivan," *International Boxing Research Organization Journal* 156 (2022): 25–26; John Boessenecker, ed., *Against the Vigilantes: The Recollections of Dutch Charley Duane* (University of Oklahoma, 1999), 127–29. My thanks to Tony Gee for this reference. *Daily Evening Bulletin*, 29 August 1856.
59. Nat Fleischer, "In the Bareknuckle Days, No. 4," 301, Nat Fleischer Papers, Notre Dame Special Collections.
60. Bill Bray, "Died True to His Pals," *Tribune* (Sydney), 15 March 1940; *Kalgoorlie Miner*, 3 November 1930; *Northern Star* (Lismore, New South Wales), 3 December 1927; *Daily Telegraph* (Sydney), 9 February 1938.
61. *Evening News* (Sydney), 22 September 1897.
62. *The Citizen*, 15 November 1856. My thanks to Robert O'Sullivan for this citation.
63. *Alexandria Gazette*, 18 June 1856.
64. *Sacramento Daily Union*, 4 June 1856; *Daily Alta California*, 2 June 1856.
65. William Newby in *Frederick Douglass's Newspaper* (Rochester), 29 May 1856.
66. Mailer's line is quoted in Donald McRae, *Dark Trade: Lost in Boxing* (Mainstream, 1996), 29.
67. Tris Dixon, *Damage: The Untold Story of Brain Trauma in Boxing* (Hamilcar, 2021).
68. *Daily Alta California*, 25 December 1852.
69. Dave Philipps, "Chronic Brain Trauma Is Extensive in Navy's Elite Speedboat Crews," *New York Times*, 12 November 2024; Dave Philipps, "Top-Gun Navy Pilots Fly at the Extremes: Their Brains May Suffer," *New York Times*, 8 December 2024.
70. David Remnick, "Kid Dynamite Blows Up," *The Hurt Business: A Century of the Greatest Writing on Boxing* (Aurum, 2013), 442.
71. *The Maffra Spectator* (Vic), 9 April 1883.
72. Dixon, *Damage*, 50, 99–102.
73. *Daily Alta California*, 2 June 1856.
74. Asbury, *The Barbary Coast*, 96.

75. Ben Tarnoff, *The Bohemians: Mark Twain and the San Francisco Writers Who Reinvented American Literature* (Penguin, 2014), 3–5, 10, 231, 237.
76. See, as representative examples, *Lowell Daily Citizen and News*, 19 June 1856; *St. Alban's Messenger*, 19 June 1856; *Massachusetts Spy*, 18 June 1856; *Alexandria Gazette*, 18 June 1856; *St. Paul Daily Pioneer*, 20 June 1856; *Portland Weekly Advertiser*, 24 June 1856.
77. *Pacific Commercial Advertiser*, 10 July 1856; *The Polynesian*, 21 June 1856.
78. See America's Historical Newspapers Database for 1856.
79. Lamb MSS, chap. 14; *New York Herald*, 29 June 1856; Gary Kamiya, "A Private Toll Road to Mission Dolores in 1851 Opened S.F. to Development," *San Francisco Chronicle*, 27 November 2020. On the history of the church, graveyard, and what follows, see Beth Winegarner, *San Francisco's Forgotten Cemeteries: A Buried History* (Arcadia, 2023), 23–33; and Z. Engelhardt, *San Francisco or Mission Dolores* (San Francisco, 1924), 350–60.
80. Matthew Dunn Testimony, San Francisco Committee of Vigilance Papers (1856), Correspondence, Depositions, etc. from the Files of the Investigating Committee, Huntington Library, San Marino.
81. *The Monitor*, 23 June 1904.
82. *New York Clipper*, 6 March 1858.
83. *Daily Alta California*, 2 July 1857; Edward David Jones Statement on "Malloy," San Francisco Committee of Vigilance Papers (1856), Correspondence, Depositions, etc. from the Files of the Investigating Committee, Huntington Library. The *Daily Alta California* of 8 January 1869 reported Mulloy was ejected from a lot by the Mission. So, Malloy and Mulloy are likely the same person.

Epilogue

1. *Freeman's Journal* (Sydney), 23 June 1906. The original tale appeared in Stella Maximo, "The Graveyard of Dolores Mission," *Overland Monthly or Out West Magazine* 47 (1906): 240.
2. *Plain Dealer*, 9 February 1877.
3. *Western Mail* (Perth), 18 February 1954.
4. Grace Karskens, *People of the River: Lost Worlds of Early Australia* (Allen and Unwin, 2020), 415; James Ryan, *Reminiscences of Australia* (Sydney, 1894), 35, 110–13. Ken Lamb convinced me this was a different character. The name Ginger carried weight after he died. One "Ginger Sullivan," for instance, fought, in the ring and out of it. A Serjeant Tones received the military medal in 1918, when he was killed for digging a communications trench between No-Man's-Land and the German lines. He also boxed in military tournaments

there, and he came in runner-up to another fighter. In the ring, he took the name "Ginger Sullivan" (see *The Referee* [newspaper], NSW, 17 April 1918).

5. *New York Tribune,* 31 March 1862.
6. "Tweed and His Congeners," *Columbian Register* (New Haven), 6 December 1873; *San Francisco Bulletin,* 22 July 1878.
7. Lorenzo Fowler, *Fowler's New Illustrated Self-Instructor in Phrenology and Physiology* (New York, 1852), 90; Samuel Wells, *How to Read Character: A New Illustrated Handbook* (New York, 1868 and 1890), 30.
8. For this and what follows, see *American Phrenological Journal,* September 1856, 49, 60.
9. *Philadelphia Inquirer,* 16 August 1890; *Sunday Times* (Perth), 12 August 1923.
10. On the séance, see *Dallas Morning News,* 26 December 1889. For the criminals, see *Pomeroy's Democrat* (New York), 28 March 1874; *New York Tribune,* 19 May 1880; *Cincinnati Daily Gazette,* 9 August 1876.
11. *New York Herald,* 16 April 1889.
12. *Cayuga Chief* (Auburn, NY), 22 January 1856.
13. William Riordan, ed., *Plunkitt of Tammany Hall* (Bedford/St. Martin's, 1994), 95.
14. Greg Heller, "Interview with Primus," *Bam Magazine,* 11 July 1997; *Primus Tracks* podcast, 30 June 2024.
15. Steven Grasse interview, 14 September 2023. Roe Jan Brewing Company makes "Sullivan Hazy Pale Ale." Rich Rosenweig brought this to my attention after he went to a tasting.
16. *New York Times,* 5 January 1877.
17. *San Francisco Bulletin,* 22 February 1877.

INDEX

Italicized page numbers refer to illustrations.

Democratic Ideals in Global Perspective

Nuremberg's Citizen Prosecutor: Benjamin Ferencz and the Birth of International Justice
Gregory S. Gordon